MW00622502

# CHRISTIAN SUPREMACY

# Christian Supremacy

## RECKONING WITH THE ROOTS OF ANTISEMITISM AND RACISM

*Magda Teter*

PRINCETON UNIVERSITY PRESS

PRINCETON & OXFORD

Published by Princeton University Press
41 William Street, Princeton, New Jersey 08540
99 Banbury Road, Oxford OX2 6JX

press.princeton.edu

ISBN 9780691242583
ISBN (e-book) 9780691242590

British Library Cataloging-in-Publication Data is available

Editorial: Fred Appel and James Collier
Production Editorial: Nathan Carr
Jacket/Cover Design: Karl Spurzem
Production: Erin Suydam
Publicity: Kate Hensley and Kathryn Stevens
Copyeditor: Dana Henricks

This book has been composed in Miller

Printed on acid-free paper. ∞

Printed in Canada

10 9 8 7 6 5 4 3 2 1

For my students at Fordham—in gratitude for inspiring this book

Teaching is never a one-way street

*When truth is buried in the earth, it accumulates there and assumes so mighty an explosive power that, on the day when it bursts forth, it hurls everything in the air. We shall see if they have not just made preparations for the most resounding of disasters, yet to come.*

ÉMILE ZOLA, *J'ACCUSE* (1898)

*History, as nearly no one seems to know, is not merely something to be read. And it does not refer merely, or even principally, to the past. On the contrary, the great force of history comes from the fact that we carry it within us, are unconsciously controlled by it in many ways, and history is literally present in all that we do. It could scarcely be otherwise, since it is to history that we owe our frames of reference, our identities, and our aspirations.*

JAMES BALDWIN, *WHITE MAN'S GUILT* (1965)

# CONTENTS

# IMAGES

[ xi ]

THIS BOOK would not have been written without at least two major factors: my move from Wesleyan University to Fordham and the COVID pandemic. Soon after I arrived at Fordham University, my colleague Doron Ben-Atar invited me to teach a class on antisemitism. Doron teaches this course at the Lincoln Center campus, so I began to offer this class at Fordham's Rose Hill campus in the Bronx.

This was fall 2016, the height of the presidential campaign. My students began to connect the rhetoric of texts we were reading about Jews and antisemitism to the rhetoric of the Trump campaign about other groups in the US. Then in December 2016, the Maysles Cinema in Harlem held an advance screening of Raoul Peck's documentary *I Am Not Your Negro* centered around James Baldwin's works and words. Watching this film and especially the clip from the 1963 PBS program "The Negro and the American Promise" made for me the conceptual similarities even starker. In that PBS segment Baldwin stated a challenge: "It is entirely up to the American people whether or not they are going to face and deal with and embrace this stranger who they have maligned so long. What white people have to do is try and find out in their own hearts why it was necessary to have a 'nigger' in the first place, because I am not a nigger, I'm a man. But if you think I'm a nigger, it means you need him. . . . If I am not the nigger here and you invented him, you the white people invented him, then you've got to find out why. And the future of the country depends on that. . . ."[1] Baldwin's quote could have been rephrased in the European context to describe "the Jew." Peck's film came out two years after a seminal book by Sara Lipton, *Dark Mirror: The Invention of Anti-Jewish Iconography*, in which she examined the invention and evolution of iconographic vocabulary to represent "the Jew" in European Christian visual culture. Having myself studied and written about both Christian views of Jews and the difference between "the Jews" created in the European Christian imagination and Jews of flesh and blood, whose lives were preserved in the archives, this quote from Baldwin struck a chord.[2] I began to explore more not only Baldwin's writing, but also Black history in the US. And as I was reading books and articles on Black history, I would frequently jot down in the margins: "cf. Jews." There were too many of those comparisons for them to be incidental, so I began thinking about these uncanny parallels for such different populations with such different historical experiences. This would be, I imagined, a project I would take up when I retired.

In the meantime, I was asked to teach a course on modern European history and decided to reimagine that course. Years ago, my colleague Debra Kaplan and I challenged historians of Europe "to remove Jews from the historiographic ghetto and weave them into the narrative of general history." We wanted to show that doing so is significant in changing our understanding even of events "which, at first glance, do not seem to have much to do with Jews."[3] So in that class I decided to tell the story of Europe and major historical events not through the traditional lens of the continent's Christian majorities, but also through Europe's religious and ethnic minorities, while also expanding the traditional geographic scope of Europe to include eastern Europe as well as western European colonies. One of the questions we probed through the centuries of historical texts and different angles of religion, race, and class was the formation of national and also "European" identities. What did the French Revolution look like from the perspective of Jews in France and people of color in French colonies? What about the Industrial Revolution? How did the idea of nationalism look when Jews were included in that story? My students, a diverse and smart group, were fantastic interlocutors, probing and challenging throughout the semester. And indeed, it was the diverse classes at Fordham that encouraged me to make connections between Jewish history and histories and experiences of other groups.

In 2019, my colleague Westenley (Wes) Alcenat and I began talking about potentially team teaching a course on antisemitism and racism. Our conversations about connecting Black history and Jewish history started after I had heard Wes speak about his project about Haiti as a Black state and a refuge for Black people living under oppression. On the surface, this sounded a lot like Zionism, which promoted a creation of a Jewish state as a refuge for Jews persecuted elsewhere in the world. But the history Wes was telling came nearly a century before Zionism. And then on a beautiful March afternoon in 2020, when we were still not sure what this new virus meant, Wes and I took a long walk along the southeast shore of Manhattan, from Battery Park to Stuyvesant Town, and started talking about the course and a potential lecture series.

My walk with Wes took place shortly after a faculty seminar about diversity and inclusion, organized by James P. McCartin of the Theology Department, had ended on Friday, March 6—what turned out to be the last day we'd be on campus for a year or more. The seminar, which included a small but diverse group of faculty from across the university, engaged in meaningful discussions on what diversity and inclusion really meant and how to make these catchphrases meaningful at Fordham, while reading works by George Yancy, Bryan Massingale, and others. It was at that seminar that I met some wonderful people, with whom I continued our conversations after the seminar ended. I am grateful to Jim for including me in the group. Without that I may not have encountered the writings of some of the scholars, whose work would prove very influential in conceptualizing this book, nor would I have met Rachelle Green, a practical theologian and a scholar whose work focuses on theological education in the context of confinement. In our conversations, Rachelle has given me insight on race and religion I would not have otherwise had.

The COVID lockdown was something we have never experienced before, and while it required a lot of adjustment, it also had a silver lining. There was not much to do, so reading and watching films filled the time. My husband Shawn Hill—my best friend and life partner—and I began Zoom movie nights with different friends. With Wes we began to explore some of the issues Wes and I were discussing in relation to our course. We all hoped that by the summer this whole disruption would be over. But the COVID pandemic continued; we continued to read books and watch films. I am grateful to Shawn for curating these amazing films and to Wes Alcenat for joining us on this intellectual adventure in the middle of a pandemic. The films Shawn found opened for all of us, I think, new areas of scholarly interests and inquiries.

My *Blood Libel* book came out just in the nick of time—the launch was at the Cullman Center for Scholars and Writers at the New York Public Library (NYPL) was on February 12, 2020—the last live, in-person event we would all have, as it turns out, for years. So, when COVID hit, I was beginning to work on my next book projects. The plan was to go to Europe in the summer to work in the archives and then come back and begin a research fellowship at the Center for Jewish History (CJH) in New York. But COVID thwarted these plans: I could not go to Europe, nor could I take full advantage of a National Endowment for the Humanities (NEH) research fellowship at the Center for Jewish History in New York because in-person research was not possible. The CJH archivists and librarians did all they could to help digitize or find digitized versions of some of the materials I hoped to work on. I am grateful Rachel C. Miller, Lauren Gilbert, and Malgorzata Bakalarz Duverger for their time and effort to accommodate my research needs remotely. But even with excellent assistance from devoted librarians and archivists, virtual research can never be as methodical as in person—even with multiple tabs open. I want to express my thanks to the NEH and the Center for Jewish History and Fordham University for allowing me to spend a year on research and writing. It was an unusual year, but there is no doubt in my mind that without this fellowship and the time it afforded me, this book would not have been written.

Thus, in the summer of 2020, just as we were all hoping for a better fall, I decided to use this time at home and write an article on the Christian trope of Jewish servitude and the myth of Jewish power as two ideas behind the rejection of Jewish equality in modern societies, in Europe and in the US. In that article I planned to discuss briefly the continuing legacy of the American history of slavery and its ramifications for Black citizenship. This was to be a summer project to tide me over till I could go back to the archives and return to the projects I planned to work on during my sabbatical. By late August, the "article" grew beyond anything any journal would accept. And so, I had to acknowledge that what I thought would be my "retirement project" began now. In September, it became clear that it would be a while before I would be able to get to the archives and in-person research and to my two other projects. The pandemic thus moved a project that I had been thinking about and reading for but intended to devote my time and energy to in a few years to the front burner.

Working from home during the pandemic, I have been deeply grateful to librarians across Europe and the US for digitizing so many historical sources I used in this book. They were available through their own platforms, HathiTrust, or Google Books. I am grateful to Amazon and Biblio.com for serving as de facto libraries, admittedly with nonreturnable books, when scholarly books were not available in libraries or online. I have bought many dozens of them, creating high and precarious piles on most flat surfaces in our apartment—academic presses must have felt a bounce!

Writing the book was a humbling experience—stepping outside one's own specialty and learning about a new field requires openness and willingness to make oneself vulnerable. Reading as much as I did won't replace decades one devotes to one's own field of expertise. I am therefore deeply grateful to Fred Appel of Princeton University Press for choosing thoughtful and knowledgeable anonymous readers for the book manuscript. The book is much stronger, and I especially appreciate the sharp critique and suggestions and prodding by the reader whose expertise was in African American studies. I have always loved peer review but with this, and my last book, where I stepped outside my own familiar area, the readers' reports were particularly helpful. The late Jeannette Hopkins showed

me how to accept even the sharpest criticisms from smart and thoughtful readers. I am grateful for the time and energy the readers put into
helping me make the book better. I tried my best; the book is no doubt
much better, though I am much aware that there is always more room for
improvement.

One thing I missed greatly during the pandemic and the writing of this
book was the ability to share my work and ideas with my colleagues. I am
therefore grateful to my friends who were willing to hear about my project during our pandemic walks, in particular Sara Lipton, Josh Teplitsky,
and Billy Weitzer. But despite lack of opportunities to share my work with
colleagues, the years of teaching and discussing these ideas with students
have been invaluable. I am grateful to the students who took my classes.
I have learned a lot from our discussions. In 2019 at the YIVO Institute
for Jewish Research, I taught a class on "History, Memory, and Law," in
which we explored three examples of turning to law and courts to deal
with historical past: France's reckoning with the Vichy regime, the recent
public trials in the US for racial crimes committed in the civil rights era,
and Poland's turn to law and legislation while facing its Holocaust era
past. That class gave me an opportunity to explore in a classroom setting,
for the first time, similarities between historical issues related to Europe's
Jewish past and the racial reckoning in the US. Ed Geffner, Judy Hol-
lander, Eleanor Lange, and Passi Rosen-Bayewitz were in that group, and
we continued some of these conversations later on. I am grateful to you for
your engagement and interest.

But the most gratitude goes to my undergraduate students at Fordham. It
is to them that I want to dedicate this book. Students in the 2018 Honors
Class in modern European history provided an inspiration for exploring
ideas in modern European history, beyond what I usually would focus
on in Jewish Studies. Sofia Anjum, Zane Austill, Elizabeth Breen, Kayla
Champion, Cathleen Freedman, Grace Getman, Kathleen Gleason, Corbin
Gregg, Carrington Gregori, Jing Han, Vincenzo Harty, Cristine Kalinski,
Brendan McErlaine, Frances Murray, Ritamarie Pepe, Jillian Rice, Lyla
Saxena, Umar Tahir, Daejah Woolery—you will probably see some of the
ideas we discussed reflected in this book. Thank you for such a stimulating
semester! Similar gratitude goes to the students in my "values seminar" on
antisemitism—over the years this class has helped me clarify my thinking about Jewish servitude and the antisemitic myth of Jewish power. I am
particularly grateful to Emily Borovskis, Sarah Cavanagh, Radley Ciego,
Emma Fingleton, Eesha Khan, Emilia Klapak, Anastasia Lacina, Michael
Liberto, Christopher Penello, Abby Ponticello, and Anthony Voka of the

fall 2018 class; Sally Brander, Katherine Courter, Isabella and Olivia Dixon, Jamie Hashem, and Clare McCabe of the fall 2019 class. Sally Brander and Clare McCabe co-curated with me an exhibit on *Media Technology and the Dissemination of Hate*, which connected aspects of the visual language present in both antisemitic and racist imagery. I appreciated our conversations as we were organizing the material—the fruit of student research in both iterations of the class from 2018 and 2019. Last but not least, students in my other classes, including in the class on antisemitism and racism, which Wes Alcenat began to teaching in 2021–2022, deserve thanks. I especially want to thank David Arizmendi, Maya Bentovim, Valerie Glass, and Kyla Hill from the fall 2021 class and Katherine Brown, Sara Castricato, Connor Chapman, Michele Daye, Lesley East, and Mika Freund from the spring 2022 class in appreciation for the way they grappled with the readings and engaged deeply with the materials and issues we discussed, which was truly inspiring. Maya, you even have a footnote in this book!

This book is really a tribute to my students and to diversity in the classroom—it leads to new thoughts, new connections, and new scholarship! I am grateful for having this opportunity to share my knowledge and to learn. Teaching is never a one-way street.

# Enduring Marks of Inferiority

ON AUGUST 11 AND 12, 2017, white supremacists, as the *Washington Post* reported, "mostly young white males," gathered in Charlottesville, Virginia, for the Unite the Right rally, ostensibly to protest the removal of the statue of confederate general Robert E. Lee by the City of Charlottesville and the renaming of the park in which the statue had stood as "The Emancipation Park."[1] The rally attracted hundreds of white protesters and a diverse group of counterprotesters, each representing different—and clashing—visions of American society and polity. On the evening of August 11, the white supremacists marched through the University of Virginia, torches in hand, chanting "Blood and soil!" "You will not replace us!" "Jews will not replace us!" and "White Lives Matter," with some donning medieval Christian symbols. The next day the events turned violent. A white supremacist drove into the crowd of counterprotesters, killing thirty-two-year-old Heather Heyer, and injuring nineteen others, while still many others were physically attacked and beaten.

During the civil trial of the organizers of the Unite the Right Rally in Charlottesville in 2021, the *Washington Post* reported, "Defendants dropped the n-word, expressed admiration for Adolf Hitler and trafficked in racist pseudoscience."[2] Two of the defendants, who represented themselves in court, cross-examined the plaintiffs and other witnesses, including their co-conspirators, one of whom they asked, "to tell his 'favorite Holocaust joke.'" Even defense attorneys "embraced the racist rhetoric." One, "repeatedly used the word 'k—' in hopes that it would 'desensitize' the jury."

The events in Charlottesville mixed antisemitism and anti-Black racism—a characteristic of the so-called "white supremacist" or "white nationalist" groups. But what has been, until recently, often missing from the coverage and description of these groups is that they represent a distinctly white Christian supremacy, which has far deeper roots than modern racism and modern antisemitism. The groups now dubbed "white nationalist" or "white supremacist," occasionally "Christian nationalist," express "Christian racial populism" through white domination over both non-whites and non-Christians.[3] Their ideology, articulated in the US through the defense of the Confederacy and through antisemitic chants, such as "Jews will not replace us," and, in Europe, through anti-Muslim and antisemitic attacks, vociferously rejects the modern idea of equality—legal and social—between them as white Christian people, on one hand, and Jews and people of color, on the other.

The two sharply contrasting visions of a state were colliding in Charlottesville—one embracing multicultural equal citizenship, another ethnonational white Christian identity. Both emerged in the Western world in the aftermath of the American and French Revolutions, but their roots run deeper. Until the late eighteenth century, European society, which included colonies, had been organized around social estates and legal pluralism—the concept of equality before law did not exist. With the Enlightenment, ideas about equality and rights began to be debated, and, following the American and French Revolutions, conceptualization of what citizenship and nationhood meant started to take shape. In Europe, two dominant ideas of citizenship and nationhood emerged: one, rooted in a political national identity, gradually and grudgingly included all those who inhabited a political state; the other, grounded in an ethnic, or ethnoreligious, identity, tended to exclude people who were not considered part of a given ethnic group. In some European states these ideas clashed, sometimes violently. In the US, similar debates about equality before law and about belonging emerged, but only a little later, as the country began to wrestle with the legal meaning of the phrase "We, the People" in the preamble to the US Constitution and the ideals of equality contained in this document and in the Declaration of Independence. But those debates were grounded in ideas about race and color.

While modern antisemitism and modern racism are, indeed, as George M. Fredrickson has argued, the outgrowth of processes associated with modernity, and while, indeed, "white supremacy attained its fullest ideological and institutional development" in the US between the 1890s and 1950s, in South Africa in the twentieth century, and in Nazi Germany, the ideology espoused by white supremacists in the US and in Europe is rooted in Christian ideas of social and religious hierarchy. These ideas developed, gradually, first in the Mediterranean and Europe in respect to Jews and then in respect to people of color in European colonies and in the US, before returning transformed back to Europe.[4] That vision of social hierarchy is built on the foundations of early Christian supersessionist theology that negated Judaism as it claimed to "replace" it, and is hence sometimes called replacement theology or replacement theory. Ancient and medieval Christians developed a sense of superiority over Jews, whom they saw as carnal and inferior, and rejected by God. Christians, they asserted, were now the new Israel, a new chosen people, spiritual and superior. Jews, then, as Geraldine Heng has argued in another context, became "constitutive, not incidental" to the formation of Christian identity; indeed, "Christian identity . . . was constructed not only in opposition to Judaism . . . but also in terms of Judaism."[5] Early Christian theology created, to use George Yancy's term, "epistemic orders" of social and religious hierarchy, in which Jews played a crucial role in the process of shaping Christian identity rooted in dominance rather than humility epitomized in Jesus's "turn the other cheek" doctrine.[6] For Christians, Jews became necessary "contrast figures" created and used to validate Christians' claims of theological replacement and superiority.[7]

With political power gained by Christians and the Christian empire taking shape in the fourth century, Christian supersessionism became Christian supremacy with its theological superiority now embedded into law and Jews specifically targeted in degrading legislation. Over the centuries in medieval Europe, Christian supremacy became more deeply entrenched in law, theology, and culture, clashing at times with historical reality, when real Jews of flesh and blood did not easily fit into the ideas Christians held about them. This Christian supremacy turned into white Christian supremacy with the colonial expansion in the early modern era, its Christian identity never lost even if individuals associated with it might not have been devoted churchgoers.

This book focuses on the interplay between law, theology, and culture, arguing that the modern rejection of equality of both Jews and Black people in the West is the legacy of Christian supersessionism, a theological concept developed in antiquity and implemented in law and policy when Christianity became a political power—its fruit Christianity's claim to superiority and dominance. Scholars of antisemitism and racism have frequently focused on theology and culture, gesturing only slightly, and sometimes not at all, toward the role law has played in that history.[8] But, as Ian Haney López has argued in the context of American law, law "transforms" ideas into "lived reality," law "reifies" them.[9] Haney López's argument about the capacity of the law to "shape and constrain how people think about the world they inhabit" can be expanded beyond American conceptions of race to premodern social and religious order.[10] According to Haney López, "Legal rules and decisions construct races through legitimation, affirming the categories and images of popular racial beliefs and making it nearly impossible to imagine nonracialized ways of thinking about identity, belonging, and difference." The same can be said about constructions of religious difference and legal affirmation of religious beliefs and hierarchy in medieval Europe. When that theological understanding of the relations between Jew/Judaism and Christians/Christianity became implemented into law, that relation transformed into Christian supremacy. Through "its coercive potential," law reified theological ideas of Christian supersessionism and superiority over Judaism.[11]

The following pages explore the relationship between Christian theology and law to demonstrate how legal and theological frameworks that were created centuries ago within Western Christianity led to social and legal exclusion of, and in modern times also a denial of equality to, Jews and Black people. The crux of the argument, then, lies in the Christian sense of superiority, a mental habit that developed first in a religious sense with regard to Jews and then transformed also into a racialized dominance, accelerating when Europeans expanded their political reach beyond Europe and established slaveholding empires in the early modern period. This was not only a cultural but also a legal transformation. Law created more tangible structures that justified and reinforced Christian domination and sense of superiority through, to quote Haney López, "promulgation and enforcement of rules that determine[d] permissible behavior."[12] This legal framework was first deployed in relation to Jews and later in relation to colonized non-Europeans of color. Paradoxically, if Christians condemned Jews and Judaism as committed to "law," it was through law that Christians turned theological exegesis into social and political hierarchy and, ultimately, also racial order. The book treats the word "supremacy" in its literal—not figurative—sense of being in "the position of supreme or highest authority or power."[13] In that sense, "supremacy" is linked to political and legal structures, which simultaneously both reflected and shaped cultural attitudes.

The ensuing chapters explore the history of the idea of Christian domination and its evolution not just into white supremacy but specifically white Christian supremacy as it exists today on both sides of the Atlantic through the lens of one motif—that of slavery and servitude. Slavery and servitude connect anti-Jewish sentiments—at first theological and in modern times also racial—with anti-Black racism. Slavery and servitude, though a legal nonracialized reality in antiquity, came to be attached to Jews as a metaphorical idiom when Christian writers began to describe Christianity's relation to Judaism and to think of Jews as doomed to "perpetual servitude." This theological idea was then translated into law, creating among Christians habits of thinking about Jews as perpetually inferior.[14] Now, the Christian idea of Jewish inferiority has become supported by both theology and law. In this rendering, centuries before slavery and servitude came to be associated with Blackness, freedom became linked to Christianity and servitude to Judaism.

In late antiquity and in the Middle Ages, Blackness was sometimes, though not always, manifested in the Christian world in negative terms as an association with ugliness, sin, or Islam, but "dark-skinned people" were still seen "as eligible for salvation," even as saints.[15] With conversion to Christianity their earlier ugliness and debasement disappeared, and their handsomeness as Christians once more visually reasserted Christian preeminence. But in the early modern period, the legally sanctioned reality of enslavement of black Africans in the European colonies created a more defined mental and legal hierarchy delineated along color lines. Freedom and liberty now came to be linked not only to Christianity but to whiteness, and servitude and enslavement to Blackness.[16] One inferior to the other.

The concept of "perpetual servitude" of Jews and the legacy of real enslavement of millions of black Africans and Black Americans then have been behind the obstinate refusal to admit Jews and Black people into a polity on equal terms.* But—and this is important to stress—while the idiom of "perpetual servitude" of Jews and the reality of enslavement of Black people share roots and remain at play within the dominant European and Euro-American Christian culture and society, one is not the cause of the other. To be sure, the idea of Jewish servitude and inferiority was articulated first, at a time when Christianity was still an emerging and

---

* I have chosen to capitalize "Black" to denote ethnicity and people of the African diaspora, who have developed a historically distinct identity, so Black Americans, Black people, but I have kept it lowercase for "black" as a color, including to describe the dark color of skin, hence black Africans. This is a choice recommended by the National Association of Black Journalists and is accepted by the *Chicago Manual of Style*. This is to correspond with a similar convention used with "Native Americans," "Arab Americans," "Jewish Americans," and so on. I do not capitalize the word "white," since that word does not denote a self-embraced ethnic identity, except for white supremacists. Instead, I use "European" or "Euro-Americans" if I want to denote whiteness as related to European identity. Though I rarely use the term "African American" to avoid de-Americanizing Black Americans, when I use the term, it is to parallel "Euro-Americans."

persecuted sect, as a form of reassurance and justification of Christianity's theological claims. Only later, after Christianity turned into a Christian supremacy, was the power of the law deployed to reify Christian conception of theological superiority over Jews. The ideology of inferiority of Jews, thus, had developed before it became embodied in law, and even then, Jews were not enslaved. In contrast, the practice of enslavement of black Africans developed at first in a military and economic context that had more to do with Christendom's expansion during the Iberian Reconquista than racial ideologies, which in fact would develop later to justify the enslavement of Africans and the resulting social, political, and economic hierarchies. As Barbara Fields has observed, "it was not Afro-Americans . . . who needed a racial explanation; it was not they who invented themselves into a race. Euro-Americans resolved the contradiction between slavery and liberty by defining Afro-Americans as a race."[17] In short, the idea of Jewish servitude emerged among a socially insecure new sect to justify a new theological idea, whereas racial hierarchies emerged from a position of power to justify the reality of slavery. Echoes of both still reverberate today.

It would be impossible to write an exhaustive history of white supremacy, as it evolved over centuries in different places and times, or even a comprehensive history of racism and antisemitism and their overlaps and distinctions. It would be similarly impossible to write a history of the role of Western Christian theology in racism and antisemitism—there were regional and denominational differences. There is also no single story of Christian antisemitism and racism. Christian beliefs were used both to justify persecution of Jews and to protect them from such persecution, even if sometimes the desire to protect was only motivated by a desire to convert.[18] Today, too, white evangelical Christians might espouse both antisemitic and racist views, while claiming to have "warm feelings toward African Americans" and expressing their staunch support for Israel.[19] Similarly, biblical texts were used both to excoriate modern slavery and to staunchly defend it. Slavers, slaveholders, and abolitionists, Black and white, often drew on the same texts to argue their opposing sides. And, today, some modern Christian theologians grapple with questions of race and racism, while others continue to espouse racist ideology.[20]

But slavery and servitude provide a lens onto confluences of racism and antisemitism and onto the role law and theology played in these histories, allowing to see through some of these difficult-to-disentangle complexities. The concepts of "servitude" and "slavery," with which the idea of Christian domination is tightly connected, help illuminate the roots of the obstinate objections to Jewish and Black social and political equality, the anxiety about Black and Jewish presence within white Christian society, and fear of their power: "Jewish power" everywhere around the world and specifically in America also "Black power" or, as it was known in the nine-teenth and early twentieth century, "the Negro rule."

The lens of slavery and servitude also provides an opportunity for a useful comparison over the *longue durée* not to find (false) equivalences or engage in competition over who was hated and who suffered more. It reveals with more clarity mechanisms and processes involved in the pro-duction and entrenchment of social hierarchy and ideas about each group that continue to persist and remain, as the events in Charlottesville dem-onstrate, seemingly impossible to eradicate.[21]

For example, because the modern history of Jews, at least in the United States and some parts of Western Europe, is that of social climb and because the myth of "Jewish money and power" is one of the most insidi-ous and enduring antisemitic myths, the attachment of the mark of servi-tude to Jews in (white) Christian society is often forgotten. But, perhaps paradoxically, this theologically rooted trope of Jewish inferiority and the idiom of servitude as it was applied to Jews for centuries help explain the very myth of "Jewish power." The antisemitic trope of "Jewish power" is a sign both of Jewish "emancipation" from the theologically grounded idea of Jewish servitude in modern times and of Christian rejection of Jewish equality and social advance. In contrast, the legacy of Black slavery and of white desire to control Black bodies undeniably still marks the lived expe-riences of African Americans even today, even of those most educated and accomplished, who continue to be seen through the prism of "the histori-cal power of the white gaze," which, as George Yancy has argued, "distorts, caricatures, oppresses, and dehumanizes Black bodies," and which denies them intellectual, professional, or political accomplishments.[22]

Thus, both the elision, in white society, of intellectual accomplishments of Black people and the myth of Jewish power are interlocked through and rooted in the trope of slavery and servitude—historically, an idiom for Jews and the de jure reality for Black people. Both represent, to use Justice Roger Taney's phrase used in his infamous opinion in *Dred Scott*, "endur-ing marks of inferiority," as understood by the dominant white Christian society. Both stem from the same root and both are tightly connected in (white) Christian habits of thought, even if that ontological link is now often forgotten.[23] Both Jews and Black people became contrast figures in Western Christian culture, serving to reinforce, as Angela Onwuachi-Willing has argued in another context, "differences in group power" and to

maintain power structures through assertions of social hierarchy by holding them in subordinate and degraded positions.[24]

While anti-Jewish hostility is documented already in pre-Christian
Greek and Roman texts, it was not marked with the anti-Jewish idiom of
servitude.[25] That idiom developed in the context of theological debates in
the early days of Christianity, when Paul evoked Isaac and Ishmael, Sarah
and Hagar, and Jacob and Esau, to explain the relationship between
Jews and the followers of Jesus. Christians were now like Isaac, children
of the promise, they were the sons of a free woman; Jews were the sons
of a slave woman, Hagar; they were like Ishmael.[26] But it was the verse
from the book of Genesis, "an elder shall serve the younger," mentioned
in the Epistle to Romans and then reinterpreted by Augustine that would
leave a lasting mark on the legal status of Jews within Christendom.[27]
In the Middle Ages, what was once a scriptural exegesis entered the law
and began to play an important role within European Christian society in
the development of what sociologist Orlando Patterson dubbed "mental
structures," shaping and hardening a Christian sense of superiority and
dominance, resulting in "unconscious habits" of thought and behavior that
remain difficult to root out.[28] This superiority was later visually depicted
in public art in the figures of the *Ecclesia*, Christianity/Church—a triumphant queen, and the *Synagoga*, Judaism/Jewish Law, a humiliated,
blindfolded maiden.

Christian theological dominance and legal and political supremacy
became a European Christian white supremacy in the era of European
expansion and Europe's exploitative encounter with non-Europeans.[29]
And even if color prejudice and negative connotations about "blackness"
had developed already in antiquity, with early Christians linking blackness with sin, and whiteness with grace, the connection between Blackness
and slavery was not made, as David Goldenberg has shown, until Muslim
conquests of parts of Africa and the increase of black African slaves within
Muslim society.[30] In Christian Europe, it was the Iberian Peninsula that
became the conduit through which European Christians developed legal
and theological justifications for the enslavement of black Africans. European Christian consciousness, both the existing color prejudice, which
developed in the context of early intra-Christian religious polemic, and
the European Christian sense of superiority, which had emerged at first
in regard to Jews, now provided fertile ground for the development of
racialized Christianity, providing epistemic justification and explanation
for the territorial, economic, and political exploitation of people in the
Americas and Africa.[31] Indeed, as M. Lindsay Kaplan has shown, "the

construction of Jewish servitude through the figures of both Ishmael and Ham help[ed] sanction and strengthen the legitimacy of Muslim servitude. The identification of the Muslim sphere of influence with Northern Africa subsequently facilitate[d] the translation of these figural discourses of enmity and servitude to black Africans in the Iberian appropriation of African lands and in the sixteenth century establishment of the trade in the enslaved people."[32] The discourse on Jewish servitude, so deeply engrained in Christian legal and theological culture, Kaplan argues, helped "transfer the notion of hereditary inferiority to Africans"; in the Americas it would become, by legal design, hereditary—indeed perpetual—enslavement.[33]

But the association of Blackness with slavery and inferiority, and the racialization of slavery took longer. In the British colonies in North America, "the law," Barbara Fields has shown, "did not formally recognize the condition of perpetual slavery or systematically mark out servants of African descent for special treatment until 1661."[34] It is no coincident that by the seventeenth and eighteenth centuries a verb stemming from the Latin *denigrare*, used in antiquity and the Middle Ages to mean making something black or dyeing something black, and occasionally also blacken or sully (a soul, for example, could be "sullied," *denigrata*, with sin), acquired in different European languages a new dominant meaning, signifying degradation, demeaning, debasement, defamation, and "blackening character," pushing out the original meaning from dictionaries.[35] In the early modern period, thus, the word *denigrare* or "denigrate" distinctly linked "black," a component of the word, with lower status. The word's changed meaning stemmed from the association between Blackness and slavery.

This process took place almost at the same time as the word "white" was beginning to gain currency to define a superior social and legal status. The English verb "to denigrate," in its meaning "to degrade" or "to demean," thus, is deeply connected with the history of European enslavement of black Africans.

Printed books—with stories and images—both reflected and helped deepen these prejudices, existing and emerging, against Jews and dark-skinned non-Europeans, searing in the European Christian imagination anti-Jewish and anti-Black stereotypes that are still at play in modern white Christian supremacist circles. But books, language, and culture were not enough. The lasting structures of racism were built into law to support the new form of slavery officially sanctioned in the European colonies, thus creating and then reinforcing the most malignant anti-Black attitudes that still endure in a white—and aspiring-to-whiteness—society.

Then and now, literature, art, and law have played crucial roles in this process. As George M. Fredrickson has put it, anti-Black racism is "the child of slavery" but it has "outlived its parent" and even "grew stronger and more independent after slavery's demise."[36]

And so, over time, white European Christians branded both Jews and people of color with "badges of servitude" and inferiority, making their full social acceptance as equals problematic. The existence of legally sanctioned enslavement of Black people had an even deeper impact on the rights of Black Americans and other people of color. Blackness became tightly associated with slavery and, by extension, with a degraded status, developing "a racial folklore," as W. E. B. Du Bois observed, "grounded on centuries of instinct, habit, and thought and implemented by the conditioned reflex of visible color."[37]

But there was an even more insidious legacy of the ideas of slavery and servitude. In the United States, the legacy of Black enslavement and Black people's inferior legal status became part of the legal fabric and language of the country's conservative jurisprudence grounded in case law and precedent. Ideas of Black equality and citizenship thus required fundamental legal changes—these sparked violent opposition among whites. And in Europe, the tenacity of theologically rooted ideas about Jewish inferiority became evident during debates over the meaning of citizenship that took place in the aftermath of the French Revolution; the weight of the idiom of Jewish servitude was so heavy that—even though Jews were never enslaved—it led to the denial of Jewish equality and challenge of their right to belong in newly forming nations. It continued even after Jews eventually, if reluctantly, were granted citizenship rights de jure as the admittance of Jews to the ranks of citizens sparked an antisemitic backlash, marked at times by what Christhard Hoffman, Werner Bergmann, and Helmut Walser Smith called "exclusionary violence."[38]

In 1796, during a debate over citizenship of Jews in the Republic of Batavia, Dutch theologian and politician Ysbrand van Hamelsveld asked, "Will we continue to regard the Jewish people as alien residents or will we go further and regard them as Dutchmen, as members of the Batavian people—in other words, not only as our fellow human beings but also as our fellow citizens—on equal footing with Dutchmen?"[39] By the nineteenth century, some Europeans—in France, Germany, and elsewhere—responded to that question in the negative. In 1819, a German writer Hartwig von Hundt-Radovsky declared that "granting civic rights to Jews was an injustice perpetrated by the government against the non-Jewish inhabitants."[40] He claimed that while the non-Jews "founded the state, defended and preserved it with their wealth, blood, and lives," Jews, "a class of morally and spiritually degenerate people (who have used the state but never benefitted it)" would soon get an upper hand over Christians. A few decades later, Bruno Bauer, a German theologian, bemoaned "the birth of a new epoch, which will cost the Christian world great pains," and asked, "are the Jews to suffer no pain, are they to have equal rights with those who fought and suffered for the new world?"[41] Bauer asserted that "the idea of human rights was discovered for the Christian world in the last century only. It is not innate to men. . . . Human rights are not a gift of nature or of history but a prize which was won in the fight against the accident of birth and against privilege which came down through history from generation to generation." As long as Jews remained Jews, they did not deserve those rights; they lived, after all, in a "Christian state." These European thinkers expressed anxieties about citizenship and equality of Jews—anxieties that emerged in Europe with the French Revolution and its ideology of "Liberty, Equality, and Fraternity," which raised questions as to whom these ideals applied.[42] Indeed, soon after the Revolution, both in France and in European territories that came under French control and influence, the breadth of the ideal raised questions about whether Jews and other previously marginalized groups, especially Black people, were eligible for citizenship and equality.

The inclusion of Jews "tested the universalist claims of the French revolutionaries," and so did "the colonial question."[43] The status of hundreds of thousands of Black slaves and tens of thousands of free men of color in the French colonies became a subject of fierce debates. White Europeans, even those committed to "liberty, equality, and fraternity," had serious misgivings about freedom and equality of Black people. One author did not even refer to the freed Black people living in the colonies as "inhabitants" or "residents," a term he seems to have reserved for white colonists. Blackness, in European minds, was indelibly tied to slavery and servitude, with the word "Negro" interchangeably used with "a slave," confirming, as the French bishop and revolutionary leader Henri Grégoire noted, that "the whites, having power, have declared, against justice, that dark skin excludes one from the advantages of society."[44]

In the US, the language and debates surrounding the status of Black Americans was eerily reminiscent of that concerning Jews in Europe— with a clear distinction of the existence of de jure enslavement of Black people as opposed to only the theologically grounded idea of slavery and servitude of Jews. The question of citizenship of people of color did not garner direct attention when the Constitution was ratified, although racial eligibility was addressed in the 1790 Naturalization Act, which limited naturalization to "a free white person," thus inscribing whiteness into the legal fabric of the country. Whiteness remained a requirement in the subsequent revisions of the law.

But the explicit question about the meaning of citizenship drew national attention only decades later. In 1820, following the admission of the Territory of Missouri to the Union, a debate erupted in the Congress over a clause in the Missouri constitution prohibiting "free people of color" from settling in Missouri in perpetuity, raising questions about potential restrictions of the rights of citizens of other states. The defenders of that clause claimed, as did Philip Barbour of Virginia, that "the Constitution of the United States was framed by the States respectively, consisting of the European descendants of white men; that it had a view to the liberty and rights of white men."[45] The Missouri debate exposed the lasting fissures around race and Black people's belonging, as well as sharp differences over the question as to who was included in "We, the people." It revealed what Judith Shklar called "enduring anti-liberal dispositions that have regularly asserted themselves, often very successfully, against the promise of equal political rights contained in the Declaration of Independence and its successors."[46] As the 2016 and 2020 US presidential campaigns demonstrated, these debates have not been relegated to the past. Over the last two centuries, these different visions periodically have clashed with each other.[47]

In the end, even after both Jews and people of color were admitted into de jure citizenship, they remained vulnerable outsiders fighting for their right to belong. And despite their demands of equality, dignity, and respect, and even despite their undisputable accomplishments and wealth, they were always reminded about their outsider and—in the eyes of white Christians in Europe and the United States—inferior position. For Jews, it was social exclusion; for Black Americans, it has been relentless efforts to undermine their citizenship rights that are still taking place, as exemplified by the denial of legitimacy of Barack Obama's presidency by questioning his birth certificate and by restrictions on voting rights passed across the country.

That outsider status is linked to that past association with slavery and servitude. As Orlando Patterson has argued, "the slave was conceived of as someone who did not belong because he was an outsider," at the same time, "the slave became an outsider because he did not belong."[48] The trope of slavery and servitude coupled, in modern time, with racial theories made the acceptance of Jews and Blacks into white Christian political

bodies difficult. The levels and intensity of that rejection varied in different times and places.

American history has been shaped by racial history and Black Americans have held a central place in that history. As Justice John Marshall
Harlan wrote in his dissent in *Plessy v. Ferguson*: "The destinies of the two
races in this country are indissolubly linked together."[49] He echoed Frederick Douglass's statement from 1854 about the United States as a land
"peopled by what may be called the most dissimilar races on the globe.
The black and the white—the negro and the European—these constitute
the American people—and, in all the likelihoods of the case they will ever
remain the principal inhabitants of the United States, in some form or
other."[50] Yet, as both historical sources and recent events demonstrate,
despite the ideal of equality enshrined in the American Declaration of
Independence, dominant American national identity has been shaped by
and grounded in racial identity and in the exclusion of Black individuals
from citizenship—with de jure discrimination of Black Americans lasting
until at least 1964 and de facto social discrimination persisting even until
today.[51] To be "American" has often been explicitly or implicitly understood
to be white.[52] This is how Senate Minority Leader Mitch McConnell sees
it. On January 19, 2022, commenting on voting laws, McConnell stated,
"The concern is misplaced because if you look at the statistics, African
American voters are voting in just as high a percentage as Americans,"
sparking a backlash.[53] Jews in the United States, by virtue of their eligibility for naturalization according to the 1790 Naturalization Act and
its subsequent versions, were not excluded from citizenship; indeed, they
were, like many other European immigrants, "white by law," even if their
social belonging has been questioned.[54]

But in Europe, modern national identities were fashioned insepara-
bly from the idea of social exclusion of Jews, which has become almost
integral to ethnonationalist ideologies that developed in the nineteenth
century and which continues. And although that exclusion of Jews failed
de jure and Jews were in fact granted citizenship in Western European
states, across Europe, "anti-liberal dispositions," to use Judith Shklar's
phrase, often clashed with the modern "promise" of equal rights enshrined
in liberal constitutions.[55]

The anxiety about the inclusion of Jews and people of color as equals in
Western society stems from the conceptions of social hierarchy and legal
structures whose roots go deep to early Christian supersessionist theology, which defined itself and Christian identity by deprecation of Jewish
ceremonies and beliefs, and then, by extension, of Jews themselves. Once

combined with political power, Christian supersessionist theology became Christian supremacy, and, in the early modern and modern era, especially, but not exclusively, in the United States, a white Christian supremacy, constructed around identity firmly rooted in whiteness and Christianity and in social rejection of Jews and of people of color, especially of Black people. So, while Robert P. Jones has recently sought to demonstrate the "legacy of white supremacy in American Christianity," this book, by taking a deeper chronological look, flips the argument to show "the Christian legacy in white supremacy," for Christian supremacy predated white supremacy and has left its mark on the legal and mental structures that continue to reverberate in what is now commonly called white supremacy.[56]

If white American identity has been shaped by the presence of Black Americans, both enslaved and free, the same can be said about Jews and Christianity and about Jews and European history—their histories, too, have been "indissolubly linked." Those "indissolubly linked" histories cannot be fully grasped without understanding the deeply rooted "mental structures" or unconscious habits that have shaped culture, social relations, and the law, along with the instincts and habits of prejudice.[57] To that long history, as James Baldwin stressed, "we owe our frames of reference, our identities, and our aspirations."[58] That long history continues to play a role in our society, causing further rifts. To paraphrase Congresswoman Eleanor Holmes Norton, understanding that history is essential to finding remedies, and to become, as Vice-President Kamala Harris has often said, "unburdened" by what has been.[59] Part of that process is understanding the central role the two marginalized groups, Jews and Black people, have played in Christian European history and imagination and in shaping European and Euro-American identity. Both Jews and Black people have been, to use Frederic Raphael's words, "the margin that runs down the middle page" of Western history.[60] And, as Glynis Cousin and Robert Fine have argued, drawing attention to earlier scholars such as W. E. B. Du Bois, it is worth "reconnecting the study of racism and antisemitism" and "overcoming methodological separatism," because "racism and antisemitism have a connected history."[61] Cousin and Fine traced that connection to European modernity. But some strands of that shared history run deeper.

While the role of Christianity has been acknowledged in the history of antisemitism, indeed the historiography of antisemitism is often a history of Christian thought, the connections between the strand of Christian thought that was shaped by Christian attitudes toward Jews and Judaism and modern anti-Black racism has often been neglected.[62] The inverse is also true: while the role of Christianity is being scrutinized in the history of anti-Black racism and white supremacy, the impact of Christian anti-Jewish attitudes on the history of racism and on the same white Christian identity that is now under scrutiny is often missing.[63] This has been so in part because studies of antisemitism have paid scant attention to discourses that do not pertain to Jews, and studies of race and racism have typically focused on the oppression of people of color, especially Black Americans.[64] While that link was not lost on scholars in the early decades of the twentieth century, since the 1960s this connection has been forgotten.[65]

But both modern antisemitism and racism continue to be linked in both contemporary white Christian supremacy and at the roots that helped shape and nourish European Christian social and mental habits and legal structures, first, as M. Lindsay Kaplan has recently demonstrated, in regard to Jews, then in similar discourse also against Muslims and black Africans.[66] Within the Christian world, over time, Jews came to be seen as contrast figures, or as Geraldine Heng put it, "figures of absolute difference," never to be fully accepted in the social or political body, even if in reality Jews were frequently not that different from their neighbors in look or status; people of color, too, became contrast figures whose exclusion came to be both determined by social values and law.[67] Jews as contrast figures became key for the development of Christian identity in the same way as Black people became key in the construction of white identity. These stories sometimes overlapped, diverged, ran parallel, or crisscrossed each other, but the history of European dominance and of white supremacy is rooted in and intertwined with the history of Christian supersessionism and Christian supremacy, and that story began with Christianity's theological relation with Jews and Judaism.

# CHAPTER ONE

# The Sketches of Social Hierarchy in Early Christian Thought

FROM THE EARLIEST DECADES of Christianity, Christian thinkers wrestled with the question of its relationship with Jews and their religious practices. Christians claimed to have their beliefs supported by the Hebrew prophecies, but Jews largely rejected these new teachings. The earliest Christian texts written by Paul already articulate this tension as the still Jewish Jesus movement was reaching out to non-Jews. Paul, a Jew and a self-described "apostle to the Gentiles," was troubled by the idea that there was only one God and the exclusive claims that this was the only God of Israel, asking, "Is God the God of Jews only? Is he not the God of Gentiles also?" and answering, "Yes, of Gentiles also, since God is one."[1] Both "the circumcised," that is Jews, and "the uncircumcised," the Gentiles, would be "justified" through faith. And though in the same passage Paul affirmed that faith did not "overthrow the law," his more elaborate reflections on the "law," or rather the Torah and commandments, created a hierarchy of values: faith representing the spiritual, and "law" representing the "earthly" or "of the flesh." One—faith and spirit—superior to the other—law and flesh, for, according to Paul, "the flesh cannot please God."[2]

Paul extended this dichotomy to the relationship between "Israelites," who rejected the idea that Jesus, who had been crucified by Romans, was a Messiah, and those who accepted Jesus as the Messiah, be they Jews like Paul himself or "Gentiles." Paul bewailed,

> I have great sorrow and unceasing anguish in my heart. For I could wish that I myself were accursed and cut off from Christ for the sake of my own brothers, my kindred according to flesh. They are Israelites,

and to them belong the adoption, the glory, the covenants, the giving of the law, the worship, and the promises; to them belong the patriarchs, and from them, according to the flesh comes the Messiah. . . . It is not as though the word of God had failed. For not all Israelites truly belong to Israel, and not all of Abraham's children are his true descendants; but "It is through Isaac that descendants shall be named for you." This means that it is not the children of the flesh who are the children of God but the children of the promise are counted as descendants.[3]

Paul then added, discussing Abraham and the promise he was granted to have a child with Sarah, "something similar happened to Rebecca when she had conceived children by one husband, our ancestor Isaac. Even before they had been born or had done anything good or bad (so that God's purpose of election might continue, not by works but by his call) she was told, 'The elder shall serve the younger.' As it is written, 'I have loved Jacob, but I have hated Esau.'"[4]

In the centuries that followed, Christian thinkers would see Paul's representation of "Esau's enslavement and his general supersession by Jacob" as an "allegory of the displacement of Jews by Christians as the chosen people."[5] The phrase "the elder shall serve the younger" would become fateful. Reinterpreted centuries later, it would help provide theological grounding for Jews' legal status in Christian Europe, with biblical exegesis serving to justify a social and political order.

Paul would return to the motif of Abraham's descendants in his epistle to Galatians, in which he articulated—much more explicitly—a social and theological hierarchy. In Galatians, seeking to dissuade judaizing Christians from following Jewish rituals and ceremonies, he wrote: "For it is written that Abraham had two sons, one by a slave woman and the other by a free woman. One, the child of the slave, was born according to the flesh; the other, the child of the free woman, was born through the promise. Now this is an allegory: these women are two covenants. One woman, in fact is Hagar, from Mount Sinai, bearing children for slavery. Now Hagar is Mount Sinai in Arabia and corresponds to the present Jerusalem, for she is in slavery with her children. But the other woman corresponds to the Jerusalem above; she is free and she is our mother."[6] Christians were now, Paul continued, the children of promise, like Isaac.[7] Jews, who continued to follow God's commandments, were, in turn, Hagar's children, "born into slavery." "But just as at that time the child who was born according to the flesh persecuted the child who was born according to the spirit, so it is now also. . . . So then, brothers, we are children not of the slave but of the free woman. For freedom Christ has set us free." Paul then commanded, "Stand firm, therefore, and do not submit again to the yoke of slavery." Christians were like Isaac, the beloved child of promise, Jews were like Ishmael, the children of a slave woman, who, though elder, did not have the same status, and indeed was even banished from Abraham's house, and thus Christians should not follow their customs.

When Paul wrote these words, the Jerusalem Temple, with its ceremonies and sacrifices, still stood and Jews still had nominal sovereignty over Judea—Paul's words, thus, had nothing to do with the loss of political sovereignty and the destruction of the Temple in Jerusalem, which would take place decades later after the Judean uprising in 70 CE. Moreover, because slavery was a part of the social and legal structures of the Roman empire, the allegory Paul deployed—contrasting a free woman with a slave woman—would have had a real social dimension, conveying a meaningful social hierarchy. With the cult in Jerusalem compared to slavery and the faith in Christ to freedom, there was no doubt what values were attached to practices and beliefs of each group—even if only through an allegory. Paul's allegorical representation would have also resonated with the Graeco-Roman thought, in which a dichotomy between master and slave was extended to the dichotomy between soul and body.[8]

Over subsequent centuries, Christian thinkers continued to delineate their relationship with Jewish scriptures and practices in what David Nirenberg called a "polyphony" of voices, with some, like Marcion, rejecting the Hebrew Scriptures altogether, and others, like Eusebius, finding a way to see Jesus as the Messiah who fulfilled scriptural prophecies; and with most "assert[ing] the validity of their beliefs by negating" those of Jews.[9] And though Paul claimed that Jews and their practices were akin to "slavery," in the first three centuries of Christianity, Jews, unlike Christians whose religion was not recognized by the Roman Empire as legal until Emperor Constantine's reign, were free to practice their ceremonies.[10]

Tertullian, a Christian writer born in the middle of the second century CE, picked up on Paul's reference to Rebecca's children, Esau and Jacob, the elder and the younger, as figures of the Jews—the "anterior" and "greater" people and Gentile Christians—the "posterior" and "lesser" people.[11] Explaining how the posterior and "lesser" gentiles overcame Jews, the elder and "greater" people, Tertullian claimed, using references to Baal and other instances of idolatry in the Hebrew Scriptures, that while "Israel" succumbed to idols and abandoned God, the gentiles, who had been idolaters, discarded their idols and converted "to the same God from whom Israel had departed." Tertullian's explanation is still quite tentative as to how and why Christians, the younger and "lesser" people, overcame the Jews. The exegesis of the passage about "two nations" in Rebecca's womb would gain greater clarity in a new political situation—in 313 CE Christianity became a legal religion and then, in 380 CE, the official religion of the Roman Empire. Augustine of Hippo, born in 354 CE, who became one of the most influential Christian thinkers "shaping how Christendom would think with Jews," would give a new exegetical punch to Paul's interpretation of the Hebrew scriptures.[12]

In Augustine's writings, the dichotomy between flesh and spirit, slavery and freedom, and the allegories previously deployed by Paul and other early Christian authors, such as Tertullian, became sharper and more explicit and refined.[13] And while most scholars have focused on Augustine's "doctrine of Jewish witness," which served to affirm the Jews' right to remain within the body of Christianity qua Jews as witnesses to the truth of Christian revelation and "the antiquity of Christian promise," his teachings, especially those developing the idea of Jewish servitude, had a profound impact on what Jeremy Cohen called "a properly ordered Christian society."[14] Indeed, as M. Lindsay Kaplan stressed, "the concept of Jewish servitude, far from being a mere corollary to [Augustine's] theology of Jews" was in fact "central."[15] Augustine was writing years after Emperor Theodosius in his Edict of Thessalonica made Christianity the religion of the Empire, and thus his vision of the relation between Christianity and Judaism were inflected by a political context that was very different from that in which Paul or even other early Christian writers had lived.

"As the sacrifice of Cain from the fruits of the earth is rejected, while the sacrifice of Abel from the sheep of their fat is accepted, so the faith of the New Testament, which praises God from the innocence of grace is preferred to the earthly works of the Old Testament." So wrote Augustine in his work against Faustus, a Manichean, articulating supersession of the New over the Old Testament, between "faith" and "earthly works," and setting up a clear hierarchy.[16] The Cain metaphor also allowed Augustine to compare Jews to Cain, stamping them for posterity with a badge of the archetypal murderer.[17] Because Cain disobeyed God, Augustine claimed, he became a "slave to sin." And so, too, the Jews, "whom these actions prefigured," failed to recognize Christ; "filled with pride over works of the law and not humbled because of their sins," they "blazed forth with hatred against him." Like Cain, Jews were envious of Christ and his sacrifice. "And so," Augustine wrote, rounding off the metaphor, "Abel, the younger, is killed by his older brother. Christ, the head of the younger people, is killed by the older people the Jews. Abel is killed in a field; Christ is killed on Calvary."

And just like Cain, Augustine continued, "the unbelieving Jewish people is cursed. . . . They wanted to be not under grace but under the law."[18] They still "carry out the works of earthly circumcision, the earthly Sabbath, the earthly unleavened bread, the earthly Pasch," and practice "in a fleshly manner the works of the law." Like Cain, "that people truly groans and trembles lest, after having lost an earthly kingdom, they also be slain by this visible death."[19] But God saved them, "the impious people of the fleshly Jews shall not perish by bodily death. For whoever destroys them in that way shall suffer seven punishments." Instead, "the Christian faithful sees well enough the subjection that the Jews merited when they killed the Lord for their proud kingdom." Indeed, just as "the Lord placed a sign on Cain so that no one who found him would kill him," so too with Jews,

> it is truly remarkable how all the nations that the Romans subjugated crossed over to the religious practices of the Romans and took up the observance and celebration of those sacrilegious rites but that the Jewish people, whether under pagan kings or under Christian ones, did not lose the sign of its law, by which it is distinguished from the other nations and peoples. And every emperor or king who finds Jews in his realm finds them with this sign and does not kill them, that is does not make them cease to be Jews, who are set apart from the community of other nations by a certain distinct and proper sign of their own observance.[20]

Jews cease to be Cain only when they "cross over to Christ."[21] Here the political became intertwined with the hermeneutical: Jews did lose sovereignty after 70 CE and all hope for rebuilding the temple after the Bar Kokhba Revolt of 132–135 CE, while Christianity, the persecuted sect, was now the religion of the Roman Empire. But since the Jews' law was a sign of Cain, Jews were to be preserved and allowed to live within Christendom.[22]

But the motif of "working the earth" was not only a metaphor; it also signaled status. In a hierarchical society, such as that of the Roman Empire, those who worked the earth belonged to the lower plebeian strata. Some may have been slaves. By returning to the verse in Genesis, "If you till the soil, it shall no longer yield its strength to you" (Gen. 4:12), not only did Augustine associate Jews with Cain, the murderer, but through this metaphor of soil he also linked them with the lowest strata of the Roman society, establishing now not only a theological but also a social hierarchy.

This social hierarchy would become even more evident in Augustine's later work, *The City of God*, in which he exploited the three biblical pairs of brothers to establish a typology of the relationship between Jews and Christians and between Judaism and Christianity: Cain and Abel, Ishmael and Isaac, and Jacob and Esau. In this work, Cain, still a symbol of "the Jews," was now associated with the "city of man," while Abel with "the city of God." And while the city of man was "in its status a servant," the "city of God" was a "free city."[23] And here Augustine returned to Paul's Hagar and Sarah as allegories for the two covenants given by God, "the old and the new," as understood through these cities. There were two meanings, Augustine argued, to the "earthly city," or the city of man: "its own presence" and its role "by its presence to signify the Heavenly City." The citizens of the earthly city were "produced by nature which is vitiated by sin," those in the "Heavenly City are brought forth by grace, which sets nature free from sin." This difference, he returned to Hagar and Sarah and their sons, "is also symbolized in Abraham's two sons: the one, Ishmael, son of the slave named Hagar, born in the course of nature, whereas the other, Isaac, son of Sarah, the free woman, was born of fulfillment of a promise. Both sons, it is true, were born of Abraham's seed," but only one, Isaac, was a symbol of God's grace and revelation of the goodness of God—this symbolized Christians; the other, Ishmael, of the earthly city marked by sin, symbolized "the carnal people of the old covenant," the Jews.[24]

Even more explicit is Augustine's exegesis of Rebecca's twins, Jacob and Esau. The key passage for Augustine was the one also used earlier by Paul and Tertullian—God's reply to Rebecca when the twins were struggling in her womb: "Two nations are in your womb, Two separate peoples shall issue from your body; One people shall be mightier than the other, And the older shall serve the younger."[25] About that last phrase—"the elder shall serve the younger"—Augustine wrote: "hardly anyone of our people has taken it as meaning anything but that the older people of the Jews was destined to serve the younger people, the Christians." It was true, he allowed, that this could refer to Idumeans, the physical descendants of Esau, "but in fact it is more appropriate to believe that the prophetic statement, 'One people shall overcome the other, and the elder shall be servant of the younger,' was intended to convey some more important meaning. And what can this meaning be except a prophecy which is now being clearly fulfilled in the Jews and the Christians?" Making this point, Augustine, clearly influenced by Tertullian, added, "It is Christ, whom the nations serve, and to whom the princes do reverence. He is lord over his brother, since his people have dominion over the Jews."[26] Augustine may have insisted this was an allegorical interpretation of these passages, but he wrote them in a new political reality marked by Jewish dispersion and loss of sovereignty, and the very recent rise of a Christian empire. That new political reality sharpened Augustine's reading of these scriptural passages, allowing him to state repeatedly that "the old covenant from Mount Sinai which 'has children destined for slavery' is of no value except in so far as it bears witness to the new covenant."[27] Supersession and hierarchy were lucidly articulated in this one sentence. Christians now had dominion over Jews.

The entanglement of the idea of Jewish witness to the verity of Christianity with the new context of a now politically assertive Christianity was even more apparent later in *The City of God*. "But the Jews," Augustine wrote in Book XVIII, "who killed him and refused to believe in him, to believe that he had to die and rise again, suffered a more wretched devastation at the hands of the Romans and were utterly uprooted from their kingdom, where they had already been under the dominion of foreigners. They were dispersed all over the world—for indeed there is no part of the earth where they are not to be found—and thus by the evidence of their own scriptures they bear witness for us that we have not fabricated the prophecies about Christ."[28] Some Jews were able to see through the prophecies and "have come to believe in him." About those "this prediction was made: 'Even if the number of the sons of Israel shall be like the sand of the sea. It is only a remnant that will be saved.'"[29] But, Augustine explained, "it follows that when the Jews do not believe in our scriptures, their own scriptures are fulfilled in them, while they read them with blind eyes. Unless, perhaps, someone is going to say that the Christians fabricated the prophecies of Christ." Augustine then pointed to Psalm 59 and its verse, "My God will let me look in triumph on my enemies. Do not kill them, or my people may forget; scatter them by your power, and bring them down."[30] According to Augustine, this verse was another prophecy:

> God has thus shown to the Church the grace of his mercy in the case of her enemies, the Jews, since as the Apostle says, "their failure means salvation for the Gentiles." And this is the reason for his forbearing to slay them—that is for not putting an end to their existence as Jews, although they have been conquered and oppressed by the Romans; it is for fear that they should forget the Law of God and thus fail to bear convincing witness on the point I am now dealing with. Thus, it was not enough for the psalmist to say, "Do not slay them, lest at some time they forget your law," without adding, "Scatter them." For

if they lived with that testimony of the scriptures only in their own land, and not everywhere, the obvious result would be that the Church, which is everywhere, would not have them available among all nations as witnesses to the prophecies which were given beforehand concerning Christ.[31]

Scholars have (over)focused on the significance and the long-term impact of this "doctrine of Jewish witness," as a doctrine protecting Jews from Christian violence.[32] But far more central to Augustine's thinking about Jews—repeated far more frequently than this idea of "the Jewish witness"—and far more impactful was his vision of the ideal social and religious order and hierarchy.[33] From his affirmation of Paul's dichotomy of flesh and spirit, to his reinterpretation of the scriptural pairs of brothers, to his repetition that Jews were "under the dominion" of the "younger people," as the "elder" brother who was a servant to the younger. Jews, Augustine frequently stressed, were "the children of a slave woman," Christians were the children of a free woman. And although scholars have tended to read Augustine in theological terms, his language and imagery had a resonance in political and social reality of the time. Indeed, some of his readers may have been familiar with the imagery of *Judaea capta*, a conquered Judea, developed after 70 CE, when the Romans destroyed the Jerusalem Temple, with Judea and the Jewish people represented in the figure of a captive, enslaved woman, weeping, with a Roman soldier, a representation of the Roman Empire, triumphantly standing behind her.[34] But in Augustine's time, Christianity had just recently asserted itself as a religion of the empire, melding the godly with the political. Jews were now not only subjugated by Romans but were indeed subject to Christian authority and power. With slavery still "more or less universal" in the Roman world, Augustine was very much aware of the power dynamic in a slave-holding society even as he was deploying slavery as a metaphor.[35] In his expositions on Psalms, *Enarrationes in Psalmos*, Augustine declared, "The elemental, daily demonstration of the power of man over man is that of master over slave. Almost every household has a display of power of this kind."[36] Similarly, in his *City of God*, Augustine outlined the social order of power and obedience, with wives obeying husbands, children their fathers, and slaves and servants their masters. Thus when Augustine repeatedly used the language of servitude, slavery, and submission in reference to Jews, he was not unconscious of what that power dynamic entailed. In Augustine's writings, then, we see more than theological hierarchy of flesh and spirit, we also see an early manifestation of a political hierarchy with

Christianity dominant over Jews and Judaism in servitude. Christian supersessionism of early centuries here is shown to be transforming into Christian supremacy.

As Roman law was adjusting to the new political reality to reflect Christian political dominance and theological preeminence, it began to display—even before Augustine composed his works—increasing discomfort with the social position Jews.[37] In pre-Christian Roman law, Jews were permitted to practice their rites—albeit with limitations, since the Romans were not eager to encourage their proselytism, and at least since 212 CE Jews were considered Roman citizens.[38] As Benjamin Isaac has shown, in the Roman Empire "subject peoples normally had a right to practice their ancestral religion."[39] But, it appears, that only Jews required special legal accommodations because of their rites: sabbath observance, dietary laws, and circumcision. Their monotheism along with these practices was seen as dangerous for the empire, thus, a balance was struck to allow only born Jews to practice their rites but ban expansion. This sanction of Jewish practices but for Jews alone is epitomized in a rescript by Emperor Antoninus Pius (138–161) and recorded by the second-century jurist Modestin, stating that Jews were permitted "to circumcise only their sons" but "if anyone shall commit it on one who is not of the same religion, he shall suffer the punishment of a castrator."[40] A few decades later, another Roman jurist, Ulpian, affirmed the legality of Jewish practices, allowing "those who practice the Jewish cult to enter offices [honores]" but imposed on them obligations "such as should not transgress their cult."[41] As did another third-century jurist, who allowed "only Jews by origin" to practice circumcision, stipulating that even Roman citizens who were not Jews would be exiled if they allowed themselves or their servants to be circumcised.[42] Doctors were to be sentenced to death if they took part in the circumcision, while Jews who circumcised their slaves "from alien nations" were to be deported or punished by death. Both Judaism and Christianity were deemed threatening to the Roman Empire, Christianity even more so because it was not associated with ancient rites of specific peoples legally inhabiting the empire but a new, expansionist religion.[43]

But after Emperor Constantine's recognition of Christianity as a legal religion, the law began to register anxieties about Jews and their position within Christian society. The discomfort was first articulated in restrictions not only on circumcising non-Jewish slaves but also on Jewish ownership of Christian slaves. In 335, Emperor Constantine prohibited Jews "from buying and circumcising a Christian slave or of any other sect whatsoever"; should such a thing occur, "the circumcised slave shall be made by measure of this statute participant in liberty and acquire its privileges; it shall not be lawful for a Jew who has circumcised a slave of aforementioned kind to retain him in slavery's obedience."[44] The law, like its pre-Christian predecessor, was still concerned with Jewish proselytism, but now making a tangible gesture to the power relations between slaves and their owners, which, according to the ancient Christian historian Eusebius "was not right that those redeemed by the Saviour should be subjected by the yoke of bondage to the slayers of the prophets and murderers of the Lord."[45] In 383, Emperor Theodosius, who made Christianity the religion of the empire, stated that "on no account shall a Jew buy a Christian slave, neither shall he contaminate him with Jewish sacraments and convert him from Christian to Jew."[46] No restriction on owning Christian slaves applied to Christian slave owners—the issue thus was not Christian slavery but Jewish ownership of Christian slaves. By the time *Codex Theodosianus* was compiled in 438, a more explicit language about power was inserted in the commentary on Constantine's 335 law: "If one of the Jews shall buy and circumcise a Christian slave or of any other sect, he shall be raised from that Jew's power [*potestas*] and remain in liberty."[47]

The anxiety about Jewish authority and power gradually also transformed laws related to Jews' ability to hold public office. In pre-Christian Roman Empire, Jews were able to hold public office and were granted accommodations for their religious observance. There was no concern about Jewish power over non-Jews, and the only concern about Jews' holding slaves was over the slaves' conversion to Judaism. But in Christian Roman imperial law, the anxiety over proselytism was increasingly mixed with anxiety over Jewish authority and power. The first explicit prohibition against Jews holding public office came in 418, declaring that "the entrance to the civil service [*militiae*] shall be closed from now on to those living in Jewish superstition."[48] Those who were already serving were to terminate their service when the term was due, while those in military service were to be deprived of all privileges. Jews were still allowed to work as lawyers. But by 425, even this ability to serve as lawyers was circumscribed, as Jews and pagans were denied "the right to practice law and to serve in state service" on the grounds that the emperor did not "wish that people of Christian law to serve them, lest they substitute, because of this mastery, the venerable religion by a sect." In 438, Theodosius II elaborated on policy regarding not just Jews but also Samaritans, pagans, and heretics—all non-Christians, adding language inflected with theological concepts, which now explicitly affirmed Christian supremacy.[49] In this

decree Theodosius asserted the imperial duty to search "for the true religion" and commanded "to establish the ceremonies of holiness to posterity, event unto eternity." To be successful, the emperor wanted to assure
that "lest the abominable sects proliferate wantonly in indiscriminate confusion in our lifetime, oblivious of the quality of our times, . . . no Jew, and
no Samaritan, nor any one constant in either of these laws, should accede
to honors and dignities, to none of them shall be opened an administration
with public obedience, neither shall he serve as a Defensor. For we consider it impious that the enemies of the Supreme Majesty and the Roman
laws shall be considered as avengers also of our laws by seizing stolen jurisdiction and armed with the authority of an ill-gotten dignity shall have the
power to judge and pronounce sentence against Christians."[50] While the
anxiety over public office was still mired in an anxiety over proselytism, it
now became clear that Jews' (and, here, also Samaritans') authority over
Christians was increasingly considered illegitimate—indeed, "ill-gotten"
and inimical to Christianity.

Church councils, too, adopted these principles, issuing canons that
prohibited Jews from holding authority over Christians while stressing
the issue of power and authority. The Council of Macon in 581–583, ruled
that "Jews shall not be appointed judges over the Christian population nor
permitted to be tax collectors, for thus Christians would be seen—God
forbid—to be subjected to them." This decree entered the highly popular
in France, Germany, and northern Italy Gallican collection of legal rulings, *Collectio Verus Gallica*, and other derivative collections, such *Collectio Herovalliana*, and the influential *Decretum* by Ivo of Chartres.[51]

But even within the imperial Christian Roman law, the legality of prac-
ticing Judaism by Jews was not questioned and the official recognition of
its validity became, to use Martha Jones's apt phrase, part of the "legal
fabric" of the Christian world.[52] "It is sufficiently established that the sect
of the Jews is prohibited by no law," decreed Emperor Theodosius in 393,
registering displeasure at "the interdiction imposed in some places on
their assemblies." He ordered his officials to "repress with due severity the
excess of those who presume to commit illegal deeds under the name of
the Christian religion and attempt to destroy and despoil synagogues."[53]
In 420, Theodosius II, citing Emperor Honorius, stated that "no one shall
be destroyed for being a Jew, though innocent of crime, nor shall any
religion whatsoever execute him while he is exposed to injury [*ad contu-
meliam*]. Their synagogues and habitations shall not be indiscriminately
burnt up, nor wrongfully damaged without any reason." [54] If there was
grievance against Jews, courts and public law, not public vigilantism, are

the proper venue, "no one shall have the power to permit himself to take vengeance." In the same decree, however, Theodosius II reiterated the limits of his protection: "But just as we wish to provide in this law for all the Jews, we order that this warning too should be given, lest the Jews grow perchance insolent and, elated by their security commit something rash against the reverence of the Christian cult." The idea of Jewish insolence now, too, became part of the legal fabric of the Christian world.

Still, the Christian Roman law accommodated Jewish religious needs, continuing the legal tradition set in the pagan Roman law. Jews, for example, were not to be summoned to courts "on the Sabbath day or on other days on which the Jews keep the reverence of their cult, for it is clear that the remaining days could suffice for the fiscal revenues and for private litigation."[55] This principle of legality of Judaism and protection from violence and disturbance, along with accommodations for religious rites, became the core feature of Jews' legal status in Christian Europe. Roman law—more than Augustine's "witness doctrine"—accounts for papal and imperial Jewry laws. Thus, while Augustine may have had, as some scholars have argued, "little concern with Jews or Judaism of his day," and while "the overwhelming majority of his pronouncements merely echo the important themes of long-established Pauline and patristic traditions," he developed his "witness doctrine" and his interpretation of hierarchical relation between Jews and Christians in the context of Roman law that affirmed the legality of Jewish religious practices among Jews, protected Jews from violence, while at the same time was beginning to register discomfort with Jews' ability to exercise power and authority over Christians.[56]

Indeed, the language found in many synodal or papal decrees of the first millennium echoed that of the Roman law, with the increasing discomfort with power relations between Jews and Christians more acutely expressed. For example, in his letter written in October 591 to Bishop Becauda of Formi and Angellus of Fundi, Pope Gregory I declared, "We forbid that the said Hebrews be aggrieved or harassed, contrary to reason. But as they are permitted to live by the Roman laws, justice allows that they should manage their affairs as they see fit, without any obstruction. They should not be permitted, however, to have Christian slaves."[57] In 598, Gregory, echoing Roman law, reiterated in a letter to the Bishop of Palermo the principle of Jews' right to live and practice their religion within confines of the law, using a phrase that would become a key phrase in papal legislation concerning Jews: "Just as the Jews [*sicut Judaeis*] should not have the freedom to presume anything in their synagogues beyond what is permitted by law, in the same way, they should not suffer any prejudice in those matters granted to them."[58] Some of the restrictions included ownership of slaves, a topic that Gregory considered "grave" and to which he returned many times.

In 594, Gregory wrote to Valentius Bishop of Luni, expressing concern about reports "that Christian slaves are held in slavery to Jews."[59] He admonished the bishop to "leave no opportunity for the simple in mind to serve in a certain manner the Jewish superstition, not so much out of persuasion as of the right of power over them," thus "no Jew should be permitted to keep a Christian slave under his ownership." Five years later, he wrote to Brunchild, the Queen of Franks, in a far more explicit manner, expressing his shock that in her kingdom Jews were permitted to own Christian slaves. "For what are all Christians but members of Christ? We all know their head, for you honor it faithfully. But what a difference, let your Excellence judge, between honoring the head and permitting his enemies to tread down his members." Gregory then admonished Brunchild to "remove this wicked evil from her kingdom, so that you should show yourselves in this matter worthier worshippers of the omnipotent Lord in that you free his faithful from his enemies."[60] A similarly explicit language was used by the VI Council of Toledo in 638, which ruled that "Jews should not be allowed to have Christian slaves, or buy them, or acquire them through gift of any man whatever; for it is monstrous that members of Christ should serve the ministers of Antichrist."[61] This wording then entered Ivo of Chartres's *Decretum*, an important work in the history of canon law.[62] Such anxieties about Jewish authority and power, in relation to public offices, especially judges and tax collectors, entered canon law through compilations by Burchardt of Worms or Gratian's *Decretales*, thus becoming part of the long legal tradition that would have an impact for centuries to come. In these legal texts and this legal corpus, Jews were marked as inferior members of society, whose presence was not questioned but whose status was to be controlled.[63]

There were no comparable laws for any other specific group in antiquity, Greek or Roman, pagan or Christian. To be sure, there was a developed legal framework to deal with the question of slavery and the status of the enslaved people, regulating manumission, court appearances, potential citizenship, which was allowed in the Roman Empire for manumitted male adults.[64] But the concept of slavery and servitude were not attached to any particular group, except, it seems, for Jews. Slaves in the ancient Mediterranean did not come from a specific region or ethnos.[65] They usually were war captives, though sometimes they were acquired through slave trade, or even self-enslavement "to escape poverty and debt. Thus, among them were those who hailed from different conquered parts of Europe or Asia, or local individuals.[66] Among them were a handful of enslaved black Africans. But in the abundance of slave laws or those dealing with subject people, there were no laws targeting people based on the color of their skin or any other characteristic. Slavery and blackness would become conceptually linked in Islamic lands and sources, whereas laws singling out individuals based on their skin color would be an early modern European invention. But in antiquity and early Christian centuries, discourses about servitude in law and theology focused on Jews; some of that discourse would later be applied to Muslims and Africans to justify their subjugation.[67]

This is not to say that ancient Greeks and Romans did not see color and held no color prejudice. As David Goldenberg has shown, ancient writers recognized that some people were fair, those hailing from the north, some were black, some "in between."[68] The third century Greek philosopher Sextus Empiricus went as far as to acknowledge the subjectivity of beauty, noting that Ethiopian men preferred women who were "the blackest and most snub-nosed, and the Persian approving the whitest and most hook-nosed, and someone else declaring that she who is intermediate both in feature and in coloring is the most beautiful of all."[69] Still, fair complexion came to be associated with refinement and elite status, while darker complexion came to be associated with uncouthness, signalling who was "high-born" and who was "low-born."[70] This was mostly because those of lower status worked outside, often in the fields in the sun, while the elites tended to be urban, sheltered from the elements.

Gradually, blackness attained a derogatory social meaning, beyond, as Goldenberg has argued, "the universal pattern of negative and positive values" attached to "black and white."[71] By the second century BCE, black and white came to be associated with what Gay L. Byron called "moral-spiritual characteristics."[72] For Philo, the Jewish philosopher from Alexandria, blackness came to be associated with evil.[73] For early Christians, it became connected with sin—a soul could be sullied (*denigrata*) with sin.[74] Two verses from the Song of Songs became a frequent reference in Christian and Jewish exegesis discussing the color of skin: "I am black and beautiful / Oh, daughters of Jerusalem" (1:5–6) and in Christian bibles verse 8:5: "Who is she that comes up having been made white?" (the Hebrew version of the verse does not mention color at all).[75] Origen, the third-century Christian writer, connected the two verses to allegorize the expansion of the

Christian church among the gentiles, asking "in what way is she black and in what way is she fair without whiteness."[76] Unbaptized gentiles were black, like the maiden, darkened by their sins, but once they "repented," their conversion "bestowed beauty" on them. "If you repent," Origen wrote, "your soul will be 'black' because of your former sins, but because of your penitence, your soul will have something of what I may call an Ethiopian beauty."

Origen's exegesis was influential. Jerome expanded on it, reflecting on the colors black and white, and attaching symbolic value to the blackness of Ethiopia. For Jerome, Ethiopia was "black and cloaked in the filth of sin."[77] But, he wrote, "At one time, we were Ethiopians in our vices and sins. How so? Because our sins had blackened [*nigros fecerant*] us. But afterwards we heard the words: 'Wash yourselves clean!' And we said: 'Wash me, and I shall become whiter [*dealbabor*] than snow. We are Ethiopians, therefore, who have been transformed from blackness into whiteness."[78] Baptism, in other words, cleansed the sins and transformed the "blackness" of sinners into whiteness. Jerome used this metaphor in another place in this homily, stating that when flax "has come forth from the ground, it is black; it has no beauty."[79] But when it is "broken, then twisted, afterwards washed. Next, it is pounded; finally, combed, and after so much care and hard work, it finally becomes white."

In a stunning and disturbing account of temptation and sin, *Acts of Peter*, a second-century apocryphal text, describes a dream in which an "Ethiopian woman . . . all black, clothed in filthy rags . . . was dancing with an iron collar about her neck and chains on her hand and feet."[80] She was a demon, whose violent killing—her head to be cut off and body "cut in pieces"—needed to be witnessed by all. She was a demonic temptation, a trope deployed in another story transmitted in the *Sayings of the Desert Fathers*, Christian monastic teachings from fourth- and fifth-century Egypt. Here the Ethiopian woman, "smelly and disgusting in appearance (*fetida et turpis aspectu*)," tempts a young monk—but her "foul odor (*foetorem*)" dissuades the young man from following worldly pursuits, for he understood that it was "the work of the devil and smelled her foul odor."[81] This story belongs to a broader genre focusing on what Susan Ashbrook Harvey called "olfactory dimensions of Christian piety," with foul smell associated with disbelief and sin, and pleasant smell with the godly and sacred.[82] Odor and blackness came to be so strongly associated with sin and the devil.

But if some of the Mediterranean and Middle Eastern Christian writers associated odor with blackness, specifically with a trope of a Black woman,

Christian writers, especially in northern Europe, would project these onto Jews. The infamous *foetor judaicus* was originally a symbol of disbelief; it would be shed with conversion to Christianity, as the sixth-century poem by the Merovingian poet Venance Fortunat tells.[83] In iconography, Jews' ugliness and darkened skins were deployed to emphasize their outsider status and perceived hostility to Christianity, and, according to M. Lindsay Kaplan, also inferiority.[84] In the moralized Bible of Saint Louis, a magnificent three-volume visual interpretation of the Bible, commissioned by Blanche of Castile for the French King Louis IX, and created between 1226 and 1234, shows dark-skinned, ugly men in its depictions of Christ's passion.[85] These darkened figures represent those who rejected and humiliated Jesus, both Roman soldiers and Jews. In the first volume, which interprets the book of Exodus and the paschal sacrifice in Christological terms, with an image of Christ's passion placed directly below the paschal lamb, none of the individuals have darkened skin—at that point in the story the manuscript was conveying they were still God-fearing Israelites. It was only after the coming and revelation of Jesus as the Messiah that their skin is darkened, for they rejected Jesus and became his enemies.[86]

And yet, the Black figure, that is a figure depicted as a realistic Black person rather than a figure marked by dark color, was not doomed in European Christian art. As the monumental multivolume work *The Image of the Black in Western Art* demonstrates, in medieval Christian art Black figures are also depicted and accepted as "eligible for salvation."[87] Depiction of Black saints, such as St. Maurice, and later in the High Middle Ages also of a Black figure among the three kings, or wise men, who brought offerings to the newborn Jesus in Bethlehem, supported the universalist vision of Christianity, as a religion offering salvation to all. But the trope of "the blackness of sin" and "the whiteness of faith" would not disappear and would prove a powerful tool for an exegetical link between blackness and slavery to be deployed by European Christians to justify the conquest and exploitation of Africans and Native Americans in the early modern period. But until then, no legal framework was devised to legislate race or color.[88] Jews, in contrast, would both remain the objects of legislation and become subjects of derogatory visual representations.

CHAPTER TWO

# Christian Supersessionism
# Becomes Christian Supremacy

EXEGETICAL LINKS BETWEEN blackness and sin, blackness and evil, did not disappear from European Christian thought, but in the Middle Ages they were often deployed against Jews, depicting them as enemies of Christ.[1] But the link between blackness and slavery, which existed in Islamic texts, did not take root in Christian writings, and certainly not in law, until, as David Goldenberg put it, "Europe discovered black Africa and began to engage in the slave trade of its inhabitants."[2] Until then, European Christians may have encountered black Africans in different capacities, especially in their encounter with the Muslim world, as "soldiers, Muslims fighting for their faith; slaves clinging to their traditional religion," even as advisors to Muslim rulers.[3] In the era of the Crusades, as Jean Devisse noted, European Christians' encounter with Black people was in the battlefield as soldiers in Muslim armies. Although Islam and its military might certainly have played a role in consolidating European Christian identity and territorial expansionist ambitions, with Muslims and Blacks encountered mostly on the frontier, its sense of superiority and dominance continued to be shaped and reaffirmed through the exegetical link between Jews and servitude developed in the first centuries of Christianity—after all, Jews lived among Christians within Europe. Indeed, the medieval explicit re-articulation of the idea of Jewish servitude came at a time of setbacks in the Crusades against Islamic territories. Jews, thus, served to affirm Christian superiority even, or perhaps precisely, in moments of defeat.

While the Roman law left its mark on legal texts from late antiquity and the early Middle Ages, the impact of Augustine's own language and hermeneutical framework that so frequently evoked the idiom of servitude and slavery about Jews was not palpably felt until the twelfth century, with only allusions appearing in the eleventh.[4] One of the first to use it was Bernard of Clairvaux in 1146. "The Jews are not to be persecuted, killed, or even put to flight," wrote Bernard, when intervening to stem anti-Jewish violence of the second crusade. "Ask those who know the sacred scriptures what they read foretold of the Jews in the Psalm. 'God,' says the Church, 'instructs me concerning my enemies, 'Slay them not, so that my people should not forget.' The Jews are indeed for us the living words of Scripture, constantly representing the Lord's passion. They have been dispersed all over the world for this reason: so that in enduring just punishments for such a crime wherever they are may witness to our redemption."[5] Bernard then switched gears to focus on hierarchy and power: "Hence the Church, speaking in the same psalm, adds, 'only disperse them in thy power and subjugate them, God my protector.' And so, it has been done: Dispersed and subjugated they are; under Christian princes they endure a harsh captivity." But, Bernard hoped, as did his predecessors, that Jews would be saved at the end by converting to Christianity and accepting Jesus as Christ. Bernard's defense of Jews against violence encapsulates the doctrine of Jewish witness: Jews should not be persecuted and destroyed because they have a role to play within Christian conception of the world as witnesses to Christian truth and their subjugation had a role to play. To quote Jeremy Cohen, "The survival of the Jews, scattered in exile and oppressed into servitude, testifies to their punishment for rejecting (and crucifying) Jesus and to the reward of faithful Christians by contrast."[6] It was the idea of Jewish servitude and subjection, and the related concern with Jewish power over Christians that left far deeper marks on Christian law, identity, and understanding of social hierarchy than Augustine's idea of "Jewish witness" confirming the truth of Christianity through their scriptures.

At first, medieval jurists only used the wording found in either imperial Christian Roman law, Church councils, or writings by early popes. For example, Pope Gregory I's *Sicut Judaeis*, which entered some canonical collections of the eleventh century, was reissued, albeit modified, by twelfth-century popes transmitting the language inherited from Roman law.[7] But it was Pope Innocent III who turned to Augustine's Paulinian hermeneutics to clad legal decrees in a theological cloak. When Innocent III reissued a revised *Sicut Judaeis*, now retitled *Constitutio pro Judaeis* in September 1199, he turned to Augustine's "witness doctrine" to justify the protection of Jews: "Although the Jewish perfidy is in every way worthy of condemnation, nevertheless, because through them the truth of our own faith is proved, they are not to be severely oppressed by the faithful. Thus, the Prophet says, 'Thou shalt not kill them, lest at any time they forget thy law,' or more clearly stated thou at any chance be able to forget Thy Law, which though they themselves fail to understand it, they display in their book to those who do understand."[8] Innocent's words acknowledged the presence of Jews within the body of Christianity and reiterated their protection, both rooted in theological justification. But doing so, the pope also reminded the faithful that Jewish religion, now called perfidy, was worthy of condemnation. This was a clear change in tone from previous papal decrees.

The affirmation of papal commitment to protecting Jews through Augustine's theological framework was not the only way Innocent III drew on Augustine's teachings. During his pontificate he evoked far more frequently those Augustinian metaphors that cast Jews in a position of "perpetual servitude" to Christians.[9] In his letter from January 1205 to the king of France, the pope wrote that "though it does not displease God but is even acceptable to Him that the Jewish dispersion should live and serve under Catholic kings until such time as their remnant shall be saved," it was "exceedingly offensive to the sight of Divine Majesty" that princes would "prefer the sons of the crucifiers, against whom to this day the blood cries to the Father's ears, to the heirs of the Crucified Christ, and . . . prefer the Jewish slavery to the freedom of those whom the Son freed, as though the son of a servant could and ought to be an heir along with the son of the free woman."[10] In this thick sentence, the pope managed to call up the tropes of Jews as Christ killers, Cain, and Ishmael, the son of Hagar. The pontiff then reiterated canon law regulations concerning Jewish-Christian relations and the proper social order, closing the letter, "Wherefore, lest through them the name of God be blasphemed, and Christian liberty become less than Jewish servitude, we warn, and in the name of God, exhort Your Serene Majesty . . . that you restrain the Jews from their presumptions . . . and try to remove from the French Kingdome abuses of this sort." The pope included incentives, such as "a remission of sins," to encourage action.

In July of the same year, in a bull *Etsi Judaeos*, Innocent III articulated most clearly his view on the position of Jews within Christendom and the power relations within it.[11] "While Christian piety accepts the Jews, who, by their own guilt, are consigned to perpetual servitude because they crucified the Lord . . . and while [Christian piety] permits them to dwell in the Christian midst . . . the Jews ought not to be ungrateful to us and not requite Christian favor with contumely and intimacy with contempt." The pope then recounted "how Jews have become insolent" and "hurled unbridled insults at the Christian faith," relating alleged reports that Jews made Christian nurses who had taken communion "pour their milk into the latrine." To stem this "insolence" and violation of canon law that prohibited Jews from having Christian servants, he urged the king of France "to restrain the excesses of the Jews that they shall not dare raise their neck, bowed under the yoke of perpetual slavery," and "to forbid them to have any nurses nor other kinds of Christian servants in the future, lest the children of a free woman should be servants to the children of a slave; but rather as slaves rejected by God, in whose death they wickedly conspired, they shall, by the effect of this very action, recognize themselves as the slaves of those whom Christ's death set free at the same time that it enslaved them." Innocent then commanded the bishops of Sens and Paris, the bull's addressees, "to warn the aforementioned king and the others to this effect and . . . to prevail upon them that henceforth the perfidious Jews should not in any other way dare grow insolent, but under the servile fear, they should always show the shame of their guilt and respect the honor of Christian faith."

Innocent III transformed, to paraphrase Ian Haney López, theological ideas and biblical exegesis into law, applying them to "lived reality" and providing legal structures for religious "dominance and subordination into socioeconomic relations."[12] As M. Lindsay Kaplan has noted, with the inclusion of *Etsi Judaeos* in canon law, the language and the concept of Jewish servitude was guaranteed broader dissemination and began to appear in the bulls and encyclicals issued by other popes as well as in other sources.[13] In 1221, for example, Pope Honorius III referred to Jews as slaves in objecting to Jews "standing in the way of Christians" and to "the slaves [having] dominion over the masters" [*servi dominis dominentur*], and urged the archbishop of Bordeaux to apply canonical statutes to prevent such "abuse" of letting Jews "grow insolent."[14] In 1233, Pope Gregory IX also registered his concern with Jews holding public office. It seemed "jarring" [*obsonum videatur*], Gregory IX wrote, "that blasphemers of Christ should exercise power over Christians."[15] And when a few months later the pope wrote to the archbishops and bishops of German lands, he added a preamble that drew attention to "the yoke of perpetual servitude" of Jews "because of their guilt" and slightly modified the language to say that "it was absurd [*cum nimium absurdum*]" that Jews as "blasphemers of Christ" should be given "power over Christians."[16] The pope then ordered these Church leaders each "in his own diocese, church, parish" to suppress completely "the above-named and similar excesses of the Jews" so that Jews "should not again dare to straighten their neck bent under the yoke of perpetual servitude in insult to the Redeemer."

These concepts of Jewish inferiority and expectations of humility before Christians thus became deeply engrained in European Christian imagination and in European secular and ecclesiastical law. Anything other than Jewish submission and humility triggered Christian leaders to call Jews insolent, arrogant, or haughty. Pope Paul IV's bull *Cum nimis absurdum* issued in 1555 bears the fruit of medieval concepts of Jewish servitude to the fullest:

> Since it is absurd and improper that Jews—whose own guilt has con-signed them to perpetual servitude—under the pretext that Christian piety receives them and tolerates their presence should be ingrates to Christians, so that they attempt to exchange the servitude which they owe to Christians for dominion over them; we—to whose notice it has lately come that these Jews, in our dear city and in some other cites, holdings, and territories of the Holy Roman Church, have erupted into insolence: they presume not only to dwell side by side with Christians and near their churches, with no distinct habit to separate them, but even to erect homes in the more noble sections and streets of the cities, holdings, and territories where they dwell, and to buy and possess fixed property, and to have nurses, housemaids, and other hired Christian ser-vants, and to perpetrate many other things in ignominy and contempt of the Christian name—considering that the Roman Church tolerates the Jews in testimony of the true Christian faith and to end [*ad hoc, ut*] that they, led by the piety and kindness of the Apostolic See, should at length recognize their errors, and make all haste to arrive at the true light of the Catholic faith, and thereby [*propterea*] to agree that, as long as they per-sist in their errors, they should recognize through experience that they have been made slaves while Christians have been made free through Jesus Christ, God and our Lord, and that it is iniquitous that the children of the free woman should serve the children of the maid-servant.[17]

Rhetorically, Pope Paul IV was indebted to Paulinian and Augustinian language, which he had received via canon law—the previous papal bulls, most notably those by Pope Innocent III; even the title *Cum nimis absur-dum* harkened back to a phrase used repeatedly by Innocent III.[18] The list of "insolences" includes items that are both rather specific, such as liv-ing in "more noble" neighborhoods, and those simply generated from the list of canonical regulations of Jewish-Christian relations. But what was new about this papal bull was the effort to implement in real life existing but mostly ignored Church rulings concerning Jews and to bring to fruition the idea of "Jewish servitude" so that "as long as they persist in their errors" Jews "should recognize through experience that they have been made slaves while Christians have been made free through Jesus Christ."

In *Cum nimis absurdum*, Paul IV did not just reiterate the concept of Christian freedom and Jewish servitude; he wanted to embody it in real life—to reify it. One of the most dramatic and tangible outcomes was the creation of a restricted Jewish quarter with "one entry alone, and so too one exit," controlled by Christian authorities. The premise of the bull was then implemented across Papal States and then in other principalities in Italy, where Jews were forced to live in ghettoes.

But outside the ecclesiastical jurisdiction, this new directive was impossible to implement. Thus, across Europe, even in Catholic areas, Jews continued to live intermixed with Christians, hiring Christian servants, and engaging in other prohibited—from the perspective of Christian theology and law—activities. The Polish-Lithuanian Commonwealth was probably, from the perspective of the Church, the most egregious example of the flaunting of these laws. Not only was the Jewish community there the largest in the world, but also Jews were integral to the Commonwealth's economy, especially in noble estates. Poland-Lithuania was representative of the "upset social order."[19] It was to this "jarring" reality that made Pope Benedict XIV issue in 1751, at the height of the Enlightenment in Europe, a stark encyclical *A quo primum*, which enumerated the "abuses" of Jews in Poland in violation of canon law and deployed a rhetoric indebted to Christian history, canon law, and traditional nonlegal sources.[20] Benedict XIV quoted Bernard of Clairvaux's letters verbatim to articulate the doctrine of protecting Jews against persecution and violence—Jews played a role in the Christological understanding of the world, for the Church triumphs "more fully over the Jews in convincing or converting them than if once and for all she destroyed them with the edge of the sword."[21] But Benedict also stressed that Bernard supported punishing Jewish "excesses" and stripping "them of the property they had taken from Christians or had acquired by usury." The pope reviewed papal statements about Jews and their place within Christendom. Christians should not serve Jews, he reaffirmed, citing Innocent III's *Sicut Judaeis*, but rather Jews should serve Christians, "Let not the sons of the free woman be servants of the sons of the handmaid; but as servants rejected by their lord for whose death they evilly conspired, let them realize that the result of this deed is to make them servants of those whom Christ's death made free." Nor should they be promoted to

FIGURE 1. Petrus Comestor, Historia scholastica, England, between 1283 and 1300. Detail of a historiated initial 'Q'(uinta) of *Synagoga* and *Ecclesia*, at the beginning of Deuteronomy, The British Library, Royal 3 D VI, f. 93. ©The Trustees of the British Museum. Public domain.

public office and have authority over Christians. Benedict XIV is considered "an Enlightenment pope," but his policies regarding Jews were regressive at a time when many Europeans were beginning to acknowledge the need for religious toleration. Benedict here reasserted the social and religious hierarchy and order that had developed over many centuries in Christian thought and law. In that hierarchy Jews remained "the sons of the slave woman" and "liberty" was only achieved through conversion to Christianity—liberty was Christian.

This social and theological hierarchy was visually embodied as part of "cathedral decorative programs" since the late twelfth century and, later, also in devotional paintings and altars in the depictions of *Ecclesia* and *Synagoga*, Church and Jewish Law (fig. 1).[22] The two were usually shown in pairs, with *Ecclesia*, a triumphant queen, seated or standing, while holding a chalice or a scepter, sometimes a church, her chin confidently up, crown on her head, and with *Synagoga* disheveled, often humiliated and blindfolded, sometimes unchastely exposing her breasts, almost always holding a broken scepter or tablets of the law, occasionally a head of a goat symbolizing animal sacrifices, her head held humbly down (figs. 2–3).[23]

In paintings, like the late-fifteenth century painting by Fernando Gallego, *Cristo Bendiciendo*, the *Synagoga*'s gown was yellow, a color symbolizing betrayal and often used to depict Judas Iscariot and later applied to Jewish badges, while the *Ecclesia*'s gown was red, symbolic of the blood of Christ and of power.[24] Displayed in public places, at entrances to cathedrals or in churches, the imagery conveyed to a greater audience what legal and theological treatises articulated to the few who could read them, embodying for all to see Christianity's triumph over Judaism. When the printing press allowed for a wider dissemination of text and images, this pair also found its way to the hands of a wider public.

The idea of such a well-ordered society was not only limited to Catholics. It also permeated into Protestant texts. Martin Luther's vitriolic *On the Jews and Their Lies* not only shows his familiarity with Augustine's works, along with extreme application of Pauline attribution of carnality to Jews, but also demonstrates the depth of the Christian expectation of Jewish humility.[25] Angry that Jews had not embraced his version of Christianity, Luther not only railed against their "obstinacy," "stubbornness," and "blindness" but also against their "disobedience," "pride," and "arrogance."[26] He conveyed, much more bluntly, the ideas articulated already in the medieval period by Innocent III and other popes, and adumbrated those expressed twelve years later by Pope Paul IV—evidence of how widespread these ideas were: "They have no reason to act this way [with hostility], since we show them every kindness. They live among us, enjoy our security and shield, they use our land and our highways, our markets and streets." [27] But the princes and lords do nothing, and "permit the Jews to take, steal, and rob from their open money bags and treasures whatever they want. That is, they let the Jews, by means of their usury, skin and fleece them and their subjects and make them beggars with their own money. For the Jews, who are exiles, should really have nothing, and whatever they have must surely be our property. They do not work, and they do not earn anything . . . and yet they are in possession of our money and goods and are our masters in our own land and in their exile." The social hierarchy, thus, was turned upside down, the Christian social order disrupted. More ominously, any material possessions and wealth Jews had was considered ill-gotten and illegitimate. Luther ended his long venomous work on Jews with recommendations of their expulsion to "their land" and their elimination from Christendom. But his ideas would not gain ground until the late nineteenth and twentieth century, when modern antisemites rediscovered this particular work and began to use it as a font of new antisemitic ideas or to justify them by grounding them in historical sources.[28]

FIGURE 2. Triptych with Synagoga and Ecclesia, ca. 1250–75, North French, The Met Museum, Gift of J. Pierpont Morgan, 1917, Accession number, 17.190.279a–e. Public domain.

Luther's language about Jews, especially those most virulent phrases, drew upon available printed works about Jews and other, more general, works with broad circulation, such as chronicles and depictions of the world, in which, both before and after the Protestant Reformation, Jews were depicted as dangerously murderous blasphemers, who defiled Christian sacred objects, killed Christian children, and in turn were then expelled or massacred as punishments for their deeds. All in all, Luther's Jews were portrayed, as they were in the widely published chronicles and cosmographies, as a threat to European Christian society.[29] Along with menacing vocabulary used to describe Jews as dangerous, demonic figures, enemies who needed to be contained and punished, these printed works also contained images that began to be disseminated in print since

FIGURE 3. Ecclesia (*left*) and Synagoga (*right*), Triptych (detail), ca. 1250–75, North French, The Met Museum, Gift of J. Pierpont Morgan, 1917, Accession number, 17.190.279a–e. Public domain.

the late fifteenth century, portraying Jews as ugly and minatory, even as brutal killers (figs. 4–5). These stories and imagery, created by elites, would wield "cultural power," demonstrating, as Anthony Bale has argued, "the frightening potency both of the imagination and the texts and images" in shaping, in the long term, mental habits of thinking about Jews among European Christians.[30]

But these Jewish characters were not the Jews Christians encountered every day. Jews in real life did not fit what the Christian imagery and ideals conveyed. Jews were neighbors, living together in the same towns, neighborhoods, even homes. They were often friends and business partners.

FIGURE 4. "Blessed Simon." Broadsheet bound with Johannes Matthias Tiberinus, *Passio Beati Simonis Pueri Tridentini a p[er]fidis judeis nup[er] occisi*. Rome: Bartholomaeus Guldinbeck, 1475, at the Bayerische Staatsbibliothek, Rar. 337. See also, Hartmann Schedel, *Weltchronik* (Nuremberg: Anton Koberger, 1493), CCLIIII verso.

Jews themselves certainly did not feel like they lived in "servitude," and that was why both Catholic and, later also, Protestant religious leaders who embraced the ideal of a properly ordered society in which Jews were to be humbled in servitude to Christians were so irked finding Jews integrated into medieval or early modern towns.

The thirteenth-century rabbi Meir of Rothenburg articulated the difference between subjugation and Jews' status in Europe: "Jews are not required to pay taxes to their overlord, unless they actually live in the domain of these overlords. For Jews are not subjugated to their overlords as the gentiles are. . . . The status of the Jew, in this land, is that of a free landowner who lost his land but did not lose his personal liberty. The definition of the status of the Jews is followed by the government in its customary relations with Jews."[31] Though Meir of Rothenburg himself died in a Christian prison, he was right, Jews did not live in servitude unlike millions of serfs; Jews were a privileged and protected group, even if they may have been called *servi camerae*, servants of the royal chamber, and even

ANNO CHRISTI.

Silverbergwerk ontdeckt.

Cometen laughdurigh.

Dorre Somer, waer door veele Bosschen

luoght men een Maet Wijn aen de Necker voor bier / aen den Rhijn voor 6. penningen.

Anno 1471. wierden ontdeckt de rijke Silver-Aderen te Schneebergh aen de Boheemsche Grensen; welcke 't Keurvorstlijck Huys Saxen een ongeloovlijck-groote Schat hebben toegebraght.

In 't volgende jaer 1472., stracks na den aenvangh / verscheen een groote vyerige Comeet, met lange swarte Stralen na 't Westen. Stond 80. dagen langh aen den Hemel. Eer deese noch verdweenen was / vertoonde sigh een andere / met een vyerige Staert tegens 't Oosten. Hier op volgde een vreeslijcke Pest / Oorlogen / en Oproeren allerweegen.

Anno 1473. was 't sulck een heete dorre Somer / dat de Bosschen van selfs in vlam geraeckten. 't Boheemer-Woud brandde thien weecken aghter een. Desgelijcks

quam 't Vyer in 't Thuringer en Swarte Woud. Veele Dorpen verdielen tot Asch; wijl men / door gebreck van Water / de brand niet kon blusschen. Evenwel was 't een taemlijck vruchtbaer jaer; en de Wijnooghst was boven maten goed.

In 't selve jaer op S. Petri en Pauli dag ontstond soodanigh een Stormwind / dat ontelbaer veel Huysen en Schuren ter neer geworpen wierden. C'Aughsburgh viel S. Ulricks-Kerck om verr'; waer door de Prediker / sijnen Capellaen, en noch 30. Menschen dood bleven. Veele Bosschen / van 't voorgedaghte Vyer noch onverseerd gelaten / wierden met de Wortel uytgeruckt. Aen de Scheepen op de Wateren geschiedde een onnoemlijcke schade.

Anno 1475. martelden de verbloeckte Joden te Trenten, op Witten Donderdagh den 23. van Martius, een arm Jongetje / ge-

ANNO CHRISTI.

in brand geraekten.

Afgrijslijcke Stormwind.

Joden martelen der Christenen.

ften Kinderen, op sulck een wijse alse Christus hebben gekruycighd. Annal. Surr.

Sprinckhanen in grouwlijcke meenighten.

noemd Simon, Soon eens Leertouwers aldaer / oud ontrent derdehalf jaer / op soodanigh een wijs als de Heere Christus gemarteld wierd; want eyndlijck nageldense 't aen een kruys. Deese Geschiedenis / in 't breed beschreven / is by andere te vinden. Even 't selve hebbense te Mota in Friaul aen een ander arm Kind gepleeght. Offe nu wel hier over haren loon ontfingen / soo hebbense echter daer door getoond hare vyandschap tegens de Christenen en der selver Kinderen; en hoe wel sy verdienen / datmen haer in de voornaemste Steeden / tot der Christenen verderf / soo sorghvuldigh handhaefd / beschermd / en als voordeel torbrengende Kostgangers geneerd.

In 't voorgemelde jaer / ontrent de Maend Augustus, quam een ongelooflijcke meenighte van Sprinckhanen uyt Hongaryen aenbliegen (na datse alles wat groen was daer afgegreten hadden) in Moravien, Polen, en Silesien, Trocken daer heenen

als een Wolck; soo datse oock selfs de Son bedeckten; wijl dit Ongediert in hare Vlught twee mijlen lengthe en eene mijl breedte sigh uytstreckte. 't Beste was / dat de Koornvrughten alreeds rijp en hard waren / waer doorse deselve weynigh beschadigen konden. Anders verteerdense alle Loof en Gras.

Anno 1576., den 12. van December, overleed Paltzgraef Frederick, Keurvorst / dien Paeng d'I., bygenoemd Victoriosus, of de Zeeghrijke; anders oock geseght de Boose d'I. Fritz; van wien wy hier boven in 't breede hebben gesproocken.

Anno 1478. stierven veelerweegen in Italien meenighten van Lieden aen de Pest. Alleen te Bresia, of Brescia, wierden door deese besmettende Sieckte wegh gerucht 20000.; te Venetien over de 40000. Menschen. Niet veel minder te Milaen.

In even 't selve jaer heeft in 't Koninghrijck Castilien haren aenvangh genoomen de van de Roomschgesinde soo hoogh geroembe Spaen-

Dood van Paltzgraef Keurvorst Frederick d'I.

Pest in Italien seer swaer.

Aenvangh der Spaensche Inquisie.

if Christian theologians and legal scholars sometimes argued that their status was in fact that of slaves.[32] In early modern Poland-Lithuania Jews were similarly protected by royal or private privileges and sometimes even held positions of authority explicitly prohibited by canon law, including tax collection. One Polish Jewish rabbi Joel Sirkes (1561–1640) remarked that because of their economic function as collectors of the tax on liquor production and sale "Jews rule and have dominion over [gentiles] and that they hold them like kings and princes," leading "to the outcry of the gentiles."[33] In Alsace, Jews—expelled from Strasbourg—found themselves living in smaller towns and villages, developing close relations with their Christian neighbors.[34] On the Italian peninsula, despite ghettoes and restrictions, Jews nonetheless participated in broader Christian culture.[35]

But all this does not mean that Jews were unaffected by the anti-Jewish rhetoric and the theological and legal ideal of a properly ordered society. As David Nirenberg has noted, "Christian ideas about Judaism might have a greater impact on those conditions of life or real Jews than anything those Jews might actually do."[36] In some places, Jews, in fact, were expelled, assigned a badge to mark them, contained in ghettos, or even massacred.[37] Still, in many other places they continued to flourish. But the long-term legacy of these words, ideas, and images would become manifest in the modern era, beginning with the Enlightenment, when new questions about identity, belonging, and race emerged first in political theory and science then in law.

# CHAPTER THREE

# A White European Christian Identity Emerges

THE TROPE OF SERVITUDE so widely applied to Jews in the Middle Ages continued to shape how Jews were perceived in early modern Europe, but its deeper influence was in the framework it provided for Christian sense of superiority. And while Jews were not actually enslaved, slavery did persist in some parts of Europe, most notably parts of the Mediterranean, and especially in Iberia, which became a theological and political laboratory on the issue of slavery, servitude, and Christian domination, creating a model that would later be applied by other European powers as they established their colonial holdings across the Atlantic.

In the Iberian Peninsula slavery endured, as William D. Phillips has shown, since the Roman times into the medieval and early modern periods, even when it largely disappeared from other parts of Christian Europe.[1] The military history of the peninsula between the eighth and fifteenth centuries, marked by fighting between Christian and Muslim forces and then followed by Christian colonial expansion in the late fifteenth and in the sixteenth centuries, was behind the persistence of the practice of enslavement.

In Islamicate lands more broadly, slavery was "a common component of society."[2] In the Ottoman Empire unfree people, captives or slaves, were found "performing diverse roles in local economies and societies," helping "the ruling regime," as Leslie Peirce has shown, maintain "its strength and stature."[3] In Iberia, parts of which were under Muslim rule from the eighth century until the end of the fifteenth, Muslims retained the system.[4] Over the centuries, the wars between Christian and Muslim forces resulted in captives held by both sides.[5] When such captives were not ransomed or exchanged, they remained enslaved. Captives seized during sea raids on the Mediterranean also produced a stream of enslaved laborers. Because slavery was so widely used across the Islamicate world, slave trade was also more developed there, extending into parts of Africa.[6]

Still, there was yet no clear racial component to slavery. In the Ottoman Empire, the enslaved people came from a wide swath of lands: the Balkans, regions around the Mediterranean, the Black Sea, as well as regions in Africa: Sudan, Ethiopia and others.[7] On the Iberian Peninsula, under both Christian and Muslim rule, slavery was, as William Phillips put it, "cross-cultural and multi-ethnic," both in terms of those enslaved and those who captured and traded them.[8] Indeed, even Miguel de Cervantes became a captive; captured at sea in 1575, he spent five years in captivity in Morocco.[9]

Despite the persistence of slavery, Iberia (or the Ottoman Empire) was not a slave society. Slavery there was never the dominant economic factor it would become in European colonies, where it developed "a predominantly commercial character" and became crucial for "the sustained economic growth of the Western world."[10] Neither did slaves in Iberia constitute a large percentage of the population. They were found among domestics, artisans, and agricultural laborers. Slavery, in other words, did not bring, as William Phillips has shown, "significant benefits . . . beyond the normal labor and services any slave owners received."[11]

But Iberian slavery, its continuation, justification, and geographic reach created solid foundations on which "the great expansion of slavery in the Americas," including the enslavement of Africans, could be built.[12] Black slaves, for example, were not unknown on the peninsula. In Al-Andalus, the Muslim territories of Iberia, some black African slaves were imported through the established African slave trade routes.[13] In the wake of the Black Death, labor shortages prompted a more sustained turn to slavery in Iberia and some Italian Mediterranean cities.[14] Christian Iberia drew their slaves mostly from the military raids into the Muslim territories during the Reconquista, capturing almost exclusively Muslims for slave labor.

The definition of the Reconquista as a crusade—a holy war against Muslims—helped justify the acquisition and retention of slaves in an era when slavery had largely declined or transformed into soil-bound serfdom within a manorial system elsewhere in Europe.[15] Drawing on Roman law, enslavement of captives in a just war was acceptable and fighting enemies of Christianity was considered a just war.

In Christendom, slave ownership had over time acquired religious significance, with ownership of Christian slaves prohibited to non-Christians.

In antiquity, it was prohibited to Jews out of fear of conversions to Judaism and concerns over Jewish authority over Christians. In the Middle Ages, that principle applied to both Jews and Muslims. In 1179, the Third Lateran Council issued a prohibition against "Jews and Saracens" having Christian slaves (*Christiana mancipia*) in their homes.[16] A telltale that this prohibition ostensibly aimed at both Jews and Muslims was rooted in anti-Jewish prohibition was a sentence, a few clauses down, reiterating that "Jews ought to be subject to Christians and be supported by them on grounds of humanity alone." In Iberia the prohibition against enslavement and ownership of Christians, for the same reasons, applied to both Jews and Muslims.[17] But while Christian Roman imperial law did not prohibit Christians from owning Christian slaves, by the late Middle Ages, enslavement of Christians by Christians also became unacceptable.[18] In fact, in 1435, Pope Eugene IV issued a bull *Sicut dudum*, prohibiting Christians from enslaving the native peoples in the Canaries who had converted to Christianity; this principle was later affirmed by Popes Pius II and Sixtus IV.[19] Since non-Christians could still be enslaved, especially if their enslavement could be justified as a result of a just war, Muslims, as both war enemies and non-Christians, constituted a majority of slaves in Christian Iberia.

Thus, by the time the first ship with enslaved Africans arrived in Portugal in 1441, foundations for justifying the enslavement of Africans had already been in place, and a year later, in 1442, came a legal shift in law that provided an explicit rationalization. That year, Pope Eugene IV issued a bull *Illius qui*. The bull, which was, as Pius Onyemechi Adiele has argued, a result of "the manipulative ploys of Prince Henry," who wanted to legitimize his slave raids in Africa, elevated the Portuguese raids on the African coast under the leadership of Henry the Navigator to the status of a crusade against "Saracens and other enemies of the Christian name," and granted indulgences to those who participated in them.[20] According to Gomes Eanes de Zurara, a Portuguese chronicler and author of a chronicle commissioned by Henry the Navigator himself, the prince wanted to seek approval of the pope for the raids and enslavement of the captives and "ask of him to make a partition with himself of the treasures of [the] Holy Church, for the salvation of the souls of those who in the toils of that conquest should meet their end."[21] The papal approval meant that Henry was able to sail ships and continue his raids of the African coast. Subsequently, dozens of ships brought enslaved Africans into Europe.

However, the question of the legality of such raids, even if justified by conversion to Christianity, continued to linger. After all, the raids were not like those on the Iberian Peninsula, which were construed as "a reconquest" of formerly Christian territories from Muslim forces and thus a "just war." Some canon lawyers did not consider it justifiable to invade militarily new territories for the purpose of conversion. Canon law, after all, prohibited conversions with a use of force—a principle developed in late antiquity in response to attacks on Jews and applied more broadly in the thirteenth century by Sinibaldo Fieschi, a jurist and future pope.[22]

In 1452, ten years after the bull *Illius qui*, with Spanish and Portuguese military activity continuing along the coast of Africa and on the recently colonized islands, the humanist Pope Nicholas V returned to the topic in a bull *Dum diversas* issued for King Alfonso V of Portugal and Henry the Navigator. For the two rulers the approval from the pope meant a license to raid the lands and enrich their coffers. For the popes, the exploits on the Atlantic helped assert their political and spiritual power, as secular rulers turned to them for approvals for military expeditions.

In *Dum diversas*, issued at a time when, in the east, Christian forces were suffering from the advancement of Ottoman Turks into the Balkans, the pope agreed to grant King Alfonso V and Prince Henry powers "to subjugate the enemies of Christ, especially the Saracens, and with a strong hand to spread the Christian faith" so that "the wrath of the enemies of Christ against the orthodox faith will be pushed back and be subjected to the Christian religion."[23] Nicholas V believed that King Alfonso and Prince Henry acted out of "devotion and Christian desire." With *Dum diversas* the pope accorded them full apostolic authority "to dispossess the Saracens, pagans and other infidels, and all enemies of Christ, of all their kingdoms, commands, dominance, other belongings, lands, towns, villas, castles" and other possessions but more crucially, "to invade, search out, capture and subjugate the Saracens and pagans and any other unbelievers and ene-mies of Christ wherever they may be, as well as their kingdoms, duchies, counties, principalities, lands, towns, villas and other properties . . . and to reduce their persons into perpetual slavery." With it came "complete indulgence for the forgiveness of sins and also to the esteemed noble com-mander, barons and soldiers and other Christian believers, who are on your side in this battle of faith and are helping you with their goods, and who, with the intention of receiving salvation are more eager to attack the enemies of the Christian faith." The bull was issued a year before the fall of Constantinople to Ottoman Turks.

After the fall of Constantinople in 1453, Christian military actions in both east and west were framed as a religious war and, since the Council of Mantua in 1459, as a crusade. Pope Pius II's speech *Cum bello hodie* at the council was both specific to the Ottoman assaults in the east and general enough to encourage action in the west.[24] "When Our Saviour cleansed the world of filthy idols and brought it the Sacred Gospel," the pope said, "he filled not just a corner of the earth, nor a single region, but almost the whole world with it." The pope then framed the Muslim attacks as geographically encompassing both east and west. In the east the Turks "occupied Cappadocia, Pontus, Bithynia, Troy, Cilicia, and all of Asia Minor. Having grown strong due to our passivity, they drove the Christians out of Asia [Minor], and, crossing the Hellespont on ships, they invaded Macedonia, Thracia, Attica, Boeotia, Phocis, Achaia, Archanania, Epirus, Paeonia, and both Moesias. In the Aegaean and Jonian Sea they seized the Cyclades and many other islands and made them the Eastern frontier of the Christians." In the west, Pius II stated "the Moors" occupied "southern Spain," adding: "These are your boundaries, oh Christians, this is how you are surrounded on all sides, this is how you are pressed into one corner, you who were once the lords and masters of the Earth. It is indeed a great empire that you have lost, with many noble cities, and many rich provinces." It was in the slumber of peace that European Christians "let the Turkish armies advance as far as Danube and Sava. It is our fault that the noble and royal city [Constantinople] is lost." It was true, the pope stressed, the enemy was strong and "will not lay down his arms before he has won or lost all. Every victory of his will be a step towards the next one until he has defeated all the Western kings, destroyed the Christian gospel, and imposed the law of Muhammad on the whole world." Pius then called all to arms, "We must go to war against the Turks: the injuries inflicted upon us cry for revenge, and the future safety of the Christians must be ensured." All Christians had to be ready, those who lived "in rich Italy, noble France, strong Spain, warlike and populous Germany."

Territory and defense of faith were now reasons for the war, Pius II continued, "since the impious sect of the Saracens and the Turks totally denies the divinity of Christ."[25] European Christians were to go to war on behalf of Christ, "to make truth shine forth." As victors "in this very just war," the pope vowed, Christians would obtain "great and inestimable" benefits: "whatever weapons, horses, garments, silver, gold, gems, servants [servos], slave girls [ancillias], territories, cities, provinces, and kingdoms that you acquire in this war," as well as "a most noble name and eternal fame." The pope also promised the crusaders "the possession of the Heavenly Kingdom and the coinheritance of Christ," granting "a plenary remission of all sins to those who fight for the law of the Lord, and with the apostolic keys We shall open the gates to Paradise," even if they were not "victorious," even if they "should fall, fighting vigorously." Decades later, in 1493, the bulls *Inter cetera* and *Dudum siquidem* would convey similar ideas of Christian expansion and rights to possess new lands, as long as these lands were not already in the possession of Christian kings, effectively sanctioning Christian supremacy worldwide.

"Just war" offered one argument used to warrant enslavement in Christian Iberia and the transatlantic world.[26] Theology provided additional underpinnings. And while the language of Eugene IV's bull *Illius qui* for Henry the Navigator was reminiscent of those authorizing crusades against Muslims, the key descriptive phrases deployed to justify the dispossession and conquest—"perpetual slavery" and "enemies of the Christian faith"—were inflected by the language and tropes developed centuries earlier in respect to Jews.

Jewish servitude was repeatedly evoked in medieval legal and polemical texts through describing Jews as "the children of a slave" and juxtaposing them to Christians, labeled as "children of a free woman."[27] This figurative description referred to the biblical figure Hagar, the slave woman who gave birth to Ishmael, and Sarah, the free woman, who gave birth to Isaac. Since Paul's use of the metaphor in his epistles, Christian theologians saw Hagar and Ishmael as representations of Jews, even though, as Augustine himself acknowledged, Jews descended from Isaac, not Ishmael.[28] But in the medieval period the name Ishmael was not explicitly applied to Jews, though the idea that Jews were "children of a slave woman" persisted. That is because after the rise of Islam, Ishmael came to be associated with Muslims. As M. Lindsay Kaplan has shown, Ishmael as the "son of a slave woman" became "a figure for both Muslims and Jews" and medieval legal scholars applied that connection in canon law.[29]

For example, if the 1205 bull *Etsi Judaeos* prohibited Jews from having Christian servants "lest the children of a free woman should be servants to the children of a slave," decades later, the thirteenth-century canonist Hostiensis extended the prohibition to Muslims and other non-Christians in his *Summa Aurea*, under *De Judaeis, Saracenis et eorum servis*, "of Jews, Saracens, and their servants."[30] The Saracens, Hostiensis argued, who wished to be so called from Sara, but "they were not born nor have their origin from her. . . . On the contrary, from Hagar, the slave of Sara," should be called "Hagarenes or Hagariens." Sara, according to the legist, was "the legitimate woman" and in her "the Church was established and therefore Pagans or Jews ought not to have under them Christians, nor children of the free woman Sara (that is Christian children) be placed to serve outside of the Catholic faith." Some decades later, the Italian jurist

Oldradus de Ponte, who also saw Jews as heirs to Hagar, was even more explicit in articulating this social hierarchy grounded in biblical exegesis:

> Sarah signifies the Holy Catholic Church, the handmaiden Hagar, the accursed sect of Muhammad which took its origins from her. Therefore, the Holy Church, symbolized by Sarah, may use the accursed handmaiden as the blessed Sarah had used her, by beating her. She may use her as her Lord commands, by driving her out and depriving her children of inheritance and possession, that they not share with the free children. For since they are the offspring of a slave woman, and are therefore themselves slaves (for the children follow the womb)— indeed, slaves reproved by the Lord—they are not legally competent to hold rights of jurisdiction, lordship or honor.[31]

Papal bulls, especially those sent to Spain, also often mentioned "Jews and Saracens" together. So, too, were the two peoples linked in the canons of the IV Lateran Council in 1215, which in canon 68 was concerned with sexual relations of Jews and Muslims with Christians.

As M. Lindsay Kaplan has demonstrated, "the subjection of Jews to Christians serves as a precedent to argue for the proper subordination of infidels to the faithful" and this link between "the Saracens" and servitude to Christians became a key idea in justification of the conquest of lands and capture and enslavement of African people and, later, indigenous peoples in the Americas.[32] Like Jews, some medieval jurists argued Saracens and pagans could be released from that servitude through baptism. The fifteenth-century Italian jurist Antonio Roselli, noting that Sarah "signified the holy mother Church" and Hagar "the cursed slave woman in whom is signified the sect of Muhammad," argued that even though "the holy church . . . has legal authority over this slave woman and pagan sect, they certainly cannot be compelled but encouraged to the faith."[33] With time "the Jewish element" disappeared, in part because by the end of the fifteenth century Jews were no longer legally allowed to live in much of western Europe; but the model that had "developed" in the idiom of Jewish servitude remained and came to be used in European imperial expansion.[34]

Conversion became the ostensible goal for conquest and enslavement of both the peoples of the African coasts and later the indigenous populations across the Atlantic.[35] In 1454, in the context of Portuguese and Spanish activity along the coast of Africa and in the nearby islands, Pope Nicholas V expressed in his bull *Romanus Pontifex*, a desire for salvation of "all nations" that dwelled across the world and a hope that it "will be agreeable to the Divine Majesty" to "bring the sheep entrusted to him by God into the single divine fold, and may acquire for them the reward of eternal felicity and obtain pardon for their souls."[36] To accomplish that "through the aid of the Lord," the pope bestowed

> suitable favours and special graces on those Catholic kings and Princes, who like athletes and intrepid champions of the Christian faith, as we know by the evidence of facts, not only restrain the savage excesses of the Saracens and of other infidels, enemies of the Christian name, but also for the defence and increase of the faith, vanquish them and their kingdoms and habitations, though situated in the remotest parts unknown to us, and subject them to their own temporal dominion sparing no labour and expense, in order that those kings and Princes relieved of all obstacles, may be the more animated to the prosecution of so salutary and laudable a work.[37]

The rest of the bull had other references to the "salvation of the souls." But the pope hoped that "the sea might become navigable as far as to the Indians who are said to worship the name of Christ," and that thus the Portuguese "might be able to enter into relation with them, and to incite them to aid the Christians against the Saracens and other such enemies of the faith, and might also be able forthwith to subdue certain gentile or pagan peoples living between, who are entirely free from infection by the sect of the most impious Mahomet, and to preach and cause to be preached to them the unknown but most sacred Name of Christ."

As the African slave trade became "lucrative" for the Portuguese in the 1460s, Castilians began to compete with them.[38] And following the Castilian-Portuguese war of 1474–1478, the Portuguese obtained, in 1479, a monopoly on African trade as part of the war settlement. By the 1480s, the royal officials became more involved in the slave trade, establishing "the House of Slaves" in Lisbon, which "administered the trade and collected royal dues."[39]

Enslaved Africans increasingly began to appear throughout the Iberian Peninsula. By the second decade of the sixteenth century, as some scholars have estimated, over 150,000 African slaves were "imported" into Europe, collapsing the previous Mediterranean slave market that had provided slaves of different ethnic and religious backgrounds.[40] As this was taking place, according to Jean Devisse and Michel Moller, a shift in the visual representation of black Africans in European art also occurred. While previously black figures might have been represented either metaphorically as figures of evil and enmity, or literally as warriors or kings, with the influx of African slaves into Europe, black Africans began increasingly to be portrayed in positions of servitude, "as servants, laborers, pages, and musicians."[41]

In these early decades some of these Africans were manumitted upon conversion to Christianity, and formed Christian confraternities.[42] But with time, especially in the Americas, conversion did not guarantee manumission, even in the Spanish or Portuguese territories, where papal directives to spread Christianity across the world was followed. Enslaved Africans remained slaves even after baptism, although the Catholic clergy made sure they attended mass, took sacraments, and complied to established norms. Over time, the Catholic Church in many parts of the colonial world became "the single largest owner of slaves," with the Jesuits becoming "major buyers."[43] Christianity no longer meant liberty.

Still, it took time for slavery to be closely associated specifically with black Africans. In the Spanish and Portuguese colonies across the Atlantic, those enslaved first were Native Americans. Columbus himself, who was "familiar with the slave markets in Spain and elsewhere in the Mediterranean," as Alan Gallay has shown, "authorized enslaving Indians to labor for the Spanish in Hispaniola" and "shipped slaves to Spain to generate funds."[44] The Spanish monarchs, initially, opposed the enslavement of native peoples, but they did not stop it even though such enslavement seems to have "conflicted with the pope's charge to Spanish and Portuguese colonizers to convert" the indigenous peoples to Christianity. It took decades to formally outlaw indigenous enslavement. In 1537, upon the urging of Bartolomé de las Casas, Pope Paul III issued *Sublimus Deus*, condemning the enslavement of "the Indians of the West and South" as if they were "brute animals."[45] The Spanish then followed with bans in 1542 and 1546 and the Portuguese in the 1570s. Although these bans did not eliminate indigenous enslavement entirely, they came at a point when African slavery began to increase due to pressing labor shortages in the colonies.[46] With the vociferous opposition to the enslavement and the abuse of Native Americans, African slaves became a preferable option—even De las Casas consented to the enslavement of Africans. Although De las Casas later changed his views and although there were others in sixteenth century who opposed African slavery, these debates demonstrate diverging attitudes toward enslaved Africans and Native Americans.[47] These divergencies would only deepen as African slaves became dominant in the Americas.

But there were, from the perspective of European slavers, also practical reasons why the enslavement of Africans became preferable: if they tried to escape, they could not blend into the native population as easily as Native American escapees.[48] The fact that slavery existed among Africans and the fact that they were either Muslim or pagan, made it easier for the Christian colonizers to justify their enslavement. With African slaves already allowed to be brought into the Spanish Antilles and the Portuguese Madeira, and with the Portuguese trading points established on the West African coast, "a delivery system" was in place that could be easily adopted to wider transatlantic slave trade as well.[49]

Iberian history is thus key for understanding the legal, cultural, economic foundations that would help establish slavery in the Americas. As Timothy Lockley has observed, there is "a clear lineage of negative racial imagery from Arabic to Hispanic [Iberian] to English thought."[50] The connection between slavery and black Africans was first made in Islamic thought, when Muslims conquered parts of Africa and amassed dark-skinned captives, by reinterpreting the curse of Ham as both the curse of slavery and Blackness.[51] In the fifteenth century this trope began to appear in Iberia. The fifteenth-century poet and chronicler, Gomes Eanes de Zurara, too, connected the African slaves he saw with "the curse, which, after the Deluge, Noah laid upon his son [Ham], cursing him in this way: that his race should be subject to all the other races of the world."[52] By the late sixteenth century, this exegetical trope became more widely accepted. In 1575 a Dominican friar, accused of heresy, in Lima spoke of a revelation he claimed to have received justifying the enslavement of Africans: "The blacks are justly captives by just sentence of God for the sins of their fathers, and that in sign thereof God gave them that color, and that the reason for their being black is not the one given by the philosophers [who explained the skin color by exposure to sun]."[53] And although the friar did not make this a curse of Ham—indeed, he linked black Africans to the tribe of Asher—he did see their enslavement and their color as a divine curse.

This connection between Blackness and slavery would be embraced by other European thinkers as European powers established their colonial economies in which enslavement of black Africans played a central role. The English, not having a history of enslavement, Lockley has argued, "imitated the systems that had already been put in place by the Spanish and Portuguese."[54] So, too, did the Dutch, who in the seventeenth century monopolized the transatlantic slave trade and occupied parts of Portuguese holdings in Brazil.[55] But following the footsteps of the Spanish and the Portuguese was not uncontroversial among the English and the Dutch, who both had a history of conflicts with the Iberian powers and saw themselves as champions of freedom, viewing slavery as a contemptible "sin" of papists, which they did not want to replicate.[56]

By the time Europeans began to expand their reach across the Atlantic, they had a firmly developed sense of religious and political superiority—Christian supremacy, in law and political structures, had already been firmly established in Europe, in part through the imposition of a theological and legal "condition of inferiority upon Jews relative to Christians."[57] The transatlantic expansion only strengthened that dominant identity. Yet, as many scholars have stressed, observing difference is not equivalent to espousing racist attitudes.[58] Assigning derogatory value to certain characteristics and peoples created fertile ground for racism to take root when coupled with power. At the beginning of European expansion, European Christian identity was not yet connected to whiteness, even though the black color had for centuries been associated with sin and even evil; but sin could, after all, be erased with baptism. The Catholic monarchs and the popes saw the colonization as an opportunity to spread Christianity across the world, by converting native populations—a much-needed boost in light of eastern losses to the Ottomans. Papal bulls sanctioning the raids in Africa and enslavement effectively authorized Christian supremacy.

But even if the Christian supremacy of the early colonial era was not yet palpably "white Christian supremacy," the desire to convert non-Europeans by Catholic powers did not preclude hierarchization of colonial Catholic society. Here, too, there was another tool already in place in Spain the statutes of purity of blood, *limpieza de sangre*. The statutes of *limpieza de sangre* were first created and applied to Jews after their mass and forced conversions in 1391 and in the early fifteenth century. The idea of purity of blood helped create a caste system that distinguished between "New" and "Old" Christians, making the past indelible by linking religion and lineage. As David Nirenberg has put it, "The conversion to Christianity of many thousands of Jews caused by the massacres, forced disputation, and segregations that marked the period between 1391 and 1415 produced a violent destabilization of traditional categories of religious identity" that led to the elevation of "genealogy to a primary form of communal memory."[59] These mass conversions raised, Nirenberg has argued, "systemic doubt about who was a Christian and who was a Jew," and reinforced "the Spanish obsession with *hidalguía*, Gothic descent, and purity of blood."[60] This doubt and distrust led to the hereditary exclusion of converted Jews and their descendants from public offices, a move that was condemned by Pope Eugene IV in 1437. The term *"sangre limpia,"* clean blood, appears to have been first used in 1449 in Toledo and would later be translated into legal restrictions.[61] But some theologians feared that "to introduce . . . difference or preference between one nation or another in the faith of

Christ would be to diminish the perfect unity of Christendom."[62] Still, the application of the purity of blood statutes was, as Robert Bernasconi has argued, different from the modern ideas of biological racism.[63]

As these debates were taking place, the Portuguese were scaling up the African slave trade. And by the time the Spanish and Portuguese expanded their territorial claims across the Atlantic, the ideas of "purity of blood," "natural Christianity," and *hidalguía*, a noble descent, were firmly in place—ripe for creation of "a 'pigmentocratic' society."[64] The concept of purity of blood was of course more broadly accepted among European aristocratic families. Historians of French colonial empire have shown that "sixteenth and seventeenth century concerns about noble purity and mésalliance, or mixed noble-commoner marriages, shaped attitudes about marriages between French colonists and Indians on the North American mainland and between French colonists and Africans in the Caribbean."[65]

But given the Catholic ideal of universal conversion in a universal church, the association between whiteness and Christianity was slow to form, even within a racialized social hierarchy. In the colonies held by the Catholic powers, Portugal, Spain, and from the seventeenth century also France, African slaves were to be catechized and baptized and non-Christians had no right to live there—Jews were excluded entirely, for they had been expelled from these Catholic domains also on the European continent. Since manumission of slaves was permitted, racialized social categories became too complicated and too fluid. In the Spanish and Portuguese colonies, wrote Timothy Lockley, "mulattoes could sometimes rise to a semi-elite status" but they were denied higher offices because they were not of "'true' Spanish or Portuguese blood."[66] French colonies, for their part, became home to the largest and the wealthiest free Black population of any European colonies.[67] According to John Garrigus, "Saint Domingue had nearly as many free people of color as whites," or about 45 percent of the population, and until the Seven Years' War (1756–1763) in which Britain defeated France, the most prominent freemen of color in Saint-Domingue were considered "white."[68]

Specifically, white Christian identity arose mostly within the English and, to some extent also, Dutch Protestant contexts, subsequently dominating the English and Dutch colonial holdings, including the territories of what would become the United States.[69] The first decades of the seventeenth century ended the monopoly on colonial possessions and African slave trade by the Portuguese and Spanish in the Americas as the two emerging Atlantic Protestant powers began to make permanent settlements—the English in Jamestown in 1607, in 1610 in Bermuda, and in 1620, Plymouth. Other colonial settlements followed.[70] In 1627 the Dutch established a colony in Guiana, and in 1630 took control over the Portuguese Brazilian port of Recife and then expanded it to Pernambuco, and then on to the island of Curaçao.[71] Enslaved Africans made up the majority of new arrivals and quickly became part of the colonial economy, especially in the Caribbean.[72] On the North American mainland, the early laborers were indentured servants from England, with African slaves only slowly becoming the dominant labor force.

Unlike the Catholic colonies, in which the policy of conversion was deployed from the very beginning, "a strong anticonversion sentiment," as Katherine Gerbner demonstrated, developed in the territories controlled by Protestant Europeans.[73] In the early years of their transatlantic endeavors, English settlers did seek the conversions of native peoples; the conversion of Matoaka, popularly known as Pocahontas, and her marriage to John Rolfe in 1614, seemed promising.[74] But in 1622, the English settlers were attacked by the Powhatans around Jamestown, along the James and York Rivers, and about a third of the English were killed. The massacre ended, as Rebecca Anne Goetz has shown, both the English Protestants' "expectation of working with Indians" and "the efforts to Christianize" them.[75] As one settler declared: "As for converting of the Infidells itt was an attempt impossible they being descended of ye cursed race of Cham." The curse of Ham became here both a racial marker and a marker of what Goetz called "hereditary heathenism," an idea that would be extended onto black Africans, who were just beginning to be brought in as slaves into the English colonies. The idea of "hereditary heathenism" worked in tandem with the idea of "hereditary Christianity," which privileged white European Christians. But in Maryland the efforts to convert the native peoples were not abandoned. This is not surprising, since Maryland was established in 1634 by the Calvert family, English Catholics who turned the new colony into a haven for Catholics, excluded from other English colonies, including Jesuit missionaries.[76]

In Protestant colonies—English, Dutch, and Danish, over the course of the seventeenth century, religious institutions were designed to exclude Africans, free or enslaved, with slave owners actively preventing the conversion of the enslaved Black people to Christianity.[77] Religion, as Katherine Gerbner has argued, came to define "mastery and whiteness," giving rise to the "ideology of Protestant Supremacy," or, more accurately, white Protestant supremacy, since the connection with Protestantism and whiteness was undeniably sound.[78] In his *History of Barbados*, published in 1657, thirty years after the English settled the island, Richard Ligon, Gerbner has shown, "consistently juxtaposed 'Negroes' with 'Christians.'"[79] Christians were white—or at least "not Negroes"—and were also associated with a free status because "Negroes" were, in Ligon's work, understood to be slaves. Christianity, freedom, and whiteness came together.

The same was observed by Reverend Morgan Godwyn, an English clergyman who lived in Virginia for some two decades before returning to London in 1681. In his book, published soon after his return from Virginia, condemning the Englishmen's opposition to conversions of both Black and native peoples and advocating "for their admission into the Church," Godwyn captured this phenomenon: "These two words, Negro and Slave, being by custom grown Homogeneous and Convertible; even as Negro and Christian, Englishman and Heathen are by the like corrupt Custom and Partiality made Opposites; thereby as it were implying, that the one could not be Christians, nor the other Infidels."[80] With "Negro" and "slave" interchangeable, or "convertible" in Godwyn's words, terms across the English colonies that embraced African slavery, the term "Christian" became "a shorthand for 'nonslave.'"[81] And "Christian" also meant "white."

This taxonomy was challenged when, some Christians, eager to missionize among the Black slaves, began to reconcile enslavement with Christianity.[82] With Black conversions, "Christian" was no longer to be synonymous with white European, and the term "white" started to be added as a descriptor and entered the colonial legal fabric, influencing the racialization of law. In 1697, the assembly in Barbados promulgated an "Act to keep inviolate, and preserve the Freedom of Elections."[83] The new law declared that "every white Man professing the Christian Religion, the free and natural born Subject of the King of England, or naturalized, who hath attained to the full Age of One and Twenty Years, and hath Ten Acres of Freehold . . . shall be deemed a Freeholder, and shall and may be capable of Electing Representatives or Vestry-Men, or of being Elected a Representative or Vestry-Man in the Parish wherein such his Estate lieth, or to serve as a Juror to try real Actions." The act excluded not only, as Katherine Gerber has noted, "non-white Christians," but also non-Christians.[84] It was a legal articulation of white Christian supremacy, which was further reaffirmed when the law was revised in 1709; this time, explicitly preventing anyone of Black extraction from becoming a freeholder.[85]

By the time the 1697 act was passed, there were dozens of Jewish fami-lies living in Barbados. By all accounts they were considered white: they were free, they held property, and some, if not all, were slaveholders.[86] One David Nemias, for example, owned twenty acres of land and twelve slaves.[87] Marked as "a Jew" in a census of 1679, he would have been disallowed from serving as an elector and juror, according to "the Act to keep inviolate, and preserve the Freedom of Elections" of 1697. With the presence of Black Christians and white Jews (although there were some Jews who were not white), the explicit reference to both Christianity and whiteness became necessary. Indeed, if Jews, as Geraldine Heng argued, were "constitutive" to the development of Christian identity, so too was whiteness built, as George Yancy has argued, "relationally" to Blackness."[88] Still, white Protestant, or white Christian, identity required both, Blackness and Jewishness.

A similar concern was articulated in Virginia. While in 1667, "Christian" still was assumed to mean "white," by 1705 the religio-racial boundaries were somewhat blurred, and law was deployed to prevent such blurring, now employing more explicit racial language.[89] In 1705, Virginia's House of Burgesses passed "An Act concerning Servants and Slaves."[90] Section XI declared that "no negros, mulattos, or Indians, although christians, or Jews, Moors, Mahometans, or other infidels shall purchase any chris-tian servant, nor any other, except of their own complexion, or such as are declared slaves by this act: And if any negro, mulatto, or Indian, Jew, Moor, Mahometan, or other infidel, or such as are declared slaves by this act, shall, notwithstanding, purchase any christian white servant, the said servant shall, ipso facto, become free and acquit from any service then due, and shall be so held, deemed, and taken." Intermarriage of "such christian servant . . . with any such negro, mulatto, or Indian, Jew, Moor, Mahometan, or other infidel," was prohibited and "every christian white servant of every such person so intermarrying, shall, ipso facto, become free and acquit from any service then due to such master or mistress so intermarrying, as aforesaid." The law was clearly concerned with social hierarchy, anxious about "negros, mulattos, or Indians, although chris-tians, or Jews, Moors, Mahometans, or other infidels" having power over white Christians—they could, after all, purchase servants "of their own complexion." The law elevated white Christianity to a position above Christians who were not white and above non-Christians. The provision was not dissimilar from that in ancient Roman Christian law, according to which a Christian slave in Jewish hands had to be released, but here it was a specifically the white Christian servant who was protected from servitude to those considered of lower social standing: "negros, mulattos, or Indians, although christians, or Jews, Moors, Mahometans, or other infidels."

Section XI of the 1705 act also expressed concern over racial and religious mixing that could lead to the increase of the free-by-birth population of color—a population whose presence begat particular anxiety among white slave holders. As a remedy, the law, in sections XIX and XX, prohibited intermarriage between free whites and free people of African descent, and, in Section XVIII, punished "any woman servant" who would "have a bastard child by a negro, or mulatto" with "fifteen pounds current money of Virginia," or risk being sold "for five years" upon the expiration of her indenture. The situation was even more dire for "a free christian white woman" who would "have such bastard child, by a negro, or mulatto"; she was similarly liable for a fine of "fifteen pounds current money of Virginia" payable "within one month after her delivery of such bastard child" or risk being "sold for five years," but her child was also destined to be a bound servant "until it shall be of thirty one years of age." This clause was based in an earlier Virginia law promulgated in 1691, which stated that "free white man or woman" marrying "a negroe, mulatto, or Indian man or woman bond or free shall within three months after such marriage be banished and removed from this dominion forever."[91] White women who had children by a man of color ("any negroe or mulatto") out of wedlock were to be punished by a fine paid to Church wardens and sold by them into five years of servitude, her child too was to "be bound out as a servant by the said Church wardens" until the age of thirty.

This angst over the potential increase of free population of color was also behind the redefinition of traditional European and English custom of patrilineality—the transmission of social status through a father. According to English law, "a child inherited the status of the father."[92] As the English Puritan clergyman Thomas Blake put it in 1644, "The child of a Noble man is noble."[93] This was redefined in 1662 in Virginia, because "doubts have arisen whether children got by Englishmen upon negro women should be slave or ffree [sic]." From then on, "the children borne in this country shall be held bond or free only according to the condition of the mother." The 1705 Virginia law reaffirmed this principle to protect slavery, adding, after a law passed in 1667, a clause about religion. Section XXXVI declared that "baptism of slaves doth not exempt them from bondage; and that all children shall be bond or free, according to the condition of their mothers." A pregnancy resulting from a sexual act between a free white man and a black enslaved woman would produce enslaved children. But, as Warren E. Milteer has shown, free people of color were most commonly born of free white women, often indentured servants themselves.[94] As a result, colonial lawmakers sought to regulate interracial sex and circumscribe the legal status of such mixed progeny.

In dealing with increasing racial and religious ambiguity due to the existence of free and enslaved people of color and of non-Christian whites, the laws began to define and protect religious and racial boundaries through more explicit modifiers, describing, for example, Christian individuals as "white Christian servants" or noting the legal status of people of color, as in "negro, mulatto, or Indian, bond or free," and through sanctions—punishment, as the laws against interracial sexual relations show, and privilege, which reified a special status hereditary European Christianity bestowed on individuals. The law restricted the service of "all servants brought into this country without indenture, if the said servants be christians, and of christian parentage, and above nineteen years of age," to five years, while designating "all servants imported and brought into this country, by sea or land, who were not christians in their native country (except Turks and Moors in amity with her majesty, and others that can make due proof of their being free in England, or any other christian country, before they were shipped, in order to transportation hither)" as slaves who could "be here bought and sold notwithstanding a conversion to christianity afterward."[95] Christianity, thus, guaranteed protection from slavery only for someone who was white.

Whiteness and Christianity also protected servants from cruelty. The law stipulated that "masters and owners of servants" should not "whip a christian white servant naked, without an order from a justice of the peace."[96] This was the first time, according to Rebecca Anne Goetz, that "Christians were legally and explicitly defined by a physical distinction—skin color—and granted certain privileges based upon color and religious identity."[97] The laws across English colonies helped assert white Protestant supremacy by the exclusion of both people of color and non-Christians from the polity and by bestowing on white Christians special privileges not granted to others that in effect elevated both whiteness and Christianity—in tandem.

This process of elevating European Christianity in the global context was made visible to readers in early modern printed books. Just as European powers were asserting their place in colonies around the world, the same chronicles and cosmographies that depicted Jews as demonic dangerous figures also increasingly began to depict non-Europeans as exotic, dangerous, and primitive, while combining innocuous texts with suggestive imagery. The printed books, in contrast to paintings, depicted

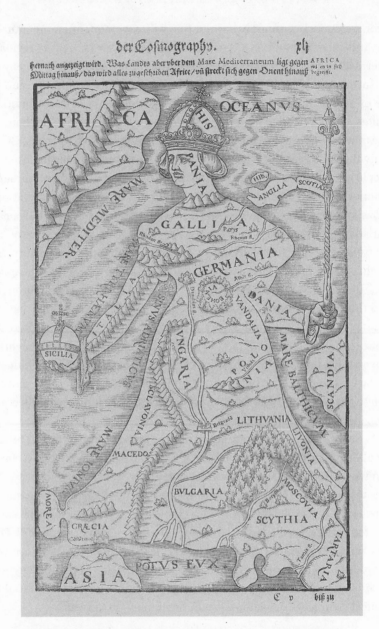

FIGURE 6. Europa Regina, Sebastian Münster, *Cosmographey: Das Ist, Beschreibung Aller Länder, Herrschafften Vnd Fürnemesten Stetten des Gantzen Erdbodens, Sampt Ihren Gelegenheiten, Eygenschafften, Religion, Gebräuchen, Geschichten Vnd Handtierungen* (Basel: Henricpetri, 1598), 54. Bayerische Staatsbibliothek, Rare 831.

the non-Europeans from Asia or Africa often naked and cruel, sometimes even as cannibals.[98] Some early examples are found in Sebastian Münster's monumental *Cosmographia*, first published in 1544, in which, at the end, are images and descriptions of peoples in Asia and, briefly, in Africa. Images found in these sections show monsters, human and animal, nakedness, and barbarity, such as chopping and roasting human beings.[99] This can be contrasted with always dressed and respectable-looking Europeans—except for Jews who, in their attire and stories about them, were always depicted in printed books as dangerous, cruel, and murderous outsiders.[100]

As Europeans began to exploit and enslave non-Europeans, their colonial triumphs and the need to justify their exploitation led to, along with the legal transformations discussed above, a transformation of European identity. The already existing sense of superiority grounded in religion and theology that developed over centuries in relation to Jews and Judaism now became combined with the new sense of superiority over the colonized and exploited people of color. The symbolic visual representation of Europe increasingly came to emphasize its dominance, Christianity, and whiteness. In 1537, Johannes Putsch created a prototype of an early modern representation of the map of Europe as a queen, Europa Regina, popularized since the late 1580s, when a version of this image entered the subsequent editions of Sebastian Münster's *Cosmographia* (fig. 6).

The inclusion of Europa Regina in Münster's *Cosmograhia* came on the heels of another important work that influenced Europeans' perception of the world—Abraham Ortelius's *Theatrum orbis terrarum*. First published in Antwerp in 1570, it reached nearly thirty editions by 1598, the year of Ortelius's death, and many more were still published thereafter. The frontispiece featured an engraving depicting four continents (fig. 7): Europa, Asia, Africa, and America. Europa sits crowned at the top, holding in her right hand a scepter and, with her left, touching an orb with a cross—its identity is clear: a Christian queen, Europa Regina. Below her are, on the left, Asia, a woman dressed in a gown, looking down with humility, and on the right nearly naked Africa. Below them, on the ground, reclines naked America, holding in her hand a head of a European man. The frontispiece conveys an unmistakable notion of European Christian superiority and dominance over the world, a notion that would become a deeply entrenched in European identity.

In 1603, five years after Ortelius's death, another important book was published, one that would have tremendous impact on the visual representation of Europe and the other three known continents—Africa,

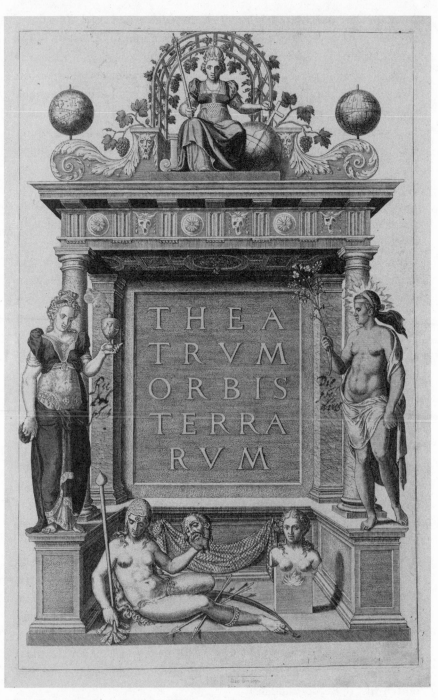

FIGURE 7. Abraham Ortelius, *Theatrum orbis terrarum* (Antwerp, Apud Aegid. Coppenium Diesth, 1570). Library of Congress, Geography and Map Division. https://lccn.loc.gov/2003683482.

America, and Asia—in art. It was the third, expanded, and illustrated edition of Cesare Ripa's *Iconologia*, a guidebook of visual motifs and allegories for painters and poets, originally published in 1593. The book included representations of a variety of concepts, such as law, knowledge, virtue, justice, and more, most presented as women. The four continents, too, were each depicted as women, and though in 1603 the imagery did not display any visible physiognomic characteristics—they were all young women—through the accoutrements and descriptions, Ripa reflected values attached to each part of the world.

Europa, like that in Ortelius's atlas, was "a woman dressed most richly in regal garments full of color, crown on her head, sitting in the middle of two cornucopias," wrote Ripa.[101] In her right hand she holds a temple, her left points to "kingdoms, different crowns, scepters, garlands, and similar things." There should be a horse with trophies, money, "most powerful arms," a book, an owl, musical instruments and more. Ripa then went on to explain the meaning of the iconography. "Europe is the first and main part of the world," he wrote referring to Pliny. "She is richly dressed in colorful regal garments, because of the richness that is in her [Europe]." The crown is to demonstrate that "Europe is always superior, a Queen of all of the world." And the temple in her right hand denotes that she embodies "the perfect and most true religion, superior to all others." Each detail in the painting was to support that. "The index finger of her left hand pointing to kingdoms, crowns, and scepters, indicate that in Europe there were the most powerful princes in the world, and the pope [*il Sommo Pontefice*], whose authority extends over everything where there is the Holiest Catholic Christian Faith, which thanks to God, has been received in the new world." The horse, the arms, music instruments, and the owl on top of the book, all "demonstrate that [Europe] has always been superior to other parts of the world in the military, letters, and all liberal arts." Other details, including paintbrushes, architectural instruments, indicate that Europe has always had genius men in arts, sculpture, and architecture.

The directions Ripa offered to painters affirmed in the figure of Europe as queen both European political supremacy—"always superior, a Queen of the world"—and Christian supremacy—"the perfect and most true religion, superior to all others." The image was not dissimilar from the image of medieval *Ecclesia*, but here it was not paired with the *Synagoga*, but rather with an allegorical depiction of the other continents, which, like the *Synagoga*, were shown as inferior. Asia followed Europe and was placed above Africa and America. When Ripa was writing, Asia was still appreciated for its spices and had not yet succumbed to European dominance. It thus earned respect. Asia was shown dressed in splendid gowns, covered in pearls and gold, standing, crowned with a garland of flowers, with "a snake on the right, a helm on the left, a bow under her feet." She was surrounded by plants of pepper and fruit.[102] Asia constituted "half of the world," Ripa wrote. The rich garment of gold and jewels represented not only the prosperity of this "most happy" land but also, he claimed, the "custom" of the people to dress thus, especially the women. This depiction stood in contrast with Africa and America, both shown as half-naked.

The description of Africa had her as a semi-nude dark woman with "frizzy and scattered hair, holding an elephant's head as a headdress," with a coral bead necklace and pendant earrings—"Moorish adornments," holding a scorpion in her right hand and a cornucopia filled with heads of grain in her left.[103] To her one side is a ferocious lion and to the other, venomous vipers and serpents. Ripa was influenced by earlier literature and representations. The elephant head was there, he explained, because it was found on a medallion of Emperor Adrian; lion, scorpion, and venomous vipers indicate that Africa is filled with those, "as says Claudiano." But for America, since it was recently "discovered," Ripa did not have ancient authors or models to draw from. He thus used more recent descriptions of the lands for inspiration. America was to be portrayed, he wrote, as "a naked woman with a dark complexion of mixed yellow, with a terrible face & a wrap, streaked with multiple colors, dropping from one shoulder across the body, covers her shameful parts"; her hair scattered, her ornaments made of colorful feathers.[104] In her left hand she holds a bow, and in her right an arrow. Next to her is a quiver filled with arrows and under her feet a human skull pierced with an arrow, which was to demonstrate, Ripa wrote, that "these barbarous people are mostly used to feed [pasciarsi] on human flesh," eating the people defeated in war and slaves they bought. A lizard, later a crocodile, would become another iconographic symbol of America.

When Ripa's work was published in Protestant countries, sometimes the language affirming Catholic supremacy was removed.[105] Iconographic changes would take place as well, as time went on. The 1603, 1625, and 1645 Italian editions did not mark color of complexion (figs. 8–11), because for Ripa, who like Münster, worked with ancient descriptions of the continent, Africa was still associated with north Africa, Libya and Egypt. The people associated with Africa were "Moors." But this was to change later in the seventeenth century, especially after the plantation economy expanded along with the transatlantic slave trade.

Law and culture reflected those changes. In 1684, François Bernier, a physician and traveler, published what is considered to be the first-ever

FIGURE 8. Europa, Cesare Ripa, *Iconologia* (1625). The author's own copy.

published work on classification of races and species in *Journal des sça-vans*, the first scientific journal in Europe, in which he argued that there were "four or five Species or Races of men so notably differing from each other that this may serve as the just foundation of a new division of the world."[106] A year later, in 1685, King Louis XIV issued the Code Noir, which sought to regulate slavery.[107] It acknowledged the growth of the number of slaves used in colonies to the point of needing new laws "for the conservation of this Colony" and "to maintain the discipline of the Catholic Church."[108] The laws focused primarily on regulating the status of Black slaves, *Esclaves Negres*, but they also affirmed the supremacy of Catholicism by demanding that all slaves be instructed and baptized in the Catholic faith and that Jews be expelled from the French colonies. The code also addressed the legal position of those who had been manumitted,

FIGURE 9. Asia, Cesare Ripa, *Iconologia* (1625).

ruling that they did not require naturalization, even if they were born elsewhere, and that they were to have "the same rights, privileges and liberties
enjoyed by persons born free." But these were not blanket equal rights.[109]
Black subjects were not allowed to receive donations from whites in the
form of peoples or property, and were they to receive anything, any such
donation would become "null and void" and would benefit the nearest
*hôpital.* The social and racial order was thus firmly established in law.

At the same time, European presses, especially in Amsterdam, were
churning out books repeatedly showing Africans, from many different
parts of the continent, as black, naked, pierced, and armed with spears.[110]
In 1668, Olfert Dapper's monumental description of Africa, written without Dapper's ever setting his foot there, was first published in Dutch, and
then in German (1670), English (1670), and French (1686) translations.[111]
Though nearly half of Dapper's book consisted of the detailed descriptions

FIGURE 10. Africa, Cesare Ripa, *Iconologia* (1625).

of North Africa—Egypt, Morocco, Algiers, and Libya—it was the other half devoted to "Negros-lant" that engraved Africa in European imagination as a black continent, inhabited by naked, dangerous—sometimes even cannibalistic—uncivilized people (fig. 12).[112] Some of the images—like those of "murderous" Jews from the early modern chronicles—once embedded in European imagination would become difficult to unlearn.[113] And so, when Dutch versions of Cesare Ripa's *Iconologia* were published in 1644, 1699, and 1700, and the English edition in 1709, it is not surprising that the image of Africa was no longer a Moorish woman but rather a naked black woman, underscoring the fact that by that time "whiteness" had become part of European Christian identity and law (figs. 13–14). This imagery spread across Europe, especially in the Holy Roman Empire and Catholic lands, committed to the idea of spreading Christianity to the rest of the world.[114] It was found on ceiling frescoes in palaces and churches,

FIGURE 11. America, Cesare Ripa, *Iconologia* (1625).

figurines displayed in parlors, and even church pulpits, like the splendid eighteenth-century high baroque pulpit in a prominent but remote Benedictine abbey in St. Lambrecht in Austrian Styria, some 40 km west of Judenburg and 120 km west of Graz. The pulpit displayed the triumph of St. Benedict pulled by the four continents, among them crowned and white Europa, brown America, and black, semi-clad Africa.

In 1753, David Hume, in his essay "Of Natural Characters," declared "the negroes and in general all the other species of men . . . naturally inferior to the whites."[115] And asserted that "there never was a civilized nation of any other complexion than white." Hume was an opponent of slavery, but that did not make him respect Blackness; his view of human hierarchy led him to diminish any evidence of Black accomplishments. "In Jamaica," he wrote, "they talk of one Negro as a man of parts and learning; but it is likely he is admired for slender accomplishments, like a parrot who

FIGURE 12. Olfert Dapper, *Naukeurige beschrijvinge der Afrikaensche gewesten van Egypten, Barbaryen, Libyen, Biledulgerid, Negroslant, Guinea, Ethiopiën, Abyssinie* (Amsterdam: Jacob van Meurs, 1668), 612.

speaks a few words plainly."[116] For Hume, there was a "uniform and constant difference" between whites and other races, and such differences "could not happen in so many countries and ages, if nature had not made an original distinction between these breeds of men." Later, Immanuel Kant, a German Enlightenment philosopher, would claim that "humanity is at its greatest perfection in the race of whites. The yellow Indians have meagre talent. The Negroes are far below them and the lowest point is the [Native] American peoples."[117] For Kant, "the Negro" was "strong, fleshy, supple but in the midst of the bountiful provision of his motherland lazy, soft, and dawdling"; white European, who inhabited "temperate zones," "most beautiful" and "happy," possessing "more beautiful body" and more intelligence.[118]

By mid-eighteenth century, thus, with the Enlightenment in full force, this white, European, and Christian identity was firmly established, and non-Europeans were visually exoticized, depicted as non-white, naked or clad in exotic garments. Giovanni Battista Tiepolo's *Allegory of Planets*

FIGURE 13. Europa, Cesare Ripa, *Iconologia* (1709), 47, fig.

*and Continents* fresco painted in 1752–1753 for Carl Philipp von Greiffen-klau, prince-bishop of Würzburg, on the ceiling of the ceremonial staircase in the bishop's palace, influenced by Cesare Ripa's *Iconologia*, displays "brown-skinned America riding a crocodile," "a black-skinned Africa mounted on a camel," "turbaned Asia on an elephant," counterweighted by Europe, "enthroned" and "regally clad," glancing up.[119]

In the allegorical portrayals of the medieval *Ecclesia* and *Synagoga* and the early modern continents, garments signaled order and hierar-chy. The regal clothes of both *Ecclesia* and Europa signaled superiority and dominance; the *Synagoga* was typically dressed like a poor maiden, while in the allegories of the continents, level of dress and undress indi-cated the level of "civilization" and world hierarchy: Europe dominat-ing others, followed by a respectable Asia, then the "uncivilized" Africa and America, both depicted as semi-naked. After the French Revolution, Liberty would take the place of the iconographic models established by

FIGURE 14. Africa, Cesare Ripa, *Iconologia* (1709), 53, fig. 209.

Europa (fig. 15) and Europa would become a personification of Liberty, while America would then be represented no longer as a "savage" naked woman but as the white and triumphant Columbia.[120] And, as Tyler Stovall has argued, Liberty was depicted as a white woman, including later in the Statue of Liberty, because it embodied a racialized idea of liberty as applicable to white people alone.[121] This white, racialized liberty had roots in "Christian liberty" developed in ancient and medieval Christian theology.[122]

As Andrew Curran has shown, the Enlightenment became a turning point for European Christian racial self-perception.[123] European proto-ethnographic literature that first emerged in the sixteenth century in relation to Jews was transformed in the seventeenth and eighteenth centuries to be more comparative thanks to the countless publications and travelogues describing different people and cultures around the world. Bernard Picart's and Jean-Frédéric Bernard's groundbreaking *Cérémonies*

FIGURE 15. *Liberté*, Jean François Janinet, 1792, Aquatint and etching,
©The Trustees of the British Museum, Registration number: 2001,0520.58.
Public domain.

*et coutumes religieuses de tous les peuples du monde* published in 1723 is the epitome.[124] Based on works available in print and adorned by impressive original though derivative copperplates, this massive multivolume book purported to be the most objective description of religious ceremonies and customs of all people in the world. It began with Jews, first describing their ancient history and customs, before moving onto contemporary Jews; this was then followed by Catholicism, Protestant denominations, Islam, and then other religious practices, including those in Africa, Asia, and the Americas. The order of the work reflected European Christian understanding of history influenced by the narratives offered in the Bible and religious histories available to readers in early modern Europe. The book, while seeking to be detached and objective, nonetheless—by the fact that it drew on previously published works, perpetuated existing preconceptions and stereotypes—Picart's and Bernard's sources of knowledge contained them. Though the book discussed different religions, it was also a reflection of hierarchy—the primacy of the Christian story. True, Jews were placed at the beginning but only because they were seen as historically the first religious group—to them the Old Testament belonged. *Cérémonies et coutumes religieuses* also reflected an increased interest in describing and categorizing the world. The interest in classifications of peoples of the world, in proto-racialist terms, began to emerge in the seventeenth century, but it was the Enlightenment in the eighteenth century with its keen interest in science and experimentations that brought a more methodical and "scientific" classification of human "races."

The motivation for such classification emerged not only from exposure to global humanity but also from the need to justify European exploitation and enslavement of black Africans. At a time when Europeans were grappling with toleration and ideas of human and natural rights—slavery presented a glaring challenge to the sincerity of these ideals. To the rescue were deployed emerging science and racial theories.

If, at first, the justification for the enslavement of Africans was conversion of the "heathen" to Christianity, with time this justification proved inadequate, especially because some enslaved populations were in fact Christianized—sometimes, like in French colonies, as required by law. European philosophers and writers began to debate whether Africans were part of human or natural history.[125] Human history had been told by Europeans through the trajectory set by the Bible and Christianity in Europe; Africans (and Native Americans) now needed to be fitted into that narrative. Theories of degeneration caused by climate were introduced, especially by those thinkers subscribing to the idea of monogenesis, which was supported by the biblical narrative tracing origins of humanity to a single source—Adam and Eve, who were always shown as white in European art. There also emerged a theory of polygenesis, arguing for the existence of multiple origins of human races. Some presented black Africans as not fully human: as machines or beasts of burden, or some barbaric species. Even the language describing them signaled otherness and difference from white Christian Europeans.

Europeans became obsessed with Blackness—desperate to establish firm differences in the nature of black Africans to justify what Europeans were inflicting on them. Even the most renown Enlightenment thinkers were unable to accept clear evidence of shared humanity. Africans had no thoughts about the past or future, they lived "from day to day," one writer noted.[126] In asserting the supremacy of white European concepts of beauty, others declared that Africans were ugly, with their wide noses, thick lips, hair that was not hair like the Europeans' "loose blond locks" at all, but rather wool.[127] (The eighteenth-century American abolitionist James Otis bemoaned that some would feel the right to "enslave a man" because he had "short curl'd hair like wool instead of christian hair."[128]) Their brain, blood, sperm, and other organs were different. Denis Diderot, for example, accepted Pierre Barrère's theory that Africans were anatomically dissimilar from whites and had "black blood and black bile."[129] Books helped disseminate these ideas, creating a body of knowledge accepted and studied by Enlightenment thinkers. But only a handful of Enlightenment thinkers, like Montesquieu or Johann Gottfried von Herder, exposed the reason behind all these intellectual efforts—profit from slave trade and slavery led to the epistemic linking of "Africanness and slavery."[130]

If Europeans disagreed over a place of black Africans within the body of humanity, such questions did not emerge about Jews at that time. Although the medieval abbot Peter the Venerable had centuries earlier questioned Jews' humanity because of their rejection of Christianity, modern polygenists and monogenists accepted that Jews and Europeans shared the past—that certainty was grounded in the shared biblical texts.[131] But with the now deeply rooted convictions about Europe as a white Christian queen, questions did arise about the place Jews—even European Jews—occupied within the newly emerging racial classifications. Much of the early modern literature about Jews was either vitriolically anti-Jewish or focused on religious polemic seeking to affirm the truth of Christianity.[132] Some works focused on Jewish history or Jewish customs and ceremonies, a genre that began in the early sixteenth century. But much of the European Christian literature on the history of Jews explored the history of "a nation chosen by God to preserve true religion until the preaching of the gospels," that is only until the rise of Christianity, post-biblical history was largely ignored.[133]

One of such exceedingly popular works was Claude Fleury's *Mœurs des Israélites*, published first in French in 1681, and then republished dozens of times in translations into Dutch, English, German, Italian, and Spanish, on average every two years in the two centuries since its first edition. Because Israelites were "chosen by God," they were "a model of human life most concordant with nature," argued Fleury. "We can see in their customs most rational manners" of life and work within society. The study of their customs helped illuminate not only "the moral but also the economic and political" aspects of society. These customs, however, were different from "our own," and as such they may be shocking, Fleury warned: the distinction between clean and unclean foods, bloody sacrifices "that disgust us," or the Israelites' proneness to idolatry.[134] That was the reason the church fathers saw Jews as carnal. "All this," Fleury continued, "together with a confused prejudice that what is the oldest is always the most imperfect, easily persuades us that these men were brutal & ignorant, and that their manners are more contemptible than admirable." But Fleury urged his readers to dispose of their prejudices, "to judge of these customs only by common sense, and by right reason," and "to leave the particular ideas of our country and our time, to look at the Israelites in the circumstances of the times and places where they lived; compare them with the peoples who have been closest to them, and thus enter into their minds."

The "past is a foreign country," wrote L. P. Hartley in 1953, "they do things differently there."[135] Fleury argued that point already in 1681: "We live in the same country where the Gauls and then the Romans lived. How far are we from each other's way of living and even from that of the French who lived seven or eight hundred years ago? And in this same century where we are, what relationship is there between our mores & those of Indians, or Chinese?"[136] Fleury described the life and customs of ancient Israelites, simple people who lived simply by their own labor, predominantly in agriculture, Fleury noted, pointing to the many stories and parables in the gospels that involve agriculture. Now, away from their lands for centuries, they became traders and usurers. Still, Fleury observed in closing, it was "among these people that the true tradition of virtue as well as that of doctrine and religion was preserved."[137] They had saints and sages, "circumcised in heart as well as body," who believed "in prophecies and God's promises," and who "waited patiently for the redemption of Israel and the reign of the Messiah." They knew that their hope should not be limited to this life, and thus believed in resurrection and the Kingdom of Heaven. The "grace of the Gospel" thus came on the heels of "such holy dispositions, it was easy to make perfect Christians of these true Israelites."[138]

While works like Fleury's affirmed the importance of Jews, or rather biblical Israelites, in human history, their focus on ancient history located Jews in Judea, or "Palestine," not in Europe. Written at a time when Europeans were also consuming books about black "uncivilized" and animalistic Africans, these books helped mark Jews as non-European outsiders. The ingrained identity of Europe as Christian and, now increasingly as Christian and white, did not allow Jews, who had lived in Europe since at least the Roman times, to be accepted as European. In 1705, one book explicitly linked Jews to "east Indians."[139]

This new exclusion of Jews from Europeanness came grafted onto the trope of the dangerous Jew disseminated in European chronicles describing the post-biblical history. Voltaire declared that "the Hebrews have always been vagrants or robbers, or slaves, or seditious," and reflecting the dominant imagery of Jews as presented in European chronicles, he asserted that "they are still vagabonds upon earth, abhorred by men."[140] He mocked their dietary practices. In 1781, Christian Wilhelm von Dohm, a German scholar, asked rhetorically, "Should a number of industrious and law-abiding citizens be less useful to the state because they stem from Asia and differ from others by beard, circumcision, and a special way—transmitted to them from their ancient forefathers—of worshipping the Supreme Being?"[141] In 1796, during the debate over Jews' citizenship in the Republic of Batavia, the Dutch theologian and politician Ysbrand van Hamelsveld, echoing Fleur, declared, "When I consult the chronicles of the Jews and the spirit of their laws, they show me a nation which, however full of shortcomings—attributable partly to the oriental climate, partly to the uncivilized state of those days, partly to their circumstances, partly to the power of prejudice—is conspicuous for its great men, excellent laws, illustrious deeds, and glorious virtues."[142] His colleague in the parliament, a Dutch politician Jan Bernd Bicker, also came to see Jews as "properly belonging to Palestine."[143] Another Dutch politician, noted that Jews' ancestors were "accustomed to the nomadic life of oriental shepherds."[144] The Enlightenment thinkers and politicians effectively de-Europeanized European Jews. By the nineteenth century, European Jews came to be seen as inassimilable and dangerous "Semites," their history relegated to biblical times, and by then European Christians had fashioned their own history and culture in religio-racial terms—they now saw themselves as white Christian Europeans.[145]

# CHAPTER FOUR

# European Christian Supremacy and Modern Citizenship

CENTURIES OF THESE RELIGIOUS and racializing ideas came crashing from the late eighteenth century with the dramatic political transformations of states from monarchies with subjects and estates to democracies and republics with citizens equal before the law. Citizenship and equality were novel ideas—there were no set models to follow, the ancient or medieval republics were not adequate. But after the American and then the French Revolutions, liberty and equality were no longer only ideas, they now were becoming a political reality embedded in each country's founding documents, both of which trumpeted liberty and claimed that "all men" are "created" or "born" equal.[1] This new political reality confronted proponents of these ideals with uneasy questions as to whom these "inalienable rights" of "life, liberty, and the pursuit of happiness" or "liberty, equality, fraternity" applied. Both race and religion played a role in these debates, though gender was a forgone conclusion. In Europe, Christian Europeans were apprehensive about the idea of Jewish inclusion in the polity.

The German scholar Christian Wilhelm von Dohm claimed in 1781 that Jews were "more morally corrupt than other nations; that they are guilty of a proportionately greater number of crimes than the Christians; that their character in general inclines more toward usury and fraud in commerce; that their religious prejudice is more antisocial and clannish."[2] But, he conceded, "this supposed greater moral corruption of the Jews is a necessary and natural consequence of the oppressed condition in which they have been living for so many centuries." These conditions "explain, although not justify, an even worse corruption"—"the spirit of the Jew to lose the habit of noble feelings." Von Dohm wondered whether Jews would be able to integrate into a new "well-ordered state" and would "do away with clannish religious opinions." Much like Claude Fleury in the seventeenth century, von Dohm believed that the biblical laws of Moses contained "goodness and utility," and for that reason the scholar supported the idea of improvement of Jews' legal status. But he equivocated about granting Jews equality with Christians. Deliberating whether Jews should be "admitted to public office," von Dohm concluded that "impartiality would demand that if a Jewish and a Christian applicant show equal capability, the latter deserves preference. This seems to be an obvious right of the majority in the nation—at least until the Jews by wiser treatment are changed into entirely equal citizens and all differences polished off." The demand for "polishing off" all differences would become later, in Europe, a secularized version of expectation for conversion found in earlier Christian texts. All in all, Jews could be reformed, von Dohm argued, embodying what Ibram X. Kendi called in the context of Black American history "uplift suasion."[3] For von Dohm it was only the "the unnatural oppression" that led to the "deterioration of their religious laws" and to the Jews' "moral corruption."

The opponents of granting Jews civil rights—and later citizenship—disagreed. Johann David Michaelis, a Bible scholar and professor at the University of Göttingen, asked, "Does the Law of Moses make citizenship and full integration of the Jew into other peoples difficult or impossible? I think it does!"[4] He asserted, "As long as the Jews continue to observe the Mosaic Laws as long as they refuse, for example, to eat together with us and to form sincere friendships at the table, they will never become fully integrated in the way that Catholics, Lutherans, Germans, Wends, and French live together in one state." It was ostensibly Jewish dietary law that prevented such integration. But a comment Michaelis made earlier revealed something else: "When I see a Jew eating pork, in order no doubt to offend his religion, then I find it impossible to rely on his word, since I cannot understand his heart." It was Jews being Jews, observant or not, whom Michaelis distrusted as citizens. He "cast doubt on the full and steadfast loyalty of the Jews to the state and the possibility of their full integration," which was prevented, he claimed, by "their messianic expectation of a return to Palestine. . . . A people which nurses these hopes will lack, at the very least, a patriotic love for the fields of their fathers." Granting Jews "rights of citizenship equal to our own," Michaelis noted, "would be a blessing for them" but would "gravely weaken the state."

Pushing back against Michaelis, Moses Mendelssohn, the renowned Jewish philosopher, identified a key cultural shift of his era. "Herr Michaelis," Mendelssohn wrote, "never speaks of Christians and Jews, but always of Germans and Jews. He does not content himself with establishing religious differences between us; he prefers to see us as strangers who will have to agree to all conditions which the owners of the land are ready to concede to us." When Mendelssohn asked, "For how many millennia must this distinction between the owners of the land and the strangers continue?" he could not have known that this cleft would become more pronounced and divisive in the decades to come. Mendelssohn captured a moment when Jews began to be seen as foreigners in countries in which they had lived for long centuries. The divisions were no longer across religious, but rather across newly emerging ethnic and racial lines.

Religious differences could, of course, be settled based on principles of religious toleration, but the questions of rights, citizenship, and belonging were new and pressing. The society, which had been organized along legally distinct estates and divided by religion, was now inventing a new social structure of equality before law and national identity. Just as Mendelssohn confronted Michaelis on the shift from religious categories of a Jew and a Christian to ethnic categories of a Jew and a German, the same questions emerged in the debates over citizenship following the French Revolution in 1789. As Lynn Hunt has noted, "French debates over citizenship and rights reveal a recurring clash between the ideals of human rights philosophy and the reality of eighteenth-century prejudices."[5] And just as the debates over the nature of Africans were meant to find justification for slavery, here too the debates over citizenship were seeking to define who was eligible, exposing how inconceivable it was that all people should have the power to make laws. As Emmanuel-Joseph Sieyès, known as Abbé Sieyès, stated, what happened in France felt "metaphysical": giving France a constitution and lodging the legislative power within the nation—not the king.[6] A solution to the conundrum was found in distinguishing between human—that is civil—rights, and political rights, or, put differently, between passive and active citizenship.

This distinction was enshrined in the very title of the Declaration of the Rights of Man and of Citizen: there were "the rights of man" and "the rights of citizen." Abbé Sieyès elaborated on the difference between "natural and civil rights" and "political rights."[7] All inhabitants, he argued, "should enjoy the rights of a passive citizen: all have the right to the protection of their person, their property, their liberty," but not all "have the right to take an active part in the formation of the public authorities: not all are active citizens."[8] Those who "contribute nothing to maintaining the public establishment," such as women, children, and foreigners, should "not actively influence public affairs." They can enjoy civil rights but only those who "contribute to public establishment" can be "true active citizens," Abbé Sieyès asserted. The question then remained who qualified.

In pre-revolutionary France only a small fraction of inhabitants was allowed to participate in the political process. Certain professions and non-Catholics—Jews and Huguenots—were excluded. In December 1789 that question returned: Should actors, executioners, and Jews be excluded from citizenship? The Declaration of the Rights of Man and of Citizen specifically banned discrimination on the basis of religious opinions, and Brunet de Latuque, a delegate from Bordeaux, which had a large population of Huguenots and Sephardic Jews, demanded that "non-Catholics who have fulfilled all the conditions . . . to be electors and eligible for office be elected to every level of administration, without exception" and "for every civil and military post."[9] And while it was soon agreed that the Protestant Huguenots qualified, objections continued to be raised about Jews. Abbé Jean Siffrein Maury objected to the assertion that Jews were a religious group—they were "a nation," he proclaimed.[10] To be sure, they should not be persecuted, "they are men, they are our brothers; and a curse on whomever would speak of intolerance! No one can be disturbed for his religious opinions." Jews should be "protected" as individuals but not "as Frenchmen for they cannot be citizens." Jews were unlike the Protestants. "Protestants have the same religion and the same laws as us, but they do not have the same creed" and thus they "enjoy the same rights." The Protestants were Christian and French; Jews could never be.

The bishop of Nancy, Anne-Louis-Henri de La Fare was even more explicit.[11] He affirmed that "all citizens are equal in the eyes of the law."[12] And under its protection and power they may "enjoy the fullness of the legitimate rights of man and of the citizen." But, he asked, should the Jews be allowed to "share, with the French citizens, the advantages of the large family of which they really are not, and cannot be, members?" Since they were expelled "from the land of their fathers" they remained, the bishop claimed, a people—persecuted and devastated—who never "mixed" with people among whom they lived. A Jew is "a foreigner to whom, during the time of this passage and his stay, France owes hospitality, protection, and security." But, La Fare asserted unequivocally, France "cannot and should not admit to public posts, to administration, to the prerogatives of the family a tribe that, regarding itself everywhere as foreign, never exclusively embraces any region; a tribe whose religion, customs, and physical and moral regime essentially differ from that of all other people; a tribe finally whose eyes turn constantly toward the common fatherland that should one day reunite its dispersed members and which cannot consequently consecrate any solid attachments to the land that supports it."[13] He then went on to list why Jews should not be granted anything but the basic civil rights: their religious observances and law create "insurmountable barriers" between them and others; they would not be able to serve in the military or any public office because of their laws and ceremonies—especially the requirement to observe the Sabbath and other holidays, which would also be an obstacle to being useful to the society; they could not partake in common meals, preventing intimate social bonding.[14] He asked, "How many obstacles and really insurmountable obstacles to the social amalgamation of the Jewish nation with the French nation emerge from the Jew's fidelity to his law?" The bishop understood that religious grounds were not sufficient for this denial of citizen rights; he thus focused on Jewish law and admonished that, "Wisdom gives the legislative body the imperative law not to grant to the Jews, whom it must always consider as foreigners among us, the quality and the rights of French citizens, and active citizens. The wish in this regard is precise. My conscience imposes on me the obligation to follow it; and make it known."[15] The bishop then noted hostility against Jews from the Christian population, even physical attacks, in the areas where they lived, "the gravest reproach which was made against them was for extending too much in the province, acquiring houses, lands, and privileges which the ancient laws did not give them." He warned the assembly not to grant Jews citizenship in order to avert "great disasters" and "misfortune."

But Jews had their advocates. Henri Grégoire, a clergyman deputy from Lorraine and since 1790 a bishop of Blois, supported admitting Jews to citizenship, but even he accepted much of the premise promoted by the Jews' opponents—that Jews were aliens, separated from Christians, whose religious practices were often incompatible with the laws of the new state.[16] He refuted some of the most spurious accusations and arguments about Jews' ineligibility for citizenship and shifted some of the blame for the state of Jews onto Christians. "Such is the incontestable genealogy of many crimes," Grégoire wrote, "and the infallible march of human nature in such cases. But the wrongs of the Jews [and] their misfortunes accuse our conduct towards them. Nations, admit that this is your work! The Jews produced the effects, you posited the causes: who are the most culpable?"[17] Grégoire sought to persuade the detractors claiming that based on the achievements of Jews in the past and of some Jews today, reforms and transformation of Jews to valuable citizens was possible. "The entire religious freedom granted to the Jews," he stressed, "will be a great step forward to reform them, and I dare say it, to convert them; for the truth is persuasive only insofar as it is gentle; the truth, they say, sometimes tears the breast which gives birth to it."[18] He was willing to be not only an "apostle" to these truths, but even a martyr. He rejected the idea that there was anything "in the moral constitution of the Jews that is opposed to any form of government whatever." And he asked, "Why don't Jews get all the prerogatives that are supposed to be granted only on merit? Why should the door of the Lycées and the Academies be closed to them, when secular sciences & compliments are not linked to the level of religion?"[19] He closed his book, summing up his argument, "After having exposed the picture of the misfortunes of the Jewish people, we destroyed many slanderous imputations with which they were charged; we have gone back to the causes which produced and perpetuated the hatred between them & the nations, which altered the physical and moral character of the Jews, we established the danger of tolerating them as they are, the need to reform them, and the possibility of achieving this. Rarely have we appealed to future experience, for the past has almost always come to support our reasoning." And he appealed to the universal principles embodied by the ideals of the French Revolution: "A new century is about to begin; may the palms of humanity adorn its frontispiece, and may posterity applaud in advance at the meeting of your courts. The Jews are members of this universal family, which must establish fraternity among all peoples; and over them, as over you, revelation spreads its majestic veil."[20] Grégoire appealed to the common humanity and religious sentiments, "Children of the same father, hide any pretext for the aversion of your brothers, who will one day be united in the same fold; open to them asylums where they can calmly rest their heads & dry their tears, & [pray] that finally the Jew, granting the Christian a return of tenderness, embraces in me his fellow citizen & his friend." But ultimately, even here, even in the argument in support of citizenship of Jews and equality regardless of religious beliefs, the framework of the state, as Grégoire understood it, was Christian. "The proposed revolution conforms to the idea of Christianity; far from being opposed to it, it is reconciled with the political, civil and fiscal laws of nations, and with their interests."[21] And thus, one had to prove "that the religious and political laws of the Jews, that their mores and their prejudices are compatible with the proposed revolution," by proving that the "parallel" would be true as well that "their current state could admit changes modeled on the religious, political and fiscal laws of the Christians." Ultimately, the framework of Christian supremacy persisted also through the French Revolution.

Many of the objections to compatibility of Jewish religious observance with the state stemmed from the claims that Judaism was grounded in "law." This in turn led to what would become a pernicious charge that

Jews formed "a state within a state." To remedy that, one of the reluctant advocates of Jewish citizenship, Count de Clermont-Tonnerre, advocated that "the Jews should be denied everything as a nation but granted everything as individuals.[22] In the end French Jews were granted the status of "active citizens," first the Sephardic Jews in January 1790, and then, in late September 1791, over two years after the proclamation of the Declaration of the Rights of Man and of Citizen and some two weeks after the passage of the French constitution, Ashkenazi Jews were included as well.[23]

Once Jewish citizenship was sanctioned in France, the debates spread across Europe. In 1793, the German philosopher Johann Gottlieb Fichte warned of the dangers of admitting Jews to citizenship, drawing on many old anti-Jewish stereotypes promoted in Christian literature for centuries that were now applied to the new political reality Europe faced after the French Revolution. Jews were "a powerful, hostilely disposed nation," Fichte claimed, "infiltrating almost every country in Europe."[24] Jews were "dreadful not because" they were "isolated and closely knit," but rather because they were "founded on the hatred of mankind." Of proponents of Jewish equality, he wrote "You speak sugar-sweet words about toleration and human rights and civic rights but you infringe upon our basic human rights." For Fichte, granting equality to Jews would impinge on the rights of Christians.

Indeed, the issue of the status of the Jews in the society was what troubled him, much like it did medieval popes, "Your loving toleration of those who do not believe in Jesus Christ [as expressed] by all the titles, honors and high positions you grant [the Jews], brings no satisfaction, for you are openly denouncing those who believe in Christ just as you do, depriving [Christians] of their civic honor and their honestly earned bread." For Fichte, opportunities opened to Jews put them in an unjustifiably high social position and by extension denied such opportunities to Christians. "Does the obvious idea not occur to you," Fichte asked, "that the Jews alone are citizens of a state which is more secure and powerful than any of yours? If you also give them civic rights in your states, will not your other citizens be completely trod under foot?" Jewish equality, in other words, was tantamount with excessive and unjustified Jewish power. In a footnote, Fichte added that Jews should be granted human rights—"for they are human," but he opposed "giving them civic rights; except perhaps," he quipped, "if one night we chop off all of their heads and replace them with new ones, in which there would not be one single Jewish idea." And even then, he advised, "I see no other way to protect ourselves from the Jews, except if we conquer their promised land for them and send all of them there." In one swoop, Fichte underscored the

Jews' exoticism and ineligibility for citizenship as Jews, granting which, he concluded, would give Jews too much power.

Three years later, the Republic of Batavia wrestled with similar questions about Jewish citizenship. Dutch politicians were asked to consider if they would "continue to regard the Jewish people as alien residents or will we go further and regard them as Dutchmen, as members of the Batavian people— in other words not only as our fellow human beings but also as our fellow citizens—on an equal footing with Dutchmen."[25] Jews could just be allowed to reside as alien residents of the Republic, guaranteed "human rights" but not "rights of Dutch citizens." Or they could "enjoy the same rights as citizens with the Dutch citizens." Like Michaelis, Ysbrand van Hamelsveld asked, "Can I say equally 'Dutch Jews, Portuguese, German and Polish Jews' as well as 'Jewish Dutchmen'? I can say, without distinction, 'Reformed, Roman Catholic (etc.) Dutchmen' and "Dutch Reformed, Dutch Roman Catholics," etc. But can I say the same of Jews without differentiation?" This semantic reflection demonstrated the deeply ingrained sense that Christians were assimilable, but Jews were not. It was an early articulation of ethno-national identity that permanently excluded Jews. Jews, the opponents of Jewish citizenship argued, did not want to be part of the Dutch nation, "They have too high an opinion of themselves to humble themselves in order to become Dutchmen." But more importantly, at play was a reluctance to Jewish equality—equality was seen as power. Jews, after all, were "merely aliens, who have no business mixing in our domestic affairs. Can we incorporate such persons as a nation, in hope that they will be liable to gratitude and hold the citizenship of the Dutch People in such high esteem that they will prefer it over their self-interest, of which they have shown themselves to be slaves?" Aliens, the opponents argued, should not be admitted to governmental posts, concluding, as did van Hamelsveld, that "collectively speaking the Jews cannot share in our Batavian social rights as citizens as long as they are Jews. If they wanted to share in them, they will have to abandon their civil laws (I do not speak of the religious) and accept our Constitution." Jews remaining Jews were not compatible with citizenship—this was a demand of civil conversion. But in the era of Enlightened thought and proclaimed abhorrence for religious discrimination, the rejection of Jewish eligibility for citizenship was couched in terms of Jewish "law."

Some Dutch politicians pushed back, underscoring the stakes. Johannes van Lokhorst expressed his surprise at the assembly's debate "whether the Jews will be admitted to partnership in the citizens' society of the Netherlands."[26] He pointed out that they could also be discussing "whether the Roman Catholic, the Calvinists, the Remonstrant, the

Lutheran, and all others who belong to this or the other denomination will be citizens." He challenged the deputies to acknowledge that if they were "faithful, as we are, to the principles of Liberty, Equality, and Fraternity," they could not "refuse" application for citizenship to anyone, for "the true Republican knows no Jew, no Malabar, no Calvinist, no Catholic, he knows only men and insofar as they live in the same country as he, he considers them all as his fellow citizens." By that measure, the Jews were both "men" and compatriots. Jacobus Kantelaar concurred, "In a society in which liberty exists and equality is respected, the rights of the citizen cannot be refused to any independent inhabitant who carries his share of the burden of the state, be he Jew, Christian, heathen or Turk [Muslim]." Kantelaar challenged the idea that Jews were aliens in a country in which they had lived for several centuries, in which they "have begotten children in to the sixth degree," "built houses, constructed pleasant homes, founded rich commercial firms," "paid extraordinary taxes." He flagged the larger question looming in that debate: that of Jewish belonging in European Christian societies. Indeed, another lawmaker, Jan Hendrick Stoffenberg, stressed that the outcome of this debate "will teach all of Europe whether we in the Netherlands honor the rights of man or only of Christian man; the rights of citizens, or only the rights of Christian citizens." In the end, on September 2, 1796, Jews in the Batavian Republic were granted, as individuals, citizenship "with rights to vote."

The questions of Jews' legal status remained an issue in several other European states and territories in the nineteenth century. Following Napoleon's defeat some regions pushed back against Jews' citizenship. In Koblenz, for example, Prussian officials produced a report on the status of Jews, claiming that the status Jews had gained thanks to the French Revolution had a detrimental effect on society.[27] The report repeated the now unshakable trope about Jews as "a nation of their own, a state within a state, firmly and imperturbably clinging to the laws of the religion," that is "in a necessarily eternal struggle with Christianity." For that reason, Jews should not be allowed to "spread" and be given "the same influence as Christians on the different institutions of the state, which, after all, are more or less in touch with the religion to which they go back or from which they proceed." The report homed in on the topic that Jews would not be productive members of society because of their current economic activities, and, while stressing Jews' supposed separation from Christians, also exhibited, like Michaelis, a contradicting discomfort with Jews who were in fact integrated and comfortable to share meals with Christians: "Those Jews, however, who move away from the positive regulations of their religion, who do not visit the synagogues, who put themselves on an equal footing with Christians in the enjoyment of meals, are far more dangerous and more damaging to the state than the true adherents of Judaism themselves." The report then proceeded to refute the argument that "the lower stage of culture in which [the Jews] find themselves, that their ugly character traits and their pernicious influence on the nations in which they live" was a result of centuries of persecutions.[28] Jews, the report concluded, were "thoroughly incompatible with the well-being and tendency of Christian states" because of "their moral teaching and their religious opinions." And therefore, the authors of the report concurred "completely with those who want to grant the Jews only human rights but not societal rights." For them Jews were foreigners, "a merely tolerated people."

The view that Jews were incompatible with citizenship, whether or not they remained observant, became deeply entrenched in European Christian imagination and reinforced, as the Koblenz report suggests and as some of the earlier voices in France and the Netherlands had shown, the perceived identity of modern states as, in fact, Christian—thereby, reaffirming Christian supremacy in modern Europe. In England, the passage of the Catholic Emancipation Act of 1829 prompted a debate about the status of Jews. There were "some 25,000 Jews domiciled in Great Britain, the majority," Apsley Pellatt, a British politician, observed, "British born subjects, [who] do not require naturalization," who were at that point "the only sect differing from the Church of England excluded from constitutional privileges."[29] In an anonymously published pamphlet, later attributed to Reverend Sidney Smith, the author scrutinized arguments against granting Jews equal political rights and the implied fear of Jewish political power.[30] The first objection was that the constitution was "essentially Christian; and therefore to admit Jews to office is to destroy the constitution."[31] The distinction, like in France, was made between civil and political rights. The Jews were not "injured by being excluded from political power," opponents argued. Indeed, "no man has a right to political power." Echoing John Locke, the opponents of Jews' citizenship rights conceded that "a man has a right to his property; a man has a right to be protected from personal injury. These rights the law allows to the Jew, and with these rights it would be atrocious to interfere." But political power was "a mere matter of favour . . . and no man can justly complain that he is shut out from it." But this was a circularly absurd argument, Smith retorted, since "if no man has a right to political power, then neither Jew nor Christian has such a right," and thus, "the whole foundation of government is taken away. But if government be taken away, the property and the persons of men are insecure, and it is acknowledged that men have a right to their property and to personal security."[32]

In England, resistance to Catholic and Jewish rights, with the former resolved that year, came from the fact that people were accustomed to think of a "Protestant" or "Christian" government to the exclusion of those who did not identify as such.[33] But, the author again echoed John Locke, the government "exists for the purpose of keeping the peace." Only those who objected to peace should be excluded, but "why a man should be less fit to exercise that power because he wears a beard, because he does not eat ham, because he goes to the synagogue on Saturdays instead of the church on Sundays, we cannot conceive." The government was not about "a man's fitness to be a bishop or a rabbi." That difference between Christianity and Judaism had "no more to do with his fitness to be a magistrate, a legislator, or a minister of finance, than with his fitness to be a cobbler." And after all, "nobody has ever thought of compelling cobblers to make any declaration on the true faith of a Christian. Any man would rather have his shoes mended by a heretical cobbler, than by a person who had subscribed all the thirty-nine articles but had never handled an awl."[34] Religion, however, had "as much to do with the mending of shoes, as with the budget and the army estimates," and, as experience had shown, "a very good Christian may be a very bad Chancellor of the Exchequer."

But the detractors, echoing centuries-old objections to Jews holding public office, feared that by acquiring rights, Jews would acquire power over Christians: "It would be monstrous . . . that a Jew should legislate for a Christian community."[35] But this was a misrepresentation, Smith posited, for the legislature would be made of both Christians and Jews, and would legislate for "a community composed of Christians and Jews." The author has effectively sketched the key difference between liberal politicians and those who feared equality—the answer to the question of who belonged to a community. If the community were Christian (or Protestant), then Jews (and Catholics) would forever be outsiders whose success in society would have been considered illegitimate, with them seen as usurpers. But if the community comprised all different peoples, then there was no fear of Jews' domination and their power over Christians. The issue was who belonged to the communal "we."

For Sidney Smith, an artificial distinction was made between civil and political power: "Civil and political are synonymous words, the one derived from the Latin, the other from the Greek."[36] Privileges themselves are power. As long as Jews could accumulate wealth, they had power. "What power," he asked, "in civilized society is so great as that of the creditor over the debtor? If we take this away from the Jew, we take away from him the security of his property." This would violate his civil rights, which even the opponents did not want to do. But "if we leave it to him, we leave to him a power more despotic by far, than that of the king and all his cabinet." The author then argued—evoking one of the most perilous anti-Jewish tropes about Jews and money—that Jews had power in politics, but their power was behind-the-scenes Jews. "It would be impious to let a Jew sit in Parliament. But a Jew may make money, and money may make members of Parliament. An elector of Penrhyn will take ten pounds from Shylock rather than nine pounds nineteen shillings and eleven pence three far-things from Antonio. To this no objection is made."[37] And yet, if a Jew "should pass the bar and sit down on those mysterious cushions of green leather; that he should cry 'hear' and 'order,'" that would be an unaccept-able "profanation sufficient to bring ruin on the country."

Smith then challenged the detractors to consider the chilling implications to the presented dilemma whether it was "our duty as Christians to exclude the Jews from political power," while Jews still "may govern the money-market, and the money-market may govern the world."[38] In such case, "it must be our duty to treat them as our ancestors treated them—to murder them, and ban-ish them, and rob them. For in that way, and in that way alone, can we really deprive them of political power. If we do not adopt this course, we may take away the shadow, but we must leave them the substance. We may do enough to pain and irritate them; but we shall not do enough to secure ourselves from danger, if danger really exists. Where wealth is, there power must inevitably be." Since this dire scenario was not an option, he examined other points that had been marshaled against Jews' equality: that they are not Englishmen, but rather "a separate people, living locally in this island, but living morally and politically in communion with their brethren, who are scattered over all the world." That was plausible but unsound, Smith declared. Other people too "have preferred their own sect to their country." Huguenots in France, for example, sought help from Calvinists elsewhere. "The feeling of patriotism, when society is in a healthful state, springs up, by a natural and inevitable association, in the minds of citizens who know that they owe all their comforts and pleasures to the bond which unites them in one community." But "if the Jews have not felt towards England like children, it is because she has treated them like a step-mother." And yet, Jews do not harbor hatred toward England, as the opponents claimed. Jews had no "rancour against the government or against their countrymen," though they were "not so well treated as the dis-senting sects of Christians are now treated in England." Jews in England, he concluded, were "precisely what our government has made them."

But there were also theological objections, Sidney Smith observed, revealing arguments that had roots in Augustine's pernicious legacy about Jewish servitude: "The Scriptures, it is said, are full of terrible denunciations against the Jews. It is foretold that they are to be wanderers. Is it then right to give them a home? It is foretold that they are to be oppressed."[39] Thus, he asked, "can we with propriety suffer them to be rulers?" Admitting Jews to citizenship would appear to go against "Divine oracles," which would be "a most atrocious crime." But admitting Jews to Parliament, the author pushed back in a tongue-and-cheek way, was not the meaning of these prophecies, for the prophecies, "whatever they may mean, do not mean that the Jews shall be excluded from Parliament." Since Jews were already "admitted to all the rights of citizens" in France and the United States, then, Smith observed, a prophecy, "which should mean that the Jews would never, during the course of their wanderings, be admitted to all the rights of citizens in the places of their sojourn, would be a false prophecy." This then could not be "the meaning of the prophecies of Scripture." If, Smith continued, the oppression of Jews is part of the punishment for "a crime which our bigots are now, at the end of eighteen centuries, urging us to avenge on the Jews—that crime which made the earth shake, and blotted out the sun from heaven," and "if this argument justifies the laws now existing against the Jews, [then] it justifies equally all the cruelties which have ever been committed against them—the sweeping edicts of banishment and confiscation, the dungeon, the rack, and the slow fire." To solve the dilemma, Smith pointed to Christ's own teachings as model to follow: "We have not so learned the doctrines of Him who commanded us to love our neighbour as ourselves, and who, when He was called upon to explain what He meant by a neighbour, selected, as an example a heretic and an alien."[40] The Parliament, Smith remarked sarcastically, should have granted equal rights to Jews on Good Friday, a "perfect" day, "on which the religion of mercy was founded," to blot "from the statute-book the last traces of intolerance" and to put an end to hostilities and "repair cruel wrongs."

But, to quote Apsley Pellatt's observation from 1829, "prejudice has ever been a stumbling-block in the way of public improvement, which unfortunately operates but too powerfully against the Jews" and so the efforts over subsequent decades to grant Jews political rights in England repeatedly failed.[41] As David Sorkin has noted, "the first bill brought to Parliament in 1830 did not pass the Commons," and when another bill finally passed the House of Commons in 1833, it "failed in the House of Lords."[42] Twelve further attempts were made, all to no avail. Over the next decades, a piecemeal approach was taken at a local level, succeeding finally to remove all disabilities preventing Jews' full political participation when in 1858 Lionel de Rothschild, after having been elected five times, finally took a seat in the Parliament.

In 1831, two years after Sidney Smith and Apsley Pellatt published their pamphlets arguing for granting Jews political rights in England, on the continent, similar sentiments were articulated in a debate between a German theologian Heinrich Paulus and Gabriel Riesser, a Jewish intellectual and lawyer. "Jewry as a social association," Paulus argued, "can no longer be aided to anything more than protection for subjects, and at the very most to protected membership in society, if it cannot, for the time being, factually accept and sufficiently prove that it no longer has reason and will to persist in its own nationality, in other words, to really, actually give this up and show—demonstrably!—that in every country every Jewish inhabitant belongs only to the nation of that particular country and no longer to the general One Jewry, as a necessarily isolated, self-preserving people of God."[43] A "protected" member of society "has no legal grounds to claim admission to full citizenship by the existing citizenry. He cannot—and may not—even be given citizenship rights in a nation as long as he—whether it be due to prejudice or for special reasons—belongs to another nation and persuades himself that he needs to constitute another nation of his own."[44] The same applies to "political and civic offices," even if a person is "capable," he would not be "qualified to hold a community director's office when he persists in belonging to another nation." Paulus posited that if Jews were to form their own state, they would institute a rule that "whoever does not nationalize himself among them by circumcision can surely not become a village judge there." He then reminded Christians "to be Christians even as citizens of the state." For "being a Christian," Paulus asserted, was "undeniably, for now, the best among the stages of civilization achieved. The more Christian the way we are governed, the better." Paulus's statement was both an assertion of Christian supremacy and a call for the total exclusion of Jews from citizenship. Allowing Jews to be citizens would "endanger" Christians, he claimed, who would "become intermixed—indeed, subordinated to this uncertain mixture—with non-Christian morals, laws, and opinions." Paulus articulated the sentiments expressed in the-now popular adage, "When you're accustomed to privilege, equality feels like oppression." The assertion that equality of Jews would be tantamount to "subordination" of Christian society to "non-Christian morals" reflected an anxiety about the loss of Christian domination, and as such was interpreted as Jewish power, usurped, illegitimate, thereby excessive. This was a manifestation of the legacy of theological Christian teachings about Jewish servitude, so indelibly seared in European Christian culture. Those who "preferred to be governed in a Jewish way," Paulus argued, should simply "convert to the Jewish nation." Jews, in their "rabbinical power of persuasion," were not capable of "helping govern us according to purely Christian law." If they wanted inclusion, Jews would have to "demonstrate that they belong solely to the country of their residence and accept the national identity of that country . . . and that they no longer consider themselves as members of a necessarily separate, self-sufficient people of God." This would be an "emphatic and tangible" renunciation—and an effective conversion.

Gabriel Riesser objected to Paulus's argument and called out the Christian theologian on the principal implication that effectively only "conversion to Christianity" would "guarantee" entrance to a "German nationality."[45] Paulus, Riesser noted, "turns a religious act into a political one." But there is a difference, "religion has its beliefs, and state has its laws." Riesser challenged Paulus to ponder "if a Catholic state were to exclude Protestants with the justification that they should be required, by converting to Catholicism, to join the 'nation of the state' consisting of Catholics? Would he not raise a mighty cry about intolerance about mixing up the authority of the state and the church?" Rather, Riesser exclaimed, "there is only one baptism that confers nationality: this is the baptism of blood in the common struggle for freedom and fatherland." And this Jews had indeed earned: "Everywhere in Germany, the Jews are obliged to military service; they were everywhere [obliged to it] even before the Wars of Liberation. In both wars Jews fought, both as volunteers and conscripts, in proportionate numbers, among the ranks of the Germans." Frustrated with the repeated claim of the opponents of Jewish citizenship that they were "foreigners" and "immigrants," Riesser asserted: "The charge that our forefathers immigrated here centuries or millennia ago is as fiendish as it is absurd. We are not immigrants, we are native born" with "no claim to a home someplace else. We are either German or we are homeless. . . . The vigorous tones of the German language and the songs of German poets ignite and nurture the holy fire of freedom in our breast. . . . We wish to belong to the German fatherland."[46] Jews in German lands would not be granted full citizenship until the unification of Germany in 1869, and no sooner had they been able to enjoy, at least in theory, equal civil and political rights, a backlash ensued in the rise of political antisemitism.

# CHAPTER FIVE

# Slavery, Citizenship, and the Legal Status of Free Blacks

THE REJECTION OF JEWISH EQUALITY revealed the lasting impact that the theologically inflected rhetoric about Jewish servitude had on European Christians. Jews may have been despised, but they were not slaves. Yet real slavery did exist in all its ugliness in European colonies, and it left a mark even on people of color who were not enslaved. The New World slavery was, as Ibram X. Kendi has argued, "killing, torturing, raping, and exploiting people, tearing apart families, snatching precious time, and locking captives in socioeconomic desolation."[1] Those who were enslaved, as Orlando Patterson has put it, had "no social existence outside of his master."[2] They were utterly powerless, wrote Frederick Douglass, "to decide their own destiny."[3] Still a child, Douglass, along with other slaves, was inventoried after the death of their master "to be valued and divided with the other property. . . . We . . . wept bitterly that day; for we might be parting, and we feared we were parting, forever. No one could tell among which pile of chattels I should be flung."[4] This experience gave Douglass "a foretaste of that painful uncertainty which slavery brings to the ordinary lot of mortals. Sickness, adversity and death may interfere with the plans and purposes of all; but the slave has the added danger of changing homes, changing hands, and of having separations unknown to other men." A few years earlier, Thomas Jefferson described that process from the slaveholder's perspective while discussing his debts and potential need to sell off some of his land and, more reluctantly, some of his slaves: "I would spare 20 negroes," Jefferson wrote to John W. Eppes, "in all from those plantations, men women and children in the usual proportions: and I should think this really more advantageous for Francis than all men.

I know no error more consuming to an estate than that of stocking farms with men almost exclusively. I consider a woman who brings a child every two years as more profitable than the best man of the farm. What she produces is an addition to the capital, while his labors disappear in mere consumption."[5] While Patterson may have overstated the "social death" of enslaved people, as scholarly works recovering the voices of the enslaved have demonstrated, it is still undeniable that their agency was severely checked by their unfree status.[6]

For Douglass that moment of division of property was a spectacle of "the intensified degradation" that lay bare the "brutalizing power of slavery," in which were assembled "men and women, young and old, married and single; moral and intellectual beings, in open contempt of their humanity, level at a blow with horses, sheep, horned cattle and swine! Horses and men—cattle and women—pigs and children—all holding the same rank in the scale of social existence; and all subjected to the same narrow inspection, to ascertain their value in gold and silver—the only standard of worth applied by slaveholders to slaves!"[7] For Jefferson, it was a business transaction; it was about monetary value not humanity. Women, as Jefferson himself noted, were valued because they could bear children for slavery, many of them, including Douglass himself, fathered by slaveholders and removed from their mothers "before the child has reached its twelfth month . . . to hinder the development of the child's affection toward its mother, and to blunt and destroy the natural affection of the mother for the child."[8] The children could then be sold, often by their own fathers, for profit—a direct result of the 1705 Virginia "An act concerning Servants and Slaves." Slavery, as Orlando Patterson put it, also "shattered relations among slaves themselves."[9]

Jews, in contrast—at least until the Nazi era in which their "social death" was implemented to prepare ground for their total annihilation— were, in premodern Europe, a legally protected group, their legal status defined within law by imperial, royal, or other privileges.[10] Even in the most unforgiving conditions, such as medieval England, where Jews were prohibited from leaving the Isle without the king's permission, or the early modern Italian ghettos into which Jews were forced from the sixteenth century, Jews were able to make decisions about their own lives. They could form communities and communal organizations, have their own courts, own businesses, marry and have children. In many other places, Jews had the freedom to move and even own real estate properties. Jewish children could grow up with their parents, without fear of being sold as chattel. With the exception of outbreaks of persecution and violence, Jewish women did not have to fear repeated rapes by Christian overlords, and when rapes did happen they were not for the purpose of producing more children. In contrast to the theoretical theologically inflected Jewish servitude, Black slavery meant utter degradation and cruelty, though enslaved Black people did all they could to retain their dignity and a modicum of agency.

Since Jews were never slaves in premodern Europe, the debates about Jews' status in Europe were about their civil and political rights; the term "emancipation" used by historians to describe the acquisition of citizen rights by Jews is therefore highly problematic and misleading, especially given that real—not symbolic or figurative—slavery existed at the very same time when debates over Jews' rights were taking place and that no one at that time would have used that term to apply to Jews.[11] In the end, Jews were admitted, if very reluctantly, to the ranks of citizens, but, as the immediate antisemitic backlash suggests, they would not be fully accepted as equal. Jews remained outsiders in part because the idea of slavery and servitude, coupled in modern times with racial theories, made their acceptance into newly forming national bodies difficult. As Patterson has argued in his sociological study of slavery, "the slave was conceived of as someone who did not belong because he was an outsider," at the same time, "the slave became an outsider because he did not belong."[12] This theory certainly applied to both Jews and Black and mixed-race people as they were "stamped" as inferior outsiders by white European Christians—even when they were not enslaved.[13] Still, as modern debates over Jewish citizenship demonstrate, Jews were not denied "human rights" but basic human rights were denied to the enslaved people of color. In the United States the idea of Black citizenship and social belonging became far more complicated than that of Jews, who were considered, to use Ian Haney López's phrase, "white by law"—that is, when they arrived in the US as immigrants, they were eligible for naturalization.[14]

The existence of transatlantic slavery forced Europeans and Euro-Americans to confront the sincerity of their principles of toleration, human rights, and even their understanding of what it meant to be a Christian, revealing in the most profound way not only the hypocrisy of European ideals of liberty, equality, and fraternity, but also, as Tyler Stovall has shown, Europeans' and European Americans' understanding of "liberty" as white.[15] If power is one antithesis of slavery, liberty and equality are another. The Europeans on the continent were shielded from the atrocities of slavery by the width of the ocean, while benefiting from the colonial economy driven by slave labor, and, thanks to that distance, they were able to engage in theoretical debates about liberty. Profit and property rights clashed with the principle of equality and human rights. But on the continent, with few slaves present, slavery was, as David Geggus put it, an issue of "political rhetoric" not "the grim reality of the colonies."[16] In 1789, after France issued the Declaration of the Rights of Man and of Citizen, an anonymous pamphlet called out these questions, noting that "the colonial question tested the universalist claims of the French revolutionaries."[17] The anonymous author allowed that with the passing of the Declaration, "no slavery should exist except for convicted criminals according to the Laws."[18] Therefore, "liberty must be restored to this multitude of unhappy beings, our brothers, albeit of different colors, that European cupidity has taken for nearly three centuries from the coasts of Africa, & condemned to eternal captivity." But, the author observed, the economic reality was such that "if the French nation completely prohibited the slave trade" and "broke the chains" of those slaves in the colonies, it would cause "too violent a shock to commerce" and cause much loss to the plantations in the colonies and the transatlantic trade "they feed." It would result in an "enormous" drop in "the revenues of the State" and "would further ruin the inhabitants of the Colonies," where "the Negro slaves make property." Thus, he added, "however odious this property may be, one cannot deprive them [the inhabitants of the colonies] of it without injustice." Moreover, if France were to do it alone, other "nations," which had sugar colonies and continued to use slave labor, "would take advantage" of France to their benefit, forcing France "to buy from them a commodity whose consumption has become absolutely necessary for us."[19] A solution would be to have an agreement with all colonial powers to abolish slavery simultaneously. But that was an impossible proposal. Another option was to turn "Negro slaves" into a service similar to that of soldiers—a temporary enlistment at the end of which they would be granted freedom. If they deserted, they would be taken back into chains. This kind of slavery, the author argued, was "not contrary to human rights, since it is contracted freely, voluntarily & for a limited term."[20] Indeed, "the Negroes [les Nègres] could not be held in irons except for a limited time" and therefore they could not be considered "slaves any more than a soldier." Like a soldier, they would "be bound to obedience for the duration of their engagement," though subjected to work "of another kind, but in proportion to their strength." The main difference between the two "types of slavery" is that "the first engagement of Negroes would not be voluntary." But the author assured that many would renew their contracts voluntarily afterwards.

The anonymous writer proposed to pass a law stipulating that "the Blacks [*les Noirs*] transported from Africa to our Colonies cannot be sold, except on the condition that the inhabitants who will buy them will give them their freedom back at the end of ten years, & then give to each Negro or Negresse a sum sufficient to pay for his passage back to his homeland."[21] Once the contract was up, the "Negro" was to be freed, with the certificate of freedom registered in court. Then they "will be made to embark on the first vessel" and depart for "the coasts of Africa." Another option would be available: the sum for passage would "be delivered to the Negro, who will be able to exercise in the Colonies such profession as he pleases, or to re-engage in the service of such inhabitant as he wishes." Those who stay would "renew thus new engagements of five years" but only after the expiration of each previous engagement. Each time, "the act of their freedom will have been delivered to them by the Judge and signed by the master they have left." This was "to prevent their masters" from abusing "their authority to force them into new engagements." Those who were already enslaved in colonies would be divided into ten classes, and each year one of the classes would be released from slavery, but each person could then enter similar contracts as those previously described. Still, the cost to "the inhabitants of the colonies," where the author estimated some 500,000 enslaved individuals were living, would be enormous.[22] The author then imagined a future where those who would return "to their homeland with some fortune which they will have gained in America, will want to enjoy in their country the comforts to which they will be accustomed, and which they will only be able to obtain by a greater consumption of several commodities from Europe." The result would be "a greater flow to the African coast of several articles of European production and manufacture, and our trade will be able to increase in this part of the world." The author hoped that his pamphlet would "give birth to [ideas]" that would lead to the betterment and "the happiness of humanity and the glory of the French Nation."

As the anonymous pamphlet demonstrates, white Europeans, even those committed to "liberty, equality, and fraternity," had serious misgivings about the freedom and equality of Black people. It was not just the economic misgivings. The author of the pamphlet did not even refer to the freed Black people as "inhabitants" or "residents," a term he seems to have reserved for white colonists. Freed people of color, in this proposal, would only be allowed to stay in the colonies under a new contract with a new "master." Thus, slavery would be technically abolished and turned into indentured servitude but Black people, should they "choose" freedom, would have to return to Africa, or remain indentured. In the British colonies, including those that became the United States, similar debates were taking place already in the eighteenth century—free Blacks were considered a problem, and one solution offered was "colonization," sometimes called "repatriation" or resettlement, even "deportation" to Africa.[23] Blackness was now indelibly tied to slavery and servitude, with the word "Negro" interchangeably used with "a slave," confirming, as Henri Grégoire noted, that "the Whites, having power, have declared, against justice, that dark skin excludes one from the advantages of society."[24]

The debate in France was influenced by a powerful lobby of French white colonists and merchants who were supplying slaves and foodstuffs to the colonies—while their interests sometimes clashed, they agreed that applying the Declaration of the Rights of Man and of Citizen to people of color in the colonies would be a disaster.[25] The representatives to the Assembly from the overseas called those who supported abolition of slavery and of the slave trade, especially the members of the Friends of Blacks, "enemies of France, the Colonies and the human race," who set "under the pretext of their passion for humanity" to subvert "the social order."[26] It could now be grasped how deeply entangled the "metropole" had become with the colonies and how dependent Europe was on the exploitation of the rest of the world they already dominated or sought to dominate.

The captains of slave ships also pushed back against the Friends of the Blacks and the anonymous pamphlet proposing the abolition of slavery and slave trade.[27] They warned, citing Pierre-Antoine Monneron, that "the cessation of this trade would starve five million French."[28] The abolitionists, the captains declared, knew nothing about the issue, and, instead, they disseminated assertions "so exaggerated that it is impossible to attribute it to someone who has the least knowledge of the slave trade."[29] The most egregious claim was that the trade killed "more than 150,000 men a year." These were unsubstantiated claims, they argued, "it is evident that all the nations that make the slave trade do not kidnap a hundred thousand blacks every year, and that they do not employ fifteen thousand men in this trade." This information was easily verifiable, the captains asserted, for it was easy to "consult the registers of the class offices, we will know exactly the number of whites that we lose to the slave trade, and the declarations recorded to the admiralties will make known that of the Negroes."[30] Drawing from a reservoir of traditionally accepted defenses of African enslavement, the captains argued that the slave trade was actually humane. They enumerated cruelties of the Africans and assured the readers that the slavers did not capture "free" Africans—only those who had already been enslaved as war captives were sold and shipped to the colonies. Doing so, the captains claimed, the Europeans were in fact saving lives, "having found the means to shield so many victims from the fury of their tyrants."[31] The "Negroes," they contended, repeating widely disseminated anti-African stereotypes, had a "ferocious and vindictive character," they engage in "cruelties in cold blood on all that is subordinate to them." Before encountering the trade with Europeans, Africans, they claimed, were cannibals (*antropophages*), with "butcheries of human flesh" visible "some distance from the seashore." The captains invited the Friends of Blacks to join them on the voyage to see for themselves.

One of the most vocal members of the Friends of Blacks, a group called by the colonists "perfidious enemies," was Henri Grégoire, an advocate of citizenship for both Jews and free Blacks.[32] In his 1789 pamphlet "in favor of the people of color," Grégoire did not just address the question of enslaved Black people but also those who were free, having "acquired their freedom in an honorable capacity, some through wise savings, others . . . from their masters, whose esteem they had captivated."[33] They were "hardworking citizens, they make the plantations flourish, there are among them large landowners, they increase the control of colonial wealth, and thereby contribute to the prosperity of the State." And yet, the whites, Grégoire wrote, were "priding themselves" in their complexion and "degrading" thousands of "estimable individuals" because of their skin color.[34] He then enumerated numerous restrictions and humiliations experienced by free people of color in the colonies, especially in Saint-Domingue, where, according to John Garrigus, "people of African ancestry [made] roughly 45 percent of the free population."[35] They were, Grégoire claimed, banned from certain trades, such as goldsmithing and medicine, and prohibited from bearing European names and forced to take African names, "so that the disparity of names establishes that of ranks."[36] And he described the humiliations. "It was forbidden to eat with the Whites," Grégoire wrote. People of color were seen humiliatingly "torn from the table of a white captain, whose first invitations they had accepted." To dance after nine o'clock, they needed "to have the permission of the police judge." They were "forbidden to use the same fabrics as whites." Police "were commissioned to execute this decree" and were "seen in public places, at the gates of even churches, tearing the clothes off persons' sexual parts, leaving no other veil than modesty." Finally, people of color were forbidden to emigrate and settle in France.[37]

All the signifiers of honor and respect were prohibited to them as well.[38] The free Black people were forbidden to use carriages with horses, under penalty of imprisonment and the confiscation of the carriage and the horse. They were excluded from all public offices, "either in the judiciary, or in the military" and could "no longer turn to the ranks of Officers, although in general they are recognized as very courageous people," Grégoire noted. "Whatever their virtues, their wealth, they are not admitted to parish assemblies." And although religion "brings all men together" and should treat all men as equals, "separate places are assigned to them." Although some of these ordinances have fallen into disuse, all of them are still "in force" and are supported by public opinion, their purpose "to remove forever mixed blood from the advantages reserved for whites."

To illustrate the deep prejudice people of color faced, Grégoire quoted a statement made in 1770 by a magistrate of Port-du-Prince, "There exists among us a class [who is] naturally our enemy, and which still bears on its forehead the imprint of slavery; it is only by strict laws that it should be led. It is necessary to call upon it the contempt and the reproach which is vested in it by birth. It is only by breaking the resilience of their soul that we can lead them to good!"[39] The whites, Grégoire concluded, conduct themselves according to these principles and even instill these sentiments in their own Negro slaves, who then—being owned by a white man—express a "tone of superiority toward the slaves of mulattoes." Even poor whites "despise" the free people of color, no matter their hospitality and generosity.

Grégoire tried to convince other deputies to grant equal rights to free people of color in the colonies—they were worthy of equality and useful to the state.[40] "No one is more agile to climb the hills and bring back the escaped Negroes," Grégoire asserted, "they are a sure support against the insurrection of the slaves: perilous commissions are sometimes given by preference to this class of men, whose bravery is known. In America's last war, they displayed their fearlessness in Savannah." Their patriotism showed even when "we wanted to stifle it."

Still the European white deputies were fearful that "people of color will become insolent if they are assimilated to us," and that the social hierarchy would be broken.[41] Grégoire summed up their concerns: whites wanted to assure that they were "the bosses" and "protectors" of the freedmen; it was from them after all that they received their freedom: "the respect of freedmen towards us was the price." As to the concern whether it was "appropriate that our slaves become our equals," Grégoire exclaimed, "I am afraid that is the end of the story. Poor vanity! I refer you to the declaration of the rights of man & of the citizen."[42] Still, for many, it was unacceptable that "the colored people [be] at the level of the Whites." But more pragmatically, Grégoire argued that rejecting citizenship of the free people of color was dangerous to the state. "A rigorous consequence of what precedes is that the rejection of people of color threatens the state with a shock capable of shaking it," he wrote. But if one were to "bridge the gap that separates them from the Whites" by "bringing the spirits together, you [would] cement the mutual attachment of these two classes, their reunion presents a mass of forces more effective to contain the slaves." [43] This would then buy time "until the opportune moment to free them." But the admission of free people of color to citizenship was concomitant to admitting them to a legislative process and the deputies, Grégoire urged, should be careful not to accept the claims from the white representatives of the colonies opposing that. He proposed a legislation that declared, "The people of color of Saint-Domingue & the other French Colonies, including the free Negroes" citizens "in the whole extent of the term, and in all similar to the Whites; consequently, they can exercise all the arts & crafts, emigrate from the Isles, attend public schools, & aspire to all ecclesiastical, civil & military jobs."[44] Grégoire ended with a plea, "Let us erase all the degrading distinctions that nature disapproves of, that religion proscribes: vice and virtue must be the only measure of public consideration, and equality the only measure of human rights. To live is nothing, to live free is everything, and would this freedom, which French warriors have gone to plant in the fields of America, be eclipsed by our Islands? No, Gentlemen, forty thousand individuals free by law, but enslaved by derogatory decrees and by prejudice, will owe you their happiness: for humanity, it will be one more triumph, and for you, one more title to glory."[45] Count Mirabeau agreed and observed that no deputy to the National Assembly ever proposed an amendment, explicitly stating that "white men alone are born and remain free."[46]

Still, even the most vocal supporters of Black rights were hedging their bets in light of the strong pushback and lobbying by the colonists and merchants. Henri Grégoire's essay dealt chiefly with the treatment of "free people of color" and their appeal for citizenship and equality, while equivocating, for pragmatic political reasons, on the question of slavery itself.[47] In February 1790, the Friends of Blacks addressed the National Assembly, rebuking the fearmongering of the colonists and the ship owners who "depict the prosperity of the colonies as inseparable from the slave trade and the perpetuity of slavery."[48] Yet, they also apologetically assured the deputies that they were "not even asking" for the liberty of Black slaves. "The immediate emancipation of the blacks would not only be a fatal operation for the colonies; it would even be a deadly gift for the blacks, in the state of abjection and incompetence to which cupidity has reduced them." It was not "yet the time to demand that liberty," they stated. They asked "only that one cease butchering thousands of blacks regularly every year in order to take hundreds of captives," demanding "the abolition of the slave trade."

Others were ambivalent even about the issue of slave trade. A British abolitionist Thomas Clarkson summarized the French advocates' dilemma: "The revolution is of greater importance to Frenchmen than the abolition of the slave trade. To secure this was their first object, and more particularly because the other would flow from it, but the revolution might be injured by the immediate determination of the question."[49] And indeed, the situation was quite delicate as the opponents of Black equality were apparently pulling no punches. Clarkson reported that some colonists published a pamphlet accusing the Friends of the Blacks in arming slaves in Saint-Domingue, reinforcing the idea that they were indeed promoting a "subversion of social order."[50]

Several issues were entangled: slavery, slave trade, and political rights for free Black men. Slave trade was pitched as a "commercial issue," and by May 1791, a "shabby compromise" was reluctantly reached about voting rights, only men of color born of both a free mother and a free father would qualify, effectively limiting political rights to a fraction of free men of color.[51] This was, perhaps accidentally, a literal application of the phrase that "all men are born free." But even this limited compromise was not fully implemented, leading to a major slave revolt in Saint-Domingue, which in turn resulted in rescinding of the limited political rights of free Blacks on September 24th, 1791. After a period of chaos and violence, a slave victory under the leadership of Pierre-Dominique Toussaint Louverture was achieved in 1793, and a year later slave trade and slavery were abolished. It was, as Franklin W. Knight observed, "a victory for colonialism and the revolution in France."[52] Indeed, after the abolition of slavery and the slave trade, Toussaint Louverture, who initially led the rebellion against France, switched sides and became a colonial governor. He remained in power in Saint-Domingue, a "semi-politically free" French colonial possession until 1803, when he was removed to France following the reinvasion of Saint-Domingue by Napoleon's troops a year earlier seeking to reestablish slavery and to fulfill Napoleon's desire to "reestablish a viable French American empire."[53] Napoleon's misadventure ended in the declaration of independence of Saint-Domingue and a creation of a second independent state in the western hemisphere in 1804—Haiti. But unlike the first independent state—the United States—Haiti was a nation without slavery under Black rule.

If the French Revolution with its ideals of liberty and equality was a catalyst for demands of equal rights for people of color in French colonies,

the Haitian revolution became a catalyst for widespread unrest that ultimately led to the end of the Atlantic slave trade and the abolition of slavery
in other European colonial possessions, and, in the US, to a backlash against
free people of color.[54] Among the whites in both the European colonies and
in the US, the Haitian revolution gave rise to the fear of, as Franklin Knight
has argued, not only Black equality but "black rule," that is, Black political
power. And in the region where the Black population outnumbered white
colonists, this had a particularly strong resonance. To be sure previous slave
rebellions had created an association between Blackness and danger, resulting in white fear of Black people, which still remains among much of white
population at least in the US. In the early nineteenth century "Remember
Haiti" became a warning across the region.[55]

The existence of slavery in the US and other European colonies complicated the legal status and assimilation of free people of color. Free
people of color were in between the politically dominant white class and
the enslaved population, a particularly difficult place when European
white identity was consolidating both on the continent and in the Americas.[56] Though free, their skin color, so profoundly associated by whites
with slavery, placed them on the outside of the white dominant society.
The fact that in France the National Assembly devoted so much attention
to eligibility to citizenship of both free people of color and Jews demonstrates the profound impact slavery—as a legal and social reality for people
of color and as an idiom applied for centuries to Jews—had on concepts
of social hierarchy that permanently marked both as inferior outsiders
to what increasingly consolidated as white European Christian identity.
(With time, the explicit religious aspect of that identity may have weakened but it remained an important cultural force.)

Since the concept of slavery is bound to the concepts of domination
and power, when attached to a group of people, now marked as inferior, it
effectively precludes their social and political equality, ultimately leading
to their exclusion from "the community," the polity, and, in modern times,
from the concept of a nation.[57] Equality was disruptive and dangerous.
As Thomas Carlyle remarked in 1853 in a screed defending slavery and
white supremacy, "In these days, the relation of master to servant, and of
superior to inferior, in all stages of it, is fallen sadly out of joint. . . . Kings
themselves are grown sham. . . . No man reverences another."[58] Carlyle
mocked equality, especially political rights. "Certainly," he wrote, "by any
ballot-box, Jesus Christ goes just as far as Judas Iscariot; and with reason, according to the New Gospels, Talmuds and Dismal Sciences of these
days. Judas looks him in the face; asks proudly, 'Am not I as good as thou?'

Better perhaps!'" He then concluded, "Without real masters you cannot have servants."

Yet, with relatively few residents of color on the continent, Europeans could largely bracket the question of citizenship and equality of "people of color"—a complicated phrase that was often applied to free individuals while the enslaved people were frequently identified simply as "Black" or "Negro"—as one applying to the colonies, where the white colonialist population was frequently outnumbered by the enslaved Black population, as was the case in Saint-Domingue, before Haiti became independent, in Jamaica, and even in some colonies on the North American continent, such as South Carolina.[59]

The angst about the presence of free Blacks in white society was so strong that in 1723 Virginia practically outlawed manumission, except "for some meritorious services," and even then it had to be "adjudged and allowed by the governor and council, for time being, and a licence thereupon first had and obtained."[60] The law also declared that "no free negro, mullatto or Indian whatsoever, shall vote hereafter have any vote at the election of burgesses or any other election whatsoever."[61] France and England made it difficult for free and enslaved Black individuals to settle in Europe. Settling in England would have been attractive since in the aftermath of the Somerset court decision in 1772, which effectively outlawed slavery on the Isle, bringing an enslaved person to its shores was tantamount to granting them freedom.[62] When the British colonies in North America rebelled in 1776, seceding from Britain and creating the United States, in no small measure to preserve slavery, the US became the only country in the western hemisphere where slavery was not a colonial but a national issue. The US was, as Tyler Stovall put it, "a slave republic."[63] (Haiti became, in 1804, the opposite, the second independent country in the western hemisphere but one in which slavery was abolished).

The US political structure and its constitution were profoundly shaped by the politics concerning slavery, even if the slave-holding states did everything they could to avoid explicit references to the subject, hiding behind general terms such as "property rights" or "state rights."[64] Political pragmatism led even those who opposed slavery to acquiesce to the pressures from slave-holding states (or colonies in the run-up to the 1776 rebellion) and agree to protect it as a status quo, thereby leaving a permanent mark on the new country's political system.

Slavery influenced the language of the declaration of independence. The clause proposed by George Mason that "All men are born equally free and independent and have certain inherent natural rights of which they cannot, by any compact deprive or divest their posterity, among which are the enjoyment of life and liberty, with the means of acquiring and possessing property, and pursuing and obtaining happiness and safety" was changed by Thomas Jefferson to "We hold these truths to be self-evident, that all men are created equal, that they are endowed by their Creator with certain unalienable rights, that among these are life, liberty and the pursuit of happiness."[65] By substituting the word "born" with "created" Jefferson was able to gesture toward the idea of natural rights, appealing to the broad ideals of the era, without evoking the idea of "birth by a woman" that could apply to all humans and raise questions about the status of those who were enslaved, or born to enslaved women and thus, according to law, were slaves by birth.[66]

Opposition to slavery came from at least two directions: the moral and religious, and the pragmatic labor protectionism. For example, for William Cox of Baltimore, who manumitted his slaves in 1768, slavery was "inconsistent with Christianity."[67] Whereas white workers and white land speculators in the US territories often opposed slavery to protect the value of white labor.[68] But even those opposing slavery and favoring abolition on moral grounds "shuddered," as did John Adams, at the idea of equality of "all men, white and black" and "the consequences drawn from such premises."[69] Though Adams considered slavery, as he wrote to Thomas Jefferson in 1821, "a black cloud" hanging over the country, he also accepted the vision often promoted by white southerners of Black violence. The image "armies of Negroes marching and counter-marching" "terrified" him.[70] Presence of free Black people was for white Americans disquieting. In 1820, a year before Adams wrote to Jefferson, the Speaker of the House, Philip Barbour of Virginia, noted that "in Virginia . . . in regard to manumitted slaves, considering them as hostile to public peace, as the brand of discord between the whites and another class of persons, it was declared, by the law, that every manumitted slave should, within twelve months after the act of manumission, leave the State, or forfeit the rights he had acquired."[71] This fear of Black people, especially those who were free, as dangerous and "hostile to public peace," would become one of the permanent stamps marking whiteness in America. So, while opposition to slavery may not always have revealed directly racial attitudes, the question of the legal status of free people of color, formerly enslaved or free born, unquestionably did.

This is what Benjamin Banneker, a famous astronomer, mathematician, and author of a popular almanac, brought up in 1791 in his letter to Thomas Jefferson.[72] Banneker, a free man of color, addressed "the greatness of that freedom" and "liberty, which seemed to me scarcely available" and contrasted the "distinguished and dignified station" in which Jefferson stood with "the almost general prejudice and prepossession which are so prevalent in the world against those of my complexion." He questioned, "If your love for yourselves, and for those inestimable laws which preserve to you the rights of human nature, was founded in sincerity, you could not but be solicitous that every individual, of whatever rank or distinction, might with you equally enjoy the blessings there of." But despite the founders' apparent conviction about "the benevolence of the Father of mankind and of his equal and impartial distribution of these rights and privileges," they were counteracting "his mercies, in detaining by fraud and violence so numerous a part of my brethren under groaning captivity and cruel oppression" and were thus "guilty of that most criminal act, which you professedly detested in others."

Indeed, the core text of the US Constitution does not mention race or color. The words "race" and "color" would only be included with the passage of the Fifteenth Amendment, in a sentence marked by negative and passive structure: "The right of citizens of the United States to vote shall not be denied or abridged by the United States or by any State on account of race, color, or previous condition of servitude." The word "citizen" appears in the original text of the Constitution twelve times, but it is not defined—it was a novelty, an unprecedented political idea, with no existing political models aside from the Roman and Greek antiquity and privileges of citizenship (e.g., Bürgerschaft) within European cities. The US Constitution was enacted before the French Revolution and its Declaration of the Rights of Man and Citizen, which did contain a clearer definition of citizenship. In 1790, a year after the US Constitution was ratified, the first step to define citizenship was made in the Naturalization Bill.[73] "Any alien, other than an alien enemy, being a free white person" residing within the US jurisdiction for at least two terms "may be admitted to become a citizen." Citizenship thus came to be linked with a "free" legal status—those enslaved were not eligible—and whiteness. But in contrast to the colonial period, during which a freeholder had to be both white and Christian in have political rights, Christianity was not required for naturalization and by extension for the status of citizens, though individual states had written Christianity into their constitutions.[74]

As a result, the debates about eligibility for citizenship were different in the US and in Europe, because ideas about citizenship were different. Race and the existence—or, later, legacy—of slavery have for centuries complicated those questions. In Europe, in the aftermath of the French

Revolution, the idea of citizenship was tied up with questions of political rights. In the US a question of what citizenship meant would not come up for debate until decades after the Constitution was ratified. And while in the US the Naturalization Bill of 1790 defined citizenship eligibility for immigrants, the US law left the question of the legal status of free Black Americans born in the United States open. Free Black Americans were, as Martha Jones noted, "not slaves nor aliens nor the equals of free white men."[75] Yet they were subjected to humiliating restrictions, including on ownership of property, guns, court testimony, or even requirements to register with the authorities and to wear a badge, "suspended by a string or ribband, and exposed to view on his breast."[76] These humiliating restrictions made clear that they, though not enslaved, were not considered equal citizens. Despite restrictions on their rights, free people of color demanded to be treated with dignity, though they acknowledged, as did free people of color in Charleston in 1791, that they could not "presume to hope" to be treated as equal with whites.[77] But the question of who was a citizen and what citizenship meant in the United States remained unresolved for decades.

# CHAPTER SIX

# The Fault Lines on
# Race, Religion, and
# American Citizenship

IN THE NINETEENTH CENTURY religion and race began to crystallize political ideas about the meaning of citizenship in the United States. The 1820 debate over the admission of Missouri into the Union put on display clashing visions of what the United States is and who belongs, while regional court cases and religious debates, in a slow-moving backlash against the ideals enshrined in the US Constitution against established religion, began to clarify a sense of a dominant religious identity. Both Jews and people of color challenged, in different ways, American white Protestant hegemony and what was beginning to shape as a white Christian republic.

The congressional debate over Missouri voiced positions about race and citizenship that would reappear again and again in major legal cases, such as *Dred Scott v. Sanford*, and in political writings, still clashing and resonating in our own times. The issue was not just whether Missouri could be admitted to the Union as a slave state, thus tipping the balance between free and slave states—the Missouri compromise and the admission of Maine addressed that. Rather, it was Missouri's constitution that proposed to ban the settlement of free Black Americans that caused a heated debate and anxiety. Representative Alexander Smyth of Virginia summarized the issue: "the Constitution of the United States contains a clause that 'the citizens of each State shall be entitled to all privileges and immunities of citizens in the several States;' and the constitution formed for the State of Missouri contains a clause making it the duty of the Legislature of that State to pass such laws, as may be necessary 'to prevent free negroes and mulattoes from coming to, and settling in, that State, under any pretext whatsoever;' and it has become a question whether the clause in the constitution of Missouri is repugnant to the Constitution of the United States."[1] In other words, the question was: Since "free persons of color were citizens" in some states, did the prohibition violate Article IV of the US Constitution?[2] The congressional debate exposed attitudes toward citizenship and race as central to the political structure of the US, threatening, as Thomas Jefferson observed, "the perpetual duration of our vast American Empire."[3] Indeed, it probed what it meant to be citizens in the Union, throwing into the open the question of who belonged to "We, the people."

Before the ratification of the Constitution of the United States, argued Representative John Sergeant of Pennsylvania, "the citizens of each member of the Confederacy were considered as citizens only of their respective State governments," but the Constitution changed that, inserting the immunities clause for all citizens, "the people of the United States . . . citizens of one Republic."[4] Missouri's clause against the settlement of free Black Americans threatened that principle, thus the very premise of the Union. "Without it, the citizens of each State, except in relation to the powers specifically delegated to the Union, would have been altogether aliens and strangers to each other," Sergeant claimed. And though much of the discussion was procedural, Sergeant, who opposed the admission of Missouri as a slave state, spotlighted the racial aspect of the question by noting the unequal treatment of free men in the United States depending on their skin color. He asked, "Suppose that constitution [of Missouri] had said that no free white citizen of the United States should come to reside in Missouri—was there any gentleman who would say that, with such a provision in her constitution, Missouri ought to be admitted into the Union?"[5]

But even with states in which free persons of color were considered citizens, it was not clear what citizenship meant. Sergeant acknowledged that "to make them citizens in any state it was not necessary they should have a right to vote," after all "more than half of the white men in some of our States did not vote, because they were not freeholders; yet no one would deny them to be citizens of those States."[6] The Missouri debate revealed how different the understanding of citizenship in the United States was from that in Europe, where the debates over Jews' citizenship focused almost squarely on political rights, with civil rights and thereby residency rights left unchallenged. In the US, even in states where free Black Americans were allowed to vote, such as New York, New Hampshire, North Carolina, and Massachusetts, there were other disabilities affecting them.

Indeed, it was granted that "the power of determining to whom the privilege of citizenship shall extend in the respective States has been vested ... in the State Legislatures, with the single exception of the right of Congress to regulate the naturalization of foreigners or aliens."[7] Since basic rights would have been denied in Missouri to Americans who were considered citizens of other states, "this clause of her constitution is repugnant to the Constitution," Sergeant continued, in the same way as it would have been, "had Missouri established an hereditary Senate, or framed a government composed of King, Lords, and Commons, acting on the same principle, I should deem it no more an impugnment, except in a higher degree, of our Constitution, than in the case now before us."[8] Missouri, Sergeant stressed, could only "become a party to our national compact, except on the terms of the compact itself. Any other union between us, as States, would create a political solecism in the Confederacy," and thus effectively undermine the Union.

But Philip P. Barbour of Virginia disagreed. Barbour asked Sergeant and others opposing the admission of Missouri—if the questionable clause of its constitution were to remain—to define citizenship before arguing that Missouri's constitution was "repugnant" to the US constitution in violating the rights of citizens of other states.[9] What "makes a citizen" and "who are the citizens"? Much like the status of Jews in Europe, the status of free Black Americans—specifically their inclusion or exclusion from the category of citizenship—provoked profound questions about the nature of citizenship and of the Union. It also forced some of the most candid political debates about race because it touched upon the visions of what the United States was as a country and society.

A citizen, Barbour proposed, "should be possessed of all at least of the civil rights, if not of the political, of every other person in the community, under like circumstances, of which he is not deprived for some cause, personal to himself."[10] Barbour then went on to explain how society sanctioned different rights and privileges to different classes of people, sketching in effect a social hierarchy in Virginia. "Every white man of Virginia who has a freehold votes. Females do not vote. But all females do not vote. All white persons in Virginia may sue and be sued, all are entitled to the great civil rights of personal liberty and the free possession and enjoyment of personal property." He noted that a young man under twenty-one years old could not make a will "but all persons under like circumstances are subject to the same disability." He challenged his colleagues to show him "an instance ... in any State in this Union, where, among white men, rights are enjoyed by some which are forbidden to others under like circumstances. It cannot be shown." But, Barbour asked, "Is there . . . a State of this Union in which colored men have all the civil rights of any other citizen in the community to which they belong?" He then enumerated conditions in Virginia and other states. "In Virginia," Barbour argued, "a colored man—yes, even a slave, and of that class over whom it was supposed, by those unacquainted with facts, that so much tyranny was exercised—is secured against at least one undue degree of personal violence. The free man of color rises higher—to the dignity of the right to sue and to be sued, to acquire property, to make contracts. He was yet under one signal political disability—he is not allowed the right of suffrage; and under an important civil disability, not being allowed to give testimony in any suit in which a white man is a party." In North Carolina, in contrast, "persons of this description are indulged in the highest political privilege, the right of suffrage, and are yet deprived of the privilege of giving testimony in any case in which a white man is a party—a privilege which can only be wrested from a white man for some cause particular to himself." Barbour concluded that "free people of color are in all the States deprived of many of the rights of white men. Was there any State in the Union in which they were in the full enjoyment of civil rights?" Massachusetts, for example, despite Black electoral franchise, prohibited marriage of "a white with a colored person." It was not on the ground of crime, the disability came "because of his color, certainly." Sarcastically, Barbour remarked, "Whom God has joined, let no man put asunder—but in old Massachusetts 'they do put asunder' the colored person who intermarries with the white." Indeed, "in the East and North, as well as in the South and West, there are certain distinctions growing out of color." There was no state in the Union, Barbour stressed, which "had declared the free man of color to be equal in his civil and political rights to the white man." For Barbour, the US was, what Edward J. Blum called, "a white republic."[11]

Barbour turned to history to explain the reasons for this disparity. "There was a time," he claimed, "when the man of color and the white man were not equal in any part of this country, even in theory."[12] The people who came "to this country from abroad were Europeans or the descendants of Europeans." They, in turn, encountered "the aborigines here." But "this other race," Barbour said of Black people, "got among us afterwards. I deeply regret that they did." And "when they came, they were slaves," added Barbour, who no doubt would have known about the arrival of first Africans in Jamestown in 1619. The representative from Virginia asked his colleagues in the House "to show the words, in any of the State constitutions, which declare that a man of color, become or born free, shall be elevated to the grade of the whites." Barbour then homed in on the right to vote. "Do you find it," he asked, "in the constitution of New York or of Massachusetts, that free people of color shall vote? No; you will find that every male person or male inhabitant shall vote; and, under this clause, it is said that free persons of color have equal rights with the whites. If upon that construction, these persons are considered as citizens, who else are not?" According to Barbour, "free persons of color have been considered a nondescript class. In some States, they have some civil rights; in others, more. In some States they have some political rights; in others, none. . . . the free people of color had civil rights, but not that they have all civil rights." For Barbour, it seemed, without laws explicitly declaring that the rights to free people of color were the same as those of whites, or explicitly granting them the right to vote, people of color could not automatically be granted the same rights as whites based on more generically worded legislation.

Returning to the question of Missouri's constitution, Barbour pondered whether Missouri, or any other state, had a right to refuse entry or residence to anyone who was not its citizen. If a person "afflicted with pestilent disease approached the shore of a State, there was certainly a right to keep him off. If vagabonds and fugitives from justice infest a State, they may certainly be expelled from it," Barbour argued, drawing dangerous parallels between free Black people and disease and "vagabonds and fugitives from justice."[13] He unapologetically affirmed that he did not misspeak:

> We in the Southern States consider this description of population [free Blacks] the most dangerous to the community that can possibly be conceived. They are just enough elevated to have some sense of liberty, and yet not the capacity to estimate or enjoy all its rights, if they had them—and being between two societies, above one [those still enslaved] and below the other [the whites], they are in the most dissatisfied state. . . . And if the time ever come when the flames of servile war enwrap this Union in a general blaze, perhaps we may have to look to them as the primary cause of such horrors. Has not a State, then, a right to get rid of them? [14]

Barbour echoed anxieties about the presence of free Black people, which Virginia had addressed just fourteen years earlier by mandating that recently manumitted slaves leave the state.[15] If Virginia was able to ban free Blacks from remaining in the state, Missouri had "as much right" to decide whether they were to be able to settle "as Massachusetts had to say that a black man shall not, within her limits, marry a white woman. Has not Missouri a right to send off beyond her limits persons of color when free? Virginia has done

it, and Missouri must have the same right as Virginia." Barbour then offered
a hypothetical scenario of what would happen if Virginia emancipated its
slaves and there would be hundreds of thousands who may want to settle in
Pennsylvania. "What would Pennsylvania say? Would she not say that free
persons of color are, by their present experience, an intolerable nuisance to
her society?"[16] And yet, if "the doctrine now contended" were to be adhered
to, Pennsylvania would have "no power to refuse them admission into her
territory." Barbour was right, other Southern states regulated the immigration of free people of color. In 1818, Georgia passed a law that prohibited
"any free person of color, (Indians in amity with the state, and regularly
articled seamen or apprentices arriving in any shop or vessel excepted), to
come into this state" under the threat of fine, imprisonment, even possible
enslavement.[17] In 1820, South Carolina made its immigration and manumission laws more restrictive, and during the 1820s, following the admission of Missouri, other Southern states followed the suit.

In his blustery speech, Barbour exposed a more fundamental question
about the nature of the United States—who belonged to "We, the people."
"Indians, free negroes, mulattoes, slaves! Tell me not," Barbour exclaimed,
"that the Constitution, when it speaks of *We, the people*, means these. The
argument in favor of including in the class of citizens free people of color
goes too far."[18] If taken to its conclusion it would then apply "equally to
the Indian and to the slave." This argument was flawed, Barbour objected.
The Constitution "was framed by the States respectively, consisting of the
European descendants of white men." Thus, "it had a view to the liberty
and rights of white men" and "with the regard to all this colored class,
it was a description of people whom that Constitution did not mean to
meddle with," except "with regard to representation." Otherwise, the Constitution "had no reference to them or their rights, real or supposed." The
framers sought to protect "merely the rights of persons and of property,
where that right existed." And as such it could only mean "We, the white
people" were the ones who "formed a Constitution to condense the will
of our fellow-citizens and to borrow the arm of a mighty people for our
protection against foreign encroachments. The poor slave and the free
man of color are sufficiently protected by the States," which could give to
them "the right to sue and be sued" and could "protect them in everything
absolutely necessary to personal comfort and the preservation of life and
property." But what the states could not "confer" on them was "the great
character of equality in all respects with the whites." According to Barbour,
equality was not only not intended by the Constitution—it was impossible;
even the states, which could "confer everything," could not do that.

The 1790 Naturalization Act served as a proof text for Barbour, "Did Congress ever pass a law to naturalize people of color? On the contrary, every word of every naturalization law speaks of whites only." Color, Barbour added, "had constantly, for centuries past, been a mark of discrimination; it had been the fate of one color to be perpetually subordinate to the other." Barbour's address was a perfect articulation of what Tyler Stovall argued was a racialized idea of liberty.[19] Based on colonial-era laws, especially in Virginia, Barbour concluded that the Constitution, though containing racially neutral language, must have intended equality for whites only. This idea of exclusive scope of the law despite broad language was not dissimilar from arguments marshaled in Europe against granting citizenship rights to Jews, though there on the basis of not race but religion, such as those by the Dutch Jan Hendrick Stoffenberg, who asked whether the Netherlands would "honor the rights of man or only of Christian man; the rights of citizens, or only the rights of Christian citizens."[20] Or, later, the assertions by the German theologian Bruno Bauer, that "the idea of human rights was discovered for the Christian world," and it was "not innate to men."[21]

Alexander Smyth of Virginia backed Barbour's argument, seeking to refute the opposition's points. "The Constitution of the United States," Smyth reiterated, "provides that the citizens of each State shall be entitled to all the privileges and immunities of citizens in the several States."[22] But this, he qualified, could "only apply to citizens who are, in their own States, entitled to all the privileges and immunities of citizens. Can it be shown that free negroes are such citizens in any one of the States as are entitled to all the privileges and immunities of citizens?" As Barbour had argued, this could not be shown, for there was no state where there were no restrictions on Black citizens. According to Smyth, citizenship consisted of "a capacity to take a freehold," "to vote in elections," and "to be elected, having the requisite qualifications of age, residence, and property." Those who enjoyed these "capacities" were citizens of the United States and to them the clause of Constitution applied. But those who did "not possess these capacities [were] not." And since, "the free negro is not entitled to those civil and political rights in the United States, or in any State that adopted the Constitution," he was not a citizen and thus the clause in Article IV of the Constitution did not apply. No state constitution or code of state laws, Smyth suggested, declared "the free negro to be entitled to all the rights of citizenship," or or accorded him "an equality in all respects as to privileges with the white citizen." Once again, the argument centered on the fact that no law specified that a free Black person was eligible to the rights of citizenship. And because "the Revolution found the negro in America a slave," no state laws granting him equality existed. "He is everywhere inferior to the white man, as well by the laws of the States as of the United States," Smyth asserted.

Smyth then proceeded to list all the disabilities to which free Black Americans were subjected. "It is not every person who is born in a State, and born free, that becomes a member of the political community. The Indians, born in the States, continue to be aliens; and so, I contend, do the free negroes." Indeed, Smyth added, as if wanting to make the point crystal clear, "a savage cannot be a member of a civilized community; he is incapable of exercising political rights; and nature seems to have made the negro a perpetual alien to the white man. Slaves are aliens. Alienage was the first foundation of slavery. Citizenship belongs to the civilized freeman." By asserting that Black Americans were "perpetual aliens," Smyth contended, echoing the language deployed against Jews in Europe, that political power belonged to whites alone in perpetuity and Black Americans could never be eligible for citizenship. This was an assertion of white supremacy to the letter of the word—only whites could have political power, akin to Christian opposition to Jewish political rights in Europe, which asserted Christian supremacy of European states. But it was also, in the nineteenth century, becoming a widely shared belief among white Protestants of different denominations, including Presbyterians, Methodists, Baptists, Congregationists, Restorationists, and other evangelicals in the US—that not only did slavery have "a biblical imprimatur" but so, too, racial hierarchy.[23]

For Alexander Smyth of Virginia, citizenship was explicitly white. Categories of people eligible to be US citizens left little to no possibility to include people of color: "1st, those subjects of Great Britain who, being entitled to all the rights and privileges of British subjects, became American citizens by the Revolution; 2d, those who were declared citizens, or naturalized by the States, previous to the adoption of the Constitution of the United States; 3d, European foreigners naturalized in conformity to the law of Congress; and I would add, 4th, the children born in the country of aliens, who were of a description that might have been naturalized."[24] The last category was explicitly "white by law" in accordance to the 1790 Natualization Act.

The debate over the admission of Missouri revealed the rift in understanding the meaning of "We, the people," a question that is still dividing Americans and Europeans alike. As Timothy Garnton Ash remarked in his book *Free World*, "When you say 'we,' what do you mean? . . . What's the widest political community of which you spontaneously say 'we' or 'us'? In our answer to that question lies the key to our future."[25] Two communities of "we" have emerged in the US, one, as Louis Adamic remarked in 1945, "for whom the United States is an Anglo-Saxon country with a white-Protestant-Anglo-Saxon civilization struggling to preserve itself against infiltration and adulteration by other civilizations brought here by Negroes and hordes of 'foreigners.'"[26] The other, for whom it was not "Protestant-Anglo-Saxon," despite English as the dominant language, but rather, a "blend of cultures from many lands, woven of threads from many corners of the world. Diversity is the pattern, is the stuff and color of the fabric." This kind of "Protestant nativism" grounded in a package of Christianity and whiteness began to crystallize in the early decades of the nineteenth century.[27] And though in the earliest iterations Christianity may not have been explicit, it became increasingly so from the 1820s onward.

Barbour's and Smyth's declarations articulating a vision of "a white republic," grounded in Protestant Christianity, did not go without a rebuke. James Strong of New York recognized "the magnitude and importance of the subject" and, refusing to accept the argument that "this description of persons are aliens," offered a rebuttal.[28] An alien, according to Strong, was someone who "owes allegiance to some Government other than that under which he lives. Allegiance to a foreign Power enters into the very essence of the term alien." But as for Black Americans, Strong asked, "To what foreign power, or to what Government, other than that of the United States, do these persons owe allegiance? If to none—then what are they, if not citizens?" Since some opponents of the idea of Black citizenship argued that Black Americans were "denizens," Strong stressed that "no one can be a denizen who has not been an alien. Denization is the modification of alienage." The New York lawmaker also objected to the claims that Missouri had the right to bar Black Americans from entry and settlement in the same way as states or local officials might ban "paupers, lepers, and persons infected with pestilence." While he conceded that persons afflicted with a disease could be barred and those who committed a crime could be banished, he rejected the idea that "a State, town, or city, could prevent the admission of a pauper as such." The fact was, he argued, that "the rights and privileges of peaceable, unoffending citizens, for whom we are expounding the law, do not depend upon the principles which determine the disabilities or punishments of criminals." Just "because a state can banish a traitor," it did not mean that it could "deport every or any harmless, unsuspected citizen." Would Pennsylvania be allowed to "exclude all the officers and troops of the Federal Government," just because it "may exclude from the city of Philadelphia persons infected with the leprosy or the plague"? If the answer was no, he concluded, then "Missouri remains undefended."

Strong then returned to the question of whether "our free negroes and mulattoes" were citizens—a question he deemed "deeply interesting, both as it respects them and the nation." [29] Barbour's definition of who a citizen was went too far. If taken to its conclusion, Strong said, it would prove "that the Jews of Maryland are not citizens of Maryland, although their fathers and their ancestors have resided there since the days of Lord Baltimore. A definition may destroy a right but never can create a right." Strong then listed "some of the peculiar and distinctive characteristics of a citizen of a State": "the right of passing, freely and unmolested, from town to town, and place to place, within the State, and the right of residing, at pleasure, in any part of the same. That these rights belong to everyone entitled to the high privilege of citizen, I think will not be denied." These rights, he continued, were "also common to all free persons, of every age and sex, within the State, except aliens, lunatics, vagabonds and criminals." [30] So, while Barbour and Smyth tried to exclude free Black Americans from the community of citizens, circumscribing that community quite narrowly, Strong's definition expanded the notion of community and citizenship quite broadly, excluding only "aliens, lunatics, vagabonds and criminals." If aliens were those who had allegiance to a foreign government, then "a slave has no country, and owes no allegiance, except to his master," could not be an alien, and, therefore, Strong asked, "if restored to his liberty, and made a freeman, what is his national character?" Strong concluded that such an individual was "a citizen of the United States." And it was "one of the inestimable privileges of a citizen of the United States to pass, unmolested, through several States, and to reside where it may best suit his health and convenience." This, indeed, was "the federal character of an American citizen." And, "if, therefore, free negroes and mulattoes are citizens of the United States, does not the constitution of Missouri conflict with the Federal Constitution although they may not be citizens of a State?"

The debate revealed an acceptance of social hierarchy and discrimination even among those who argued that free Black Americans were citizens. Objecting to Barbour's argument "that a citizen means a person who is entitled to all the civil rights of others in like circumstances, unless deprived of some of them for personal reasons" and that "discriminations existed, in a variety of instances, and in different States, between the white and Black people," Joseph Hemphill of Pennsylvania declared that "discriminations are familiar to us, in the several States, both as to political and civil rights; but it never was believed that they effected a total extinguishment of citizenship."[31] For instance, "some citizens are entitled to vote, and others are not. Some are exempted from serving in the militia, or on juries for various reasons." Clergy were citizens, but in Tennessee they could not "hold any office in the civil department of this State"; women were also citizens, but they did not "fall within the given definition, particularly in the sense in which it is intended to operate on political rights."

Hemphill then delivered a commanding justification for Black Americans' entitlement to claims of citizenship, reminding his colleagues—as we are reminded today in The 1619 Project—of the role Black Americans have played in the history of the United States since its founding:

When our different constitutions were formed this class of people lived among us not in the character of foreigners; they were connected with no other nation, this was their native country, and as dear to them as to us. Thousands of them were free born, and they composed a part of the people in the several States. They were identified with the nation, and its wealth consisted, in part, of their labor. They had fought for their country, and were righteously included in the principles of the Declaration of Independence. This was their condition when the Constitution of the United States was framed and that high instrument does not cast the least shade of doubt upon any of their rights or privileges; but on the contrary, I may challenge gentlemen to examine it, with all the ability they are capable of, and see if it contains a single expression that deprives them of any privileges that is bestowed on others. They have a right to pursue their own happiness, in as high a degree as any other class of people. Their situation is similar to others, in relation to the acquirement of property, and the various pursuits of industry. They are entitled to the same rights of religion and protection and are subjected to the same punishments. They are enumerated in the census. They can be taxed and made liable to militia duty; they are denied none of the privileges contained in the bill of rights; and, although many of these advantages are allowed to a stranger, during his temporary residence, yet, in no one instance is a free native black man treated as a foreigner. When they enjoy all these rights, civil and religious, equally with the white people; and when they all flow from the same constitutions and laws, without any especial designation or reference to them, I have a curiosity, to learn upon what principle any right can be singled out, as one of which they are to be deprived. . . . As citizenship has not been defined in any of the conventions, or by any of the wise assemblages of men in this country, it would be rash in me to attempt to give anything like a confident definition; but, if being a native, and free born, and of parents belonging to no other nation or tribe, does not constitute a citizen in this country, I am at a loss to know in what manner citizenship is acquired by birth.[32]

Hemphill then quoted the fourth article of the Confederation, ratified in 1781, that mentioned "free inhabitants of each of these states." The phrase "free inhabitants," Hemphill explained, "includes every free inhabitant whether black or white, and clothes him with all the privileges of a citizen."[33] His proof that there was no racial preference implied for whites under that provision was the fact that South Carolina wanted to add the word "white" to the text of the Confederation to read "free white inhabitants" but it was voted down, "ayes 2, noes 8, one State divided." This was express evidence that "there were other free citizens besides white citizens" and that "free negroes and mulattoes were, from early times, considered as citizens, and composed a part of the people who chose the delegates to frame the Federal, Constitution."

Regretting that this issue was even raised, Louis McLane from Delaware disagreed: citizenship could not be assumed for free Black people.[34] "In a country," McLane stated, "where there are slaves who can become citizens, the middle condition of a man passing from slavery to citizenship can be no otherwise designated than by the terms here employed, since his freedom does not necessarily import citizenship." There were gradations of status: "a negro slave" was someone "who owes a lasting service to a master," "a free negro" someone "who has been set free by his master," but "the appellation of a citizen belongs to a higher condition and fuller rights." McLane expressed discomfort with the idea of Black citizens. "To my ear," he said, the term "black or negro citizen" had "the sound of novelty." The term "free negro" was used "in contradistinction both to slave and citizens" like "freedman among the Romans," denoting "the middle condition between the bondsman and the Roman citizen." Applying the term "citizen" to all, would devalue it, since equality was out of the question. McLane agued, "if we design to discriminate between citizens of different color, we should use the terms white citizens, or black or negro citizens."

McLane begged to distinguish between federal and state citizenship, since "the free negroes and mulattoes in the United States are not that description of citizens contemplated by the Constitution of the United States as entitled to Federal rights."[35] To be sure they had "certain rights," even "many," and these he "cherished" when "consistent with the safety of the white population." But these rights were "of a local nature, dependent upon the gratuitous favor of the municipal authority of the States, and liable to be curtailed or enlarged by those authorities; they are limited to the State granting them, and [they] confer no claim to similar privileges and immunities purely federal." Thus, it was not enough to "show that a free negro may be admitted to the enjoyment of some rights of citizenship in a particular State but they must also show that he is of that description of 'citizens' to whom the Constitution meant to guaranty equal rights in every State." This, of course, McLane asserted, could not be shown. "A consideration of the nature of citizenship and the principles of the Federal Union will show that the free negroes in our country have no such pretensions [to claim immunities on a federal level, thus, to claim citizenship]."

McLane's idea of citizenship spoke to the political "we" Timothy Garton Ash mentioned—it was about who belonged to a civic community. "A person," McLane declared, "to be a 'citizen' under one Government, must be a member of the civil community, and entitled as matter of right to equal advantages in that community. His rights result from his association with it, and of which nothing short of his own will or misconduct can deprive him. They are rights independent of the political power, and inalienable."[36] McLane then referred to Hugo Grotius and his argument that citizens were "members of a civil society." As such they were distinguished from "inhabitants"—strangers allowed to settle, and "the perpetual inhabitants . . . who have received the right of perpetual residence. These are a kind of citizens of an inferior order." It was to these last two classes that "Indians, free negroes, and mulattoes" belonged. But for the representative from Delaware the "civil society" was white, and Black people and Native Americans were excluded:

> Every one in any degree acquainted with the history of the first settlement of these States must know that the association was of white people—Europeans and their descendants. The idea of a mixture was at no time tolerated; even the aboriginal Indians were not received as a competent part of the civil or political community; but the country was settled, and the society formed, by a white population. It was essentially a white community. In its origin the black population could have formed no part of it, and throughout its progress the invincible barrier to a mixture of white and black, and the positive regulations of society, have perpetually excluded them. They could not, therefore, upon the principles of the association, and in the nature of things, be entitled

to equal rights. The American race [*sic*] came to the country posterior to the whites, and their original condition most unhappily was that of slaves. As such, they were clearly without the pale of the society.[37]

Even manumission could not change that—that was an act of the owner, and it was prohibited, for example in Virginia.[38] There was no state in the Union, McLane asserted, "in which it is declared, by positive enactment, that free negroes shall be entitled to claim all the rights of citizens, and be entitled 'equally to participate in the advantages of the civil' or political 'society.'"[39] Only "some express statutory decision" could change that. The American slaves, even when freed, could never become part of society, McLane declared. Unlike Roman bondsmen, who "were of the same color as the rest of the population" and if freed could assimilate into the population, "servitude is not [the] only distinguishable feature" of the slaves in America, "they never can mingle or assimilate with the white population, more than oil with water. The liberation of the slave from his master pushes him from the shore, on an element where he is a stranger on which he can make but little progress." The Black population would be perpetually excluded from the polity—they could not belong, McLane and others insisted, to the white republic.

The argument Louis McLane from Delaware offered highlights both the differences and similarities between the social and political status of Jews and people of color. If Jews in Europe were considered unassimilable because of their religion, people of color were considered unassimilable because of the color of their skin. Both were excluded from the communal "we," but only one could not change it at all.[40] Moreover, discrimination based on religion became intellectually and politically unacceptable, allowing Jews in the end to gain citizenship de jure, even if de facto they continued to be excluded from the ranks of full citizenship, even if conceptually both European states and the United States understood themselves implicitly and, in some cases, explicitly, as Christian polities. But skin color—whiteness and blackness—did become part of legal fabric in both colonial and early republic laws, with ramification continuing to reverberate in social and political discourse even today. And in the United States, Jews as Europeans could be naturalized and thus enjoy full rights of citizenship. Jews were, therefore, considered "white by law," though whether they belonged to the polity, that remained, as we shall see, a debated question.

McLane concurred with Barbour that the words "We, the People," "broad as they appear . . . were limited" and "did not include the slaves, nor the Indians, because they referred only to those who were members of our civil community."[41] There was no reference "to the free negroes in the country," they were, in fact, "expressly excluded from the advantages of their naturalization laws" and "no positive law has incorporated these people with the civil society." Free or enslaved, people of color were perpetual outsiders—permanently excluded from the polity: "There is no instance in history of any attempt at a mixture with white and black; the natural sense and feeling of all nations have been universally averse to it, and in any country where there is found a weaker caste of people who cannot, by any possibility, mix and assimilate in common with the stronger, their rights can never be the same."

By referring to "nature" McLane precluded any possibility of change. Acceptance and integration would be unnatural, because associations were "founded in the natural sense of community," the exclusion of people of color from positions in public offices and associations "is not the result of incapacity, or the humbleness of their station: for the poorest white man often fills some office of trust and profit; but this is the result of other deeper causes."[42] With the term "racism" unknown at the time, McLane came as close as it was possible to acknowledging racism and emotions linked to it as a reason for the exclusion of Black people from "immunities and privileges" of citizenship.[43] Racism was the key to discrimination; laws simply reflected that. These discriminations, McLane noted, were "called for by the feelings of society." Why, he asked, could not "a free negro be a witness against a white man, as a foreigner or an Indian may?" It was "because the custom of society, having drawn a discrimination between the white and the black, disparaging to the latter, the law deems it safe and wise to deprive him of the means of gratifying feelings which such a condition might engender." And though some of these restrictions might be found "in some only of the states; but the most important one is found in all, rooted in the heart of the people and enforced by the laws."

Intermarriage was a case in point, both on the emotional and legal level, proving, according to McLane, that Black people were not considered citizens.[44] No state allowed intermarriage, even in places where Black free men had the right to vote. There were, McLane argued, "few men" who would not "revolt at such union," and "no state of society in which such a union would not be reprobated."[45] But "to guard against the possibility of a different feeling, the laws come in aid of and enforce the prohibition." Were Black people to "form part of the civil society, which in such a case would be composed of a motley population consisting of all the variety of color" and where they thereby were "entitled to claim equal rights, by what authority can the right of forming a marriage contract be annulled?" The prohibition of intermarriage, "because the strong sense of the community is against it," demonstrated that Black people were not "members of the civil community" and could "never become so." This, McLane concluded, "closes the only legitimate avenue to their amalgamation," "strengthens and sanctifies the moral feelings of society," and "keeps the black man forever without its bosom, and perpetuates his discrimination."

The congressman from Delaware once more reiterated that "the Constitution was the work of States composed of a white population."[46] After all, when the country was settled, it was "essentially a white community." The Constitution was, thus, "designed to secure their interests chiefly," guaranteeing immunities only to those "who had perfect rights in one State." The Constitution "was intended to make the United States a common country for such as were full members of the particular States." Free Black people were not part of that collective, McLane stressed; they were "a distinct class everywhere, and the creatures of local and municipal policy; certainly, of an inferior order, and enjoying such rights as the policy of the particular State might think proper to confer." They were "merely inhabitants, who had not attained to the condition of citizens and enjoyed only partially the privileges appertaining to the former class."

Defending Missouri's right not to allow free Black people to settle, McLane asked, "Why force upon [Missouri] an evil which every other State is aiming to shake off? Why compel her to receive a population which cannot assimilate with her citizens; which retard the growth and prosperity of her empire; which are dangerous to her peace, and quiet, and safety, and upon which she must heap odious and continued disabilities, as the lesser evil?"[47] McLane's language reflected the sense of threat Black people presented to the whites and to the white supremacy they wanted to protect—"odious and continued disabilities" were a price to pay.

McLane's soliloquy was not left unchallenged. Representative Rollin Mallary of Vermont called attention to the constitution of his state adopted after Vermont was admitted to the Union in 1791, which declared that "that all men are born equally free and independent; that no male person, born in this country, or brought from over sea, ought to be holden, by law, to serve any person as a servant, slave, or apprentice, after he arrives at the age of twenty-one years; nor female, in like manner, after she arrives at the age of eighteen years."[48] Mallary addressed the question of the general language of liberty that was used by Barbour and others to argue that people of color, by not being explicitly mentioned, were not intended to be included in the clauses concerning citizenship and liberty.

Mallary emphatically stated that the constitution did not "declare that all men except negroes and mulattoes 'are born equally free and independent;' it does not declare, Mr. Speaker, that no person except negroes and mulattoes shall be holden to servitude. The language is broad and comprehensive as the race of man." People of color in Vermont, Mallary observed, "were received and acknowledged as citizens when the constitution was formed, under which the rights and privileges of every citizen are protected."[49]

William Eustis of Massachusetts added his voice to the chorus challenging Barbour's interpretation of the meaning of the words "We, the people."[50] The exclusion of "Indians, free negroes, mulattoes" from the meaning of "We, the people" would not have been possible at the time. If such exclusion had been intended, Eustis noted, "the preamble ought to read 'We the white people,'" and to this "the members of the convention who formed that constitution, from the Middle and Northern States, could never have consented, knowing that there were in those States many thousands of people of color, who had rights under it." These people were free, and not simply "free from their masters." They "also became freemen of the State and were admitted to all the rights and privileges of white citizens." Since Barbour and Smyth demanded to see evidence that Black free people had the same rights and privileges as whites, Eustis obliged. In Massachusetts, Black citizens enjoyed "all the broad and essential rights of citizens—the right, in common, with the whites, to hold real and personal estate; the right of course to hold and convey land; the right of trial by jury; the right to the writ of habeas corpus; and, in this Government, the all-important right of the elective franchise . . . by the laws and constitution of Massachusetts, they are considered as citizens equally with the whites." Eustis emphatically reiterated, based on "incontrovertible facts" and "actual and long continued practice that blackmen and mulattoes, in Massachusetts at least, are citizens, having civil and political rights, in common with the whites." Whiteness was, Eustis conceded, still the standard to which other groups were compared, but he had no doubt that, by law and practice in Massachusetts, people of color were equal to whites.

Missouri was admitted to the Union, under the Missouri Compromise, in 1821. Four years later, the issue of free persons of color was addressed by the General Assembly of the State of Missouri in an "Act concerning Negroes and Mulattoes."[51] Section 1 defined who was "a mulatto"—"a negro" did not need to be defined—as a person "of whose grandfathers or grandmothers any one is or shall have been a negro, although all his or her other progenitors, except those descending from the negro, shall have been white persons ... and so every such person, who shall have one fourth or more negro blood, shall in like manner be deemed a mulatto."[52] Section 4 directly responded to the objections voiced by John Sergeant and others in 1820: "hereafter no free negro or mulatto, other than a citizen of some one of the United States, shall come into or settle in this state under any pretext whatever."[53] If a complaint were made against an individual before a justice of the peace, they would have to produce "a certificate, attested by a seal of some court of record in some one of the United States, evidencing that he is citizen of such state." Should the individual be unable to produce such a certificate, the justice "shall command him to depart the state" within thirty days. Should the person not depart, the justice "may commit him to a common goal," thereafter they would be examined by a court, which in turn could sentence the individual to "ten lashes on his or her bare back, and order him to depart the state; and if he or she shall not depart, the same proceedings shall be had and punishment inflicted, as often as may be necessary, until such person shall depart the state." This clause, though ostensibly addressing the concerns voiced by some of the congressmen in 1820, effectively sanctioned harassment of free persons of color, forcing them to present on demand a "certificate, attested by a seal" of their citizenship in other states, and should this be unavailable, granting the state the right to abuse them physically with corporal punishment until they left the state. Those bringing "a free negro or mulatto" without a certificate would be fined $500 (over $13,000 in today's dollars) for every person brought. The letter of the law thus complied with the constitution, but the spirit and the application of the law stayed the same as in the original constitution and made Missouri an inhospitable state for free people of color, with requirements almost impossible to satisfy.

The arguments presented in the congressional debate over Missouri were eerily reminiscent of those that had taken, or were taking, place in Europe in regard to Jewish citizenship. Both Black citizenship in the US and Jewish citizenship in Europe touched the nerve of a more profound question of national belonging—what it meant to be a nation, who belonged, who the "we" was. The self-identity of Europeans both in the US and on the continent became centered on Christianity and whiteness, both of which were deemed nonpareil—Jewishness and Blackness disrupted that. In the United States and in European colonies, Jews, for a short while were considered "white," or, in some cases, "off-white." Some even owned plantations and slaves, but in some of the states and colonies, like Barbados, Jews did not have the same rights as white Protestant Americans and suffered from some legal disabilities. In the US, some of these legal disabilities were removed only after the ratification of the Fourteenth Amendment.[54] There were also in the Caribbean mixed-race Jews, and their legal status was complex and dependent on lineage and local laws.[55]

But even though the American Constitution was, as Edward Blum and Paul Harvey put it, "Christless," the cultural framework of reference—including some state constitutions and the colonial legal fabric—was dominantly Christian.[56] It became even more explicitly so over the decades of the nineteenth century, with westward territorial advancement and the expansion of slavery that coincided with the growing opposition to enslavement across the Atlantic and within the United States. Christianity and the Bible became powerful tools of defense against anti-slavery agitation helping define "proslavery Christianity."[57] Still, while many white Americans were indeed uneasy about slavery itself, Barbour, McLane, and Smyth were right: the majority of whites in the US, even those opposing slavery, would agree, as Alexander Smyth asserted, that free Black people were "everywhere inferior to the white man" and were thus "not entitled to those civil and political rights" that white citizens possessed.[58] Ending slavery—albeit gradually—was more broadly accepted, but equality was resoundingly rejected, and not just by Southerners. The argument was not just legal, it was also religious.

Many European Americans would have agreed with the lawmakers in Kentucky, who argued in 1836 that it was "through the mysterious dispensation" of God's Providence that "dominion has been given to the white man over the black."[59] And for some proslavery Christians, abolitionist activism was tantamount to politicizing Christianity. A fictional preacher in John H. Van Evrie's parody declares, "Then I forsook Christ and took up politics. . . . I taught people to hate each other. . . . I preached the negro and Abolitionism instead of Christ and salvation."[60] Opposition to slavery was increasingly cast, among proslavery Christians, as anti-Christian—a process that would come to matter after the Civil War.

Defense of slavery and racial hierarchy came hand in hand. In his 1853 pamphlet, John Van Evrie, a committed defender of slavery and racial hierarchy, asserted that the transatlantic slave economy was divinely ordained: "The world, civilization, the wants of society, the comfort and well-being of the millions of Christendom required the products of the tropics and of the West India Islands. The Creator has ordained that these products can only be forthcoming through the labor of the negro; the demand was imperative, and the labor was furnished."[61] In the 1861 expanded version of this work, Van Evrie added a more explicit argument about racial hierarchy cast within a Christian framework of reference. "It is doubtless," he wrote, "the design of the Almighty that the Caucasian and negro, under certain circumstances which will be considered elsewhere, should exist in juxta-position, and therefore a specific knowledge of this race, and its true rela-tions to our own, is the most vital and indeed transcendent question or consideration that was ever presented to a civilized and Christian people. Nor can this be delayed or pushed aside, for even now the nation is rapidly drifting into serious difficulties and possibly terrible calamities."[62] The calamities would come because of "the misconception prevalent in regard to the negro's nature and his true relations to the white man."

Because slavery was a national issue and because polemic for or against it was framed within the Christian moral framework, it was easy to for-get that, according to the US Constitution, the United States was not a Christian nation. And yet, Christianity and appeals to Christian values permeated political and social discourse, sometimes implicitly or explic-itly excluding Jews from the civic community. In 1824, in the blasphemy case *Updegraph v. Commonwealth*, Justice Thomas Duncan writing for the court, asserted that "Christianity, general Christianity, is, and always has been, a part of the common law of Pennsylvania."[63] It was, however, different from an established religion, and different from the place Chris-tianity had in Europe. It was, Duncan stated, "Christianity, without the spiritual artillery of European countries; for this Christianity was one of the considerations of the royal charter, and the very basis of its great founder, William Penn; not Christianity founded on any particular reli-gious tenets; not Christianity with an established church, and tithes, and spiritual courts; but Christianity with liberty of conscience to all men." Indeed, Willam Penn's 1682 "Act of Liberty of Conscience" affirmed only "christian liberty." He established Pennsylvania's Christian framework by setting "every first day of the week, called the Lord's day" as a day on which "people shall abstain from their usual and common toil and labor" not only so they could have a better disposition "to read the scriptures of truth at home or frequent such meetings of religious worship abroad as may best suit their respective persuasions," but also so that "looseness, irreligion, and atheism may not creep in under pretense of conscience in this prov-ince."[64] According to the act, anyone who would "speak loosely and pro-fanely of almighty God, Christ Jesus, the Holy Spirit, or the scriptures of truth" would be fined. Penn's "Charter of Liberties" issued in 1701 removed some of the explicitly Christian references but reiterated the eligibility of "all persons who also profess to believe in Jesus Christ, the saviour of the world, . . . , notwithstanding their other persuasions and practices in point of conscience and religion, to serve this government in any capacity, both legislatively and executively, he or they solemnly promising, when lawfully required, allegiance to the King as sovereign and fidelity to the proprietary and Governor."[65] Justice Duncan then concluded in *Updegraph* that "this great body of laws" was issued "for a Christian country and Christian people" since "[i]nfidelity was then rare, and no infidels were among the first colonists."[66] In fact, Duncan noted, it "was justly observed by the learned Chancellor of the associated members of the Bar of Philadelphia, in the city of Philadelphia, in his address to that body, 22d of June, 1822, the number of Jews was too inconsiderable to excite alarm, and the believers in Mahomet were not likely to intrude." Ultimately, Duncan argued Christianity had become the fabric of "the common law, incorporated into the great law of Pennsylvania, and thus, it is irrefragably proved, that the laws and institutions of this state are built on the foundation of reverence for Christianity." Although Penn's religious criteria as a requirement for public office was removed from the US Constitution, "the constitution of the United States has made no alteration" regarding "the common law doctrine of Christianity, as suited to the condition of the colony, and without which no free government can long exist. Under the constitution, penalties against cursing and swearing have been exacted. If Christianity was abolished, all false oaths, all tests by oath in the common form by the book, would cease to be indictable as perjury." The state then, though part of the US and under the US Constitution, was implicitly Christian, and Jews residing in the commonwealth were considered, or implied, to be "infidels."

Three years after *Updegraph v. Commonwealth*, in 1827, Ezra Stiles Ely, a Presbyterian preacher in Philadelphia, openly called on "Christian freemen to elect Christian rulers."[67] In his sermon, Ely danced around the constitutional rights against an established religion. "God," Ely stated, "requires a Christian faith, a Christian profession, and a Christian practice of all our public men; and we as Christian citizens ought, by the publication of our opinions, to require the same."[68] But, since Ely believed that it was "the duty of all our rulers to serve the Lord and kiss the Son of God," it was "manifestly the duty of all our Christian fellow-citizens to honour the Lord Jesus Christ and promote christianity by electing and supporting as public officers the friends of our blessed Saviour." This did not mean that "Jews and Infidels" should have no rights. On the contrary, Ely granted "that Christians have the same rights and privileges in exercising the elective franchise, which are here accorded to Jews and Infidels" and that "every citizen is eligible to every office, whatever may be his religious opinions and moral character; and that every one may constitutionally support any person whom he may choose." But Ely rejected the idea that such citizen would be "without accountability to his Divine Master for his choice; or that he may lay aside all his Christian principles and feelings when he selects his ticket and presents it at the polls." Christian citizens then should "acknowledge" God not only on the Sabbath at the "Lord's table" but also "on the day of public election" in choosing "a Chief Magistrate." Ely listed the Christian denominations considered "true Christians," whose members would be acceptable as "Christian rulers," and suggested voting en bloc: "If three or four of the most numerous denominations of Christians in the United States, the Presbyterians, the Baptists, the Methodists and Congregationalists for instance, should act upon this principle, our country would never be dishonoured with an avowed infidel in her national cabinet or capitol."[69]. The coalition could be expanded to "add the members of the Protestant Episcopal church in our country, the electors of these five classes of true Christians, united in the sole requisition of apparent friendship to Christianity in every candidate for office whom they will support, could govern every public election in our country, without infringing in the least upon the charter of our civil liberties." German Christians in Pennsylvania and Ohio and the Reformed Dutch Church in New York and New Jersey also stood for "the fundamental truths of Christianity." The result of such alliance would be a Christian leader, at times "a Baptist, at another an Episcopalian, at another a Methodist, at another a Presbyterian of the American, Scotch, Irish, Dutch, or German stamp, and always a friend to our common Christianity." Such alliance would ensure that the country would not "ever suffer an enemy, an open and known enemy of the true religion of Christ, to enact our laws or fill the executive chair." But such "Christian rulers will not oppress Jews or Infidels; they will kiss the Son and serve the Lord; while we have the best security for their fidelity to our republican, and I may say scriptural forms of government." Electing "men who dare to acknowledge the Lord Jesus Christ for their Lord in their public documents," Ely noted, would "pick no infidel's pocket, and break no Jew's neck."[70] Neither would it be a "violation of our national constitution, if our members of Congress should quit reading of newspapers and writing letters on the Lord's day, at least during public worship in the Hall of Representatives"; "reverence for the Sabbath and the worship of Almighty God . . . would not convert them into tyrants; it would not make our national government a religious aristocracy; it would not violate our federal constitution." Ely concluded his sermon, "We are a Christian nation: we have a right to demand that all our rulers in their conduct shall conform to Christian morality; and if they do not, it is the duty and privilege of Christian freemen to make a new and a better election. May the Lord Jesus Christ for ever reign in and over these United States, and call them peculiarly his own."

The sermon did not sit well with some Pennsylvanians. Ezra Stiles Ely was called "before the Senate of the Commonwealth of Pennsylvania, with advocating the UNION of CHURCH AND STATE, and the establishment of a predominant religious sect by civil authority."[71] But Ely denied it. "An avowed enemy to Christ," he noted, "has the political liberty of being an infidel in his opinions; of preferring an infidel for his civil ruler; and of giving his vote in aid of the election of an infidel." But as a Christian he preferred "a Christian to an infidel."

Even abolitionists saw the nation as fundamentally Christian and sought to appeal to its Christian moral values. William Garrison questioned, for example, whether there were "two Christs," one representing "submission and non-resistance for black man," the other "rebellion and conflict for the white man."[72] Since 1850, the mast of Garrison's *Liberator* featured a commanding central Christ figure, who, as Edward Blum and Paul Harvey have observed, "beckoned to a kneeling black slave with his right hand and scolded a white slave owner with his gaze" (fig. 16).[73] The *Liberator*'s Christ was white.

And then there were the Sunday laws or attempts to issue them—Christianizing the weekly rhythms for all Americans.[74] The letter of the Constitution was one thing; the popular sentiment was another.

It is thus not surprising that Jews too came to be seen as outsiders, not quite fitting in, easily forgotten, frequently marginalized. Garrison, for example, excoriated Mordecai Manuel Noah, a fifth-generation American Jewish politician from New York, for his support of slavery, calling him "a Jewish unbeliever, the enemy of Christ and Liberty."[75]

But as Euro-Americans, Jews were citizens, who could use the tools this status provided to push back. In 1812, for example, Governor Henry Middleton of South Carolina called on "all Christian denominations to have services in their respective churches" to celebrate a day of thanksgiving.[76] The Jewish congregation of Beth Elohim in Charleston felt excluded and intervened, reminding the governor of the existence of a Jewish community in the state. The governor apologized for the oversight and invited Jews to join "in a devotional action that would assuredly be most acceptable to the Almighty."

A similar situation took place in 1841, when Jacob Ezekiel, a Jew born in Philadelphia, protested President John Tyler's use of a phrase

FIGURE 16. *Liberator*, June 1, 1860. Author's own copy.

"Christian people" in his appeal to Americans to mourn the death of President William Henry Harrison.[77] Ezekiel felt that President Tyler excluded non-Christians from the notion of "the People of the United States," and noted that while he was "fully conscious that a denomination of a 'Christian people' exists in this country as in others," there also existed "a Jewish People," and "a People who neither profess Judaism or Christianity but [were] believers in a Supreme Being and Creator of universe whom they adore." He pleaded with Tyler not to exclude non-Christians from "matters of a National Character" and for the sake of "our Common Country" to modify or at least explain that those "who do not profess Christianity" were welcome "to participate in the fact which you have most properly recommended to be observed on the 14th of May next by the People of the United States."

In his response, President Tyler apologetically assured Ezekiel that "in speaking in the first paragraph of the duties of the Christian people" he in "no way" meant "to imply that similar duties should not be performed by all mankind" and stressed that "for the people of whom you are one" he felt "none other than profound respect," a respect on account of "the wisdom which flowed from the lives of your prophets" and "holy records [that] bear witness to the many instances of divine favour and protection of the God of Abraham and of Isaac and of Jacob, God of the Christian and of the Israelite."[78] Reassuring as the president may have been, his letter did not seem inclusive of contemporary Jews in America—rather the president's stated "respect" was nothing more than Christian supersessionist appreciation of the Hebrew scriptures.

But three years later, in South Carolina, even that kind of respect was missing and the tone became more bellicose in a similar confrontation.[79] In the fall of 1844, Jews there were reminded of the Christian supremacy of the state, when in a proclamation establishing the third day of October a thanksgiving day Governor James H. Hammond called on "citizens of all denominations to assemble at their respective places of worship, to offer up their devotions to God, their creator, and his Son Jesus Christ, the Redeemer of the World."[80] Worse, the governor assumed that it was the duty of "all Christian nations to acknowledge at stated periods their dependence on Almighty God." Jews, considering themselves as "as American freemen," protested that "the tenor" of the proclamation "excluded the Israelites of this city and State from his invitation to public prayer and thanksgiving." They first reached the governor through private letters. But when these efforts failed, they addressed him in an open statement published in the newspaper *Southern Patriot*.

In that open letter the Jewish leaders explained why they felt excluded from the governor's declaration as well as the ramifications of this exclusion.[81] The proclamation was "utterly repugnant to their feelings—so violative of the accustomed privileges." They did not want to engage in a discussion over "doctrinal points" but rather they proposed "to test the position you have assumed, by that constitution, which you have sworn to support" along with "the Constitution of the United States," both of which "present a glorious panoply of defence against the encroachments of power, whether its designs be bold or insidious." They were adamant that "under its universal and protecting spirit," Jews did not seek "toleration" but their rights. The constitution of South Carolina offered the governor "a salutary instruction," for it guaranteed that "the free exercise and enjoyment of religious profession and worship, without discrimination or preference, shall for ever hereafter be allowed within this state to all mankind." The Jewish leaders charged the governor "with such obvious discrimination and preference, in the tenor of your proclamation, as amounted to an utter exclusion of a portion of the people of South Carolina." In this sternly worded letter, the signatories warned about the potential consequences of tolerating such discrimination and preference, not just for Jews but also for many others:

> From your perversion of it, what monstrous evils might arise? [I]f your Excellency could be justified in so framing your proclamations as to shut out the religious privileges of the Israelites, where are we to find the line of limitation? Instead of representing the whole people of the state in their various tenets and creeds, the governor would make his own opinion the standard of orthodoxy, be it what it may. Episcopacy and Presbytery would in turn exclude each other, as the views of the functionary who may happen to fill the chair might lead. Individual prejudice or prepossession would usurp the place of the constitution. An orthodox Protestant governor might exclude all who do not come up to his peculiar standard of faith; and the Catholic, the Unitarian, the Israelite, and numerous other sects, may find their privileges discriminated away, and their most cherished opinions crushed or slighted by a gubernatorial preference.[82]

The state constitution was "a palladium that throws its broad and protecting influence over all who abide beneath it" and "guarantees TO ALL, in its own expressive phrase, 'without discrimination or preference,' the free and full enjoyment of every right, civil and religious." Jews, the letter stated using a lofty sacralized rhetoric, "cherish its principles next to the Holy Testimonies of our God! It is a noble covenant of Liberty, won and consecrated by the blood of Heroes. The temple is pure and the shrine is sacred." And for that reason, it had to be guarded against desecration by "the errors or misdeeds of those in authority," which, in turn, "cannot pass unnoticed, or unrebuked." And that was why the Charleston Jews wanted to "record this our solemn and emphatic protest against your proclamation, as unsanctioned by the letter or spirit of the Constitution, as offensive and unusual in language, as exclusive, arbitrary, and sectarian in its character." In closing, the signatories, reminded the governor that his "term of office is about to expire" and hoped that to preserve his reputation, he would "remove the impressions which the act in question has made upon the minds of a large portion of your constituents."

The governor would express no remorse and no apologies.[83] Initially, he wrote, he had hoped to avoid this controversy, but when the letter demanding apology, signed by "over one hundred of the most respectable Israelites of Charleston," was published, he felt he needed to respond. In a tersely worded letter, Hammond confessed that "the simple truth" was that "at the time of writing my Proclamation it did not occur to me, that there might be Israelites, Deists, Atheists, or any other class of persons in the State who denied the divinity of Jesus Christ." Thus, his words were not intended to "wound the feelings of such individuals." But, the governor stated bluntly, "Had I been fully on my guard, I do not think I should have changed the language of my Proclamation!" He offered "no apology" because "up to this time, I have always thought it a settled matter that I lived in a Christian land! And that I was the temporary chief magistrate of a Christian people. That in such a country and among such a people I should be, publicly, called to an account, reprimanded and required to make amends for acknowledging Jesus Christ as the Redeemer of the world, I would not have believed possible, if it had not come to pass." He felt that if he excluded "the name of the Redeemer" from his proclamation, the proclamation would no longer be a "Christian proclamation" and as such "it might, justly, give offence to the Christian People, whom it invited to worship." Like the Jewish signatories, who pondered the consequences of including religious, denominational language in the proclamation, the governor pondered the consequences its omission. "If in complaisance to the Israelites and Deists, his name must be excluded, the Atheists might as justly require that of the Creator to be omitted also; and the Mahometan or Mormon that others should be inserted. I feel myself upon the broad ground that this is a Christian community; and that as their chief magistrate it was my duty and my right in conformity with usage, to invite them to return thanks for the blessings they enjoy, to that Power from whence, and that Being through whose intercession they believe that they derive them." Indeed, the governor unflinchingly asserted, "The civilization of the age is derived from Christianity, that the institutions of this country are instinct with the same spirit, and that it pervades the laws of the State as it does the manners and I trust the hearts of our people. Why do we observe the Sabbath instituted in honour of Christ? Why do our laws forbid labour on that day or the execution of civil process? [I]t is because we are, and acknowledge ourselves, and wish to be considered, a Christian people." Hammond did not think he violated the constitution by wording his proclamation the way he did. Jews were, after all, not compelled to worship contrary to their faith, and "those who did not choose to accept my invitation, were at full liberty to decline it, and if the Israelites refused to open their Synagogues, I had no complaint to make—no penalty to exact."

As the governor was closing his lengthy response, he articulated the sentiment that combined both the long-standing theologically grounded Christian anti-Jewish prejudice and the core of what religious equality meant in modern society.[84] Had the Jews stopped at simply refusing to open synagogues on the day the governor proclaimed as a day of thanksgiving, "such a manifestation of their disapproval of my Proclamation would have been the more severely felt by me, because of its dignity and its consonance with true religious feelings as I apprehend them." And even if, "inheriting the same scorn for Jesus Christ which instigated their ancestors to crucify him," Jews "would have felt themselves degraded and disgraced in obeying my exhortation to worship their 'Creator,' because I had also recommended the adoration of his 'Son the Redeemer,' still I would not have hesitated to appoint for them, had they requested it, a special day of Thanksgiving according to their own creed." But this was not, the governor continued, "what the Israelites desired. They wished to be included in the same invitation to the public devotion with the Christians! And to make that invitation acceptable to them, I must strike out the cornerstone of the Christian creed, and reduce the whole to entire conformity with that of the Israelites; I must exhort a Christian People to worship after the manner of the Jews."

The governor's response powerfully illustrates not only the persistence of Christian theological anti-Jewish tropes but also the resulting social hierarchy of Jews and Christians. The removal of specifically Christian references was deemed "worship after the manner of the Jews," clearly demeaning for Christians, for as Hammond stated, it was "reducing"

Christian worship "to entire conformity with that of Israelites." It also highlights the way Jews' presence in Christian society was considered threatening to Christianity and Christian identity—tantamount to de-Christianization, even if, in American law, religion, unlike race, was not a factor in entitlement to citizenship rights. While Jews saw the removal of specifically Christological references as broadening the scope of the proclamation to include Jews, Hammond saw this demand as an unacceptable demand to "narrow it down to the exclusion of ninety-nine hundredths of my fellow-citizens" and an effective discrimination "in favour of the Israelites." He thus declared that "neither the Constitution, nor my public duty, would allow me to do this, and they also forbid me to offer any apology for not having done it." Jews' gains were thus the Christians' loss. Neither side mentioned race.

The confrontation about the polity, here, was framed in religious terms. For Hammond, civic nationalism was bound with Protestant Christianity. For Jews, his declaration was a violation of the very premise of the American Constitution and religious equality. Jews were caught in the middle. They were white, or at least "white by law," but they were not Christian. White supremacy made "whiteness the normative model," allowing "white people to ignore race," and be "burdened" by it. But in nineteenth-century US, Protestantism, with all its different denominations, had become a normative religious model.[85] Governor Hammond, and President Tyler before him, had never had to consider or examine their own religious identity within the context of the civic community. Just as people of color provoke an examination of whiteness, Jews in the midst of a Christian society challenged Christian hegemony and normativity, forcing Christians to examine their own social privilege and dominance, while simultaneously bearing, as Naomi W. Cohen put it, "the discomforts foisted upon non-Christians in a Christian America."[86]

James H. Hammond's response was forwarded to a committee of Jewish leaders in Charleston, which issued its own report and a response to the governor, with a mandate to make it public. The committee stated that after the governor's proclamation had been issued, a prominent leader of the community "addressed a letter to his excellency, couched in the most respectful language. Had the governor been pleased to instruct his secretary to acknowledge either of these, simply declaring their exclusion an oversight, the matter would have been dropped at that point."[87] But regretfully, "the positions taken by the Israelites" in their letter to the governor were "erroneously construed and misstated in his reply." Their protest—they wanted to clarify—was not about his reference to "Jesus

Christ the Redeemer" but rather to the fact that because of such "framing" of his proclamation, Jews "were entirely excluded from 'a participation in the religious observances of the occasion.'" The committee observed that the governor could have simply extended the invitation "as is customary, to all other denominations." It was a common practice everywhere, "even in monarchical countries . . . for rulers to call on every denomination to offer up prayers at their respective places of worship." And this would have been satisfactory. But the issue was far more serious.

The governor mentioned "Jews," "Atheists," "Mormons," "&c. &c." to emphasize the numerical contrast with the Christian majority, but, as the Jewish leaders noted, "the constitution has nothing to do with the relative numbers of the citizens—with popular or unpopular modes of faith." American law was not about majority's exclusion of a minority. "If either of these classes of citizens formed nine-tenths of the population, and the other tenth were Christians, with the present constitution, his Excellency, under his view, must exclude the minority of Christians, and interpret Mormonism, or any other ism, as the religion of the state." The committee felt, "as citizens of this state, and of the United States," they "would be unworthy of the rights secured to them, in common with all others, if they did not protest against the principles set forth in the governor's letter, which if admitted, would form a base sufficient to measure away their rights, and the rights of others, for what affects you now, might at another time be fatal to the rights of other minorities."[88] They were wary that with "such invasions silently creeping in, some future proclamation may make farther discriminations, expressing what the executive means by Christianity, and who are Christians." But more to the point, they argued that "the worst species of wrong is the partial one that aims at the few; that abandons principles and strives to please numbers." As Jews, "few or many, popular or otherwise," they hoped "to be found always upholding those principles, wherein as American citizens, they of right are at issue with the interpretation of the spirit of the laws as expressed by the governor," believing that "the state government, like that of the United States, is a government of equal rights in religious privileges, as in all other things," and not as the governor's position suggested, "a government of tolerance, enabling rulers to give or to withhold." Such a policy "would be an outrage on the constitution, and on the character of the patriots who made it free and equal, and on our countrymen around us, if any contrivance should make it otherwise."

The committee was also troubled by the governor's "language which they deem calculated to excite the worst of feelings in our country,"

especially, "his allusion to the crucifixion of Christ."[89] They saw it as "tending to excite the prejudices of eighteen hundred years against a small portion of his constituents." The Jewish community recognized its vulnerabil-
ity and appealed to "their fellow-citizens of all denominations to support
them in the declaration . . . in defence of the humblest of them, should
fanaticism, or outrage of any kind, (which Providence avert,) ever assail
them."

In January of 1845, the editors of the Jewish periodical *Occident*
published the documents prefacing them with an introductory text that
asserted Jewish equality and citizenship. Like the signatories of the letter to the governor, the editors presented themselves as "lover[s] of true
and rational civil and religious liberty," without as much as a nod to the
existence in their own town and state of enslaved people who could not
lay claims to liberty.[90] Jews were, the editors wrote, "emphatically citizens of the state, not alone by grant of law, but because they themselves
have striven for the independence of the land. . . . If, therefore, the other
inhabitants have a right to the consideration and the liberties which they
enjoy, the Jews have it equally so; especially as they come not to ask any
exclusive privileges, but to be left in possession of the immunities which
the constitution guarantees to all, and to be allowed to join in the joys, the
sufferings, and aspirations of their fellow-citizens." The editors remarked
that "Governor Hammond showed himself but little acquainted with his
duties of a governor of a free people, by forgetting, or not heeding, the
existence of a numerous body of men who are generally so well known
as the Jews of South Carolina, some of whom have been legislators in
the very capitol at Columbia, from which he dictates his proclamation."
Hammond, they argued, "was clinging in his imagination to times never
known in this country since its freedom was established, which proscribed
persons for their speculative opinions, and hence he forgot that there were
such people as Israelites within the bounds of the state of South Carolina."

By focusing on religion, Jews were able to claim their right to citizenship and equality—something unavailable at the time to even free Black
men—and to contend "that, as far as religion is concerned, the majority
has no rule whatever over the minority by any right, either reasonable or
constitutional."[91] It did not matter, they stressed, "in this respect whether
the majority be Christian or Jewish; the constitution knows nothing of
either" and in the Constitution, "the fundamental charter of the United
States, neither Christianity nor Judaism is mentioned by name. Consequently, neither can be said to govern the land, neither can be said to tolerate the other. The constitution found us living side by side upon the soil

of America; both Jews and Christians had sacrificed blood and treasure in the achievement of the independence of the Union." Emphatically and self-confidently, they declared, "The Jew is not tolerated in this country; he belongs to the constitution, which assures him the privilege of worshipping God as his conscience dictates to him."

Ostracized as Jews may have been or felt socially or politically, they were still considered citizens able to exercise their rights—each time pushing back against discrimination and exclusion, and against the vision of the United States as, to quote a Kentucky paper from 1860, "a monument of power of Christianity and civilization."[92] In contrast, the issue of Black citizenship, and the adamant rejection of Black equality in society and law would continue to plague the United States. As Judith Shklar has put it, "The struggle for citizenship in America has . . . been overwhelmingly a demand for inclusion in the polity, an effort to break down excluding barriers to recognition, rather than an aspiration to civic participation as a deeply involving activity."[93]

# CHAPTER SEVEN

# Contesting Black Citizenship and Equality

THE RACIAL HISTORY in the US has often been told through the prism of slavery. With this focus, it is a story that allows for a narrative redemption that culminates with the Emancipation Declaration and the eventual abolition of most slavery through a constitutional amendment. But, as the Missouri debate demonstrates, the racial history told through the lens of attitudes toward free Black people is far more revealing and offers a history that is much less redemptive, since citizenship rights of free Black Americans have been repeatedly challenged, their membership in the civil and political community frequently denied. The questions raised and attitudes voiced in the Missouri debate and, decades later, in 1857 in the critical *Dred Scott v. Sandford* case have continued to resurface even, or perhaps in particular, after the Civil War ended with the abolition of slavery. Many European Americans considered Black Americans, as Chief Justice Roger B. Taney wrote in *Dred Scott*, as "beings of an inferior order, and altogether unfit to associate with the white race either in social or political relations, and so far inferior that they had no rights which the white man was bound to respect."[1]

Both the arguments articulated by Chief Justice Taney in *Dred Scott* that effectively extended slavery to the free states and the dissenting opinions by Justices John McLean and Benjamin Robbins Curtis echoed those voiced in the Missouri debate of 1820.[2] The case was brought by Dred Scott, a Black man born enslaved in Virginia, who moved in 1830 with his owners to Missouri, a slave state newly admitted to the Union, and then, in 1836, from Missouri to Illinois, a free state, whose constitution explicitly stated that "neither slavery nor involuntary servitude shall hereafter be introduced into this State otherwise than for the punishment of crimes whereof the party shall have been duly convicted," and "any violation of this article shall effect the emancipation of such person from his obligation to service."[3] From Illinois, they were moved to the Wisconsin Territory that was, according to the Missouri Compromise, a free territory, before returning to Missouri.

While the court considered issues of jurisdiction, it also addressed questions of legality of slavery, citizenship, and the limits of congressional powers. Dred Scott claimed that he had gained freedom upon arrival in Illinois and through his subsequent residence in the Wisconsin Territory, and thereby upon the return to Missouri he was no longer enslaved but in fact was a citizen of the state, and thus able to sue in federal court. Justice Taney focused on the question of citizenship, turning to what might today be called an originalist argument, "to determine who were citizens of the several States when the Constitution was adopted" based on "opinion of the court, the legislation and histories of the times, and the language used in the Declaration of Independence," as well as "the state of public opinion in relation to that unfortunate race which prevailed in the civilized and enlightened portions of the world at the time of the Declaration of Independence and when the Constitution of the United States was framed and adopted."[4]

Taney phrased the legal question under consideration as "can a negro whose ancestors were imported into this country and sold as slaves become a member of the political community formed and brought into existence by the Constitution of the United States, and as such become entitled to all the rights, and privileges, and immunities, guaranteed by that instrument to the citizen, one of which rights is the privilege of suing in a court of the United States in the cases specified in the Constitution?"[5] In his argument the justice then returned to the question voiced in the Missouri debate about the meaning of "We, the people."[6] Taney argued that the words "people of the United States" and "citizens" were synonymous, pertaining to "the political body" and included those who held "the power and conduct the Government through their representatives." Black people, he claimed, were not "included, and were not intended to be included, under the word 'citizens' in the Constitution, and can therefore claim none of the rights and privileges which that instrument provides for and secures to citizens of the United States." On the contrary, he added, asserting white supremacy, "they were at that time considered as a subordinate, and inferior class of beings who had been subjugated by the dominant race, and, whether emancipated or not, yet remained subject to their authority, and had no rights or privileges but such as those who held the power and the Government might choose to grant them." Matter-of-factly, Taney declared that "this opinion was at that time fixed and universal in the civilized portion of the white race"; it was "an axiom in morals as well as in politics which no one thought of disputing or supposed to be open to dispute." In fact, "men in every grade and position in society daily and habitually acted upon it in their private pursuits, as well as in matters of public concern, without doubting for a moment the correctness of this opinion."[7] And "in no nation was this opinion more firmly fixed or more uniformly acted upon than by the English Government and English people." The English, Taney recounted, "not only seized" Black people in Africa and "sold them or held them in slavery for their own use, but they took them as ordinary articles of merchandise to every country where they could make a profit on them." In the British colonies, everywhere, including in "the thirteen colonies which united in the Declaration of Independence and afterwards formed the Constitution of the United States," enslaved Africans were "an article of property, and held, and bought and sold as such." Taney cited a number of colonial laws demonstrating "the degraded condition of this unhappy race" in order to show "that a perpetual and impassable barrier was intended to be erected between the white race and the one which they had reduced to slavery, and governed as subjects with absolute and despotic power, and which they then looked upon as so far below them in the scale of created beings."[8] The justice then added that "no distinction in this respect was made between the free negro or mulatto and the slave, but this stigma of the deepest degradation was fixed upon the whole race." For Taney, like for Virginia's Philip Barbour and Alexander Smyth and other supporters of the admission of Missouri, to consider Black people, even if free, as part of "We, the people," was inconceivable.

Taney's language stressing the "perpetual and impassable barrier" and "the stigma of the deepest degradation," marking Black people as the standing at the lowest levels "in the scale of created beings" reflects the depth of racism, indebted to the Enlightenment era taxonomies of race, that has been so difficult to overcome. Taney was unapologetic about his views, they were for him quite ordinary, emerging from the cultural and political history that Europeans brought to the colonies; they were at the foundation of the United States. For him these were "historical facts" reflecting "fixed opinions concerning that race."[9]

The exclusion of Black people from the polity was central to Taney's legal argument and to his ability to reconcile the fundamental paragraph in the Declaration of Independence—"We hold these truths to be self-evident: that all men are created equal; that they are endowed by their Creator with certain unalienable rights; that among them is life, liberty, and the pursuit of happiness"—with the existing reality of slavery and discrimination against free people of color. According to Taney:

> The general words above quoted would seem to embrace the whole human family. . . . But it is too clear for dispute that the enslaved African race were not intended to be included, and formed no part of the people who framed and adopted this declaration, for if the language, as understood in that day, would embrace them, the conduct of the distinguished men who framed the Declaration of Independence would have been utterly and flagrantly inconsistent with the principles they asserted, and instead of the sympathy of mankind to which they so confidently appealed, they would have deserved and received universal rebuke and reprobation.[10]

There was no doubt, Taney argued, that the framers were "great men—high in literary acquirements, high in their sense of honor, and incapable of asserting principles," who "perfectly understood the meaning of the language they used, and how it would be understood by others," who "knew that it would not in any part of the civilized world be supposed to embrace the negro race, which, by common consent, had been excluded from civilized Governments and the family of nations, and doomed to slavery." Taney's words were a reflection, in a legal opinion of the US Supreme Court, of the sense of racial superiority and dominance that developed over the centuries in European and Euro-American white identity, visually depicted in printed books showing Africans as uncivilized and subservient, with Europa as the Queen of Civilization and Liberty as a white woman. Here, in Taney's view, European colonists and white citizens of the United States were an extension of that Europa on the American continent, establishing a legal system that reflected that social and racial hierarchy, seeing "the unhappy black race" as nothing but "property."

Taney echoed an argument articulated in 1820 by Representatives Barbour and Smyth that the Constitution was formed only by those who were members of "political communities in the several States," its great objective "to secure the blessings of liberty to themselves and their posterity."[11] Black population, according to Taney, were not members of that political community—they were "articles of merchandise," even those who "had been emancipated at that time," though very few in numbers, "were identified in the public mind with the race to which they belonged, and regarded as a part of the slave population rather than the free." In Taney's mind, the mark of slavery was not lifted with manumission and legal acquisition of freedom—it was indelible. Blackness was, in his mind, an eternal sign of servitude and inferiority.

Taney was not alone in this view—after all, the case was decided by the majority of justices, with only two dissents. His opinion was an unapologetic expression of white supremacy. If others argued, both in the Missouri debate and in the dissent in *Dred Scott*, that free Black people had been, in fact, considered citizens in several states at the time of the formation of the United States, Taney maintained that it was "impossible to believe" that rights and privileges guaranteed in the US Constitution "were intended to be extended to them."[12] Doubling down on the exclusion of Black Americans from the polity, the chief justice added, "As relates to these States, it is too plain for argument that they have never been regarded as a part of the people or citizens of the State, nor supposed to possess any political rights which the dominant race might not withhold or grant at their pleasure." Thus, even the rights that some Black Americans may have possessed in some states were granted at the "pleasure" of "the dominant race" and could equally be withheld at their will. These rights, Taney argued, were not inherent, they could be taken away just as easily as they were granted. The power lay with the white population. This was a textbook example of an expression of white supremacy—but this interpretation was eerily reminiscent of the precarity of the status of Jews in premodern Europe, where they held rights and privileges, which in turn could be withheld at the whim of the ruler in power.

For Taney, examples of state-imposed disabilities on the free Black population in different states—intermarriage, membership in militias, travel passes—were "mark[s] of inferiority and degradation."[13] For the chief justice, "the legislation of the States therefore shows in a manner not to be mistaken the inferior and subject condition of that race at the time the Constitution was adopted and long afterwards, throughout the thirteen States by which that instrument was framed."[14] It was impossible, he claimed, to think that these states "regarded at that time as fellow citizens and members of the sovereignty, a class of beings whom they had thus stigmatized, whom . . . they had deemed it just and necessary thus to stigmatize, and upon whom they had impressed such deep and enduring marks of inferiority and degradation." It was thus not plausible that when the representatives of these states "met in convention to form the Constitution, they looked upon them as a portion of their constituents or designed to include them in the provisions so carefully inserted for the security and protection of the liberties and rights of their citizens."

The existence of such disabilities imposed by European Americans on Black Americans was evidence of intentionally imposed Black inequality. Taney's opinion against Dred Scott was meant to affirm this "original" intent. If Black people had been considered citizens, Taney maintained, they would have had "the right to enter every other State whenever they pleased, singly or in companies, without pass or passport, and without obstruction, to sojourn there as long as they pleased, to go where they pleased at every hour of the day or night without molestation, unless they committed some violation of law for which a white man would be punished; and it would give them the full liberty of speech in public and in private upon all subjects upon which its own citizens might speak; to hold public meetings upon political affairs, and to keep and carry arms wherever they went." Doing so, given the existence of both free and enslaved populations, would have "inevitably" led to "discontent and insubordination among them, and endangering the peace and safety of the State. . . . It is impossible . . . to believe that the great men of the slaveholding States, who took so large a share in framing the Constitution of the United States and exercised so much influence in procuring its adoption, could have been so forgetful or regardless of their own safety and the safety of those who trusted and confided in them." Taney here openly acknowledged, as modern scholars have repeatedly shown, the centrality of slavery and racial thinking at the time of the founding of the republic.

Justice Taney was emphatic in answering, in the negative, the question "whether a person of the African race can be a citizen of the United States, and become thereby entitled to a special privilege by virtue of his title to that character."[15] He insisted that "no one, we presume, supposes that any change in public opinion or feeling, in relation to this unfortunate race, in the civilized nations of Europe or in this country, should induce the court to give to the words of the Constitution a more liberal construction in their favor than they were intended to bear when the instrument was framed and adopted." Doing otherwise "would be altogether inadmissible in any tribunal called on to interpret it," but a potential path for change lay in a constitutional amendment. For now, while the Constitution "remains unaltered," it had to be interpreted "as it was understood at the time of its adoption." The baggage of cultural attitudes toward race, shaped by European law, literature, and philosophy, thus, weighted heavily on European Americans' ability to include Black people in their conception of community, civil or political. For them America was white. The presence of Black people disrupted this white republic.

Taney was not incorrect in his reading of racial attitudes in the eighteenth century among Europeans and European colonists in America,

and, as such, the recounting of these attitudes in his ruling, even as a justification to deny Dred Scott and his family freedom, is not where most
of the damage of this case lies. Rather, it is in his reification of the view
that the position of Black people as inferior, stigmatized by their color
and status, was "perpetual" and "enduring," as intended by the framers
of the constitution and early laws of the new country. Based on the language of the laws passed at the time, most clearly the Naturalization Act
of 1790, Taney was able to argue, "citizenship at that time was perfectly
understood to be confined to the white race; and that they alone constituted the sovereignty in the Government."[16] Taney, however, granted that
Congress could change that, and they did after the Civil War by passing
the Fourteenth Amendment.

The majority of the Supreme Court concurred with Chief Justice Roger
Taney, with some justices issuing their own concurring opinions, focusing on different points of interest, such as property rights, the meaning
of the word "citizen," or the lack of "positive laws" affirming Black citizenship. Drawing on examples from European law that supported Taney's
interpretation of history and language, Justice John Archibald Campbell
asserted that "the American Revolution was not a social revolution. It did
not alter the domestic condition or capacity of persons within the colonies,
nor was it designed to disturb the domestic relations existing among them.
It was a political revolution, by which thirteen dependent colonies became
thirteen independent States."[17] The point Campbell made was implicitly
contrasting the American Revolution with the French, which resulted in
major social transformations, including the reluctant abolition of slavery
and the invention of inclusive citizenship. There were, however, two dissents. One by Justice John McLean, and another by Justice Benjamin
Robbins Curtis. They would push back against some of the points raised
by the majority, deploying similar historical methods as did Chief Justice
Taney but to argue the opposite side.

In his dissent Justice John McLean focused on two key points—the
citizen status of freemen and territorial limits of slavery laws. McLean
argued that freemen were in fact citizens and chastised his colleagues for
claiming "that a colored citizen would not be an agreeable member of society."[18] This was, he wrote, "more a matter of taste than of law." After all,
McLean noted, "several of the States have admitted persons of color to
the right of suffrage, and, in this view, have recognised them as citizens,
and this has been done in the slave as well as the free States." He contended that slavery laws were local laws, not in effect in across the whole
of United States and its territories. He cited, as if to refute his colleagues'

use of European sources, European laws, noting that "there is no nation in Europe which considers itself bound to return to his master a fugitive slave under the civil law or the law of nations. On the contrary, the slave is held to be free where there is no treaty obligation, or compact in some other form, to return him to his master." McLean offered a different understanding of the legal context at the time of the framing of the Constitution, demonstrating territorial limitations of slavery and state rights to prohibit slavery entirely. The justice maintained that "a master" who had taken "his slave" to a territory or state that prohibited slavery effectively emancipated the enslaved person.[19] This was exactly what happened to Dred Scott. Other court cases, which had addressed a similar question, McLean asserted, "settled the question."

The second dissenting justice, Benjamin Robbins Curtis, returned to the question of citizenship: "whether any person of African descent, whose ancestors were sold as slaves in the United States, can be a citizen of the United States."[20] The question was pertinent to the issue of federal court jurisdiction over the case. "If any such person can be a citizen," Curtis stated, "this plaintiff has the right to the judgment of the court." There was no reason to deny Dred Scott such a right, "for no cause is shown by the plea . . . except his descent and the slavery of his ancestors."[21] Justice Curtis rejected Chief Justice Taney's argument that the facts "that he is of African descent, and that his parents were once slaves, are necessarily inconsistent with his own citizenship in the State of Missouri within the meaning of the Constitution and laws of the United States." If Taney claimed that there were no Black citizens at the time of the adoption of the Constitution, Curtis argued otherwise. There could "be no doubt," Curtis wrote, that "at the time of the ratification of the Articles of Confederation, all free native-born inhabitants of the States of New Hampshire, Massachusetts, New York, New Jersey, and North Carolina, though descended from African slaves, were not only citizens of those States, but such of them as had the other necessary qualifications possessed the franchise of electors, on equal terms with other citizens."[22] Curtis then proceeded to cite court cases from North Carolina, a slave state with a sizable free Black population, to demonstrate this point. In 1838, for example, the Supreme Court of North Carolina declared in a lengthy, but worth quoting in full, historical passage that:

> according to the laws of this State, all human beings within it, who are not slaves, fall within one of two classes. Whatever distinctions may have existed in the Roman laws between citizens and free inhabitants,

they are unknown to our institutions. Before our Revolution, all free persons born within the dominions of the King of Great Britain, whatever their color or complexion, were native-born British subjects—those born out of his allegiance were aliens. Slavery did not exist in England, but it did in the British colonies. Slaves were not, in legal parlance, persons, but property. The moment the incapacity, the disqualification of slavery, was removed, they became persons, and were then either British subjects or not British subjects, according as they were or were not born within the allegiance of the British King. Upon the Revolution, no other change took place in the laws of North Carolina than was consequent on the transition from a colony dependent on a European King to a free and sovereign State. Slaves remained slaves. British subjects in North Carolina became North Carolina freemen. Foreigners, until made members of the State, remained aliens. Slaves, manumitted here, became freemen, and therefore, if born within North Carolina, are citizens of North Carolina, and all free persons born within the State are born citizens of the State. The Constitution extended the elective franchise to every freeman who had arrived at the age of twenty-one and paid a public tax, and it is a matter of universal notoriety that, under it, free persons, without regard to color, claimed and exercised the franchise until it was taken from free men of color a few years since by our amended Constitution.[23]

The court in North Carolina thus admitted that change happened over time: at the time of the passage of the US Constitution Black freemen were indeed citizens, and it was only recently that they were disenfranchised and their citizenship rights restricted. In 1844, that same court reiterated that it was "beyond all controversy that persons of color, descended from African slaves, were by that Constitution made citizens of the State, and such of them as have had the necessary qualifications have held and exercised the elective franchise, as citizens, from that time to the present."[24]

Changes in the constitutions of other states demonstrated similar development, Curtis continued. In 1789, the year the US Constitution was ratified, Black free men were considered citizens but with time restrictions were added. New York, for example, in 1820, added "certain qualifications prerequisites for voting, which white persons need not possess," or New Jersey, which "by its present Constitution, restricts the right to vote to white male citizens."[25] These changes, Curtis emphasized, could "have no other effect upon the present inquiry, except to show that before they were made, no such restrictions existed; and colored in common with white persons, were not only citizens of those States, but entitled to the elective franchise on the same qualifications as white persons." Curtis refused to go into discussion of "opinions of that period respecting the African race," and declared that "it would not be just" to the framers of the Constitution, "nor true in itself, to allege that they intended to say that the Creator of all men had endowed the white race, exclusively, with the great natural rights which the Declaration of Independence asserts." Instead, he wanted to focus on "substantial facts evinced by the written Constitutions of States, and by the notorious practice under them," which "show, in a manner which no argument can obscure, that in some of the original thirteen States, free colored persons, before and at the time of the formation of the Constitution, were citizens of those States." To prove his point, the justice used the same argument as Joseph Hemphill did in the 1820 debate over Missouri, demonstrating that when South Carolina moved to amend the fourth article of the Articles of Confederation in 1778 to secure "the privileges and immunities of general citizenship" to whites only, it was voted down by eight states, with only two supporting it. Curtis thus could "find nothing in the Constitution which, proprio vigore, deprives of their citizenship any class of persons who were citizens of the United States at the time of its adoption, or who should be native-born citizens of any State after its adoption; nor any power enabling Congress to disfranchise persons born on the soil of any State, and entitled to citizenship of such State by its Constitution and laws." But this was not a voting rights case. Curtis's argument about citizenship was to support the question over jurisdiction. Indeed, he conceded that he did not consider "the enjoyment of the elective franchise essential to citizenship, there can be no doubt it is one of the chiefest attributes of citizenship under the American Constitutions; and the just and constitutional possession of this right is decisive evidence of citizenship."[26]

Justice Curtis was adamant that the phrase "We, the people" included people of color. The Constitution was not "made exclusively for the white race," but for "the people of the United States, for themselves and their posterity."[27] And because "free colored persons were then citizens of at least five States, and so in every sense part of the people of the United States, they were among those for whom and whose posterity the Constitution was ordained and established." Still, Curtis allowed for some inequities. For him, citizenship did not mean entitlement to "all the privileges and immunities of citizens in the several States." For example, "a naturalized citizen cannot be President of the United States, nor a Senator till after the lapse of nine years, nor a Representative till after the lapse of seven years, from his naturalization." Nonetheless, once "naturalized, he is certainly a citizen of the United States." The justice cited the District of Columbia among other examples of disabilities imposed on citizens. The district's residents, though citizens, were not "eligible to the office of Senator or Representative in Congress." Moreover, not all citizens had political rights. "In all the States, numerous persons, though citizens" could not vote or hold office, "either on account of their age, or sex, or the want of the necessary legal qualifications." But they were citizens, since, Curtis stated, "the truth is, that citizenship, under the Constitution of the United States, is not dependent on the possession of any particular political or even of all civil rights." There may be differences across different states in which rights were granted to their citizens. "But," Curtis stressed, "whether native-born women, or persons under age, or under guardianship because insane or spendthrifts, be excluded from voting or holding office, or allowed to do so, I apprehend no one will deny that they are citizens of the United States." Thus, the justice concluded, if "free born native citizens of states are citizens of the United States" and if "free colored persons born within some of the States are citizens of those States, such persons are also citizens of the United States."

*Dred Scott*, as scholar Martha Jones has observed, became "a shorthand for a broader struggle over race and rights, one in which black Americans claimed to be citizens of the United States."[28] Eleven years after *Dred Scott*, in the aftermath of the Civil War fought relatedly over the question of slavery, citizenship would be extended to "all persons born or naturalized in the United States" through Section 1 of the Fourteenth Amendment. *Dred Scott* was effectively overturned, at least on the legal level. But the Fourteenth Amendment did not succeed in overturning the culture that produced *Dred Scott*. The "white republic," as Edward Blum put it, "fell" but it was "reforged" through the work of Protestant evangelical Christians from the North and the South and bolstered by both violence and laws.[29]

The passage and ratification of the Fourteenth and, later, also the Fifteenth Amendment, provoked a backlash marked by vehemence, discrimination, and elimination of any advances gained during the Reconstruction era, establishing a pattern that would dog US history ever since—with a backlash following any event signifying racial progress. The passage of the Reconstruction amendments accomplished, as Luke Harlow has shown, "what was impossible before."[30] It united white Americans and "created cultural and political solidarity with the white South." Ground for this solidarity had been prepared even before the war—evangelical Protestants, though maintaining "strident and robust denominational differences," did not differ much on the question of "slavery, race, or the nation."[31] Even those supporting the Union, after the Emancipation proclamation was issued in 1862, began to question what the Union and the war meant, seeing the war, as Harlow put it, as fought "to establish the freedom and supremacy of the black race in the South, and confer on free negroes . . . that perfect equality with ourselves, whether personal, social, civil, or political."[32] Those who supported these policies, the opponents argued, were acting against both the Constitution and the Bible, both of which recognized slavery. For the white evangelical Christians, Emancipation and then later also the Reconstruction Amendments went against God's preordained social order.

The trauma of the war and the white racial solidarity that strengthened after the war had ended provided an opening for both reconciliation between formerly opposing forces and a backlash against Black citizenship. The racist religion of the antebellum period became "racist unity" that "paved the way for the emergence of a dominant white Democratic political bloc."[33]

But there were also postwar voices of unity who were not necessarily embracing the Southern ideology but rather were embracing more benign hope for reconciliation and forgiveness. Northern preachers, like Henry Ward Beecher, pleaded with their supporters not to "be disappointed or startled because you see in the newspapers accounts of shocking barbarities committed" on the now freed Black Americans, and asked for "patience with Southern men as they are, and patience with Southern opinions as they have been, until the great normal, industrial, and moral laws shall work such gradual changes as shall enable them to pass from the old to the new."[34] A uniting theme was Christianity, with its motifs of "forgiveness, sacrifice, and atonement," which, according to Edward Blum, "suffused a broader culture."[35] A powerful epitome of this approach was on display in an engraving by J. L. Giles, titled "Reconstruction," printed in 1867 (fig. 17). It offered an allegorical hopeful vision of "an American nation reborn after four years of bloody civil war."[36] At the center of the engraving stands a pavilion, whose domed roof, featuring a map of the *united* United States, is placed on top of a frieze depicting the three branches of the US government. The roof structure is supported by pillars representing states that remained in the Union with new pillars symbolizing the Confederate states shown in the process of re-installation. Under the dome are prominent figures "of the present age" from the North and the South, embracing and shaking hands, "congratulating each other

FIGURE 17. Allegory of reconciliation between the North and the South, "Reconstruction," engraving by J. L. Giles (c. 1867), printed by Francis Ratellier, 171 Broadway, New York, NY, The Library of Congress, LC-DIG-pga-01366 (digital file from original print), https://lccn.loc.gov/2004665356.

on the happy results of the Reconstruction and becoming United on the true basis of a Free and Independent Republic," among them the tall figure of General Robert E. Lee is shown embracing a shorter General Ulysses S. Grant.[37] On top of the domed roof sits the American eagle, carrying an American flag and shield. Above, the sky is filled with historical figures no longer alive, among them past presidents, chief justices of the US Supreme Court, including Roger B. Taney, and even non-Americans, such as Joan of Arc and Simón Bolívar. The souls are flanked by Justice and Liberty, shown as white women. The engraving sought to convey a new nation being (re)built under the Reconstruction as "One Country and One People" with equality of races, symbolized by two images: one at the bottom center an image of the future—two babies, black and white, lying in cradles under the American eagle carrying the American flag; the other, a faint representation to "The Spirits of a Black, and a White man as they leave the GRAVE. Showing the souls of both alike in the future." And while Horatio Bateman envisioned a representation of peace at the center top, in the midst of the departed souls, J. L. Giles represented "peace" with the image of Christ. The new United States was thus a Christian nation.

This was a utopian vision—the equality of races never achieved, the years following the war *not* marked by peace, justice, and liberty but by an immediate backlash to the Reconstruction and its amendments. But the image did catch the increasingly powerful national ideology built around Christianity and whiteness. Within a few years of the war's end, northern evangelical churches expressed or passed resolutions to unite with churches in the South. To achieve this unity they had to compromise the ideals and hopes of the more perfect union as represented in the post-war amendments and, so poignantly, in J. L. Giles's engraving. The advocates for reconciliation in fact promoted a "racially hierarchical society."[38] The United States was tested, but with slavery gone so was the issue of most contention for white Christian Americans. As Northern Methodist church leaders declared already in June 1865, "The great cause which led to the separation from us . . . has passed away, and we trust the day is not far distant when there shall be but one organization which shall embrace the whole Methodist family of the United States."[39] White Southerners would have none of it, especially since such a union would require the acceptance of Northern rule. To accept the re-union would be "to adopt their political creed and receive the mark of the beast."

The Presbyterian *Free Christian Commonwealth* was even more explicit in explaining the Southern evangelical resistance to reunion: "While the existence of slavery, in its civic aspects be regarded as a settled question, an issue now gone . . . the lawfulness of the relation as a question of social morality, and of Scriptural truth, has lost nothing of its importance."[40] The "dogma" of abolition was "unscriptural and fanatical"; it was "one of the most pernicious heresies of modern times."

Southern evangelical Protestants were unwilling to let go of the idea that "the system of negro slavery in the South" was "a Divine institution," which the Southern churches were "to conserve."[41] So while slavery might have been gone with the passage of the Thirteenth Amendment, commitment to it as "a divine appointment" among Southern Christians remained, even hardened with the passage of the Civil Rights Act and the Fourteenth and Fifteenth Amendments.[42] Kentucky's journal *Christian Commonwealth* called the Reconstruction amendments "New Negrophile Erastian Crusade" and found "making an inferior race predominant over a superior one" repugnant. The advancement of free Black Americans, claimed two Presbyterians, John Bailey Adger of South Carolina and George James Atkinson Coulson of Maryland, "thrust upon the hearts and consciences of a Christian nation," created "a perplexing and threatening" problem for white Southern Christians.[43] Two South Carolinian Presbyterian preachers asserted that "the elevation of the black people to a position of political and social equality with the whites" was "simply an impossibility" for "God has constituted the two races as to make their equality *forever* impossible." With slavery effectively outlawed, white Southerners and their allies became committed to fulfill what they saw as a divine design to prevent Black Americans to achieve equality and enjoy fully the rights of citizenship. It was not just a civil matter; for them, it was also a matter of faith.

It was evident, both before and after the war, that freedom from bondage was not considered as tantamount to citizenship, let alone equality, legal or social.[44] The ratification of the Thirteenth Amendment in 1865 did not change that. The Civil Rights Act of 1866 and the Fourteenth Amendment needed to be passed, resolving—at least in legal though not in cultural terms—the debate that had marked the deliberations over Missouri in 1820 and the *Dred Scott* case and affirming that Black Americans were indeed citizens. But even here, the question of what citizenship meant in the United States was not fully resolved—citizenship did not guarantee political and civil rights for everyone, and for Black Americans, whiteness still dominated the legal and cultural framework. The language of the 1866 Civil Rights Act weighed the rights of "citizens of every race and color," a phrase that should have included everyone, against the rights "enjoyed by white citizens."[45] This wording amplified a privileged status of white citizens and whiteness as a standard by which rights and privileges of others were measured. As such, the Act with its framing perpetuated a mark of inequality of non-white citizens. Whiteness was, and remained, "the normative model" in law and culture.[46]

But Black freedmen hoped for true equality, "the same rights, privileges, and immunities as are enjoyed by white men . . . nothing more" and "nothing less."[47] They demanded of white people, as did the delegates to the State Colored Convention in Alabama in 1867, the year Giles published his engraving, "to surrender unreasonable and unreasoning prejudice." With the Civil War over, and the Reconstruction on the way, they argued, "the law no longer knows white nor black but simply men." The Alabama delegates wanted to be able "to ride in public conveyances, hold office, sit on juries, and do everything else which we have in the past been prevented from doing solely on the ground of color." They were not demanding anything extraordinary. Some states already granted these civil rights to Black Americans, but political rights and electoral franchise as rights guaranteed by the Constitution were only accorded in the Fifteenth Amendment, ratified in 1870.[48]

With the passage of the Fifteenth Amendment, Black Americans immediately began to register to vote and to participate in the political process both as voters and as candidates running for office. Just in Alabama, as the delegates to the State Colored Convention observed in 1867, "one-half of the voters [were] black men" and they expected to exercise that power.[49] During the Reconstruction, some "two thousand black men served in office at every level of government, including two US senators and twenty congressmen."[50] In 1895, Thomas E. Miller, a Black congressman from South Carolina summed up, in his now-iconic speech, Black political success during the Reconstruction: "We were eight years in power. We had built schoolhouses, established charitable institutions, built and maintained the penitentiary system, provided for the education of the deaf and dumb, rebuilt the jails and courthouses, rebuilt bridges and reestablished ferries. In short, we had reconstructed the state and placed it upon the road to prosperity."[51]

But the white population was determined to protect racial hierarchy and inequality. Black Americans' participation in the political process came to be seen as "Negro rule" by whites, Southerners and Northerners alike, and became a boogeyman to scare the white population and turn them against acceptance of Black Americans as equal—a legacy still plaguing the American political and social landscape.[52] Already in 1874, Thomas Nast published a front-page cartoon in *Harper's Weekly*. Depicted in it were caricatures of plump Black politicians screaming at each other, whites exhausted in the background, and a distraught Columbia, standing in front of a sign "Let us have peace," admonishes them. "You are aping the lowest Whites. If you disgrace your race in this way you better take back seats."[53] Though Nast depicted bad "colored rule," as W. E. B. Du Bois noted, commenting on Thomas E. Miller's speech, what white Southerners "feared more than bad Negro government" was "good Negro government."[54]

The backlash was ferocious. Whites organized to prevent Black men from voting, by legislation and outright violence—terrorism, massacres, and lynchings that resulted in the deaths and injuries of thousands of Black Americans. The year Giles published his utopian "Reconstruction," in Kentucky alone, a Union slave state, there were 324 attacks against Black Americans, including 20 murders.[55] There was the Colfax Massacre on Easter 1873; the Vicksburg Massacre of 1874; the Clinton, Mississippi, massacre of 1875; the Danville Riot of 1883, and many more.[56] All this was done in the name of Christ, in defense of the purported racial hierarchy ordained by God. As Blum and Harvey have put it, "The most belligerent sons of former Confederates clothed the Son of God as they did their horses—in white. He became not just a member of the Ku Klux Klan but its original founder."[57] The Klan, according to Charles Reagan Wilson, "fused Confederate and Christian symbols"; it was "a vital organization of the religion of the Lost Cause."[58] They felt summoned "to deliver the South from 'that wild orgy of corruption, graft, thievery, and lust miscalled Reconstruction'" and "to restore 'good and civil order.'" For them, "Christianity and civilization lay in the balance." That message was powerfully reiterated in the final scene of the 1915 film *The Birth of a Nation*.

In 1890, during the Constitutional Convention in Mississippi, Solomon S. Calhoon, a judge, could not be clearer about the Southerners' end goals when he said, "We came here to exclude the Negro. Nothing short of this will answer."[59] And another judge, Joseph Bledsoe Chrisman, cried out, "My God! My God! Is there to be no higher ambition for the young white men in the south than that of keeping the Negro down?" One such young politician, James K. Vardaman, was indeed explicit about the ongoing efforts to disenfranchise Black voters and maintain white supremacy. "There is no use to equivocate or lie about the matter," he said at the convention.[60] The constitutional convention "was held for no other purpose than to eliminate the nigger from politics; not the 'ignorant and vicious,' as some of the apologists would have you believe, but the nigger." Vardaman, who that year became a congressman, knew that though the language of the new constitution might have been "race neutral," the real animus behind white political efforts was in fact racism, and he was also, as his own words show, eager to expose some who may have shared the sentiments and intentions but were more polite and less explicit about them. The future congressman thus explicitly threatened that if political measures to restrict Black political engagement failed, "we will resort to something else."[61]

In the United States, the backlash against the Fifteenth Amendment and Black suffrage did not take long (and it continues till today).[62] Intimidation, violence, terror, and gradual disenfranchisement of Black voters became the hallmark of what would become known as the Jim Crow era, as captured, for example, in cartoons published in *Harper's Weekly* just before the 1876 presidential elections. In one by A. B. Frost, two white Southerners intimidate a Black voter to vote for the Democratic ticket by pointing guns to his head, as a crowd of white men looks on from behind, "You are as free as air, ain't you? Say you are or I'll blow yer black head off," read the caption.[63] In the background, two white men on horses are dragging a Black man to the polls. A week later, on October 28, 1876, *Harper's* published a cartoon by Thomas Nast, "**He** wants change too," also depicting pre-election violence (fig. 18).[64] Here, a Black man with a rifle stands next to the bodies of Black men, women, and children, and burned down buildings labeled "home," "work shop," and "school house." Behind the man are excerpts from Southern publications. "To the Negroes (at Cheraw, SC)," stated one, "we the white people are able and ready to protect all of your race who choose to vote for Democrats we make no threats; but we do claim that South Carolina belongs to her native sons. And by eternal God we intend to have it." Another, said to be from *Raleigh Sentinel*, edited by Josiah Turner, threatened violence, focusing on Black political power as undeserved and disruptive for the white supremacist social order: "Evidently, it needs to be a Democratic administration in the South to keep a negro in his place. . . . And so long as that party [Republicans] insists that the negro shall govern without respect to his natural right which inheres in intelligence and governing capacity these slaughterous outbreaks may be expected."

In 1879, the *Atlantic Monthly* expressed anxiety over "the system of universal suffrage," that threatened the power of educated "Anglo-Saxon" elites.[65] In the aftermath of the Civil War "men found themselves face to face with a pure democracy from one end of the country to the other." The recently expanded "voting population," through "almost unlimited immigration of adult foreigners, largely illiterate, of the lowest class and of other races" and the addition of "at one stroke four millions and more of ignorant negroes to our voting population in the South," the magazine argued, led to distrust of the electoral system and the government. "Thirty or forty years ago it was considered the rankest heresy to doubt that government based on universal suffrage was the wisest and best that could be devised. . . . Such is not now the case." The editors concluded that "the democratic principle . . . reached its culmination about 1850." They conceded that "direct disenfranchisement" was "out of the question," but suggested that "the reading and writing qualification, and an increased poll tax" could be considered as a solution to limit the electorate. If ignorant voters "threaten[ed] the general welfare and endanger[ed] the cherished political system of the country," they had to "be educated." But if they could not "be educated sufficiently," they had to "be limited." The editors ended ominously, "Nothing is surer than that if these limitations, when

FIGURE 18. Thomas Nast, "**He** wants a change too," *Harper's Weekly*, October 28, 1876.

they become necessary, are not made peaceably and reasonably, they will sooner or later be made by violence." These efforts to disenfranchise Black voters through law and violence became a long-term project that was, according to historian Alexander Keyssar, "a slow Thermidor, a piecemeal rolling back of gains achieved in earlier decades."[66]

"Keeping the negro in his place" by undermining both the Reconstruction era constitutional amendments and the post-Civil War Civil Rights Act became, as Thomas Nast's cartoon illustrated, a widespread effort in both the South and in the North, though perhaps with different intensity. Despite the law, discrimination against and refusal of service to Black (as well as Jewish) Americans became common not only in the South but also in the North. According to Edward J. Blum, white Protestants in the North were on the forefront of "reforging the white republic," through promotion of reconciliation with the Southerners. Indeed, even former abolitionists, like Harriet Beecher Stowe, became "apostles of forgiveness" and "advocate[s] of white reconciliation and racially hierarchical society."[67] In the process, through the use of the language of Christianity and brotherhood, they contributed to the forging of an idea of Americanness that was both white and Protestant—a white Christian republic that was also uncomfortable with both Black and Jewish Americans. But Black and Jewish Americans would continuously push back demanding the fulfillment of the promise of equality—Jews from the perspective of freedom of religion, struggling "for a religion-blind and secular state," Black Americans demanding equality regardless of race.[68]

In 1883 the Supreme Court addressed the legal questions of such racial inequity in the *Civil Rights Cases*, encompassing five cases of discrimination against Black Americans by private businesses that included "the denial of equal accommodations in inns, public conveyances, and places of public amusement."[69] The *Civil Rights Cases* addressed situations that appeared to violate the Enforcement Act, the Thirteenth and Fourteenth Amendments, and the Civil Rights Act of 1875, with the last one promising to "recognize the equality of all men before the law, and hold that it is the duty of government in its dealings with the people to mete out equal and exact justice to all, of whatever nativity, race, color, or persuasion, religious or political."[70] The 1875 law sought to assure "that all persons within the jurisdiction of the United States shall be entitled to the full and equal enjoyment of the accommodations, advantages, facilities, and privileges of inns, public conveyances on land or water, theaters, and other places of public amusement; subject only to the conditions and limitations established by law, and applicable alike to citizens of every race and color, regardless of any previous condition of servitude." Violators and those who aid them were to be punished by "the sum of five hundred dollars to the person aggrieved" and were to be "deemed guilty of a misdemeanor, and, upon conviction thereof, shall be fined not less than five hundred nor more than one thousand dollars, or shall be imprisoned not less than thirty days nor more than one year."

In the *Civil Rights Cases*, Justice Joseph P. Bradley delivered the court's majority opinion, ruling Sections 1 and 2 of the Civil Rights Act of 1875 unconstitutional, and thereby validating discrimination by private entities.[71] By arguing that the law on which the lawsuits were based was unconstitutional, the court denied standing to the prosecution of the cases. "The essence of the law," the court argued, "is not to declare broadly that all persons shall be entitled to the full and equal enjoyment of the accommodations, advantages, facilities, and privileges of inns, public conveyances, and theatres, but that such enjoyment shall not be subject to any conditions applicable only to citizens of a particular race or color, or who had been in a previous condition of servitude." Thus, the court argued, the law was not meant to guarantee equal access to all facilities, but rather "the purpose of the law [was] to declare that, in the enjoyment of the accommodations and privileges of inns, public conveyances, theatres, and other places of public amusement, no distinction shall be made between citizens of different race or color or between those who have, and those who have not, been slaves."[72]

The majority opinion was grounded in a very narrow interpretation of the Thirteenth and Fourteenth Amendments. The Fourteenth Amendment, on which Civil Rights Act and the plaintiffs relied, was, in the majority opinion, only applicable to the states, not to private individuals.[73] The justices argued that "it is State action of a particular character that is prohibited. Individual invasion of individual rights is not the subject matter of the amendment."[74] Justice Bradley interpreted also the Enforcement Act and the Civil Rights Act quite narrowly, saying that these measures were "clearly corrective" and "intended to counteract and furnish redress against State laws and proceedings, and customs having the force of law, which sanction the wrongful acts specified."[75] Bradley argued that "civil rights, such as are guaranteed by the Constitution against State aggression, cannot be impaired by the wrongful acts of individuals, unsupported by State authority in the shape of laws, customs, or judicial or executive proceedings."[76] Without state authority, "the wrongful act of an individual" was "simply a private wrong, or a crime of that individual; an invasion of the rights of the injured party, it is true, whether they affect his person, his property, or his reputation; but if not sanctioned in some way by the State, or not done under State authority, his rights remain in full force, and may presumably be vindicated by resort to the laws of the State for redress." Individual discrimination was not illegal; violation of only a limited number of right was prohibited to individuals:

> An individual cannot deprive a man of his right to vote, to hold property, to buy and sell, to sue in the courts, or to be a witness or a juror; he may, by force or fraud, interfere with the enjoyment of the right in a particular case; he may commit an assault against the person, or commit murder, or use ruffian violence at the polls, or slander the good name of a fellow citizen; but, unless protected in these wrongful acts by some shield of State law or State authority, he cannot destroy or injure the right; he will only render himself amenable to satisfaction or punishment, and amenable therefor to the laws of the State where the wrongful acts are committed.[77]

This was a narrow list of rights the justices deemed were guaranteed to citizens. And, therefore, the majority claimed, in all such cases, "the Constitution seeks to protect the rights of the citizen against discriminative and unjust laws of the State by prohibiting such laws," but not against "individual offences." According to the court, the Civil Rights Act was unconstitutional because the Fourteenth Amendment referred to the states and in declaring "that all persons shall be entitled to equal accommodations and privileges of inns, public conveyances, and places of public amusement, and imposes a penalty upon any individual who shall deny to any citizen such equal accommodations and privileges," the law under consideration made no "reference to adverse State legislation on the subject." With the Civil Rights Act deemed unconstitutional by the court, the plaintiffs had no legal basis to sue for discrimination.

But the plaintiffs also argued that discrimination they had experienced violated the Thirteenth Amendment, which had abolished slavery and involuntary servitude, because discriminatory treatment marked them with "badges of servitude." Here, too, the court narrowly interpreted the Thirteenth Amendment, claiming that this amendment was "self-executing," needing no additional legislation, in that "by its own unaided force and effect, it abolished slavery and established universal freedom."[78] And while the Congress could enact legislation to obliterate slavery and erase its "badges," the court asked whether "the denial to any person of admission to the accommodations and privileges of an inn, a public conveyance, or a theatre does subject that person to any form of servitude, or tend to fasten upon him any badge of slavery." There was no "similarity," the majority suggested, between servitude and "a denial by the owner of an inn, a public conveyance, or a theatre of its accommodations and privileges to an individual, even though the denial be founded on the race or color of that individual." Justice Bradley doubted that "any slavery or servitude, or badge of either" arose "from such an act of denial."

Bradley then proceeded to another narrow interpretation, this time of the meaning of slavery and citizenship. "The long existence of African slavery in this country," he wrote, "gave us very distinct notions of what it was and what were its necessary incidents. Compulsory service of the slave for the benefit of the master, restraint of his movements except by the master's will, disability to hold property, to make contracts, to have a standing in court, to be a witness against a white person, and such like burdens and incapacities were the inseparable incidents of the institution."[79] The Thirteenth and Fourteenth Amendments "wipe[d] out these burdens and disabilities" and secured "the fundamental rights" of citizenship, which included "the same right to make and enforce contracts, to sue, be parties, give evidence, and to inherit, purchase, lease, sell and convey property as is enjoyed by white citizens." But the amendments were not meant to address "the social rights of men and races in the community, but only to declare and vindicate those fundamental rights which appertain to the essence of citizenship, and the enjoyment or deprivation of which constitutes the essential distinction between freedom and slavery." The majority thus insistently concluded that "such an act of refusal has nothing to do with slavery or involuntary servitude, and that, if it is violative of any right of the party, his redress is to be sought under the laws of the State, or, if those laws are adverse to his rights and do not protect him, his remedy will be found in the corrective legislation which Congress has adopted, or may adopt, for counteracting the effect of State laws or State action prohibited by the Fourteenth Amendment." Justice Bradley added, trivializing discrimination and the impact of slavery on social relations, "it would be running the slavery argument into the ground to make it apply to every act of discrimination which a person may see fit to make as to the guests he will entertain, or as to the people he will take into his coach or cab or car, or admit to his concert or theatre, or deal with in other matters of business or intercourse."

Blind to—or unwilling to see—the legacy of slavery in the United States and the significance of racial discrimination, the court seems to have wanted to see the abolition of slavery and the granting of citizenship to Black Americans through the Thirteenth and Fourteenth Amendments as something final, said, and done, not to be dealt with again. "When a man has emerged from slavery," Bradley wrote for the court, "and, by the aid of beneficent legislation, has shaken off the inseparable concomitants of that state, there must be some stage in the progress of his elevation when he takes the rank of a mere citizen and ceases to be the special favorite of the laws, and when his rights as a citizen or a man are to be protected in the ordinary modes by which other men's rights are protected."[80] The fact that the justices saw protection from discrimination as making Black Americans "the special favorite of the laws" and that such law was outside "the ordinary modes by which other men's rights are protected" signaled that the court saw this type of legislation illegitimate and the mere pursuit of equality for Black Americans as "special treatment," in violation of equality itself. To leave no doubt, the majority concluded, that "mere discriminations on account of race or color were not regarded as badges of slavery," and thus, legislation curing discrimination was unconstitutional since such discrimination did not violate the Thirteenth and Fourteenth Amendments. (Two years before the *Civil Rights Cases*, in *Bradwell v. State* [83 U.S. 130, 1873], Justice Bradley concurred with the majority opinion ruling that refusal "to grant to a woman a license to practice law" did not violate any "provision of the federal Constitution." The court argued that "God designed the sexes to occupy different spheres of action, and that it belonged to men to make, apply, and execute the laws, was regarded as an almost axiomatic truth.")[81]

Justice John Marshall Harlan issued a lone dissenting opinion, objecting to the majority's ruling as "too narrow and artificial" and focusing on protecting the powers of the Congress to issue corrective legislation. He also probed the deeper and more pernicious legacy of slavery.[82] The Congress, Harlan argued, was "not restricted to legislation for the execution of its expressly granted powers, but, for the protection of rights guaranteed by the Constitution."[83] He then turned to case law to explore the meaning behind the two key amendments on which the *Civil Rights Cases* rested and argued for a much broader interpretation. "The Thirteenth Amendment," Harlan contended, "did something more than to prohibit slavery as an institution resting upon distinctions of race and upheld by positive law. . . . [It] established and decreed universal civil freedom throughout the United States."[84] But, Harlan asked,

> Did the freedom thus established involve nothing more than exemption from actual slavery? Was nothing more intended than to forbid one man from owning another as property? Was it the purpose of the nation

simply to destroy the institution, and then remit the race, theretofore
held in bondage, to the several States for such protection, in their civil
rights, necessarily growing out of freedom, as those States, in their discre-
tion, might choose to provide? Were the States against whose protest
the institution was destroyed to be left free, so far as national inter-
ference was concerned, to make or allow discriminations against that
race, as such, in the enjoyment of those fundamental rights which, by
universal concession, inhere in a state of freedom?[85]

It was, Harlan implied, absurd to think that the states that had enslaved
these people could be relied on to protect their rights as citizens. That was
why the Congress stepped in and issued the Civil Rights Act—to address
"burdens and disabilities which constitute badges of slavery."[86] And so,
the Thirteenth Amendment was intended not just to eradicate the institution of slavery but also "its badges and incidents." Slavery, after all, "rested
wholly upon the inferiority, as a race, of those held in bondage, their freedom necessarily involved immunity from, and protection against, all discrimination against them, because of their race, in respect of such civil
rights as belong to freemen of other races."[87] And since Congress had the
"express power to enforce that amendment by appropriate legislation," it
had the right to "enact laws to protect that people against the deprivation,
because of their race, of any civil rights granted to other freemen in the
same State, and such legislation may be of a direct and primary character,
operating upon States, their officers and agents, and also upon at least
such individuals and corporations as exercise public functions and wield
power and authority under the State."

Harlan thus sought to expand the meaning of the Thirteenth Amendment and the law, which the majority interpreted as only applicable to the
states, at least to institutions, which, though private, "exercise public functions." Case law also supported the plaintiffs' claims. Harlan highlighted
previous court rulings that prohibited innkeepers from "selecting" their
guests.[88] Any private property "affected with a public interest . . . ceases
to be *juris privati* only," and that applied to railways and theaters at issue
here.[89] The justice stressed that the granting of citizenship to Black Americans guaranteed to them "exemption from race discrimination in respect
of any civil right belonging to citizens of the white race."[90] Citizenship, he
explained, "necessarily imports at least equality of civil rights among citizens of every race in the same State" and it was "fundamental in American
citizenship that, in respect of such rights, there shall be no discrimination
by the State, or its officers, or by individuals or corporations exercising

public functions or authority, against any citizen because of his race or previous condition of servitude."

One of the main purposes of the Thirteenth and Fourteenth Amendments was, Harlan argued, citing *Ex parte Virginia*, "to raise the colored race from that condition of inferiority and servitude in which most of them had previously stood into perfect equality of civil rights with all other persons within the jurisdiction of the States." Harlan repeatedly stressed the fundamental right to "exemption from discrimination," and implored that "exemption of citizens from discrimination based on race or color, in respect of civil rights, is one of those privileges or immunities [that] can no longer be deemed an open question in this court."[91] To reiterate the role the Congress played, Harlan contended that "to secure equal rights to all persons, and, to insure to all persons the enjoyment of such rights, power was given to Congress to enforce its provisions by appropriate legislation."[92] The majority ruling sought to limit the Congress's power to do that.

Harlan then passionately turned to the question of the government's role in regulating social relations—and thus the question of bigotry and racism. The justice conceded that "government has nothing to do with social, as distinguished from technically legal, rights of individuals. . . . No government ever has brought, or ever can bring, its people into social intercourse against their wishes."[93] And if individuals choose not to engage in social relations with one another, "even upon grounds of race, no legal right of a citizen is violated by refusal of others to maintain merely social relations with him." But states, corporations, or "individuals wielding power under State authority for the public benefit or the public convenience" were not allowed to "discriminate against freemen or citizens in those rights because of their race, or because they once labored under the disabilities of slavery imposed upon them as a race." This was consistent with "the freedom established by the fundamental law or with that equality of civil rights which now belongs to every citizen." The Civil Rights Act of 1875, Harlan argued, was meant to secure and protect those "legal, not social, rights." These rights included the right of Black Americans "to use the accommodations of a public highway upon the same terms as are permitted to white citizens." These were "no more" social rights than the "right under the law to use the public streets of a city or a town, or a turnpike road, or a public market, or a post office, or his right to sit in a public building with others, of whatever race, for the purpose of hearing the political questions of the day discussed." Harlan vehemently objected to the assertion that the use by "colored citizen . . . upon the same terms as is permitted to white citizens" of the "public highways, or public inns, or places of public amusement, established under the license of the law" was "an invasion of the social rights of the white race." Harlan did not just challenge white supremacy. He also objected to creation of "white spaces" and the exclusion of Black American from them through discrimination and the infringement of the rights of citizenship.

In his dissent, Justice Harlan unmasked racism as the unspoken real reason behind both such discriminatory treatment of Black Americans and the court's ruling rejecting their claims. Harlan especially pushed back against the concluding remarks by Justice Bradley that legislation meant to prevent discrimination was treating Black citizens as "the special favorite of the laws." There was nothing special about those laws, Harlan stressed. The Civil Rights Act was "for the benefit of citizens of every race and color."[94] In fact, "what the nation through Congress sought to accomplish in reference to that race is what had already been done in every State of the Union for the white race—to secure and protect rights belonging to them as free-men and citizens, nothing more." But law and the power of Congress were not the crux of the problem; the main problem was, as Harlan saw it, "the difficulty . . . to compel a recognition of the legal right of the black race to take the rank of citizens, and to secure the enjoyment of privileges belonging, under the law, to them as a component part of the people for whose welfare and happiness government is ordained." Black Americans, according to Har-lan, were excluded by many whites from the concept of "We, the people." But for him they were unquestionably part of the idea. Harlan warned that although "today" it was "the colored race which is denied, by corporations and individuals wielding public authority, rights fundamental in their free-dom and citizenship," the court's narrow interpretation of the Constitutional amendments could potentially lead to discrimination, "at some future time," against "some other race." But if, Harlan added, closing his dissent, "the con-stitutional amendments be enforced according to the intent with which, as I conceive, they were adopted, there cannot be, in this republic, any class of human beings in practical subjection to another class with power in the latter to dole out to the former just such privileges as they may choose to grant." As Harlan understood the problem, it was true that the Reconstruc-tion Amendments were to "raise" Black Americans from their "inferior state," but legal equality meant that no one could have power to discriminate or "dole out" privileges to another. He rejected the majority's contention, which echoed the sentiment already made by Chief Justice Taney in *Dred Scott*, that rights "might or might not" be withheld or granted at the pleasure of "the dominant race." For Harlan, rights were not a matter of a whim.

Like Harlan, Black leaders understood what the court ruling in the *Civil Rights Cases* meant. John Mercer Langston, the founding dean of Howard University's law school, protested, saying, "The Supreme Court would seem desirous of remanding us back to that old passed [*sic*] condition."[95] According to Frederick Douglass, "The whole essence of the thing is a studied purpose to degrade and stamp out the liberties of a race. It is the old spirit of slavery and nothing else." They were right. The *Civil Rights Cases* would leave an imprint on American jurisprudence. In 1948, in the landmark case *Shelley v. Kraemer*, the court noted that "since the decision of this Court in the Civil Rights Cases, 109 U. S. 3 (1883), the principle has become firmly embedded in our constitutional law that the action inhibited by the first section of the Fourteenth Amendment is only such action as may fairly be said to be that of the States. That Amendment erects no shield against merely private conduct, however discriminatory or wrongful."[96]

Justice Harlan was surely aware of the prevailing sentiments in the US at the time, and in his warning he may have been alluding to another act of Congress, passed just a year before: the Chinese Exclusion Act, which prohibited the immigration of Chinese laborers on the grounds that "the coming of Chinese laborers to this country endangers the good order of certain localities" and excluded the Chinese from US citizenship by declaring that "hereafter no State court or court of the United States shall admit Chinese to citizenship."[97] The Chinese Exclusion Act, and the subsequent Supreme Court decisions upholding it, were, as Gabriel Jackson Chin has shown, motivated by racism and "had effects similar to domestic racial discrimination, by disadvantaging" and excluding, as did later *Plessy v. Ferguson* for Black Americans, another group of "nonwhite Americans."[98] But Chinese immigrants were also non-Christians, their presence, much like Jews and Black Americans, disrupted the then-widely accepted vision of what it meant to be an American.

In March 1882, in the middle of the debates about the Chinese Exclusion Act, *Harper's Weekly* published a cartoon by Thomas Nast titled "Which color is to be tabooed next?" depicting two Irish men, Fritz and Pat, discussing the new anti-Chinese law, the caption stating: "If the Yankee Congress can keep the *yellow* man out, what is to hinder them from calling us *green* and keeping us out too?"[99] Increasing xenophobia coupled with the failure of the Reconstruction strengthened and emboldened white supremacy—that the US was a white nation for people with European Christian roots was now affirmed by the Supreme Court and the Congress. (In 1892, Justice Brewer would even state in *The Church of Holy Trinity v. United States* that "a volume of unofficial declarations to the mass of organic utterances" demonstrated that this was "a Christian nation."[100]) Newspapers, magazines, pamphlets, and books in turn promoted these ideas broadly, embedding them more deeply among white Americans and European immigrants who were gradually assimilating and aspiring to dominant whiteness.[101] European immigrants were considered "white by law" and allowed to be naturalized. Asian immigrants, in contrast, were repeatedly excluded from the legal "whiteness," even if their education, language, religion, and even skin color matched the ideal of "a white Christian nation." This was the case, for example with Takao Ozawa, who was born in Japan in 1875, came to California in 1894, and twenty years later, in 1914, sought to become a naturalized citizen.[102] Ozawa was educated at the University of California at Berkeley, then moved to Hawaii. In his petition he declared that, though born in Japan, he was "a true American." He did not register himself, nor his marriage, nor his children with the Japanese diplomatic mission in Honolulu, even though "all Japanese subjects are requested to do so."[103] Instead, he reported all these matters to the American authorities. Moreover, he stated that he did not "have any connection with any Japanese churches or schools, or any Japanese organizations"; he sent his children to American schools, used English at home—his children thus could not speak Japanese at all, and attended an American church. Given that naturalization law was based on whiteness, he asserted that he was white—many Japanese were "particularly white-skinned . . . whiter than the average Italian, Spaniard or Portuguese." By any measure Takao Ozawa was "white." Even the court conceded that "he was well qualified by character and education for citizenship."[104]

Nonetheless, the court rejected Ozawa's petition. Objecting to Ozawa's assertion of whiteness, Justice Southerland, who authored the court's opinion, observed that the wording in the 1790 Naturalization Act was

> employed . . . for the sole purpose of excluding the black or African race and the Indians then inhabiting this country. It may be true that those two races were alone thought of as being excluded, but to say that they were the only ones within the intent of the statute would be to ignore the affirmative form of the legislation. The provision is not that Negroes and Indians shall be *excluded*, but it is, in effect, that only free white persons shall be *included*. The intention was to confer the privilege of citizenship upon that class of persons whom the fathers

knew as white, and to deny it to all who could not be so classified. It is not enough to say that the framers did not have in mind the brown or yellow races of Asia.[105]

The wording of the 1790 act that limited naturalization to "free white persons" was to "ascertain" first of all who was to be included and only then "as a necessary corollary that all others are to be excluded." Now, the court continued, the word "free" was no longer pertinent, it "has long since ceased to have any practical significance, and may now be disregarded." What remained of that wording was "the words 'white person.'" The court argued, to counter Ozawa's claim to whiteness based on his qualifications, that "these words import a racial, and not an individual, test" and declared that "the test afforded by the mere color of the skin of each individual is impracticable, as that differs greatly among persons of the same race, even among Anglo-Saxons, ranging by imperceptible gradations from the fair blond to the swarthy brunette, the latter being darker than many of the lighter hued persons of the brown or yellow races. Hence, to adopt the color test alone would result in a confused overlapping of races and a gradual merging of one into the other, without any practical line of separation." Thus, based on previous cases, in both federal and state courts, the justices concluded that "the words 'white person' were meant to indicate only a person of what is popularly known as the Caucasian race."[106] And since Ozawa was "clearly of a race which is not Caucasian" he was not eligible for citizenship, notwithstanding "the briefs filed on behalf of [the] appellant [which] refer in complimentary terms to the culture and enlightenment of the Japanese people." And though the court did not disagree with "this estimate" of Ozawa, that had no bearing on the decision of the court, which had "no function in the matter other than to ascertain the will of Congress and declare it." The law was the law, and only the Congress could change it. But, as Ian Haney López has noted, "Ozawa's argument undermined the basic division of humans into races."[107] By rejecting it, the court thus effectively declared that Americans can only be those of European descent—race, however construed, not skin color made individuals eligible to become Americans. The court engaged in "the gradual process of judicial inclusion and exclusion" and also legitimized anti-Japanese animosity, blessing it "with the weight of enlightened opinion confirming Japanese racial difference at law." But the court also exposed what it meant when people did not fit into the "black and white" dichotomy of race in America—such individuals, as Richard Delgado and Jean Stefancic have argued, became "marginalized, invisible, foreign, un-American."[108]

The legal cases concerning the civil rights of Black Americans and naturalization were intended to protect white Euro-American supremacy. But
while the immigration cases reaffirmed the Euro-American vision of what
it meant to be an American, the cases affirming restrictions on the citizen
rights of Black Americans were aimed at, as John Mercer Langston put it,
"remanding" Black Americans "to that old passed [sic] condition."

The fear and rejection of Black equality and full political participation,
coupled with the fervent desire to block it, is evident in an essay titled
"Shall Negro Majorities Rule?" and published in 1889 by a staunch opponent of the Reconstruction amendments, Senator John Tyler Morgan of
Alabama.[109] In that essay, Morgan lambasted political rights for Black
Americans and sought to justify their gradual disenfranchisement "by
whatever means," even if "unlawfully."[110] Morgan opposed any "elevation"
of Black people and combatted laws that, in his eyes, "demand[ed] the
humiliation of the white race, or the admission of the Negroes to a dangerous participation, as a race, in the affairs of our government."[111] Though
the two "races" were "brought together here on terms of political equality," Morgan reiterated, they were "not equal or homogeneous." In fact, to
remove "the bar to union" between whites and blacks would be "to lower
the whites to the level of the intellectual, moral, and social condition of
the Negroes. It would be to destroy the white race."[112] For Morgan, and for
other white supremacists, any gains of Black Americans were to the detri-
ment of whites—a zero-sum game.

Morgan deemed Black people as "dependent and inferior." "Negroes
have as distinctly shown their aversion to any relaxation of race ties and
exclusiveness," wrote Morgan echoing antisemitic tropes hurled at Jews
accusing them of Jewish clannishness and reluctance to comingle with
Christians.[113] The aversion, Morgan maintained, was "mutual, and, in a
general sense, fixed." The "Negro question" was both "a race question" and
a political question related to the "political power accorded to the African
race." As voters, enfranchised Blacks were "without merit or capacity" now
"indued with power to influence the destiny of the whole country through
their votes." But they were also "dangerous," the senator claimed, for they
were voting, admittedly not unlike whites, "with [their] race at every
opportunity."[114] Black electoral franchise was a mistake; it was an "experi-
ment" that had "cost the country too dearly to admit."[115] And people in the
South, Morgan maintained, could testify "as to the dangers of the ballot
in the hands of the Negro race. Twenty years of experience, beginning
with eight years of the horrors of enforced Negro rule, has demonstrated
to them that a relapse into that condition would be the worst form of

destruction." The white fear, as articulated by Morgan, of Black people as citizens and voters was evidently quite potent.

Black people would again find allies, Morgan predicted, who would join "for the purposes of plunder," as they did in 1866–1877.[116] Such combination would bring, "if it were successful, the domination of the Negro race in the invaded States. They would furnish the power, and their mercenaries would furnish the skill, through which the capture of the State governments would be accomplished. Power thus gained could not be enduring." The white race, Morgan asserted, was "unconquerable," even "if it never raised an arm in forcible resistance to such a degradation," it would fight "through the silent but omnipotent influence of public opinion" so that "all who fostered such a warfare on the honor of the race would perish." For all its doom about "Negro power," the passage asserts Black inferiority and the need for white, or mixed race, allies. In the twentieth century, Jews would come to be seen as such allies, conspiring against the white Christian society.[117] And in fact, the language Morgan deployed about Black power, danger, and domination was reminiscent of antisemitic language propagated around the same time in Europe, especially in France and Germany, where antisemites were drumming up the fear of "Jewish power." In the United States, however, the conviction about Black inferiority gave Morgan a sense that without assistance from others Black people could not hold on to power—the "white race" was "unconquerable."

But the fear of race mixing remained. The state-imposed political equality and social contacts, Morgan claimed, would result in the "infusion of blood of the Negro race into the white race" and would "Africanize our people in their social instincts and in their ideas of government."[118] But he hoped that "public opinion," which he saw as "the mightiest agency in free self-government," would "ultimately dispose of the Negro question according to the enlightened judgment and the will of the white race in the United States."[119] For him, "equality before the law" was only a phrase, "this condition [was] impossible without equality in the opinion and conscience of the white race" and that was unattainable.

A year later Senator Morgan attacked the Reconstruction era amendments in an essay titled "The Race Question in the United States." The amendments, Morgan wrote, were intended to help "the negro race to rise to social and political equality with the white race in this country."[120] He lashed out against "constant but futile efforts on the part of the negro race and their political masters to force them, by political pressure and by acts of Congress, upon the white race as equals and associates in their domestic relations," once more reasserting Black inferiority and the need for "political masters." The senator did not fear that "the highest class of white people shall consort with the lowest class of negroes." Rather, he expressed a concern that "where the conditions of wealth, education, culture, and position are equal, discrimination against the negro shall cease." This was for him unacceptable. The differences between the races were "arranged by the hand of the Creator." Most troubling for Morgan was Black people's "political power and their social aspirations," because he thought they, as "an inferior race," had little to offer. The inferiority went beyond "all the physical distinctions;" even in their "native land," he claimed, they "never made a voluntary and concerted effort to rise above the plane of slavery, they have not contributed a thought, or labor, except by compulsion to aid the progress of civilization." In a language again echoing that used by European antisemites, Morgan proclaimed that "nothing has emanated from the negroes of Africa in art, science, or enterprise that has been of the least service to mankind. Their own history, at home, demonstrates their inferiority when compared to that of other people."[121] Thus, Black people were "unprepared and disqualified" from "the full rights and powers incident to citizenship."

"The aversion between the races," Morgan claimed, was caused by the Reconstruction constitutional amendments that "forced" equality between the races, "infus[ing] its virus into the social and political affairs of the country, where it will be, forever, a rankling poison."[122] The push for equality in turn caused rivalry. As long as "the slave laws" existed holding "the negro to his daily work," making him "temperate," enforcing "subordination," repressing "crime and misdemeanor," the Black man was "a safe and harmless neighbor." There was "no cause for social or political rivalry with white people," nor was there "friction between the laboring classes in the South," for "the slave did not aspire to such an attitude." The Black people's "inferiority and dependence," Morgan remarked, inspired "in all classes of white people, that sort of Christian benevolence that compassionates, always, the poorest and least attractive of the human family." What Morgan offered was a romanticized harmony wrapped in white paternalism conditional upon Black people's remaining in their place. Indeed, Morgan claimed that this harmony was replaced with "antagonism" when "the possibility of the future social equality, or union of the races, under political pressure" arose.

The most dangerous threat to the previous social order was "the ballot in the hands of the negro race," which, the senator argued, "has been relied upon as a substitute for personal worth, industry, and good conduct, to life the inferior race to the same level plane with the superior race." The danger lay "in confiding to negro voters the representation of white families in the ballot box," and giving such power "to the negro race, no matter how they may use it, only increases race antagonism." Political power and social equality of Black people were to blame for the troubles that "afflicted the country." Black people had to be reminded about their place in society and disabused of the "aspirations" of equality. Morgan argued for legal and social structures—in education, economy, and at the ballot box—to do just that.

These were not fringe views, they were mainstream opinions—John Tyler Morgan was, after all, a senator. On his death, his colleagues praised Morgan, together with Edmund Winston Pettus, a fellow senator from Alabama, who died soon after Morgan, on the floor of the House of Representatives as a devout Christian man, defender of "Anglo-Saxon civilization," who "when the unfortunate period came in the history of America, when reconstruction, with attendant evils was forced upon the people of the South . . . showed the way to liberation from oppression, and pointed out the course by which the people of [Alabama] came again into the possession of their own, and the blessings of a white man's government and Christian civilization."[123] This was an explicit expression of white Christian supremacy, with racial hierarchy endorsed by the highest public figures in the country and, as the *Civil Rights Cases* suggested, sanctioned by courts.

In 1896, thirteen years after the *Civil Rights Cases* and seven years after Senator Morgan's treatise was published, the US Supreme Court issued a ruling in what became a landmark case *Plessy v. Fergusson*, upholding the constitutionality of segregation laws that were being passed in Southern states since the 1880s.[124] *Plessy v. Ferguson* was designed to challenge the constitutionality of a Louisiana law passed in 1890 that provided separate carriages on the railway for white and Black passengers and threatened fines or imprisonment of passengers "insisting on" occupying "a coach or compartment other than the one set aside for the race to which said passenger belongs."[125] The plaintiff, Homer Plessy, who was one-eighth African American, purchased a first class ticket and took a seat in a car for white people. He was removed and charged with a misdemeanor. The plaintiff's attorneys argued that segregation diminished the social reputation of the person of color and thus perpetuated "the essential features of slavery," thus, in addition to violating the equal protection clause in the Fourteenth Amendment, it also violated the Thirteenth Amendment, which prohibited slavery and servitude. But the US Supreme Court decided that the Louisiana law did not violate these amendments and ruled, as it had in the *Civil Rights Cases*, that segregation in private—not state—settings was legal. Justice Henry Billings Brown issued the majority opinion for the court. Only one justice, John Marshall Harlan, dissented, as he did in the *Civil Rights Cases*.

The court majority ruled that what happened to Homer Plessy was not a violation of the Thirteenth Amendment—merely implying "a legal distinction between the white and colored races—a distinction which is founded in the color of the two races and which must always exist so long as white men are distinguished from the other race by color—has no tendency to destroy the legal equality of the two races, or reestablish a state of involuntary servitude."[126] As for the Fourteenth Amendment, Brown argued that "the object of the amendment was undoubtedly to enforce the absolute equality of the two races before the law, but, in the nature of things, it could not have been intended to abolish distinctions based upon color, or to enforce social, as distinguished from political, equality, or a commingling of the two races upon terms unsatisfactory to either."[127] Legal equality did not mean social acceptance. Brown referred here to the same "social feelings" that Louis McLane from Delaware flagged decades earlier during the Missouri debate as "rooted in the heart of the people and enforced by the laws."[128] Still, Justice Brown declared that "laws permitting, and even requiring" segregation of the two races "do not necessarily imply the inferiority of either race to the other."[129] In fact, shrewdly referring to a case in Massachusetts to avoid arguments that racism was a characteristic of Southern former slaveholding states, Brown pointed to "the establishment of separate schools for white and colored children" in places where "the political rights of the colored race have been longest and most earnestly enforced." Thus, the court concluded, "the enforced separation of the races, as applied to the internal commerce of the State, neither abridges the privileges or immunities of the colored man, deprives him of his property without due process of law, nor denies him the equal protection of the laws within the meaning of the Fourteenth Amendment."[130]

But reputation was property, argued the plaintiff. In response, Brown was forced to admit that whiteness had superior value, but Plessy, as a man who was considered Black, did not suffer damages, for he could never claim the value of whiteness. The plaintiff, Brown argued, claimed "in error" that in a racially mixed community "the reputation of belonging to the dominant race, in this instance the white race, is property in the same sense that a right of action or of inheritance is property." The court was "unable to see how this statute deprives him of, or in any way affects his right to, such property." If he were "a white man and assigned to a colored coach, he may have his action for damages against the company for being deprived of his so-called property." But as "a colored man," he was "deprived of no property, since he is not lawfully entitled to the reputation of being a white man." Thus, for all his earlier claims that "laws permitting, and even requiring" segregation did not "necessarily imply the inferiority of either race to the other," Brown now admitted that the court did indeed deem the Black "race" inferior, and associating a white person with it would cause damages to the white person's reputation, and thus to his economic position.[131]

In spite of this admission, Brown doubled down on trying to refute the claim that "the enforced separation of the two races stamps the colored race with a badge of inferiority."[132] This was a "fallacy," Brown asserted, blaming "the colored race" for "choos[ing] to put that construction upon it." The assumption, the justice continued, "that social prejudices may be overcome by legislation, and that equal rights cannot be secured to the negro except by an enforced commingling of the two races" was also wrong. The meeting of "the two races" as equals could only "be the result of natural affinities, a mutual appreciation of each other's merits, and a voluntary consent of individuals." But equal rights before the law did not guarantee social equality. "Legislation," Brown concluded, "is powerless to eradicate racial instincts or to abolish distinctions based upon physical differences, and the attempt to do so can only result in accentuating the difficulties of the present situation. If the civil and political rights of both races be equal, one cannot be inferior to the other civilly or politically. If one race be inferior to the other socially, the Constitution of the United States cannot put them upon the same plane." The issue emerging from Brown's opinion was structural racism within the law versus personal bigotry. Brown defended the law—thus affirmed the racism within legal fabric—by leaning on the existence of personal prejudice for justification. If law could not eradicate "racial instincts," it should stay in place affirming them. Structural racism remained in place.

Justice John Marshall Harlan passionately dissented, exposing the disingenuousness of Brown's argument and putting his finger, as he did in the *Civil Rights Cases*, on the core racial issues behind the court majority's opinion. Harlan pointed to a broad principle that "in respect of civil rights, common to all citizens," the US Constitution did not "permit any public authority to know the race of those entitled to be protected in the enjoyment of such rights."[133] As he had argued in the *Civil Rights Cases*, here, too, Harlan saw a much more expansive meaning in the Thirteenth Amendment than the court majority, who applied it narrowly to formal slavery that was abolished by this very amendment. According to Harlan, "the Thirteenth Amendment does not permit the withholding or the deprivation of any right necessarily inhering in freedom. It not only struck down the institution of slavery as previously existing in the United States, but it prevents the imposition of any burdens or disabilities that constitute badges of slavery or servitude." Harlan understood that what lay behind the segregation laws—"badges of slavery or servitude"—was both the inability, or unwillingness, to accept the legal equality of people of color, and the rejection of the Reconstruction Amendments. Indeed, when it became clear that the Thirteenth Amendment was not adequate, Harlan continued, the Fourteenth was passed, guaranteeing citizenship and equal protection to all born or naturalized in the United States. The justice then applied what might today be deemed as "originalism" for liberal purposes to show that the Reconstruction era amendments had a specific intent to combat white resistance to Black equality. "These two amendments," Harlan wrote, "if enforced according to their true intent and meaning, will protect all the civil rights that pertain to freedom and citizenship." The Fifteenth Amendment, which guaranteed political rights, articulated the intent more explicitly: "race, color or previous condition of servitude" were not to impinge on citizen rights and equal protection of the law. These amendments, Harlan stressed, "removed the race line from our governmental systems." But if Harlan demanded that the amendments be enforced according to the spirit of the law, the other justices sought to limit their scope as much as possible to the dry letter of the law.

But even in court opinions seeking to affirm equality, the language conveyed deeply rooted and difficult to shed ideas of racial social hierarchy. Quoting from *Stauder v. West Virginia* (1880), a case that addressed the exclusion of Black Americans from juries in criminal trials, Harlan argued that these constitutional amendments "had, as this court has said, a common purpose, namely to secure 'to a race recently emancipated, a race that through many generations have been held in slavery, all the civil rights that the superior race enjoy.'" The law in the United States was to be "the same for the black as for the white," with "all persons, whether colored or white," equal before the law, and with people of color, "for whose protection the amendment was primarily designed," protected from discrimination "made against them by law because of their color."[134] Harlan specifically addressed the issue of legal discrimination rather than personal bigotry that was addressed by the majority. Although the affirmation that "all persons, whether colored or white, shall stand equal before the laws" appeared to buttress racial equality, it also effectively reinforced racial divisions and inequality. Racial inferiority was inscribed in a sentence aimed at ostensibly affirming equal rights stating that Black Americans should have the "the civil rights that the superior race enjoy."

For Harlan the argument that there could be something "separate but equal" was dishonest. "Everyone knows," Harlan wrote, "that the statute in question had its origin in the purpose not so much to exclude white persons from railroad cars occupied by blacks but as to exclude colored people from coaches occupied by or assigned to white persons."[135] The exclusion then was not equal. The core of the issue was that "the white race deems itself to be the dominant race in this country . . . in prestige, in achievements, in education, in wealth and in power."[136] But, Harlan invoked a political ideal, under the law and the Constitution, "there is in this country no superior, dominant, ruling class of citizens. There is no caste here. Our Constitution is color-blind, and neither knows nor tolerates classes among citizens. In respect of civil rights, all citizens are equal before the law. The humblest is the peer of the most powerful." And this was the principle that the court's decision undermined in reaching "the conclusion that it is competent for a State to regulate the enjoyment by citizens of their civil rights solely upon the basis of race," instead of accepting that "the law regards man as man, and takes no account of his surroundings or of his color when his civil rights as guaranteed by the supreme law of the land are involved." The ideal Harlan articulated has yet to be attained.

Justice Harlan clairvoyantly warned that *Plessy v. Ferguson* would, "in time, prove to be quite as pernicious as the decision made by this tribunal in the *Dred Scott Case*," which, in ruling that

> the descendants of Africans who were imported into this country and sold as slaves were not included nor intended to be included under the word "citizens" in the Constitution, and could not claim any of the rights and privileges which that instrument provided for and secured to citizens of the United States; that, at the time of the adoption of the Constitution, they were "considered as a subordinate and inferior class of beings, who had been subjugated by the dominant race, and, whether emancipated or not, yet remained subject to their authority, and had no rights or privileges but such as those who held the power and the government might choose to grant them."[137]

Harlan noted that although the constitutional amendments were supposed to eradicate "these principles from our institutions," as the case before the court demonstrated, in some states the intention of the amendments was not accepted and "a dominant race—a superior class of citizens" continued "to regulate the enjoyment of civil rights, common to all citizens, upon the basis of race."[138] As such, this decision, the justice stressed, was bound "to stimulate aggressions, more or less brutal and irritating" and "the belief that it is possible, by means of state enactments, to defeat the beneficent purposes which the people of the United States had in view when they adopted the recent amendments of the Constitution."

Harlan then turned to the racist perception of danger that Black Americans supposedly posed to whites. "Sixty millions of whites," Harlan wrote, "are in no danger from the presence here of eight millions of blacks. The destinies of the two races in this country are indissolubly linked together, and the interests of both require that the common government of all shall not permit the seeds of race hate to be planted under the sanction of law."[139] Legislation such as the one enacted in Louisiana only serves to "create and perpetuate a feeling of distrust between these races," because "the real meaning" behind such legislation was the premise "that colored citizens are so inferior and degraded that they cannot be allowed" to share public spaces, such as train cars, "occupied by white citizens." Harlan then exposed the hypocrisy of American jurisprudence: "We boast of the freedom enjoyed by our people above all other peoples. But it is difficult to reconcile that boast with a state of the law which, practically, puts the brand of servitude and degradation upon a large class of our fellow citizens, our equals before the law. The thin disguise of 'equal' accommodations for passengers in railroad coaches will not mislead anyone, nor atone for the wrong this day done."[140] Separate would never be equal.

The crux behind both the Louisiana law mandating segregation and the court's ruling on its constitutionality demonstrated, Justice Harlan wrote, that "the dominant race" was "disturbed at the possibility that the integrity of the white race may be corrupted, or that its supremacy will be imperiled" by social integration of Black and white citizen.[141] For Harlan, the Louisiana law "conceived in hostility to, and enacted for the purpose of humiliating, citizens of the United States of a particular race" and was "inconsistent with the personal liberty of citizens, white and black, in that State, and hostile to both the spirit and letter of the Constitution of the United States." The law was in effect devised as a recoil from the Thirteenth and Fourteenth Amendments. And, Harlan concluded,

if laws of like character should be enacted in the several States of the Union, the effect would be in the highest degree mischievous. Slavery, as an institution tolerated by law would, it is true, have disappeared from our country, but there would remain a power in the States, by sinister legislation, to interfere with the full enjoyment of the blessings of freedom to regulate civil rights, common to all citizens, upon the basis of race, and to place in a condition of legal inferiority a large body of American citizens now constituting a part of the political community called the People of the United States.[142]

Harlan must have known, even if he did not say it in his dissent, that what lay behind the newly passed laws and the court rulings was the fulfillment of the old vow of so many Southerners to do what they could to affirm the racial hierarchy they believed was divinely ordained.

Justice Harlan was right in *Plessy*—as he was in 1883 in his dissent in the *Civil Rights Cases*. The law was enacted "in hostility and for the purpose of humiliating" Black citizens. *Plessy* justified policies and social practices of discrimination that came to be known by its innocuous and "silly expression 'Jim Crow,'" but that was in fact an era of "racial terror."[143] The dissenting justice understood what we now call structural racism, "inferiority" enforced by "sinister legislation," and not simply expressed through personal prejudice and social exclusion. It was only with *Brown v. Board of Education* in 1954 that law began to align with Harlan's voice of dissent. As Gabriel Jackson Chin noted, *Brown v. Board of Education* "marked the beginning of the modem era of American constitutional law by introducing the presumption against racial discrimination."[144] And yet, both before and after the landmark case of 1954, legal discrimination and acts of horrific violence were part of Black Americans' everyday experience. Until *Brown*, the courts had unapologetically affirmed white supremacy—it was "white supremacy" in the legal sense because racism had left such a deep mark on jurisprudence in the US. And although *Brown v. Board of Education* ended the legal sanction for racial discrimination and enforcement by law of that which was "rooted in the heart of the people," as Representative McLane put it in 1820, it did not eliminate discrimination and violence against Black Americans. But it did make it more difficult and less acceptable, at least legally.

# CHAPTER EIGHT

# Backlash against Jewish Equality

THE BACKLASH AGAINST CITIZENSHIP and overall equality of Black Americans before law was almost contemporaneous with the backlash, in Europe, against the citizenship of Jews, which manifested itself in the rise of modern political and racial antisemitism.[1] It did not leave the United States and its Jews untouched, although the legal context was very different on both sides of the Atlantic. The 1870s proved pivotal. The majority of Jews lived in eastern Europe, where they did not have citizenship. But in western and central Europe, by 1870 Jews had gained it. Of those, the majority lived in what became, in 1869, Germany. German Jews' path to civic equality was marked with false starts and reversals. In reaction to Napoleon's defeat in 1815 came violence and a retraction of rights gained under the French influence. It was not until the unification of German states in 1869 that Jews became citizens, with restrictions based on religion removed and legal discrimination eliminated. By then the Jewish population in Germany had reached over half a million. Male Jews could now enter any profession and enjoy full political rights. And just as it happened in France earlier in the century, so, too, in the German lands, Jews began their climb on the social ladder, entering spaces and professions from which they had been excluded.

By the last quarter of the nineteenth century, racial attitudes had become ingrained in European Christian society—Jews were seen as unassimilable "oriental" aliens, their Europeanness denied. In 1880, for example, Heinrich von Treitschke, a German historian, claimed that "there has always been an abyss between Europeans and Semites, since the time when Tacitus complained about the *odium generis humani*," and "there will always be Jews who are nothing else but German-speaking orientals." And though von Treitschke urged Jews to "adjust to the customs and ideas of their Christian fellow-citizens," for many European intellectuals, it did not matter how acculturated or even assimilated Jews might have become—they were not accepted as part of the German nation. In 1881, philosopher Eugen Karl Dühring declared the "Jewish question" to be a "race question," which, he wrote, "would still exist, even if every Jew were to turn his back on his religion and join one of our major churches. Yes, I maintain that in that case, the struggle between us and the Jews would make itself felt as ever more urgent. . . . It is precisely the baptized Jews who infiltrate furthest, unhindered in all sectors of society and political life. It is as though they have provided themselves with an unrestricted passport, advancing their stock where members of the Jewish religion are unable to follow."[2] The same happens with unconverted Jews "as soon as all civic rights and opportunities become available." Then, they "force themselves into all aspects of social and political life just like those who have converted to Christianity." This leads to a closer contact with non-Jews. And "this takes place despite the fact that in society there is never an instance in which the members of the Jewish religion are made completely equal." But such "infusion of Jewish quality" was, Dühring claimed, "incompatible with our best impulses."

This social climb and success of Jews came to be perceived, as it was in the medieval and early modern periods, as insolence and ill-gained power; it went against centuries of repeated assertions in Christian theological teachings and premodern laws that Jews should be subjugated and inferior to Christians. This was behind Dühring's assertion that "there is never an instance in which the members of the Jewish religion are made completely equal."[3] Jews' social climb also came at a time of great upheavals. Industrialization, with the rise of urban centers and large new department stores, led to the decline of smaller towns and impacted smaller businesses and entrepreneurs. In addition, new media—the newspapers—came to dominate the way news and information was disseminated and consumed. Though Jews were not the only industrialists, bankers, entrepreneurs, or newspaper men, their very presence among these financial and intellectual elites made them visible, especially since their presence was disproportionately higher than their population size, triggering what came to be known as political antisemitism. Antisemitism became, according to Shulamit Volkov, "the cultural code" for anti-modernist backlash.[4]

In 1879, Wilhelm Marr, a failed German journalist and the author of the seminal pamphlet *The Victory of Judaism over Germandom*, created a party whose name included a neologism, "Antisemites' League." The word "antisemitism" and the concept were self-consciously invented to distinguish what Marr and others were doing from earlier anti-Jewish sentiments; both the word and the concept spread rapidly across Europe and beyond. According to historian Richard Levy, within the next fifteen years "variants of *antisemitism, antisemite,* and *antisemitic* made their way out of the German-speaking world into nearly every European language."[5] Modern antisemites eschewed premodern religious prejudice and saw themselves as reacting to new modern political reality. Wilhelm Marr even asserted "When it comes to religious persecutions, I take even the Jews under my unconditional protection."[6] Antisemitism was different. As another pamphlet, titled *Elect No Jews,* which Marr published in 1879, suggests, the issue was political rights and social success. Indeed, that same year, a German politician, Adolf Stöcker, declared that "the Jewish question" had been a "burning issue," with everyone "the orthodox and the free thinker, the conservative and the liberal" writing and speaking about it "with equal violence."[7] And none of them treated "Jewry as the apple of discord because of religious intolerance but because of social concern. . . . Social evils are visible in all the limbs of the body politic."

In *The Victory of Judaism over Germandom,* Marr raged that in the nineteenth century Jews raised to "pre-eminence" so much so that it was not they who merged with "Germandom" [*Germanenthum*] but rather it was Germandom that turned into Jewry [*Judenthum*].[8] Marr built on the earlier dichotomy of spirit and flesh, redefining it into "idealism" and "realism," with idealism attached to Christianity and "realism" to the Jews, whom he called "Oriental aliens," and their "Semitic cunning and realistic spirit of business."[9] This "business realism" then helped Jews "dominate" Germans who "earned their bread by the sweat of their brow"; "the rule of Jewish realism" came "at the expense of everything idealistic."

The indignation over Jews' reluctance to engage in agriculture harkens back to the trope of Cain who was to till the soil as part of his punishment—Jews in Christian tradition since Augustine were associated with Cain. By engaging in business, Jews began to occupy social spheres that were not intended for them, and, egregiously, according to Marr, from the eighteenth-century, they began to demand more—the so-called "freedom of religion."[10] But that this was a religious question was a "delusion," Marr argued. The quest for toleration, as exemplified by German writer and philosopher Ephraim Lessing, was "a wrong philosophical path." For Marr, the "Jewish question" was not a religious question, because "the Jewish 'confession' was nothing more than the statutes of a people that formed a state within a state" that "demanded very specific material advantages for its members." It was instead a "sociopolitical question" related to political equality.[11] "In civic life [*bürgerlichen Leben*] Jewry, in fact, had long since achieved a dominant, leading position." It was a lie perpetuated for 1800 years "that it was a question of belief and freedom of conscience, one lied again and again and so the sociopolitical invasion of Jewry into Germanic society received its legal consecration through the emancipation of Jews." It was thus not about religion, Marr explained. Jews demanded "equal political participation in the legislation and administration of the same state. . . . This and nothing else has been the core of the Jewish emancipation question after all shimmering phrases have been peeled off."[12] The result was that the "unconditionally alien Jewish domination was ushered into the Germanic state." And, today, Marr continued, "without a blow of a sword, on the contrary, politically persecuted through the centuries, Jewry has become the social-political dictator of Germany." Religion, thus, was in Marr's mind, a ruse to get political rights in an era when religious toleration was an accepted argument.

The acquisition of citizenship by Jews, in Germany and elsewhere, which was by then misleadingly called "emancipation," was a historical turning point, argued Marr and other antisemites. Equality before law gave Jews access to opportunities they would not have otherwise had and led, Marr claimed, to Jewish "dominance"; France was "Jewified," he declared, so was England, as the presence of "the Semite Disraeli" in English government demonstrated.[13] Jews achieved "the highest dignities in the state"; they were "the best citizens of this modern, Christian state," which now abided by their interests. Marr then warned his readers, "Four generations will not pass before there will be absolutely no state office, even the highest not excluded, that would not have been usurped by the Jews." But Jews, whom he called "Semitic aliens" (*semitischen Fremdlinge*), were not to blame, it was Christians, whom Marr addressed, who "elect the alien masters in your parliaments, you make them legislators and judges, you make them dictators of the state financial systems."[14] At the end, Marr bemoaned that it was the Christian Germans who were "the vanquished, the subjugated" and Jews who had the power. "Germandom" was now, he went on to say, in a state of "sociopolitical enslavement" [*sozialpolitische Knechtung*] to Jews, "hands and foot, head and heart, from the palace to the hut."[15] Marr's cry of outrage about what he saw as an upside-down social order was similar to those voiced by Christian leaders in the premodern period who bemoaned Jewish "insolence." He ended his pamphlet in a tone of "stoic resignation"—Germans now "sigh" under Jewish "rule" just as Jews had previously "sighed under our rule." The "apocalypse" had arrived, Marr wrote, Jews were "the masters, we are the servants"—the exact opposite of the dictum trumpeted over centuries by European Christians in law and literature that "the elder shall serve the younger."

Similar sentiments were heard in Italy, even before Marr's essay. Like Germany, Italy had also recently unified and granted full citizenship to Jews. In 1873, one Italian paper *La Frusta* run a piece claiming that "after ten years of sad experience, that the only race of people who could draw profit, protection and advantages from this great chaos called the Italian revolution, was the Jewish race."[16] There were Jews "in Parliament, Jews in municipal offices, Jews everywhere. . . . In the hands of the Jews [are] nationality, faith, privileges, honors, future, everything." The achievements of the Jews had became a fodder for antisemites.

Marr's and *La Frusta's* words reflect the impact of the centuries-old idiom of Jewish servitude on "mental structures" of European Christian society that could not accept Jews in any but subservient positions, and anything else—equality—was considered excessive power.[17] Power, as Orlando Patterson argued, was the antithesis of slavery. Thus, equality granted to Jews signified a release from their servitude and came to be perceived as a usurpation of power and encroachment on the rights of others. Jewish equality seemed to Marr and fellow foes of Jewish citizenship like unearned power because equality opened to Jews domains of achievement and honor previously reserved to Christians. And honor, as Patterson has argued, was "intimately related to power," only enhanced by having someone to dominate. Jewish equality, which resulted in the Jews' exit from the inferior (legal) position, felt to Marr and other antisemites as their own degradation and loss of honor of the "master" status that Christians had previously enjoyed.[18] Like white attitudes toward Black Americans' success, it was a zero-sum game. From a Christian theological perspective, Jews were not worthy of honor, they were to be "humbled" and humiliated as was the *Synagoga* standing next to the *Ecclesia*. Now, citizenship put the *Synagoga* on an equal plane with the *Ecclesia*. This transformation was to Marr tantamount to Christians being turned into "the servants." Just how much this connection of honor and power was engrained in European culture is exemplified by a comment, given in a different context—about the concept of freedom in slaveholding colonies, "Masters of slaves, they are jealous and proud of their own freedom; which is to them not merely an enjoyment, but a dignity and rank."[19]

In 1880, a year after Marr published his pamphlet, antisemites circulated a petition, "the Antisemites' Petition," pushing back against Jews' social climb and demonstrating that, modern as they were, they did not eschew the premodern framework of social order.[20] The petitioners claimed that "The Jewish hypertrophy conceals within itself the most serious dangers to our national way of life." The power dynamic was now flipped: "We see the Jew as master and the native-born Christian population in a servile position." Jews were exploiting the Christian workers. "Everywhere," they claimed, "it is only the calloused hand of the Christian that is active." Echoing, no doubt unintentionally, the words of Pope Paul IV, the petition asserted that now, with Jews up on the social ladder, "the proudest palaces of our cities belong to the Jewish masters (whose fathers or grandfathers crossed the borders of our fatherland as peddlers and hawkers)," as well as "the rural estate—this highly significant and conserving basis of our state structure—is falling into Jewish hands with ever greater frequency."

Palaces and especially rural estates were historically held in the hands of aristocracy in Europe, so a reference to those insinuated that Jews had usurped their place in society. It was, as the petition stated, "the massive penetration of the Semitic element into all positions affording power and influence," raising a question, "What future awaits our fatherland if the Semitic element is allowed to make a conquest of our native soil for another generation as it has been allowed to do in the last two decades?" They contended, drawing sharp religious and racial boundaries, that "if the inward connection between German custom and morality and the Christian outlook and tradition is to be maintained, then an alien tribe may never, ever rise to rule on German soil. This tribe, to whom our humane legislation extended the rights of hospitality and the rights of the native, stands further from us in thought and feeling than any other people in the entire Aryan world." The danger Jews posed to "the national and religious consciousness of our people" came from the press and access to "state offices," which were obliged to guard over the idealistic goods of our nation." Professions such as "teacher and judge," which were "inaccessible to Jews until very recently," were again to "be closed if the concept of authority, the feeling for legality and fatherland, are not to become confused and doubted by the nation." With Jews in these positions, "the Germanic ideals of honor, loyalty, and genuine piety" was being "displaced to make room for a cosmopolitan pseudoideal." The Christian German nationalism clashed with the ideal a liberal state, which could be pluralistic, or as the antisemites called it "cosmopolitan."

To prevent the German nation from being "consigned to economic servitude under the pressure of Jewish money power" and "national decadence one step at a time under the influence of Jewry's materialistic outlook," the antisemites demanded that "the immigration of alien Jews be at least limited, if not completely prevented"; "the Jews be excluded from all positions of authority; that their employment in the judiciary—namely as autonomous judges—receive appropriate limitation"; "that the Christian character of the primary school—even when attended by Jewish pupils—be strictly protected," with only Christian teachers allowed to teach. These demands and reasoning echoed the Christian theological and legal framework that had emerged already in late antiquity, during the Roman period. The reference to "Jewry's materialistic outlook" was a modern idiom referring the traditional idea of Jewish "carnality." The outrage about alleged "Christian servitude" and demands to remove Jews from public offices and courts resembled the discomfort with Jews' authority over Christians expressed in much of Christian legislation and polemical works.

Equality before law was seen as a propeller to power and domination, but Jews were supposed to be humble and subservient. "Pray, a little more modesty!" exclaimed Adolf Stöcker, in response to a German Reform rabbi's sermon saying that "Israel's mission and gift is to be the lighthouse on humanity's sea of thought."[21] Pointing his spotlight onto the Jewish community in Berlin, Stöcker bemoaned their size, "good circumstances and increasing power," which he ascribed to "a profitable intellectual energy" and refusal to "participate in our German Christian interests."[22] As such, they "constitute[d] a real danger." They dominated "finance, banking, and commerce"; the press was "in their hands"; and they "push[ed] into institutions of higher education beyond all proportion." Stöcker then demanded, "Pray, a little more equality!" Stöcker implied that Jews were haughty by avoiding "handicrafts and manufacturing,"; "hard and bitter," and preferring "the lucrative and easy occupations." They even "have pressed into the judiciary, which does not speak well of our justice system." He then threatened, "If modern Jewry continues as before to employ the power of the press and of capital to ruin the nation, then a catastrophe is ultimately unavoidable"; and demanded, "Israel must give up the desire to be master in Germany." Stöcker proposed measures intended to address "the social maladies that Jewry brought with it."[23] Regulation of capital, the stock market, which boomed in Germany in the second half of the nineteenth century, and the mortgage system; prominence of Jews, especially in the newly expanded Frankfurt Stock Exchange, prompted these calls. Wanting to lessen what he saw as the "disproportionate" influence of Jews, he sought "restitution of the denominational census so that the disproportion between Jewish wealth and Christian work can be established, limitation

of appointment of Jewish judges to their proportion of the total population," and "dismissal of Jewish teachers from our primary schools so as to
strengthen the Christian-German spirit." This was Stöcker's understanding of "equality."

Arrogance and lack of humility was also a motif picked up by a German
historian and nationalist, Heinrich von Treitschke, who wrote a series of
essays about Jews and their place in German society.[24] He was troubled
with the rise of Jews in Germany, which he called "a young society," in
numbers and in "social power."[25] Once "emancipation" was achieved, "they
brazenly insisted" on their "certificate" and "demanded the literal parity in
everything and everyone, and they no longer wanted to see that we Germans are a Christian people and the Jews are just a minority among us."
He was not alone in his distress; even in the "best educated circles," von
Treitschke claimed, one could hear a cry: "The Jews are our misfortune!"

What triggered von Treitschke to write these essays was a history of
Jews written by the Jewish historian Heinrich Graetz, which highlighted
Jews' accomplishments and spotlighted their persecution by Christians. Its
tone, according to von Treitschke, was "indescribably insolent and mali-
cious," making him question whether Graetz could be considered a German.[26]
No, he could not, he was "a stranger," "an Oriental who neither understands
nor will understand our people" and who "has nothing in common with us"
except for "citizenship rights" and "our language," which he used "to slander us." He saw Jewish identity and Jewishness as "racial arrogance," which
had no place in modern Germany, and asserted that Jews played no or
at best "subordinate" role in German society and culture—until recently.[27]
Jews, von Treitschke stressed, should be thankful to "the new Germany" for
their "liberation," but instead of "gratitude" there was a growing "spirit of
arrogance."[28] He closed his essay from January 1880, with a note of pessi-
mism and assertion of Christian domination: "The German Jewish question
[Judenfrage] will not be solved completely, the relationship between Jews
and Christians will not be truly friendly until our Israelite fellow-citizens are
convinced by our attitude that we are and want to remain in the Christian
people."[29] Von Treitschke's sentiment was not dissimilar from that voiced by
proponents of racial segregation in the United States, both indebted to the
concepts of servitude and inferiority.

Liberal intellectuals understood the danger of this rhetoric. Theodor
Mommsen, a German classicist at Berlin University, diagnosed the problem and pushed back against von Treitschke and his interpretation of
history.[30] Jews were Germans, just like Mommsen and von Treitschke.
"What gives us," Mommsen asked, "the right to remove our compatriots

who are of this or that group from our German ranks?" The country was entering "upon a dangerous path" in dividing the nation into "unequal" tribes, "German Occidentals and Semitic blood." He did not deny differences between Jews and Germans and seems to have accepted the racial de-Europeanization of Jews, but such differences were due to "the thousand-year oppression of the German Semites by German Christians" from which Jews developed some of the undesirable manners.[31] This was all verifiable in historical sources. Still, Jews were part of the German culture, with "a few percent of Israel . . . added to the Germanic metal."[32]

Mommsen was alarmed by von Treitschke's cry: "Jews are our misfortune," which was picked up by many, from "the pant selling youths" to "men from the ranks of the most educated."[33] Von Treitschke's pamphlets frothed up antisemitism and "every Jew of German nationality understood and had to understand" that von Treitschke regarded them "as second-class citizens." If the petition of antisemites were to be implemented, Mommsen remarked, it would claw back "emancipation" and exclude Jews "from all official (authoritative) positions." Given von Treitschke's "political and moral influence," this rhetoric was dangerous. Mommsen concluded, "It goes without saying that our nation is bound by law and honor to protect the principle of legal equality, both from open breaches of law and from administrative fraud."[34] This duty "in no way depends on the good behavior of the Jews." But Jews cannot be protected from "the feeling of strangeness and inequality with which even today the Christian German often treats the Jewish one." This, Mommsen stressed, "carries a danger for them as well as for us—the civil war of a majority against a minority, even as a possibility, is a national calamity." In the Mommsen-von Treitschke's debate, two visions of a nation clashed—one a Christian German nation, which had no place for Jews, and the other a liberal inclusive nation, in which all citizens were equal before law. The goal of antisemites was not dissimilar to those in the US who fought against the Reconstruction and the constitutional amendments that granted citizenship rights to Black Americans.

A similar clash took place in France. As Robert F. Byrnes noted in 1948, "the connection between foreign antisemitism as an intellectual influence and a model and the movement in France is unmistakably clear, because conservative and Catholic newspapers and journals in France gave wide publicity to those campaigns abroad."[35] But the process was much more drawn out in France, where Jews had been citizens in France since 1791. As Maurice Samuels has recently argued, "Jews have played an outsized role in the French political imagination" since the French Revolution, providing

"French thinkers with a forum for debating the nature of citizenship and the state, as well as the meaning of Frenchness itself."[36] Though Jews constituted only a tiny fraction of the French population—in 1889 just 0.17 percent—they rose to high social positions, becoming quite visible, especially in Paris.[37] There were Jews who were judges, ministers, generals, deputies in the French parliament, prefects, and more. Jewish intellectuals were found in French cultural institutions, and Jewish business elites participated in global and national enterprises, becoming also some of the most prominent patrons of the arts. And although already in the 1840s there were three Jewish deputies to the National Assembly, it was during the Third Republic, which emerged out of the French defeat in the Franco-Prussian war, that, according to James McAuley, Jews "enjoyed a greater level of civic engagement and public visibility . . . than at any other point in modern French history."[38]

But this high level of success and the Jews' ability to create individual and communal identities that melded "Frenchness and Jewishness," which they saw as symbiotic, also made them vulnerable to the emerging virulent antisemitism and reactionary backlash.[39] It did not matter how Jews saw themselves; a large part of the French society never accepted them as French—for them, these Jews' "Jewishness" was incompatible with Frenchness. Jews did not belong to the French national narrative as conceived by these conservatives. Rather, Jews were seen as displacing invaders. "The Jew," wrote Petrus Borel, a French writer and art critic, in 1844, "is increasingly invasive in art as he is in commerce. Time is not far off when that race, formerly banned and burned, will have so decimated and subjugated us that our cities will no longer have but a little corner in their slums reserved for the last Christians, relegated there in misery and shame, just as in the Middle Ages they had a Jewish ghetto where the last dregs of Judea rotted."[40]

In the second half of the nineteenth century, especially in light of the dramatic social, political, and economic transformations of the 1860s and 1870s, antisemitism became "a vehicle" of "grievances and discontent in French society," and modernization came to be seen as "Judaization," that is, according to Pierre-André Taguieff, "de-Christianization."[41] The presence of Jews in prominent positions made it easy for reactionaries to focus their attacks on them and blame every social and economic ill on Jews. Jews disrupted the order of what these reactionaries believed was their Christian society.

But it was the Franco-Prussian war, which ended in 1871 with a humiliating defeat of France and the collapse of the Second Empire that amplified the sentiments. France lost Alsace-Lorraine to newly unified Germany and was forced to bear German military occupation until the French government could pay a "hefty" war indemnity amounting to five billion francs.[42] This peace settlement was negotiated by Alphonse de Rothschild, a prominent Jewish financier, at the Château de Ferrières, Rothschild's property that the Germans had seized during the war. Out of this context the Third Republic emerged, giving rise to French reactionary revanchism and grievances, amplified by the new media—the newspapers, and increasingly directed at Jews.

Then, in January 1882, a Catholic bank, Union Générale, that had been founded in 1878 as a counterweight to Protestant and Jewish banks, collapsed, leading to a stock exchange crash. Some four billion francs "vanished into thin air."[43] By then an antisemitic republic of letters had already been in place. In Germany, the antisemitic league was active; in Italy, newspapers, such as the *La Civiltà Cattolica*, began publishing articles promoting anti-Jewish conspiracies. In France, anti-Jewish publications began to appear. They cross-pollinated each other, drawing attention to "Jews' domination" and the danger they supposedly presented. In France, even Émile Zola, a committed republican and would-be defender of Alfred Dreyfus, the wrongly accused of treason French Jewish officer, was not immune to antisemitic ideas.[44]

Anti-Jewish conspiracies explaining the collapse of Union Générale found in France a fertile ground. In 1880, an obscure Provençal publisher rediscovered a seventeenth-century publication of forged letters between Jews in Arles and Constantinople, which itself was based on an earlier sixteenth-century Spanish forgery of letters from Toledo, alleging Jewish conspiracy against Christians.[45] The topic was then picked up by a French priest, Emmanuel Chabauty, who amplified them in his 1882 publication *Les Juifs, Nos Maîtres!* (Jews, Our Masters!). Chabauty had been interested in anti-Jewish conspiracies. In 1880, he published, under a pseudonym, a book about Freemasons and Jews.[46] For Chabauty, the French Revolution was a Jewish-Masonic plot to achieve "universal domination," and to destroy "Christian ideas" and "the Christian social order." "Our enemies were Jews," Chabauty wrote, and to ignore it was to be complicit in "the triumph of the Jew" and the "installation of anti-Christ" as the "king of the world." In his 1882 book, Chabauty also cited articles from *La Civiltà Cattolica* as proofs that the ideas he presented were not figments of his imagination.[47] It was "obvious," Chabauty wrote, "that this is the great danger, at the present time, for the Catholic Church and Christian society in general, and probably for France in particular."[48] It was not just the "Talmudic Jews," but rather modernized Jews who were consciously chosen as to be part of the plot.[49] Adolphe Cremieux, a Jewish leader who also served as the French Minister of Justice in 1848 and then in 1870–1871, and the *Alliance israélite universelle*, which he founded, were a case in point. A year later, in 1883, Chabauty founded a short-lived periodical *L'Anti-Sémitique*, whose tag line was "Le Juif, voilà l'ennemi!" (The Jew, here is the enemy!).

Though antisemitism as a political movement took immediate root in Germany, in France the pace was slower, with antisemitic publications struggling in the first years of the 1880s. Still, they prepared receptive ground and provided "the perfect setting" for antisemitic ideas to go mainstream, which is what happened when, in 1886, Édouard Drumont, then editor in chief of *Le Monde*, published his massive two-volume book *La France juive*, "A Jewish France." After the publication, the book's initial sales fell flat—apparently only twenty-five copies were sold during the first week.[50] But on April 19, journalist Francis Magnard drew attention to the book on the front page of *Le Figaro*, a major Paris paper. Magnard saw the book as "threatening," for it contained "the germ of a Catholic socialism" and called out Drumont for being "in the grip of a particular obsession that makes him see the Jew wherever other monomaniacs see the police, the Jesuits or the Freemasons. Also, considering them as a danger for France, he quietly asks for the confiscation of all the property of the Israelites, bankers or merchants of lorgnettes."[51] Magnard suggested that given Drumont's role as the editor in chief of *Le Monde*, "considered as the quasi, official journal of the Archdiocese of Paris," he must have consulted with the archdiocese before publishing his book.

Magnard's anti-Catholic insinuations, in turn, drew a firestorm and a defense of Drumont in Catholic publications. Within days, the two thousand copies of the first printing of *La France juive* "melted away," and by the end of 1886 over one hundred thousand copies were sold, with some two hundred editions of the book published by 1914.[52] The book received an enthusiastic reception from Catholic journals and helped consolidate a conservative Catholic strand of French antisemitism. Drumont was called "a great Christian, sound scholar, and strong patriot," his book "precious."[53] This enthusiastic reception delighted him.[54]

Drumont's work was innovative in its attack on the Third Republic. As James McAuley has persuasively argued, Drumont weaponized a manufactured nostalgia against Jews, inspiring a deep hate. Drumont's mélange of political and cultural attack was particularly powerful. He was not just a journalist but also an antiquarian, an author of a book *Mon vieux Paris*,

"My Old Paris," which McAuley called "a nostalgic reverie for a lost city." The book's goal was, as Drumont put it, to defend "our traditions, our faith, our heritage of beliefs and ideas—all that constitutes the very souls of the Fatherland."[55] For him, the old Paris was devastated with innovations such as railways, department stores, and modern buildings. And Jews were to blame. Modern capitalism was a form of unearned Jewish domination.

Drumont's was "material antisemitism," manifested through material aspects of French heritage and what Drumont saw as "a Jewish invasion of France's cultural patrimony."[56] For him, as McAuley put it, "Jewish owner-ship or 'occupation' of [French] historic objects and places was ultimately an act of aggression"; "an act of Jewish violence," because by purchas-ing objects associated with French national heritage, "Jews such as the Rothschilds inserted themselves into a national narrative that they then undermined from within." France became Jewish—a point that Drumont emphasized in *La France juive*. It was, as he called it, "Republic juive," a Jewish republic, a result of "a Jewish conquest." As Jacob Katz observed decades ago, unlike the German antisemites, who wanted to realize anti-semitic goals "within the prevailing system," Drumont "denied the legiti-macy" of the existing political system and authority.[57] For him, the Third Republic was "usurpatory" and "void of legitimate or intrinsic authority" and republicanism was a Jewish plot. He was happy "to put the Jew in the spotlight, to bring him out of his vague humanitarianism and show him as he is: stoking the fire of persecution with all the strength of his lungs, with all the bellows in his newspapers."[58] Drumont, according to Mau-rice Samuels, "conceived of the nation in fundamentally antiuniversalist terms: Frenchness was determined by blood, soil, and religion, and Jews were by definition excluded from it."[59] Moreover, in Drumont's mind, the positions Jews held were illegitimately attained, their power, in turn, dele-gitimized the government. This sentiment was grounded in traditional social hierarchy built on the expectation of Jewish social inferiority—the fruit of the dictum "the elder shall serve the younger," as interpreted in Western Christendom. And so Drumont wanted to turn "La France aux Français," "France for the French," as the tag line of *Le Libre Parole*, an antisemitic paper Drumont founded in 1892 stated.

To prove the republic's illegitimacy, Drumont made a concerted effort to highlight Jews within the Third Republic's institutions and to question their loyalty to France. For him, for example, the collapse of the Catho-lic bank Union Générale was "a veritable coup d 'état for the benefit of the Jewish bank against an association of French capitalists, the ministry delivered the country, hand and foot, to German finance," taking money from "so many French" and delivering it to a Rothschild—an opinion shared by Émile Zola until his views became more nuanced in the 1890s.[60] And then, in 1892, two years *before* the pivotal Dreyfus Affair, in which a French Jewish officer was wrongly accused and convicted of treason, Drumont drummed up suspicions of disloyalty of Jewish officers in the French army.[61]

The acrimonious Dreyfus Affair, lasting twelve years, changed, according to McAuley, the "landscape of French public discourse," antisemitism now became more widely accepted.[62] If for the French Jews, Frenchness and Jewishness were not only compatible but even symbiotic—Jews were, as Pierre Birnbaum stated, *fous de la Republique*, "crazy for the Republic"— the Dreyfus Affair and antisemitism unleashed by Drumont "mobilized these categories against them," and raised "existential questions for the future of France."[63] Jews' Frenchness was now deemed "inauthentic." They could never be French, just "facsimiles of Frenchmen," according to the antisemites.[64]

France never really recovered from the identity crisis that erupted in the last three decades of the nineteenth century. In the end French republican universalism failed and Jews' Frenchness was rejected; they themselves were made "expandable."[65] While some of the elite Jews, such as the Comondos, the Reinachs, or the Rothschilds, whose story has recently been told by James McAuley, donated in the 1920s and 1930s their magnificent art collections to the Republic as a testimony of their commitment to the French state and its patrimony, in the 1940s, with the collapse of the republic and the rise of the reactionary Vichy government, set on erasing, in collaboration with the Nazi regime, the principles of republicanism and Jewish citizenship, they were deported to Auschwitz for being Jews, even when their identities were more complex, even though they felt French.[66]

In eastern Europe, and especially in the tsarist Russian empire, where there was no citizenship for anyone, antisemitism did not manifest itself in political terms, as a rejection of Jews as citizens, as it did in Germany and France, but rather in anti-Jewish violence, provoked by a nationalist anti-Jewish propaganda. In 1881–1882, a wave of over two hundred pogroms swept through the southwestern provinces of the Russian empire that had suffered from famine and economic crisis, with dozens killed and much property destroyed.[67] The pogroms spread from cities to smaller towns and villages. They revealed that the idealism of the liberal reforms of Tsar Alexander III failed. And like in the West, Jews, both those who were educated and integrated into Russian society and those who were poor and insular, were rejected by Russian and Ukrainian nationalists.

After two decades of quiet, another pogrom, in 1903 in the Bessarabian city of Kishinev (today's Chişinău, the capital of the Republic of Moldova), not only exposed the deadly power of antisemitic propaganda but also marked the beginning of a century that would prove to be the bloodiest in Jewish history. The Kishinev pogrom, according to Monty Penkower, was "a turning point in Jewish history. . . . Its varied legacy is with us."[68] On Easter Sunday, according to the Orthodox Christian calendar, mobs of Christians, mostly young men, began to attack Jews. After two days of rioting, over forty Jews were killed, hundreds were wounded, and dozens raped. Several succumbed to their wounds, days later. Homes and businesses were ransacked or outright destroyed, turning thousands of Jews homeless. The pogrom shocked the Western world, Jews and non-Jews alike. News spread rapidly, thanks to the efforts of a Jewish community leader Jacob Bernstein-Kogan, who used the telegraph to notify international newspapers about the violence in Kishinev. Soon headlines in London and New York reported news about the pogrom.

The effect of the pogrom and its legacy were far more long lasting than fleeting headlines around the world. The Russian word *pogrom* became rooted in the English language to mean an organized violent attack or massacre aimed at a specific group of people. Moreover, the Kishinev pogrom provides a link to the most notorious antisemitic conspiracy, *The Protocols of the Elders of Zion*, which as Steven Zipperstein has recently established, was penned by the main inciter of the pogrom, Pavolachi Khrushevan.[69] *The Protocols of the Elders of Zion* described the world of "Jewish domination," an imagined effect of an uncontrolled rise of Jews in European society and a clear inversion of the proper order in which Jews were supposed to live in subjugation, servitude and with eternal gratitude to Christians.

The idea of "Jewish power" became an obsession of antisemites around the world. The *Protocols* claimed that the ideals of the French Revolution of "Liberty, Equality, and Fraternity" were a Jewish plot, "the worms that gnawed at the welfare of non-Jews, everywhere undermining peace, calm, community, common values, and thereby destroying the foundation of their domination."[70] Fulfilling these ideals and dismantling traditional structures led to the Jews' "triumph" and their ability to "exploit" non-Jews whom they turned into "castrated sheep." The forgery explicitly dubbed Jewish equality as implemented after the French Revolution through legal equality of citizenship "Jewish domination." The idea took root. And, when Adolf Hitler and the Nazis came to power, they immediately took steps to dismantle the legal framework of Jewish citizenship by gradual elimination of laws that guaranteed Jews equal rights and privileges. To do so effectively, they found a model—the US and its treatment of Black and Native Americans.[71]

While the nineteenth century was for Jews in the West a century of social climb, for Jews in eastern Europe it was a century of demographic growth and pauperization, with social advancement limited only to a small group of Jews.[72] That pauperization helped reinforce Christian anti-Jewish attitudes of contempt and a sense of Christian superiority, it came at the time when the social rise of some Jews enflamed, as *The Protocols of the Elders of Zion* demonstrates, a fear of Jewish power and with it, as a Polish writer would note after the World War II, "aversion, hostility, envy, threats." The pauperization of millions of Jews in eastern Europe reinforced that aversion and perception of Jews as unassimilable aliens.[73]

In the United States the situation was a little more complex, at least until the 1870s, which coincided with the backlash against the Reconstruction, the beginning of the Jim Crow era, and the process of "reforging of the white republic," or perhaps more accurately "white Protestant republic," since reconciliation between the North and the South—at the expense of the civil rights of Black Americans—was promoted by white northern Protestants. For white Protestants, as Edward J. Blum has shown, "American nationalism, whiteness, and Protestant Christianity had been powerfully bound together."[74] But until the 1880s, the Jewish population was relatively small and affluent, residing predominantly in the South. To be sure, even before the 1880s, with whiteness and Protestant Christianity defining the American white identity and white supremacist ideology and drawing racial and religious boundaries, Jews were religious outsiders, marked, in Christian eyes, by theological inferiority. But, given the Jews' European roots, they were "white by law" and thereby were American citizens.[75] As such, Jews tried to combat the pernicious notion of the US as "a Christian nation" by turning to the constitutional protection of freedom of religion.

But the specter of the idea that the United States is a Christian nation has not disappeared, as anxieties and hostilities against non-Protestant denominations, which developed in the nineteenth century, continue to persist.[76] In 1892, the Supreme Court in a unanimous decision authored by Associate Justice David J. Brewer concerning a violation of the Alien Contract Labor Act included a statement "this is a Christian nation."[77] In 1905, Brewer doubled down on this point in his publication, *The United States: A Christian Nation*, in which he argued that from the earliest days of European settlement in the Americas Christian values permeated culture and law. He declared that Christianity was "the best of all religions," and claimed that in none of the earliest laws adopted in America was Judaism anything more than "tolerated" as a "special creed."[78] Both the court decision and especially the justice's publication elicited a pushback from Jewish leaders who understood that even such casual remarks had a potential to exclude Jews from polity and endanger their place in American society, making their "integration as fully equal citizens . . . illusory."[79] But for Brewer, as he tried to show through a historical discussion of law in America, Protestant Christianity was normative. It was, as Naomi Cohen put it, "a Christian nation by heritage, culture, and values."

The noted cartoonist Thomas Nast captured that hostility to non-Protestant denominations in one of his cartoons, which depicted two monstrous creatures crawling, "at the foot of liberty," over the Capitol, one marked "Roman Church," the other "Mormon Church." The caption said, "Religious liberty is guaranteed: but can we allow foreign reptiles to crawl all over us?"[80] While Mormonism was a new religion, Catholicism, though present and visible in Maryland, entered American political and religious consciousness with the mass Irish migration in the middle of the nineteenth century. The Irish and Mormons, like Jews and Chinese, challenged the Euro-Protestant supremacy. But the Chinese, Blacks, and, increasingly also, Jews, also challenged that supremacy at a presumed racial level.

When the wave of Jewish immigrants from eastern Europe began to arrive in the early 1880s, the ground was already primed for antisemitism to take a deeper root in the US, reinforced now even more strongly by the "reforging" of the white Protestant republic. Before then, Jewish immigration to the United States was that of affluent Sephardic or German Jews. Jews were considered white and at issue was only their religion and social acceptance.[81] In the South, Jews, in particular, those in Charleston, South Carolina, shared sensibilities and racial attitudes with their affluent Christian neighbors.[82] They excluded non-white Jews from their congregations, some held slaves, and during the Civil War, joined the Confederate forces. Indeed, notwithstanding the clash in 1844 with Governor Hammond of South Carolina, a German Jew visiting the South remarked on white solidarity in the South, which included Jews. "The southern states," he wrote, "outdid, in many respects, northern states in hospitality. The white inhabitants felt themselves united with and closer to other whites—as opposed to the Negroes."[83] In the North, Jews had also lived successful lives, including German Jews who arrived in the first half of the nineteenth century, becoming quite affluent and prosperous, yet even then, they remained outsiders.

One of the first publicly noted antisemitic incidents took place in the United States in 1877, the same year as the Senate held its hearings on Chinese exclusion and just two years after the passing of the 1875 Civil Rights Act, which mandated that "all persons within the jurisdiction of the United States shall be entitled to the full and equal enjoyment of the accommodations, advantages, facilities, and privileges of inns, public conveyances on land or water, theaters, and other places of public amusement" regardless of "race and color," and "any previous condition of servitude."[84] The incident reminded American Jews that they were not as "white" and equal as they aspired to be. In June of that year, a prominent Jewish businessman, Joseph Seligman, who "had socialized as a financial equal with Astors, Vanderbilts, and Whitneys," was denied access to a luxury hotel—the Grand Union Hotel—in Saratoga Springs on account that he was Jewish.[85] When he arrived with his family to spend the summer there as he had in the previous ten years, Seligman was informed that Judge Henry Hilton, a lawyer and an executor of the will of the owner of the hotel, A. T. Steward, who had died the previous year, had "given instructions that no Israelites shall be permitted in future to stop at this hotel."[86] The *New York Times* reported that Seligman was astonished and asked for clarification, "Do you mean to tell me that you will not entertain Jewish people?" The manager responded, "That is our orders, Sir." Seligman wanted to know the reasons for this discrimination of Jews: "Are they dirty, do they misbehave themselves, or have they refused to pay their bills?" None of this was the reason, the hotel manager explained. "The reason is simply this: Business at this hotel was not good last season, and we had a large number of Jews here. Mr. Hilton came to the conclusion that Christians did not like their company, and for that reason shunned the hotel. He resolved to run the Union on a different principle this season, and gave us instructions to admit no Jew." The manager "personally . . . was very sorry, inasmuch as Mr. Seligman had patronized the hotel for so many years, but the order was imperative." Left without accommodations, Seligman returned home to New York and wrote to Hilton, threatening a boycott of his businesses— hotels and stores.

Jewish leaders felt they could not let the matter rest. As the *New York Times* reported, what happened in Saratoga was new and dangerous: "In this century, when the proscription of the Jews in other countries was dying out, it would be shameful to permit it here. There had been at times in the community a desire to slight the Jews, but hitherto this feeling had been confined to ignorant people—'to the small vipers . . . but now the big snakes have attacked us, it is that that we awaken and defend ourselves.'"[87]

The *Times* contacted Henry Hilton to hear his side of the story.[88] While Hilton did admit that the hotel staff "had been instructed to carefully discriminate as to their guests" and "Mr. Seligman fell under this discrimination," he denied that Seligman was "ejected from the Grand Union." Hilton claimed, it turns out falsely, that Seligman had been "boarding at the Clarendon," another hotel in Saratoga Springs, waiting for the Grand Union to reopen. "He came over, and 'in an ostentatious manner,' it seems, demanded the best apartments. If Mr. Seligman had come to Judge Hilton personally, the latter would have perhaps seen to his accommodation." Hilton thought Seligman and other Jews were attempting to step above what Hilton considered their appropriate social position. The hotel was designed to be a model hotel "for the families of the better and more exclusive classes of society." Two million dollars were invested in this hotel, which accommodated 2,500 guests. The hotel was to be "a family home, where men could leave their families during their absence with perfect security and satisfaction," Hilton said. What mattered for business were "the wishes and prejudices of the only class of people who can or will support a hotel like this most. The hotel is run for them, and not for those they dislike." And Seligman belonged to the "class" with whom the guests of Grand Union, "especially the female portion of them" did not want to "associate" or "be forced to meet, even under the etiquette of the dining-room or parlor of a public hotel."

Hilton insisted that it was the "fault" of the Jews themselves for their own discrimination and were not, with a few exceptions, "not wanted any more at any of the first-class Summer hotels." It was their "vulgar ostentation, a puffed-up vanity, and overweening display of condition, a lack of those considerate civilities so much appreciated by good American society, and a general obtrusiveness that is frequently disgusting and always repulsive to the well-bred" that "brought the public opinion down." Their presence in establishments was, Hilton claimed, ruinous. "The hotel men all over the country were awakening" and soon "a man of this type" would not "find admittance at all to such hotels as the Buckingham, the Windsor, those at Sharon Springs, Saratoga and elsewhere." Admitting Jews was "a severe tax of judgment of the proprietors of these places," though he granted that some "Hebrews," such the old Americanized families, "the Hendricks and Nathans," were welcome.

The incident and Hilton's unabashed explanation for what had happened in Saratoga Springs the week before caused "a profound sensation" and prompted reactions from other hotel managers and patrons.[89] "The general position taken," the *Times* reported, was "decidedly opposed to that of Judge Hilton, although there are a few hotels in this City where

Jewish custom is openly discouraged on grounds similar to those stated by Judge Hilton." But others admitted to discriminating "closely," while being "careful not to openly base such discrimination on grounds of race," which in 1877 was prohibited by both federal and state law. The Grand Union in Saratoga did not budge under the scandal. They justified their action "by the demands of their business" and the desire to bring "a different class of customers from that which the Jewish people bring." Joseph Seligman and his family were "not the only ones whom they have denied rooms." The hotel admitted that "several prominent Hebrew merchants and lawyers are among the number." Seligman for his part threatened to sue the Grand Union hotel "under the Civil Rights bill."

But Hilton remained unapologetic.[90] When the *Times* contacted him again after the report had been published, he explained that he had taken the step "after long and conscientious deliberation." Like Seligman, Hilton understood that what he had done was unprecedented and believed that "every proprietor of a first-class Summer hotel will hail with joy the break which this precedent has made for them . . . scores of these proprietors would long ago have done just what I have done, if they had dared to do right and had been independent enough, financially, to take the step which prudence has for a long time been insisting should be taken." Hilton said to the *Times* reporter that "by scurrility of his newspaper defense," Seligman proved that he did "really belong to the class of 'Jews' to which I properly assigned him."

Hilton wanted to humiliate Seligman. Seligman's wealth, he said discussing financial affairs that A. T. Stewart had with Seligman and Seligman's financial firm, was illegitimate—a fruit of "the practice of the veriest Shylockean meanness."[91] As were his social aspirations. "Should the Seligman 'Jew' be excluded from certain first-class hotels?" Hilton answered, "emphatically, yes." It was not "at all because he is a Hebrew but because he is not wanted" by those "who support the hotels and for whose especial benefit the hotels are built and conducted." And there was "nothing" wrong about it, Hilton asserted. Indeed, "Hebrews" were not "proscribed" because of their religion, "there is no religious standard raised." Hilton, like many Christians in the US and in Europe, distinguished between the idealized ancient Hebrews and Jews. For Hilton, Hebrews were respectable religious individuals; "Jews," as Sharon Oster has shown, were "the nouveau riche," and they were not welcome.[92]

Hotels, Hilton maintained, were "run for a particular class of patrons" and as such they "must conform . . . to the wishes and prejudices of these patrons or go down." Hilton then gave an example of a hotel that charges a certain amount ("$4"), that amount signals that they do not want people who were unable to pay that amount, and those people would go else-where (to a "$2" hotel), without complaining. But Seligman had money to pay. Here, Hilton revealed the obstinate power of social hierarchy and of anti-Jewish stereotypes. Seligman did not belong, even if he could pay for the class of accommodations he desired. "He shoves his person upon respectability," Hilton said. It was not about religion. "Seligman 'Jew,'" according to Hilton, "represents nothing that is standard Hebrew; he is to the Hebrew what a shyster is to the law profession—he is the 'Shee-ney.' He has made money; he must advertise it in his person." As a person "of low origin," his instincts were "of the gutter, his rags—his principles smell—they smell of decayed goods or of decayed principle." He was "too obtuse or too mean to see his vulgarity." Hilton kept going, calling Selig-man "shoddy—false—squeezing—unmanly"; "vulgar," "worthless," "vain," and "devoid of merit;" "puffed out with as much importance as he is poor of any value." Seligman's financial success became his "only token . . . to push himself upon the polite."

.Seligman was way out of his rank, Hilton continued, drawing once more on stereotypes that echoed old theological tropes of Jewish "carnality":

> He comes to the Grand Union big with himself and little with every-body else in the decent world; planks down his cash with his royal order, and having never seen respectable food, he can't get enough to eat unless he gorges down his unpracticed throat six meals a day, and then for fear folks will not know that he is an old epicure, he protrudes his ill-shaped pod into the gaze of very unfortunate person in his path who has open eyes and then goes to his room and prepares himself for next day's gluttony by ridding himself of his torturing load all over the furniture, with groans at its loss that disturb every decent person within 10 rooms on every side of him.[93]

Whether Hilton was aware or not of the roots of the anti-Jewish motifs he evoked; smell, gluttony, groan so loud as to disturb the polite society—all harkened back to medieval anti-Jewish tropes: the *foetor judaicus*, or the Jewish smell, carnality, and sound pollution.[94] All signaled the lower social and theological rank of Jews. "They have deserved the common con-tempt," Hilton added. It was thus "no wonder that Americans are down on the Seligman 'Jew.'" Hilton turned Seligman into a caricature. He was no longer Joseph Seligman, the elite businessman from New York; he became "Seligman Jew," a stand in for all Jews, deserving the contempt of the "Americans." Jews did not belong in white, "polite" American circles. "People won't go to hotels where the Seligman 'Jew' is admitted," Hilton concluded. "And hotels if they would thrive must keep out those who would ruin their existence. The very fact that the Seligman 'Jew' makes such a fuss because people don't want his society, and makes such a noise to force himself where he is unwelcome, instead of going elsewhere, proves him to be just what I have described him." The uppity Jew, seeking to be equal, was not welcome. The affair underscored the default meaning of the term "American" as both white and Christian, superior to others. Seligman too seems to have understood it that way when he wrote to Henry Hilton the day he was refused accommodations at the Grand Union hotel.[95] The reason he and his family were given for refusal of service was that there was "prejudice among Americans against people of [Jewish] persuasion, which had injured the Union [hotel] to that extent last season that head-quarters proposed to 'roast them out,' namely, to tell them all, without exception, that all rooms except garret chambers were engaged." The offer of "garret chambers" was meant to mark the Jews' lower and marginalized, servile status.

This sentiment was shared by others. On June 21, the *Times* published several letters in support of Hilton. One described the Howard Hotel in Long Branch, which "was so overrun by Jews that Americans and others avoided it."[96] The hotel was nearly bankrupt, the anonymous writer noted, until owner "saved himself by refusing accommodations" to Jews. The letter-writer praised Hilton for what he had done, saying that his efforts "will redound to the reputation of your house and fill it with the best and most desirable patrons."

Hilton's rant against "the Seligman Jew" and the specific vocabulary stressing vulgarity and money making was likely a conscious inversion of claims made by Joseph Seligman in his letter to Hilton, in which Seligman accused Hilton of "vulgar prejudice," and warned him, pun likely intended, that he was "no judge of American character. The civilized world [was] beginning to be more tolerant in matters of faith and creed or birth than you believe or would have them."[97] This new "civilized" world despised "intolerance, low cunning, and vulgarity"; it refused to "patronize a man who seeks to make money by pandering to prejudices of the vulgar." Seligman regretted that Hilton, who had just recently taken over the Grand Union Hotel, was "running the Union [hotel] at a loss," pointing to Hilton that he was a bad businessman—his other ventures were also losing money—a point reiterated also by the organizers of the Hotel Keepers' Union of the Park Avenue Hotel in New York, managed by Henry Hilton.[98]

Seligman's attorney argued that Hilton's steps to exclude Seligman and Jews were rooted in Hilton's own envy.[99] Hilton's statement in the *Times* about Seligman was projection: "In all he does, there is too much *Hilton*, and not too much Jew." Hilton ruined A. T. Stewart's businesses. Everything Hilton has handled since Stewart's death was "colored by Hilton—Hilton, all Hilton." In contrast, Seligman was "really and acceptedly the head of the Jewish people in this country, and all the Jews are proud of him." He was "socially and financially too high to be pulled down one jot by any man of Judge Hilton's calibre." The attorney then listed the long list of envy-inducing accomplishments. Seligman had been "a prominent Commissioner of the Board of Education"; he was at the time of the affair, "president and leading mind of the Rapid Transit Company," "leading Director in many of the best banks in this City," "a principal leader of every charitable institution of every sect started in this community, and is a leading member of the Republican Party and Vice-President of the Union League Club, into which Judge Hilton has vainly sought admittance—always getting black-balled—and hence, perhaps, much of his pique." The attorney asserted that "so high does Mr. Seligman stand in national reputation that, although when Gen. Grant was here, the Union League, the Century, and other of the best clubs, tendered him receptions, Mr. Seligman's Delmonico supper was the only one accepted from the whole splendid list." Seligman's brothers were also accomplished, one was the head of the Hebrew Benevolent and Orphan Asylum Society, "the largest eleemosynary institution of the kind in the world," and the other was "a leading Director of the Emanuel Congregation at Forty-third-street and Fifth-avenue, the largest Jewish church in the United States." So high was Seligman's reputation that there was "no Jew in New York or elsewhere who would not be proud to be what Judge Hilton sneeringly calls a 'Seligman Jew.'" The attorney expressed puzzlement between Hilton's distinction "between a Hebrew and a Seligman Jew." He mockingly speculated that Hilton's "etymological education is on a par with his aesthetical culture." This harsh judgment stemmed from Hilton's term as Parks Commissioner, when "he suggested whitewashing the bronze statutes in the Park during the hot weather of Summer, and objected to the purchase of a valuable collection of fossils for the museum on the ground that no one wished to have anything to do with old bones. Judge Hilton always was a bigot." The lawyer also pointed out that Hilton lost his reelection for a judgeship thanks to "the efforts of lawyers and others of foreign and Hebrew birth whom he systematically snubbed while on the bench." The steps he has taken managing Stewart's estate were thus an expression of long-standing grudges and prejudice.

The attorney hoped that "Judge Hilton and his nefarious intolerance shall be together and forever crushed out" and added that "the legal remedies for

Mr. Seligman and other Jews are ample under the Civil Rights bill, which prescribes a fine of $500 and an imprisonment of from one month to one year for every outrage upon an American citizen like this Saratoga one." But the attorneys representing the staff at the Grand Union Hotel dismissed Seligman's threat of litigation as "good enough for law students and moot courts but . . . too amusing to deserve serious consideration."[100]

The next day, Hilton doubled down, reiterating that this was not a question of religious discrimination, but "only a question of what class of guests are socially wanted at the hotel" and "of property."[101] The question that had to be decided was whether an owner of a summer hotel had "the right to conduct his house on his own principles" and whether he had a right "to manage his property" in such a way as to attract "the best class of patrons" to "stop with him," or whether he had to "keep them away by being forced to take as guests a class with whom neither he nor they will associate. Must a valuable hotel be run for those who can and will support it or for those whose patronage is ruinous." According to Hilton, the Grand Union Hotel was to be "run for the best class of American Summer guests, and that these people do not like to associate with Jews of the Seligman type, and will not patronize a hotel where, out of etiquette or necessity, they are compelled to be in their company." As a result, "this class of Jews must stay away." He was not going to budge: "This was the decision." He complained that "the Americans are a very democratic people, and their democracy is broader at public houses than in their private homes," so "when a certain class of people have become so offensive, socially, to Americans," they are willing to "remain away, at a disadvantage, from a favorite resort, merely to avoid the company of this class," and it was "a fact" that they had "very good reasons for their exclusiveness."

What Hilton did was not about what Seligman and Jews were or what they did. As the Swedish scholar of antisemitism Hugo Valentin argued in 1936, it did not matter if Jews acted "in this way or that . . . it is not Jews who are hated, but an imaginary image of them, which is confounded with the reality, and the Jews' actual 'faults' play a very unimportant part in the matter."[102] Indeed, to quote philosopher George Yancy, "The white gaze sees, what it constructs."[103] Seligman, the respected and successful businessman, found himself objectified and distorted: he became Seligman "Jew." What Yancy has explored in the context of Black bodies applies to Jews as well: "Whiteness is that according to which what is nonwhite is rendered other, marginal, ersatz, strange, native, inferior, uncivilized, and ugly."[104] Seligman entered white Protestant spaces, and while he may have considered himself white and deserving equality, that was not what

Hilton, a representative of white Protestant hegemonic culture saw. Hilton saw "a Jew," a historical construct of Christian imagination, and to him he was, as Yancy argued about the Black body in white society, "marked and inscribed in derogatory terms . . . marginalized and derailed within the space of the white body politic."[105]

The Hilton-Seligman controversy did not die down for at least a month; it even became part of Henry Hilton's legacy—noted in his obituary.[106] But the matter did not go to court as threatened and, two years later, in 1879, the Manhattan Beach affair erupted.[107] A New York newspaper reported: "The war against the Jews, which was carried on at Saratoga two years ago, is apparently to be revived at Coney Island."[108] A New York developer, Austin Corbin, wanted to create a fashionable resort on Coney Island and decided to follow Henry Hilton's steps and exclude Jews. Here, too, a threat of legal action alleging violation of Section 1 of the Civil Rights Act of 1875 was made, but like in the Seligman-Hilton affair, no lawsuit appears to have been filed. It was only the *Civil Rights Cases* in 1883 that settled the matter in a way that likely pleased Henry Hilton and Austin Corbin—the Supreme Court justified race-based discrimination in private businesses, ruling the Civil Rights Act unconstitutional.

Some decades later, at the beginning of the twentieth century, another scandal broke out; this one, in connection with the Lake Placid Club founded by Melvil Dewey, the New York State Librarian, best known for the Dewey decimal system. The club, founded in 1895 and self-characterized as "a congenial club," excluded anyone "against whom there is any reasonable physical, moral, social or race objection, or who would be unwelcome to even a small minority," as well as "invalids, whose presence might injure the health or modify the freedom or enjoyment of others."[109] In the 1914 handbook an explanation about "this standard" was added, stating that the Lake Placid Club had "many Southern members, so negroes can be admitted only to servants quarters; for no one has a right to entertain as his personal guest any person who would clearly be an 'undesirable' who would be rejected by the membership committee."[110] This was "a chief advantage of a strictly private club," allowing for "the social life" to be "free from the embarrassment which the law enforces on public hotels." And while the federal courts at this time allowed for segregated hotels, New York State laws prohibited discrimination in accommodations. Though the exclusion of Jews was not mentioned in the Lake Placid Club's *Handbooks*, it was mentioned in its circulars, in which a phrase was added to the exclusion paragraph: "This invariable rule is rigidly enforced; it is found impracticable to make exceptions to Jews or others excluded, even when of unusual personal qualifications."[111] More implicitly, the club banned "stock tickers," had a piggery, and advertised local churches.

Melvil Dewey was proud of his club, but its rules led to his forced resignation as the New York State Librarian.[112] In 1903, as in previous two years, the New York Libraries Association's Library Week was scheduled to take place at the Lake Placid Club. One of the librarians attending was Henry M. Leipziger, who noticed a circular that included the clause about the exclusion of Jews from the resort. Leipziger left the club in protest and consulted with Jewish lawyers in New York City, including Louis Marshall, an attorney responsible for making the Adirondacks and the Catskills a protected "forever-wild" region, and also an owner of a club in the nearby Saranac Lake. In January 1905, the Regents of the University of the State of New York received a petition "asking for the removal of Melvil Dewey as the State Librarian," who was also "the President of the Lake Placid Company," which "runs the club."[113]

The petitioners, among them Louis Marshall, cited the circular, which explicitly discriminated against Jews, and reminded the regents that there were about 750,000 Jews in the state, "a large proportion of them are taxpayers, who contribute their quota to the support and maintenance of the institutions of the State, the payment of the salaries of public officials, including that which is paid to Mr. Melvil Dewey, as the State Librarian." New York Jews took "pride in the State and its government"; they devoted "their energies and their intellect to the development of its resources, and the fostering of its industries"; strove "to raise the standard of public intelligence to cherish learning; to promote arts, sciences, and literature"; and "sought to advance the cause of education as great an extent at least as any part of the citizenship of this Commonwealth." Having listed Jews' contributions to the state, the petitioners noted, as if representing all Jews, that Jews felt "therefore, that they have a right to demand that one, who as a public servant represents all the people of the State, of whom they are part, so long as he remains such a servant and receives compensation from the State Treasury under the sanction of your honorable body, shall not, with impunity, pander to the lowest prejudices of which man is capable."[114] The "intolerable spirit" of Lake Placid Club's circular, the petitioners wrote, was "a far-off echo of the ignorant brutality of medieval times." Fortunately, they concluded, though there were "sporadic instances where drunken rowdies have given evidence of similar sentiments by pulling the beards of aged and defenseless men," and "cases where shortsighted innkeepers have refused accommodations to Jews," such intolerance, "thus far . . . has gained no footing in this State."

But the petitioners made clear that it was not just about discrimination against Jews in hotels and clubs, it was "understood that a number of social clubs have exercised their undoubted privilege to exclude from membership those of the Jewish faith." With those "they had no concern." What they were objecting to was that Dewey was "a high ranking public official . . . placed . . . at the head of an important branch of the educational system of the State, one to whom the youth are accustomed to look for instruction and guidance, for precept and example." But "either from motives of religious or racial hostility, or from considerations of pecuniary greed, or from ignorance or bigotry," this official forgot "himself and the duties which he owes to the entire public as to spread through the land a publication which tends to make of the Jew an outcast and a pariah." In such a case, the petitioners demanded, the state and the regents could not "afford to trifle with the offender or allow an infamous precedent to be established." There was thus only one solution: "to remove from the service of the State the official whose act undermines the very foundations of our governmental system." They noted that if Dewey did so against Jews, there was nothing stopping him from doing it against others, "the Catholic, the next day the Methodist," violating "the most sacred sentiments of all the people of the State." The petitioners argued that "as the President and the stockholder of the Lake Placid Company," Dewey could "adopt whatever policy he desires, but he must not at the same time remain the State Librarian" or use this position for advertising his company as he did in his circulars: "Mr. Melvil Dewey, the President of our company is Librarian of the State of New York."

In his response to the regents, Dewey asserted that "the allegations that are serious are based on misapprehension of the facts" and those that are "true are not serious."[115] Dewey admitted that the club since its founding indeed did not accept Jews as members, and the language that Leipziger and the lawyers petitioning the regents objected to was inserted in 1901 because "it was discovered that a family, highly recommended, regularly introduced and admitted, with an English name, were Jews." Upon this discovery, Dewey explained, the council members of the club decided that the family could not come and "wrote the family frankly." They were apparently "thanked politely for the consideration that saved the embarrassment of coming where [the family] could not be welcome." The librarian explained that the council then decided to add the explicit language "to guard against similar misunderstanding" because "the rule on race objection had not impressed this family as excluding cultivated and desirable Jews." Dewey noted that in his official capacity as a state librarian he held no "race or faith" prejudice and "Jews have been and are among the most valued members of my staff and among the ablest students in our library school," they have even been to Dewey's house, and he was sure that "every one of them will vouch for as warm a welcome and as fair treatment both personal and official as accorded to any Christian." As a bona fide of his professional openness, Dewey noted that the only other time he was attacked was when the library had issued wall pictures for New York schools, he acquiesced to "protest of certain rabbis" and "omitted the Sistine Madonna and five other famous Christian pictures recommended by prominent artists and critics." The Lake Placid Company, too, he noted, "has given some of its most valuable patronage to Jews, and three times sold real estate at Lake Placid to them." Dewey then addressed the points raised by the petitioners, concluding that "all allegations except for the exclusion of Jews do not accord with facts that it is a social club not a hotel, and that I have been scrupulously careful not to confuse my official position with the club."

In February, the regents conducted a hearing and later in the month a committee submitted a report on the "facts" of the case but no recommendations.[116] Following the report, the regents offered "the formal and severe public rebuke" for Dewey's conduct, and censured "the publication by an officer of the Education Department of the expressions complained of in the petition concerning an important class of people, which also has official representation under the board, furnishes large support to the State, and has many youth in the schools." They also admonished Dewey that his "further control of a private business . . . conducted on such lines is incompatible with the legitimate requirements of his position in the service of the educational interest of the State of New York."

Though it was only a slap on the wrist, the regents' statement accepted all points offered by the petitioners, including the acknowledgment of the respectable social standing of Jews, underscored by the fact that a Jewish member was now a member of the board. The board said nothing about other forms of discrimination by the club. The outcome got a mixed reception, but the petitioners were content that they "succeeded in establishing the principle . . . that a public officer could not, directly or indirectly, identify himself with any movement that smacked of anti-Semitism."[117] But a pamphlet issued in the aftermath of the affair in defense of Dewey demonstrated the persistence of some long-lasting anti-Jewish feelings and shone light on the role political power played in fight for respectability. "Jews are too important an element nowadays," the pamphlet explained, "to be against by anybody who holds a public position; Jews may be despised, but their votes are respected."[118] And this was a key reason for the silence on anti-Black discrimination and a swift reaction to antisemitism. Jews were voters, they thus had access to political power. Black Americans' right to vote was contested and restricted; their political influence was therefore limited.

But the rules at the Lake Placid Club would not change—the language in the circulars would, however, have to become vaguer: "The Council after this outbreak will probably avoid the word Jew again in any rule again, but will surely maintain its absolute right to reject from membership any person not desired by the Club."[119] The message was received: overt antisemitism was unacceptable; it had to be concealed in respectable and unsuspicious terms. Still, by the fall of 1905, Melvil Dewey submitted his resignation to the regents, effective January 1, 1906. Thereafter, Dewey moved to Lake Placid where he ran the club with unchanged rules, leading to yet another flare-up on the eve of the 1932 Winter Olympics, when Jews objected to state funds being funneled to Dewey's company to build an Olympic bobsled run on the property of the Lake Placid Club.[120]

For Dewey and other members of the Lake Placid Club, Jews were both a race and a religious group, unacceptable even if "cultivated and desirable." But, as the incident with the unnamed family that prompted the insertion of the explicitly anti-Jewish language in the Lake Placid Club circular suggests, affluent Jews considered themselves white and associated the Lake Placid Club's racial exclusion clause as applying only to people of color and not to them. They may have been white, in look and wealth, but they were not considered equal. Despite their social aspirations, achievements, and level of integration, they were not acceptable to many white Christian Americans, even those committed to issues of education or even social justice.

A similar incident took place in 1911, when Rabbi Stephen Wise was invited to speak at the annual Lake Mohonk Peace Conference, which was founded in 1895 and hosted annually off-season at the high-class Lake Mohonk Mountain House resort owned by Quaker brothers, Albert and Alfred Smiley.[121] "Upon making inquiry," Wise told his congregants, he discovered "that the Lake Mohonk Mountain House, the proprietor of which is the host of the conference, 'does not solicit Hebrew patronage'; in other words, denies accommodation to Jews during the Summer months."[122] The conference had been attended by Jews before. Wise contacted some of the regular Jewish attendees and informed them, "I would not for a moment think of accepting for myself in May the hospitality which is denied to my people in July and August," and pleaded that "no self-respecting Jew ought to be willing to accept [*sic*] such hospitality even for an hour." Some of the Jews who had attended the conference offered "explanations" for their participation and for the hotel's policies, but Wise found them to be "lame and impotent excuses for the attitude of the hotel." The Quaker organizers of the conference tried to persuade Wise that the hotel and the conference were "distinct institutions." They claimed that "the owner of the hotel and the host of the conference," Albert Smiley, "deplored what seemed to be a business necessity in that it seemed to discriminate against men," such as Rabbi Stephen Wise himself.

But Rabbi Wise was unmoved. He wrote to the conference and fellow Jewish participants, expressing his moral outrage and highlighting the contradiction between the Conference's goals and its venue's discriminatory practices. "It is vain to hope for a cessation of war as long as men suffer racial antipathies and religious animosities to go unchallenged. War, after all, is not a thing of arms and armies. War is a thing of the human heart, and arms merely execute the purposes of the souls of men. If we can get slaughter out of the hearts of men war will speedily cease."[123] He added that he had long admired "Mr. Smiley as a high-souled servant of the race, as a noble example of American citizenship," it thus caused him "a real grief . . . to find him yielding, even in the least degree, to one of those prejudiced which lie back of the wars to the extermination of which he has dedicated his life." In a sermon Wise delivered to the congregation in the aftermath of this exchange, the rabbi reflected on the biblical verse, which he also quoted in his letter, "Peace, Peace, when there is no peace" [Jeremiah 6:14 and 8:11]. "One of Israel's prophets," Wise said, "has for all time stigmatized pseudo peace advocates in telling of the false prophets who cry peace, peace, when there is no peace." Such "peace-at-any-price men" bartered their souls "not so much for peace as for that spurious thing which Milton calls ignoble ease and peaceful sloth"; they forgot that "the work of righteousness shall be peace, the work of peace is not always righteousness," and such peace was "not life's highest good." But because, Wise warned, "the Jew has been burdened by the centuries of woes innumerable he is in peculiar peril of crying out peace, peace, when there is no peace," and that was a "morally imperiling temptation." Referring to the Dreyfus affair, in which a French Jewish officer was falsely accused and convicted of treason, Wise noted that "panic-stricken" Jews compromised "supreme moral" principles and "stooped to the base of expediency of counseling silence even at the cost of the martyrdom of one Jew, rather than subject all Jews to the possibility of danger." Wise in a surgically sharp language then emphasized that he had "no quarrel with the Peace Conference," but

as long as it met in a place that participated "in a vulgar and godless discrimination against a whole people," it undermined "its own high purpose
and in a very real sense comes to bring not peace but the sword." Wise's
quarrel, he said, was "with such fellow-Jews as are ready without demur or
protest, to acquiesce in this conduct." Such quiet acquiescence pointed to
"an even graver moral remissness in the silent endurers of the deed than in its
doers."[124] The rabbi then hit at the social standing of the Jews: it mattered not,
he said, "how distinguished be the place of these Jews in public or private
life." With stature comes responsibility. Indeed, "the higher their place or
position, the loftier is their duty and the more commanding their obligation jealously to safeguard the honor of their people."

This whole controversy was, for Wise, about moral issues. Had it
been just about "moneymaking hotel keepers," the affair would have been
"wholly negligible."[125] But the Lake Mohonk Peace Conferences sought to
lead on moral issues and inspire others. There could be no international
peace "as long as an inter-racial bitterness and inter-religious animosities
are unconquered." Indeed, Wise stressed, "even if war should cease this
day and the sound of weapons be heard no more, even if the prophecy of
the Hebrew seer be fulfilled that swords be beaten into plowshares and
spears into pruning hooks," there would still be "war upon earth as long
as peace be not rooted in good-will and comity and fraternity." At the root
of the war were not so much "land hunger or territorial greed," but rather
"racial and religious and National hostilities of which anti-Semitism is at
one and the same time the most persistent and Christless example." Wise
closed confronting the organizers' hypocrisy, "They have no right to feign
to be makers of peace between nations who in very truth are war perpetu-
ators between faiths and races." For Wise, such peace was no peace at all.
But some Jews did not have the same courage as Louis Marshall and his
partners in the Dewey affair or Rabbi Wise in the Mohonk Conference
case, fearing that standing up to anti-Jewish prejudice would increase
antisemitism by confirming the antisemitic stereotypes of arrogant Jews,
as the backlash that ensued when Jews reacted to Justice David J. Brewer's
*The United States: A Christian Nation* had shown.[126]

The conference in Mohonk did take place that year, but its tone was not
inclusive at all. The participants affirmed the United States as a Christian
country and declared, as one pastor did, that "the world needed a Christian
union."[127] And the policies at the Lake Mohonk Mountain House did not
change after the confrontation with Rabbi Wise. The managers continued to discourage Jewish patrons and contacted other hoteliers to inquire
about potential "undesirable guests."[128] The resort even kept a report and

lists of such guests. At times, "a few Jews crept in," a 1917 report said, that was because, unlike Black Americans, Jews were white and, as Cindy Sondik Aron noted, "those with anglicized names found it easier than African Americans to evade discriminatory rules and visit gentile resorts."[129] The Great Depression changed the fortunes at the Mohonk Mountain House, and although the resort began to admit Jews, the management regretted that Jews (and Germans) were now found among the guests.[130]

In Europe, too, certain resorts prided themselves on excluding Jews. For example, Borkum, "the most beautiful ornament on the North See," had a song announcing that it was to remain "free of Jews."[131] Borkum was not an exception, many other resorts on the North Sea and the Baltic, in the Hartz Mountains, and the Black Forest began to exclude Jews in the 1870s, as if to remind them that they were not equal even though they had just acquired full German citizenship.[132] Resorts that did accept Jews often found themselves mocked or stigmatized for their inclusion, which is what happened to Carlsbad and Marienbad.[133] German scholar Frank Bajohr has argued that the "resort antisemitism" has played a role in mentally preparing Germans for later total exclusion and persecution of Jews by the Nazi regime.[134] By the late 1930s, Jews had no place to vacation in Germany.

In the United States, such discrimination would also continue until the passage of the Civil Rights Act in 1964, with hotels and establishments across the country excluding Jewish and Black patrons by advertising "exclusive," "restricted," "Christian," or even "gentile" clientele, and in the South, with far more degrading spaces and signs, such as "Whites Only" or "Colored Only," specifically designed to exclude and humiliate Black Americans, and to disabuse them of the idea that they were equal citizens.[135] In the north, while no signs like that were visible, discrimination against Black travelers existed as well, as experienced in 1905 in Asbury Park in New Jersey, by Dr. William Crum, a collector for the Port of Charleston. Crum had been confirmed to his position by the Senate just in January of that year after an acrimonious process in which his race played a key role because, as the *New York Times* reported in April 1904, "the nomination of a negro to be Collector of the Port is in the highest degree offensive to the people of Charleston," stirring up "excitement and anger in South Carolina and throughout the South."[136] Vacationing in Asbury Park, William Crum wanted to rent a wheelchair for his wife to take her to the boardwalk. The proprietor "J. L. Schneider refused to order any of his white lads to push the chair, but said that Dr. Crum might have it if he would wheel his wife himself."[137] Affronted, "Dr. Crum refused in a gentlemanly manner and left." The case was reported by the *New York Times*, no doubt because of the high profile of Dr. William Crum. But such indignities were common at the time, which is why both Jews and African Americans sought out businesses in which they were welcome, sometimes even establishing resorts that catered to their needs.

As the Dewey affair in Lake Placid and the Crum affair in Asbury Park plainly show, there was a major difference in the status of Jewish and Black Americans. While both incidents were reported in the press, there were public consequences for discrimination against Jews, but only acquiescence to the discrimination against African Americans. Indeed, a month before Rabbi Stephen Wise's protest against the Lake Mohonk Mountain House, a scandal erupted in regard to Colonel John R. Marshall, a Black commanding officer of the Eighth Infantry of the Illinois National Guard. Colonel Marshall was sent, according to the *New York Times* report, "as one of the National Guard officers from that State to serve a tour of duty with the division of regulars mobilized here under command of Major Gen. William H. Carter."[138] While Colonel Marshall's name was sent, it was not revealed that "he was a negro," and "the discovery of Col. Marshall's race caused a stir, because under the instructions issued by the War Department . . . the National Guardsmen are to be assigned for purposes of instruction and also for tentage and mess purposes to officers of equal rank in the regular service." There were several officers of equal rank to Marshall but none wanted to associate with him. Marshall was then assigned to the Eighteenth United States Infantry, in which "50 per cent of officers are Southerners," the *Times* reported.[139] An officer of equal rank to Col. Marshall, with whom Marshall was to partner, was from North Carolina. As a result, the *Times* recounted, "the colored officer has his meals sent to his tent, while the North Carolina Colonel and the other white officers assigned to the regiment mess with regular officers. The negro keeps to himself most of the time." The equal rank did not make Marshall equal.

An editorial comment in "The Topics of the Times" section acknowledged "a radical and fundamental incongruity between making a man a soldier, entitled to the respect deserved by one trained and ready to sacrifice his life in defense of the Nation, and at the same time treating him as unworthy to sit on the same seat in a street car with citizens theoretically possessing not one right or privilege he lacks."[140] But at the same time, the editors concluded that "apparently it is impossible to reconcile theory and practice." Moreover, because "there seems to be little likelihood that negro soldiers, with their inevitably well-developed appreciation of their own worth and importance, will ever submit gracefully or permanently to discriminations of the 'Jim Crow' kind, the wisdom of having any negro soldiers at all is at least debatable." The editors allowed that Black soldiers were "good soldiers, as everybody admits, and as they have many times proved in both peace and war, but somehow they do not fit well with the Nature of Things as They Are." The expectation that Black Americans would "gracefully or permanently" submit to whites, despite their achievements and rank, and the conclusion that they did not "fit well with the Nature of Things as They Are" was a tacit endorsement of, or at least an acquiescence to, the American racial status quo.

This editorial comment elicited a response from one Ruth Hampton, who spoke up against editors' conclusion that "the negro soldier does not fit in."[141] It was "true," Hampton wrote, that a Black soldier did not "submit with good grace" to the "outrageous Jim Crow laws in the South designed only to humiliate and degrade him, along with the other members of his race." He was assigned to "the most undesirable posts" and "discriminated against in every way possible on all occasions." And yet, despite such humiliations, she firmly noted, such a soldier "still fondly cherishes the delusion that under the Star-Spangled Banner he must go forth to serve his country and give his life when need be, because he loves it and knows no other home." Hampton contrasted the treatment of a Black soldier with that of immigrants from Europe who were at the time coming into the United States in great numbers. Whereas the Black soldier "is barely tolerated," "the flotsam and jetsam of Europe flowing into the country in a continual stream may become citizens, join the army and are treated with all the consideration denied to him." These immigrants, whom she called "serfs, criminals, and other undesirables," were "welcomed into this country, given every opportunity to improve themselves," and were "offered all the rights and privileges of American citizenship in its fullest meaning." They "may aspire to its highest offices," and yet the Black soldier, who was "inextricably mixed with the history of the country and its people," was "denied practically everything worth living for." She condemned the *Times* for being "on the wrong side of the question in advising that the negro soldier be dismissed from the army."

While Hampton expressed increasingly common anti-immigrant views, she also captured the opportunities afforded to European immigrants, including Jews, to improve their lives and fortunes in the new country. She articulated the reasons behind the myth of the United States as a land of opportunity, "the golden land," or in Yiddish "goldene medine," and captured, if only implicitly, why Jews also felt confident to demand equal treatment as citizens. American Jews stressed their difference through the lens of religion—freedom of which was guaranteed by the Constitution. They demanded equality based on that principle.

To be sure, racial questions were raised about Jews and sometimes Jews themselves acknowledged those. But they were different from those facing Black Americans. That difference was captured at a Republican luncheon that took place in New York a month before the scandal over Colonel Marshall's assignment.[142] At that event, according to the New York *Times*, "the evils of racial prejudice were denounced" by three speakers, "Dr. Emil G. Hirsch of Chicago [who] spoke for the Jews, Prof. Masujiro Honda for the Japanese, and Prof. W. E. B. Du Bois for the negroes." While Hirsch condemned race science and Honda focused on anti-immigration laws, Du Bois highlighted structural racism within the justice system that treated Black Americans differently from whites. And so, while Jews may have been pulled into the debates over race, may have been objects of bigotry, in contrast to legally sanctioned discrimination against Black Americans, there were no laws targeting Jews specifically. Moreover, Jews could pass. As Franz Fanon would observe in *Black Skin, White Masks*, "The Jew can be unknown in his Jewishness . . . he is a white man, and apart from some debatable characteristics, he can sometimes go unnoticed."[143] Or as the film *Gentlemen's Agreement* would try to show after World War II, a non-Jew could pass as a Jew as well.

American legal framework helps explain why there were such public consequences for antisemitism and not for anti-Black discrimination. Race as legitimate grounds for discrimination was inscribed in law, religion was protected by law. Moreover, as the Dewey affair demonstrated, the real and perceived power of the vote was also crucially important. Although there had been restrictions in certain states on Jewish voting rights in the antebellum period, by the time the Dewey affair took place, Jewish citizens as voters could exercise that power in the US without being systematically disenfranchised.[144] This was not the case with Black citizens, who have faced violence, legal and logistical challenges ever since the moment they acquired electoral franchise. Legal protection against religious discrimination coupled with voting power gave Jews a sense of confidence strong enough to push back.

The position Black Americans were in was not comparable on legal, social, and economic level. They have continually faced dogged efforts to limit their citizenship rights. The same year when Colonel Marshall was forced to eat alone in his tent despite his rank, when Rabbi Stephen Wise boycotted the Mohonk Conference, and Hirsch, Honda, and Du Bois protested "the evils of racial prejudice," a congressman from Georgia,

Thomas W. Hardwick, introduced a bill "for the repeal of the Fourteenth Amendment to the Constitution" with a goal, as the *New York Times*'s headline noted, to "abolish negro vote."[145] Antisemitism and anti-Jewish discrimination in the United States was tacit and often veiled in euphemisms or behind-the-scenes schemes, such as "restricted clientele" in hotel advertising, but there were no separate entries to public buildings or separate water fountains designated for Jews only—that would come later, in Europe in the 1930s, following the Nazi rise to power in Germany, and with the implementation of Nuremberg laws, copycat practices spreading across Europe, including Italy and Poland. In Poland, for example, in the second half of the 1930s, significant infringement on Jewish rights took place. Even in the 1920s, Jewish citizenship and equality before the law was considered by some Poles as an unjust imposition by foreign powers at the end of World War I, whose own track record on equal rights was questionable.[146] But, in the 1930s, following the death of Marshal Józef Piłsudski and the rise to power of ethno-nationalist parties, Jews, as another Polish writer noted, would soon be "completely pushed to the position of Negroes in America— with separate seats in trams, with separate waiting rooms at stations etc."[147] But he added that Americans did not treat only "Negroes as something inferior and worthy of contempt," some also discriminated against Jews, posting "No Jews admitted" signs in hotels.

Thus, when Joseph Seligman was arguing in 1877 that "the civilized world [was] beginning to be more tolerant in matters of faith and creed or birth," despising "intolerance," he was overly optimistic.[148] In Europe, the word "antisemitism" would be invented in just two years after Seligman uttered these words, giving rise to the new antisemitic movement, leading to the Nazi regime and the destruction of European Jewry.[149] In the US rising anti-Jewish sentiments coincided with the post-Reconstruction anti-Black racist backlash and with virulent anti-immigrant sentiments. All this helped bolster the notion that "true" Americans were white Protestants, others were undeserving of citizenship and equality.

In the South, the Klan affirmed those values, violently targeting Black Americans, sometimes along with, to quote scholar Charles Reagan Wilson, "Jews, Catholics, foreigners, and those Protestants who were deemed moral degenerates."[150] Some of those attacks were violent, especially against African Americans, who were regularly subjected to lynchings and terror; some incidents were an expression of nonviolent prejudice, and some—especially in regard to Jews—were examples of polite exclusion, or, to use Deborah Lipstadt's term, "dinner party antisemitism."[151] But unlike anti-Catholic or anti-Jewish bigotry, anti-Black discrimination was structural—it was not only part of the culture; it was also built into law and the justice system, and as such, it was, as the *New York Times* editorial comment illustrates, widely accepted.

But the pattern of discrimination closed the circle connecting the US and Europe when Nazi legal scholars came to the United States to study US race laws in order to find justification for anti-Jewish laws they wanted to pass in Germany.[152] The Nazis were particularly interested in questions concerning restrictions of citizenship and in anti-miscegenation laws. They saw American jurisprudence as a model, if imperfect, to follow and justify their own measures. As James Whitman has shown, the Nazi interest in American jurisprudence reveals a long American history of a conscious "work-around" the principle of equality and citizenship in order to hide "the depths of American racism."[153] The Nazis readily recognized that American law was trying to protect white supremacy and saw through this web of "covert devices and legal subterfuges" that were designed, according to Whitman, "to preserve the façade of compliance with the Fourteenth Amendment."[154] They also understood the two clashing strands of American values articulated from the earliest years of the republic: the abstract concept of equality or "formalistic liberal egalitarianism" standing against "realistic racism," which affirmed white supremacy.[155] The Nazi jurists and legal scholars saw through the fissure dividing Americans torn between idealistic equality and racism. And while Americans were engaging in what the Nazis called "*Umwege*, devious legal pathways" to sustain a racist system of citizenship, the Nazis wanted to use these principles and create an "open system of racist citizenship"; they were not ashamed of their antisemitism and racism.[156] Indeed, they proudly flaunted it.

Already in 1920, the Nazi Party Platform advocated restrictions on citizenship, with only "a person of German blood . . . a *Volk*-comrade" eligible, explicitly excluding Jews, and demoting them to the status of "foreigners."[157] Later, in his *Mein Kampf*, Hitler criticized the liberal conception of citizenship. "Today," he wrote, "the right of citizenship is acquired primarily through birth *inside* the borders of the state. Race or membership in the *Volk* play no role whatsoever."[158] Hitler complained that even "a Negro" who resided in Germany could "thus beget a 'German citizen.'" So, too, "any Jewish child, or Polish child, or Asian child can become a German citizen without further ado." Becoming a citizen was like "joining an automobile club." Hitler wanted for the racial considerations to play a more decisive role.

When Hitler and the Nazis came to power in 1933, they began to pursue the project of legal "denaturalization" of Jews, first the east European Jews, then with the Nuremberg laws all others; their citizenship became invalidated and they were then gradually eliminated from public life and public spaces. And while American segregation was not the Nazis' prime interest, by the late thirties, it was also implemented in some places in Germany, marking some spaces with signs "*Juden sind nicht erwünscht*" (Jews not welcome here), as did a village of Behringersdorf, which placed such a sign on its outskirts.[159] Over the next several years, as Jews were gradually excluded from the civic society, violence also increased, and the Nazi propaganda churned out publications and films to justify these moves.

The Nazi political and ideological influence was also felt beyond Germany. In Poland, as Joel Cang wrote in 1939, the Polish Nationalist Party, the Endeks, embraced principles that represented "Nazi principles interchanged and mixed with Polish peculiarities and local coloring," calling for "the complete elimination through expulsion or otherwise, of all Jews from Poland.[160] But when challenged on the grounds that violence and antisemitism "contradict[ed] the principles of Christianity," the Endek party's response was: "We have not the slightest need to write about antisemitism being contrary to Christianity. Such a reproach is simply laughable. It arises from the complete ignorance of the traditions and principles of the Catholic church in that matter." The Endeks were not incorrect. Christianity and the legal and theological structures it created played an important role in the history of anti-Jewish attitudes.

But even the more moderate Christian Labor Party, whose leadership included General Józef Haller, the economist Stanisław Grabski, and other major political figures of interwar Poland, espoused similar policies. At the 1938 congress in Katowice, the party's program declared: "This party will fight for the complete elimination of Jews from industry, trade, and business. The party will support the tendencies for a complete cultural separation from the Jews but definitely opposes all racial theories and denounces all attempts to solve the Jewish problem in Poland through terror. As the best solution of the Jewish problem the party regards mass emigration of the Jews."[161]

This was an ideological and legal prelude to the attempt by Germans at the total annihilation of European Jews. By 1945, some six million European Jews had perished, most of them in death camps the Nazis set up in occupied Poland. This was an unprecedented act of methodical industrialized annihilation aimed at a particular group of people. While there had been examples of genocides and ethnic cleansings, and racially or ethnically motivated, even systemic, violence before, such planned systematically executed murder aimed at elimination of an entire Jewish population was unprecedented.[162] But we are getting ahead of the story.

# CHAPTER NINE

# Visualizing Social Hierarchy

THE NINETEENTH CENTURY brought major breakthroughs in mass media technology. The development of chromolithography coupled with rotary and the offset printing technology allowed for mass production of color images. Added was the increasingly cheap paper, made of wood pulp. Newspapers began to publish not just text but also cartoons. Cartoonists in the US and in Europe began to respond to contemporary events and engage in political and social commentary, capturing, and often also reproducing patterns of discrimination and exclusion. In the US, their stinging sketches recorded and reflected not only anti-Black racism, but also racialized anti-Jewish, anti-Chinese, anti-Catholic, and even anti-Mormon attitudes.[1] In Europe, Jews were frequently a sole target.

Political antisemitism in Europe and the Jim Crow era in the US were a backlash against citizenship and equality of Jews in Europe and Black Americans in the US. But in the United States, the racist backlash coincided with a wave of immigrants, from Asia in the West and from eastern and southern Europe in the East, releasing a new anti-immigrant virulence characterized by anti-Catholic, anti-Jewish, and anti-Chinese attitudes, and forcing the white Protestant society to grapple with the newcomers and the changing make-up of the country.[2] The Chinese became a category not easily fitting into the racial hierarchy structured so rigidly along black and white lines. Indeed, even the seventeenth-century traveler, François Bernier, considered them as "véritablement blanc," truly white, with caveats that their physique differs in the shape of their eyes, which Bernier described as "small pig's eyes," and faces, "flat" with "three hairs for a beard."[3]

In 1877, during congressional hearings on Chinese immigration, a white Protestant pastor, who was arguing for Chinese exclusion, observed "the practical superiority of slavery over Chinese immigration, as an impelling force for good."[4] Slavery, he argued, "compelled the heathen to give up idolatry" and "the adoption of Christian forms of worship, resulting in universal Christianization." But, not being slaves, "the Chinese have no such compulsion and they do not do it. . . . The Chinese have no such influence tending to their conversion, and rarely—one or two in a thousand—become Christian." The pastor was evidently sympathetic to Black citizenship and suffrage, arguing that "slavery took the heathens and by force made them Americans in feeling, tastes, habits, language, sympathy, religion and spirit; first fitting them for citizenship, and then giving them the vote," but he held different views about the Chinese. For him "the Chinese feel no such force [to become American]"; they remained "in character and life the same as they were in Old China, unprepared for citizenship and adverse in spirit to our institutions." For the pastor, as Helen H. Jun has shown, part of Americanization was becoming a Christian. His language about incompatibility of the Chinese with American citizenship and the "spirit of our institutions" was eerily similar to that used against Jews in Europe. Jews, too, were portrayed as "oriental" aliens in spirit to the European Christians; they, too, were "unassimilable."

With the Chinese Exclusion Act passed in 1882, Chinese immigrants became legally ineligible for citizenship, those who were in the United States were deemed "aliens," a status affirmed in 1893 by the same Supreme Court justices who would rule on *Plessy v. Ferguson* just three years later. The 1893 Supreme Court ruling supporting the Chinese Exclusion Act and sanctioned the deportation of immigrants "lawfully residing in the United States" if the Congress deemed "their race . . . undesirable."[5] The anti-Chinese sentiments were not unfamiliar even to Justice Harlan, who in his passionate dissent in *Plessy* used an example of a "Chinaman" to underscore injustice done to Black Americans. "There is a race," Harlan wrote, "so different from our own that we do not permit those belonging to it to become citizens of the United States. . . . I allude to the Chinese race."[6] And yet, "by the statute in question, a Chinaman can ride in the same passenger coach with white citizens of the United States, while citizens of the black race in Louisiana, many of whom, perhaps, risked their lives for the preservation of the Union" were considered "criminals, liable to imprisonment, if they ride in a public coach occupied by citizens of the white race."

The reigning anti-Chinese sentiments, which led to the passage of the Chinese Exclusion Act, were a part of the same sentiments that defended white Protestant supremacy against those challenging it on a religious or racial level, leading to anti-Black violence, antisemitism, and anti-immigrant animus. In 1871, Thomas Nast of *Harper's Weekly* published a cartoon called "The Chinese Question" (fig. 19).[7] At the center stands Columbia, a white woman symbolizing America, facing right toward a crowd of boorish-looking armed white men. Behind them in the background, a tree with a noose is seen right next to a burned down "Colored Orphan Asylum." Placards can be seen in the crowd: "If our ballot will not stop them coming to OUR country, the bullet must;" "Blood . . ."; "We rule . . ."; and "Our rights." At Columbia's feet is a crouched figure of a crying Chinese man, whose head she touches with her right hand, her left clutched in a fist. She stands in front of a wall covered with anti-Chinese statements, targeting the Chinese as cheap labor and religious outsiders: "Coolie, Slave, Pauper, and a Rat-Eater"; a quote from a supposed trade union resolution: "The importation of Chinese BARBARIANS into the country must be stopped by a ballot or a bullet"; a quote from Wendell Phillips: "The Chinaman works cheap because he is a BARBARIAN and seeks gratification of only the LOWEST, inevitable wants"; "They are dishonest and false and vicious, immoral heathenish"; "John Chinaman is an IDOLATER and HEATHEN"; "Chinese paganism has by its fruits practical immorality fouler by far than that known among any European or Christian people." Columbia's response to these statements and the crowd reaffirmed American ideals: "Hands off, Gentlemen! America means fair play for every man." Anti-Chinese sentiments thus seized not only upon the issue of cheap labor but also upon that religious motif, marking the Chinese as pagan or heathen, and, thus, as both racial and religious outsiders.

If Nast's cartoons represented relatively liberal views, many magazines were less charitable toward those they perceived as inferior outsiders. In July 1887, *Life* published an anti-immigrant double-spread, glorifying the pilgrims who arrived in 1620, and vilifying those who arrived in 1887: the poor, the crippled, the Jewish.[8]

Some seized on the idea of "undesirable clientele" in resorts, as did *Life* in the summer of 1885. In a July issue, a double-spread cartoon depicted, on one page: "Scene: Fashionable resort. Time: Mid-Summer," showing a resort overrun by caricatures of Black men, while, on the other, the privileged whites were doomed to spend their summer on "Fifth Ave."[9] Later in the summer, the magazine published another double-spread cartoon titled "Some Summer Styles."[10] One scene depicted stereotyped "savage" semi-nude black men, with thick lips, round earrings, with a short grass skirt, working as wait staff at a resort. Below, a fat man with a big nose is shown smiling at a fashionably dressed woman, her wealth indicated to viewers

FIGURE 19. Thomas Nast, "Chinese Question," *Harper's Weekly*, February 18, 1871, 149. Public domain.

by a shiny brooch and dollar signs drawn on her clearly expensive dress—
an unmistakable stereotype of a Jew eyeing a rich woman for her money.

Magazines, joke books, postcards, and songsters began to disseminate
widely racist imagery, targeting all considered outsiders. For example, I & M
Ottenheimer Publishers in Baltimore, Maryland published a series of ten
joke books, including "Coon Jokes," "Irish Jokes," "Hebrew Jokes," and
"Blackface Minstrel Jokes," each filled with demeaning stereotypes. With
the rise of the postcard in the 1890s, postcards, too, became a vehicle for
transmission of degrading imagery expanding their geographic reach. In
these Black figures had cartoonishly large lips, wide noses, were often fat
and ugly, typical of what Henry Louis Gates Jr. termed "Sambo art"; they
were, as Gates put it, "embodiments of all that was the reverse of Truth and
Beauty, the Good and the Civilized" (fig. 20).[11] Such images were not only
produced for entertainment, they were also produced to sell commercial
products—the types that only reasserted racial hierarchy: soaps, cleaning
products, rice ("Uncle Ben's"), pancake flour ("Aunt Jemima"), cream of
wheat, and others. Americans were ubiquitously exposed to this imagery.

Similar iconography developed for Jews. In Europe, it blossomed in
the last decade of the nineteenth century and the first three decades of
the twentieth, especially in France during the Dreyfus affair, with postcards and magazines like *La Libre Parole* and others churning out caricatures for mass consumption.[12] In the US, it appeared in postcards and
magazines, especially in juxtaposition with white Christians. *Life* magazine, founded in 1883, its tagline "Humorous, Satirical, Refined," depicted
refinement only in images of the white bourgeois upper-class society,
while the rest, those considered "non-white," such as Black Americans,
Jews, immigrants, or Native Americans, were depicted as revolting or
laughable. In Europe, the visual degradation of the Jew had, of course,
as Sara Lipton has shown, a long history that was tied to the transformations within medieval Christian theology. Like "Sambo art" in the late
nineteenth century and in the twentieth century, which depicted African
Americans as "the reverse of Truth and Beauty, the Good and the Civilized," traditional Christian iconography's disfigurement of Jews to portray
them as ugly was about affirming Christian truth and amplifying its rejection by Jews; that is what is behind the invention of the Jewish nose.[13] But
in the modern era, anti-Jewish iconography lost its theological meaning
and became racialized.[14] Jews were depicted as fat, thick lipped, with big
noses, and darker complexion and hair (fig. 21).

In some instances, Jews and Blacks were linked, as objects of ridicule
and racial fear. In one such postcard, a fat, bald, unsightly Jewish man is

FIGURE 20. A trio of racist postcards published by E. Nash in 1905, postmarked 1906. It features racist iconography that draws on visual tropes introduced in the early modern period. Fordham University.

FIGURE 21. "Just to pass time." An antisemitic postcard, mailed in Pennsylvania in 1906. Fordham University.

shown marrying an equally fat black woman, her face featuring exaggerated lips and nose. The caption says, "What will the harvest be?"[15] Another, from Germany, depicts two scenarios of a German man marrying outside his "race." In one, he is shown marrying a dark-haired Jewess, fat and big-nosed, their children, too, with dark hair and big noses; in the second, a German married a black woman, depicted as fat, with exaggerated thick lips, big nose, and Afro-textured hair; their children all black, with similar features.[16] Another one, mocking Darwin's theory of evolution, displays a monkey, a caricature of an African man—bald, naked, with exaggerated lips and large round earrings, and an elegantly dressed Jew, with big nose that cannot be hidden behind his smart European clothes.

Mixing the races was seen, since the Enlightenment, as "degradation" of the white race, its apogee was manifested in the Nazi era in books, popular press, cartoons, children's books, and films. Adolf Hitler himself imagined "the black-haired" Jew "lurk[ing] in wait for the unsuspecting girl whom he defiles with his blood, thus stealing her from her people. . . . Just as he himself systematically ruins women, he does not shrink from pulling down the blood barriers for others, even on a large scale. It was and it is Jews who bring the Negroes into the Rhineland, always with the same secret thought and clear aim of ruining the hated white race by the necessarily resulting bastardization, throwing it down from its cultural and political height, and himself rising to be its master."[17]

In the US, cartoons linking Jews and African Americans depicted Jews as tricksters and Blacks as dimwits, easily duped by Jews. In the July 9, 1885 issue of *Life Magazine*, for example, a cartoon, titled "Convincing," depicted a stereotyped Jew, perhaps a tailor: fat, bald, big nose, trying to convince a young Black man that his misfitted pants looked fine. Both speak in heavily accented and incorrect English.[18] The depiction of a Jew as a fraudster was quite common. That same year, *Life* published a cartoon of a lady selling a bag of rags to "a ragman," depicted with a big nose and speaking with an accent, "Madam, shust dventy four pounds."[19] To which the woman responded, "Ye old scoundrel it weighs over forty, for OI weighted it meself." The "ragman" then retorts, "B—lieve me, Madame, I vould n't sheat a child. But, my scales vil only vay dventy-four pounds."

Improper speech, deformed look, marked Jews, Black Americans, and the Chinese as outsiders. Frederick Douglass noted the impact. "When a black man's language is quoted," Douglass said, it was done "in order to belittle and degrade him."[20] "His ideas," he continued, "are put into the most grotesque and unreadable English, while the utterances of negro scholars and authors are ignored." This imagery of Jews as tricksters and Blacks as dupes planted seeds of what in the second half of the twentieth century would become an antisemitic and anti-Black trope of Jewish support of Black civil rights in order to disrupt white Christian American society. It returned in 2018 in an RNC ad run in MN-01 depicting George Soros and Colin Kaepernick as "agents of chaos."

The caricatured images of Jews and Black people were frequently juxtaposed to elegant and respectable depiction of white European Christians. In a 1900 book, an American polygenist minister, Charles Carroll published a book arguing that "the Negro" was not a human, could not have come from a human descent but was "a beast."[21] The book's first image is of "The Morning of the Creation of Man," a direct ray of light connects "Heaven" with Adam and Eve, depicted as white and conforming to nineteenth-century white aesthetic standards of beauty.[22] The ray of light is described as "Direct Line of Kinship with God"; the caption reads, "Where does the line of kinship between God and Adam and Eve connect with the Negro?" the subsequent images drove the point home. In the next image in the book, we see a white Jesus Christ on top, with a caricature of a Black man, conforming to aesthetic norms of "Sambo art" next to a white man.[23] The text says "Christ-The Son of God. Man was created in the image of God. Is the negro in the image of God's son, Christ?" The racial similarity between Christ and the white man conveyed the idea that white people were the true children of God; "the Negro" could not

FIGURE 22. "The VIRGIN MARY and the CHILD CHRIST. Could the Child Christ possibly be of the same flesh as the Negro," in Charles Carrol, *"The Negro a Beast," or, "in the Image of God"* . . . *The Negro Not the Son of Ham*. St. Louis: American Book and Bible House, 1900, 104. Fordham University.

possibly be one. An image of a white Mary Virgin with a white baby Jesus and a "Sambo" infant made a similar point: black, exaggerated lips, kinky hair; the caption: "The VIRGIN MARY and the CHILD CHRIST. Could the Child Christ possibly be of the same flesh as the Negro?" (fig. 22). So, too, did an image, at the end of the chapter on "Convincing Biblical and Scientific Evidence that the Negro is not of the Human Family," depicting white Adam and Eve, with a black "Sambo" boy at their feet, and the caption "ADAM and EVE in the GARDER of EDEN. Is the negro an offspring of Adam and Eve? Can the rose produce a thistle?" The book then included images of white parents with Black children—ridiculing the idea of Black humanity; it ended with an image of a Black man raping a white woman—visually affirming the common at the time charge "of assaults by negros upon white women" that had justified, as Frederick Douglass said, "lawless vengeance," "frantic rage and savage extravagance," and led to numerous lynchings.[24]

Theatrical posters also conveyed similar ideas. In 1905, a theatrical poster for *The Frisco* depicted "a lecherous but well-dressed black man," following and "ogl[ing]" in the most exaggerated manner a young, elegantly dressed, refined white woman."[25] As did a 1906 poster for *The New Smart Set* (fig. 23).

FIGURE 23. *The New Smart Set*, U.S. Lithograph Co, and
Smart Set. ca. 1906. Cincinnati; New York: U.S. Lithograph
Co. https://www.loc.gov/item/2014635570/.

This portrayal of Black men as dangerous and lustful was made even
more real in the new medium—the film. *The Birth of the Nation*, released in
1915, portrayed, in the words of historian Leon Litwack, "impudent, ungrateful,
venal black men, their ambitions bloated by emancipation and civil rights,
terroriz[ing] helpless whites, shoving them off sidewalks, blocking their
access to the ballot boxes, and leering at their women."[26] The film included
an attempted rape of a white woman, combining in one story an image of
Black men's "lust after political power or white women."[27] This imagery and
real-life anti-Black accusations and lynchings were designed, as Douglass
observed, "to check the nomination and supremacy of the negro and to
secure absolute rule of the Anglo-Saxon race."[28]

So, too, in Europe, antisemitic imagery was used to drive the point of
both Christian Europeans' racial superiority over Jews, and, like the American imagery of the "black rapist," the perception of Jews as dangerous and

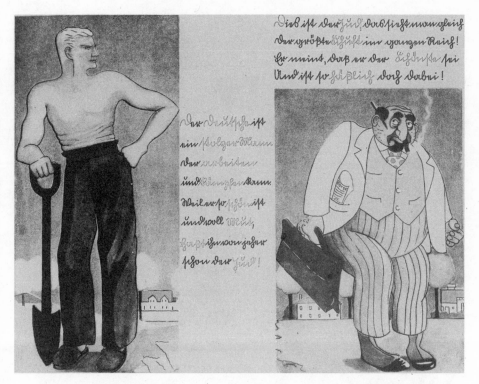

FIGURE 24. Elvira Bauer, *Trau Keinem Fuchs auf Grüner Heid und Keinem Jud bei Seinem Eid: Ein Bilderbuch für Gross und Klein* (Nuremberg: Strürmer-Verlag, 1936), 2. Fordham University.

lecherous villains, endangering the purity of European Christian women, which reached an apogee in the Nazi propaganda from the 1920s on.[29] Some of it was influenced by American media. For example, the Jews' supposed lust for power and for German women was articulated visually in a 1940 Nazi-produced historical drama and blockbuster *Jud Süss* about Joseph Süss Oppenheimer, an eighteenth-century court Jew, who socially and politically climbs in the realm of the Duke of Württemberg, ruining the realm and seducing and raping a daughter of a prominent Württemberg official. The film was made to justify murderous Nazi policies and rally the Germans behind them. Nazis had promoted these ideas through cartoons and books since the 1920s.[30]

The depiction of the ugliness and lecherousness of Jews also made it into children's books. A children's book published in 1936 to translate the Nuremberg laws for a child's mind depicted an ugly, fat, thick-lipped Jew, with dark complexion, leaving no doubt who the superior race was.[31] Right at the beginning a young strapping German is juxtaposed to a fat ugly Jew, the rhymed text draws attention to the two (fig. 24):

FIGURE 25. Elvira Bauer, *Trau Keinem Fuchs auf Grüner Heid und Keinem Jud bei Seinem Eid: Ein Bilderbuch für Gross und Klein* (Nuremberg: Strürmer-Verlag, 1936), 12.

Look at the two and compare! . . .
The German is a proud young man,
Able to work and able to fight.
Because he is a fine big chap,
For danger does not care a rap,
The Jew has always hated him!
Here is the Jew, as all can see,
Biggest ruffian in our country;
He thinks himself the greatest beau
And yet is the ugliest, you know!

Later in the book, the Jew is shown trying to date a German woman (fig. 25). The text and imagery again draw attention to his ugliness and lecherous behavior:

What a creature is the Jew.
Not even his own women he likes.
To share himself a German wife
He thinks just cute. You bet your life!

FIGURE 26. Elvira Bauer, *Trau Keinem Fuchs auf Grüner Heid und Keinem Jud bei Seinem Eid: Ein Bilderbuch für Gross und Klein* (Nuremberg: Strürmer-Verlag, 1936), 18.

> Look at Jew and girl right here:
> 'Tis sure he can't be thought her peer!
> Compare him with this German Frau.
> He cuts a pitiable figure now!
> I would the Jew had sense to own
> He'd best leave German girls alone.
> Try his own "kalle" instead.

Toward the end, the book turns to German schools, rejoicing the removal of Jews, as they were through the Nuremberg laws (fig. 26):

> It's going to be fine in the schools at last,
> For all the Jews must leave.
> For big and small it's all alike.
> Anger and rage do not avail
> Nor utmost Jewish whine nor wail
> Away with all the Jewish breed.

'Tis the German teacher we desire.
Now he leads the way to cleverness,
Wanders and plays with us, but yet
Keeps us children in good order.
He makes jokes with us and laughs
So going to school is quite a joy.

The imagery too makes a clear racial point: Germans are beautiful, their complexion fair, their hair blond; Jews are ugly, their complexion dark, their hair black.

And it did not matter that Jews or Black Americans did not look or behave the way the mass-produced popular culture depicted them; when they were encountered, that is how they were seen.[32] What Henry Louis Gate Jr. has said about "the collective image of the black person in American popular culture" as "function[ing] like a visual mantra reinforcing the negativity of difference" marked by "twin poles of repugnance and fascination" can be equally said about antisemitic imagery produced in Europe and in the United States, especially in the nineteenth and twentieth centuries.[33] Indeed, the goal of both anti-Black and antisemitic imagery was "to naturalize the visual image" of Black people and Jews "as subhuman" and thus inferior.[34]

The language used to describe Black Americans was often similar to that describing Jews in Europe. For example, with only slight revisions, the description of Black people in *Williams v. Missouri* (1898) could be applied to Jews. "By reason of its previous condition of servitude and dependencies," the court stated, "this race has acquired or accentuated certain peculiarities of habit, of temperament, and of character, which clearly distinguished it as a race from the whites. A patient, docile people; but careless, landless, migratory within narrow limits, without forethought; and its criminal members given to furtive offences, rather than the robust crimes of whites."[35] Like Jews in Europe, Black people in the US were described as "landless" and "migratory," in essence, as not belonging. They were suspected and accused of crimes against Christian Europeans. Both were seen as "unassimilable," if for different reasons, and the idea of unassimilability was reinforced through antisemitic and "Sambo" imagery. And there were of course differences. The essence of the differences is epitomized in two similar US postcards from the first decade of the twentieth century (fig. 27). One depicts a watermelon turning into a black man's head, the cut in the watermelon becoming his red, exaggeratedly large, open mouth: "Evolution: From a watermelon into Coon."[36] The other depicts the similar evolution of a sack of money that turns into a Jew.[37]

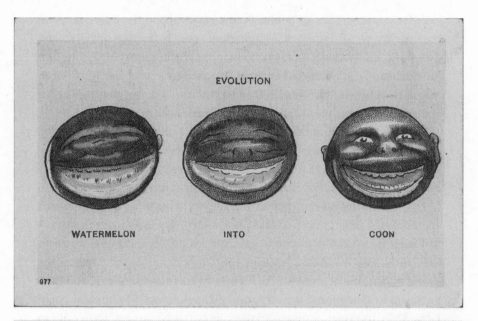

FIGURE 27. Two postcards: "Evolution Watermelon," post-stamped 1909, and "Evolution of a capitalist," post-stamped 1910. The author's own collection.

Black Americans and Jews pushed back against such visual stereotypes and portrayals of them as "inferior races."[38] Already in 1854, Frederick Douglass flagged this visual contrast. In his essay "The Claims of the Negro Ethnologically Considered," he noted that it was "fashionable now, in our land, to exaggerate the differences between the negro and the European" in order to present the hierarchy: "the *highest* type of the European, and the *lowest* type of the negro."[39] Douglass astutely pointed out that "the European face is drawn in harmony with the highest ideas of beauty, dignity and intellect," with "features regular and brow after the Websterian mold." In contrast, "the negro," Douglass continued, was depicted "with features distorted, lips exaggerated, forehead depressed—and the whole expression of the countenance made to harmonize with the popular idea of negro imbecility and degradation." He lamented that he had "never seen a single picture in an American work, designed to give an idea of the mental endowments of the negro, which did any thing like justice to the subject." Douglass returned to that subject in his 1894 speech "Lessons of the Hour": "Even when American art undertakes to picture the types of two races it invariably places in comparison not the best of both races as fairness would dictate, but it puts side by side in glaring contrast the lowest type of the negro with the highest type of the white man and calls upon you to look upon this picture and then upon that."[40] The same could be said for the visual representation of Jews and white Christians both in Europe and in the United States, reaching the zenith the 1930s and 1940s.

To counteract this flood of derogative imagery, Jews and Black Americans began to promote their own ideals and visual representations. In Europe, the Zionist movement that emerged as a response to rising antisemitism began to promote the image of a "new Jew": muscular and masculine, a far cry from the deformed stereotype depicted so widely in popular media. Max Nordau, famously, decried Jews' degeneration and promoted the idea of a "new muscular Jew."[41] The fin de siècle Jewish artists began to create images of fit and attractive Jews (fig. 28), and Zionist photographers took photos of Jews in Palestine engaging in physical and productive labor, in the fields or in crafts.[42] Affluent European Jews, for their part, commissioned portraits by famous artists such as Pierre-Auguste Renoir or Gustav Klimt.

For American Jews, struggling for acceptance and respectability, such opportunity emerged with the Chicago World's Fair of 1893, organized at the height of east European Jewish migration and growing antisemitism in the US, to show arts and accomplishments of Jews across the globe. The exhibit highlighted the work of the French *Alliance israélite universelle* and was a "cornucopia of crafts, art, and student accomplishments"[43] The report of the exhibition prepared for the Congress by the Department of Education acknowledged the tacit goal behind the exhibit was to challenge anti-Jewish stereotypes.[44] The report discussed the schools supported by the Alliance, noting that they "did not present a denominational

FIGURE 28. Ephraim Moses Lilien, "Die Gesänge des Jehuda" *in Juda: Gesänge von Börries, Freiherrn von Münchhausen mit Buchschmuck von E. M. Lilien* (Goslar, Germany: F. A. Lattmann, 1900). The author's own collection.

character" and "their aims are purely educational, and they try to avoid the narrow spirit of exclusiveness."[45] The Alliance, the report noted, "has taken up the difficult task of assisting the moral and intellectual development of Jews, of encouraging the acquirement of professions and trades, and of struggling against their ignorance and faults, frequently the result of ill-founded prejudices." But the association worked "outside of political and religious questions, direct[ing] its activity, according to a circular published, principally to the work of education." Its schools were "founded on the modern demands of education," eschewing traditional schools, like the Talmud Torah, "which is of a sectarian character." The exposition at the Chicago World's Fair was "filled with a quantity of articles." But it was "the exhibits of agricultural institutions [that] excited special interest, as they proved that with proper education the young Jews were capable of taking an interest in agriculture, for which in Russia they generally show an aversion." It is clear from this report that though the exhibit focused on the work of *Alliance israélite universelle* in the Mediterranean, its goal was to show that Jews could be productive members of society, neutralizing antisemitic stereotypes of Jews as avoiding "productive" physical labor, preferring easier ways to make money.

Black Americans too began to focus on the promotion of the "new Negro."[46] But while Jews did not feel the need to affirm their intellect—their achievements and "cleverness" were, after all, what irked antisemites—and focused on the body and trades, African American intellectuals focused on intellect and respectability; they did not need to show Black ability to do physical work, that was a given. Both groups were counteracting the stereotypes that were epitomized in the two postcards depicting the evolution of a watermelon and a sack of money. The 1893 Chicago World's Fair, according to the report to the Congress, featured exhibits about "negro education," but it showcased the Hampton Institute of Virginia, a Black educational institution attended by Booker T. Washington, praising it for teaching "the red and the colored men useful trades—printing, blacksmithing, wheelwrighting, shoe-making, and tailoring, and the finished articles exhibited are uniformly well done."[47] A year later, Frederick Douglass expressed his frustration with the invisibility of Black intellectuals. In his "Lessons of the Hour," he bemoaned the fact that whites would attend "white negro minstrels with faces blackened with burnt cork," but few would be seen at "a lecture by an intelligent negro."[48] And so, seven years later, when the 1900 World's Fair in Paris featured "The American Negro Exhibit," it looked different.[49]

Organized by Daniel Alexander Payne Murray, the Assistant Librarian of Congress, in collaboration with Thomas Colloway, a lawyer and educator, and W. E. B. Du Bois, at the time, a professor of sociology at Atlanta University, the exhibition displayed "charts, maps, and graphs recording the growth of population, economic power, and literacy among African Americans in Georgia," along with over five hundred photographs selected to show Black Americans at "homes, businesses, churches and communities," challenging white stereotypes "of blacks as impoverished, lazy, and ignorant."[50] The organizers wanted, as David Levering Lewis has put it, "to set the great white world straight about Black people."[51] The photographs showed African Americans as doctors, members of the board of directors of manufacturing companies, men and women dressed in fashionable clothes, in respectable bourgeois settings; they were "cynosures of all the characteristics and virtues of which most whites, either in ignorance or from bigotry, believed most blacks of be devoid."[52] As Shawn Michelle Smith has argued, W. E. B. Du Bois and his partners devised the exhibit and chose the photographs to "function as a counterarchive that challenge[d] a long legacy of racist taxonomy, intervening in turn-of-the-century 'race science'" and providing "competing visual evidence."[53]

Similarly, across the country, Black photographers, most famous of them James Van Der Zee, photographed Black Americans projecting their achievements and respectability.[54] Some of those images were also sold as postcards (fig. 29). But these respectable images, as Black intellectuals observed, "were so vastly outnumbered that they did not have a meaningful chance at countering the fabrication of racist imagery."[55]

The struggle of Black middle and upper classes for respectability, especially in the North, was made more difficult by the Great Migration, when millions of Southern, mostly poor, rural, and uneducated Black Americans moved to northern cities. As Henry Louis Gates Jr. noted, "The Old Negros . . . came flooding, further exacerbating class differences within the black community."[56] These affluent and successful Blacks were fearful of being associated with the newcomers, a dynamic that was strikingly similar to that among American Jews, who struggled for respectability and then were faced with the mass migration of poor, undereducated, and unacculturated Jews from eastern Europe. Both the Black newcomers from the South and the Jewish immigrants from the east confirmed to white Christians in the US the antisemitic and anti-Black stereotypes that were already deeply ingrained in popular imagination, "fixed upon them," to quote Henry Louis Gates Jr., "like hoods or masks." These dangerous stereotypes helped justify not only social and legal exclusion and discrimination, but also, in the US, widespread lynchings of Black men, and, in Europe, the antisemitic violence and then, later, the Nazi murder of Jews.

Despite hopes expressed by Joseph Seligman in 1877 and Du Bois's proud exhibition in Paris, the twentieth century was marked by even more virulent anti-Black and antisemitic violence. In 1920, W. E. B. Du Bois, under whose leadership the NAACP, an organization established in 1909 to fight anti-Black violence, began to collect statistics on lynchings, wrote about the impact of centuries of degradation on Black and white Americans: "One cannot ignore the extraordinary fact that a world campaign beginning with the slave-trade and ending with the refusal to capitalize the word 'Negro,' leading through a passionate defense of slavery by attributing every bestiality to blacks and finally culminating in the evident modern profit which lies in degrading blacks—all this has unconsciously trained millions of honest,

FIGURE 29. A photograph of an unnamed man, Richmond, Virginia, Davis Studio. The author's own collection.

modern men into the belief that that black folk are sub-human . . . a mass of despicable men, inhuman; at best, laughable; at worst, the meat of mobs and fury."[57]

The same can be said about the impact mass-produced, antisemitic imagery, written works, and propaganda that unleashed a new level of derogatory stereotyping of Jews in Europe and in America. But if in the US the antisemitic imagery might have been in the category of depicting Jews as unpleasant but laughable, in Europe, especially under the Nazi regime, which also refused to capitalize the word "Jew," film and print depicted Jews as despicable and vile, as rapists and dangerous enemies of the state, deserving expulsion or total annihilation. The visual propaganda, it turned out, served as a backdrop to the mass killings that were to follow.

# CHAPTER TEN

# The (Stunted) Reckoning

THE TWENTIETH CENTURY, as George M. Fredrickson has noted, brought both "climax and retreat" of racism and antisemitism.[1] World War II left millions dead, among them six million European Jews, who were degraded, ghettoized, enslaved, and then methodically murdered. The vast number of dead and the very systematic genocide during World War II revealed where the path of hatred leads humanity. "In the beginning was the word," the narrator of a 1948 film called *Strange Victory* said over footage of Hitler speaking, "the end—rubble."[2] The systematic annihilation of European Jews, including over 90 percent of Polish Jews, forced a reckoning with ideas and attitudes that made these unprecedented crimes possible. The scope of the crimes committed during the war also prompted broader reconsideration of social and religious values dominating Western society. The decades that followed also forced "a re-examination," as the editor of *Ebony* put it in the context of the Black struggle for civil rights, "of the Christian faith which brought forth the idea that skin color was not a true measure of a man's humanity."[3] After World War II, Christianity was on trial.

But a true reckoning was not possible, neither in Europe, nor in the United States. While some were willing to confront their own complicity or at least that of their own society and culture, the majority were not ready for this introspection. It was easy to execute the worst of the Nazi leaders. Yet, as *Strange Victory* emphasized, that kind of reckoning was not enough.[4] The moment of euphoria over victory was fleeting. "We rounded them up," Saul Levitt narrated in the film. "We dug them out. We got Quisling and all the other quislings. . . . We collected all the little killers. The little ones and the big ones. We had them," Levitt said over the footage of Goering. Showing the images from the Nuremberg trial, the narrator continued, "And we made a new law to fit a new crime. The crime of killing a whole people by your own idea that you were better than they were. The crime of profiting from murder. Of teaching a whole nation to murder. Of ordering murder. And what's the penalty for child murder? We tried to make the punishment fit the crime, but we only hanged them."

The reckoning was anticlimactic and unsatisfying, not only because Hitler himself was not caught or because the punishment was not commensurate to the crimes committed. The issues ran far deeper. As the narrator of *Strange Victory* noted, "And if Hitler died, why does his voice still pursue us through the spaces of American life?"[5] The victory achieved in 1945 rang hollow. "Nobody knows for sure where the victory is. Lost, stray or stolen," the film ended with these words spoken over the sequence of images from American streets, spliced with images of Nazi camps, "White Only" signs, and others. "It isn't here. And if we won, why do we look as if we lost? Why is the news still bad? Not enough victory to go around. Too many quotas. Too many invisible yellow stars. Not enough housing to call it a victory. Not enough peace to call it peaceful. Too much fear. Too many raw deals. Not enough hope to call it a victory. So, the battle is still on. Without guns now. The old hard battle. And if we want victory, we still have to get it." *Strange Victory* highlighted the pervasive racism and antisemitism in America—of political leaders and ordinary people who looked the other way, or perhaps complacently participated in the system of prejudice and oppression, or quietly whispered words of bigotry, lived in or patronized "restricted" establishments, or violently and gleefully engaged in lynchings. All this taking place even after the most horrific war in history. *Strange Victory* did not let anyone off the hook. No one could hide, everyone was responsible, in America and in Germany, and everywhere else. *Strange Victory* with Saul Levitt's narration echoed Jeremiah's "Peace, peace, when there is no peace."

A year before *Strange Victory* was released, Charles Abrams, a lawyer and author of *A Housing Program for America*, reported in *The Commentary*, a newly established Jewish magazine, on the rise of restrictive covenants in the United States.[6] "Eighty years after Gettysburg," Abrams wrote, "and two years after Hitler, the proposition that all men are created equal is again being whittled down, and in the area perhaps most crucial for a future democratic America—the area of our neighborhood life." The trend was troubling, because "the weight of judicial authority here in the United States of America now holds that white landowners may freely band together to bar Negroes from a place to live, that Christians may shut out Jews, that Protestants may ban Catholics." With such discrimination now also supported by the FHA, Abrams argued, "the involuntary ghetto may soon be an unalterable American institution." Racism and discrimination were built into space, allowing "decent citizens" to buy homes "without [a] touch of conscience."

There was much work to be done for the victory to be fulfilling; there was still much despair. But there was also hope. Through the lyrical meditation on newborns and the meaning of childhood, Leo Hurwitz's *Strange Victory* conveyed both hope and despair. Hope because hatred and prejudice are learned, not innate. Children, the new generation, were a hope for change. In a sequence showing newborns of different races and ethnicities, a soft female voice is heard speaking: "And we speak to this hope. We whisper to it the first lullaby. Rest. And listen to me deep in your slumber, you hope of mine. Does our light hurt your eyes? Is this place strange? . . . I swear to you by the tides going in, going out, by the way moon changes to night changes to morning. By the sun promised to this earth forever." As the camera shows images of white and Black newborns, she reiterates: "I swear to you: You belong here. For this is the right place. And you are loved. . . . Created. Each from the same dark into the same light. This is us. We tend to forget these small strange beginnings. The promise. The becoming. The unforeseen. This too is how we are. We are made and we make. Columbus in a way. Each one of us. Holding a new world within the borders of our arms. Discovering them with our own hands."[7] The woman's voice then asks questions, which she joyfully answers, "And where will you go? Oh, you'll go everywhere. And what will you do? Oh, you'll do everything." The images show modern advancements in technology, dams, airplanes, an orchestra, a city viewed from the plane; babies, but no longer newborns; then toddlers. "And what will you do? Well, I told you, you'll do everything. . . . And how big is the world? How high? And how fast will you go? How far? And where to? . . . And whose world is it? It's yours for the making. It's yours. . . . It's for you. The world and what we made of it. It's for you."[8] There were no limits to the children's potential.

But there was also despair—precisely because hatred and prejudice are not innate, but learned from the moment we are born.[9] Leo Hurwitz's *Strange Victory* offered a sobering meditation on despair crashing the hope and the dreams. A male voice is heard reciting racial and ethnic slurs, as film footage shows a doctor lifting newborns by their legs and slapping them after birth. A woman's voice whispers in the background: "I've got nothing against them. . . . Some of my best friends are Jews." The male narrator soon picks up, "Voices sometimes crude. Sometimes polite. Really one voice. Stealing across the birthday like a shadow. This sound . . . of our customs and our daily barbarisms. Call it the voice of custom. Whoever you are we welcome you. You are now part of the human race. . . . You are now part of the United States in the fifth decade of the twentieth century. You belong here," the voice says over a shot of a Black baby in a cot next to a white baby. "You have come to share our world. And I have some words of advice to you. I am going to put some plain facts before you. . . . There are many things you must learn in order to get along. First, who are you? You know that there are differences among you, which are important. The color of your skin is important," the narrator says over the footage of a white baby. "The slant of your eyes," over the image of an Asian baby. "The breadth of your nostrils," over a Black baby. "The shape of your nose," over a Jewish baby. "These are facts. We also separate you by your names. What's in a name? O'Connell. Goldberg. Wilson. Yes, there are differences among you, which will last all your life. They are as good as written," the voice says ominously over images of patient cards, with names and symbolic stamps: Richard Johnson, stamped WXP, "White Christian Protestant. All other things being equal, the best breaks will come your way." Rosalie Jordan, stamped with NXP, "Negro Christian Protestant. There are fourteen million of you. You will live a special life in this country. And I advise you to pay careful attention to what I will say later." Joseph O'Connell, stamped WXC, for White Christian Catholic: "If you are Catholic, there will be some people who won't think well of you, although actual persecution isn't practiced right now." The camera pans to another newborn, "There are some four million others who work at some jobs and live in certain districts. But their choices will be limited," the narrator says over a card for one Samuel Hershkowitz, stamped, WJ, White Jewish. "If you are Jewish, you are one of them." As the camera zooms out to show all these newborns, the male voice pronounces the painful truth, "And no matter how many times, you will recite the Declaration of Independence. No matter how often you invoke the Thirteenth, the Fourteenth, and the Fifteenth Amendments, no matter what you hear on the Fourth of July, and whatever rights the laws give you, whatever they say in churches," the camera pans over the image of crying babies, "whatever you were taught in classrooms, these are the facts you will live by. This is how it is now for you who are now a part of the human family in the United States of America in this decade." How hard facts are is shown through painful images of segregated South, ads seeking "white tenants only" or "white girls" for housekeeping, and through signs for "restricted" communities. The painful truth is that "the world is already arranged for you. Facts." These were the ways in which the systemic racism has been perpetuating the social hierarchies that have undercut the hope for each child's potential to be able "to go anywhere."

The hardest world awaits the Black newborn: "Now that youngster over there, when your eyes begin to focus, you will discover many things. A house is where you eat, sleep, and grow."[10] And as the camera pans over to a canopied entry to a fancy apartment building, the male voice says, "You won't live in a house like this. You will live somewhere else." Here the camera shows a dilapidated house, next to an empty lot. "Afterwards you'll go to work," the narrator speaks over a street sequence with white people in professional clothes, "but you will rarely show up in a crowd coming out of the main entrance. As a janitor or a porter, you will use the freight entrance. In some parts of this country, they write it all out on signs," the voice says over a sequence with shots from the South and the signs "colored entrance," "for colored only," and "white only."

The message is reinforced by a story of a Tuskegee pilot, Virgil Richardson, returning home from Europe.[11] While in Europe he was one of the liberators; at home, he is greeted with violence and degradation, and no jobs for which he is well qualified and which should belong to him. While he receives an appointment for a job interview, once he arrives, he is told by a secretary that "all the pilot openings are filled. I am sorry." Both the secretary and the airman know this is not true and what it is all about. And the narrator's voice lists the statistics: "In the airlines of post-war America there are no Negro pilots. No co-pilots. No navigators. Only a thousand Negros flew in the war against Nazi Germany. We only let a thousand fly. But the old job mopping the floor in the men's room is still open. A Negro flyer. A million soldiers. A people of fourteen million who are still waiting for their share of the victory." In adding the sentence "we only let a thousand fly," the filmmakers made sure that the point did not get lost—it was not about abilities and qualifications, it was about the barriers that the white society and the United States government put in place.

Indeed, as Black veterans returned, expecting to partake in victory, they were denied the benefits of the post-war years.[12] The way the GI Bill was structured, giving local officials and counselors authority to direct vets to the benefits meant that many Black veterans were denied the benefits white veterans received. The Veterans Administration, for example, applied the same rules for housing that the FHA had, excluding Black vets from eligibility for mortgages. As one veteran would later remark, "If I was man enough to fight the war, I'm man enough for everything else."[13]

But that was not a view shared by white employers. In March 1946, *The Commentary* ran a piece on employment and race.[14] It quoted some Southern employers to demonstrate how discrimination and existing race hierarchy affected hiring. "You may not pick the man who is best qualified for a particular job if his skin is of the wrong color. You may not put a good white man in this job if the job is traditionally a colored man's job, and, at the same time, you cannot put a colored man in a white man's job even if he is twice as efficient and three times as productive as his white competitor for the position." The conclusion was obvious: discrimination was "bad business" everywhere, not only in the South, and it was bad "also for consumers and taxpayers."

Virgil Richardson, thus, was not alone. His story echoed that of so many others. According to Will Thomas, writing in 1946 in *The Crisis* about a Black veteran, "Bitterness had scalded him almost immediately [as] he stepped from the big plane onto his native soil."[15] Thomas conveyed the hopes Black servicemen felt at the end of the war "that by now people would understand that Negro soldiers were dying in precisely the same fashion as were their fellows in arms. And presumably they were dying for precisely the same symbol, the same cause"; they hoped that when they returned home, they would have "earned at least the goodwill of *all* his American brothers." But that hope was shattered—what they found was "the old hate, contempt and condescension." In Europe, they flew fighting an armed enemy, "you killed him or he killed you. But back at *home* you did not need to seek the enemy with flaming guns to get killed. All you had to do was to say the wrong thing; to refuse to say the thing you were expected to say. A few words could bring violent, sudden death, at home. If you were brown, they could. Just a few words. . . . Down South a few words could get you killed." But many of the Black veterans were determined to fight for the full citizenship that was promised to them. One of them declared, "I know the price. . . . If I could go there and make sacrifice with my life. . . . I was willing to do it here, if it meant death."[16]

Just a month after Will Thomas's piece appeared in *The Crisis*, on July 18, 1946, a Black World War II veteran, Maceo Snipes, was shot dead on the porch of his mother's house in Taylor County, Georgia, as a retribution for casting a ballot in the Democratic primaries the day before—the first primary since the Reconstruction in which Black Americans could vote.[17] As the only Black person to cast a vote in this county, he paid with his life. The day after his murder, a note was posted on an African American church, "the first Negro to vote will never vote again." No one was held accountable for the murder, as local authorities exonerated a person accused of the murder. This violence was a backlash against Black voters during the first election season following the US Supreme landmark decision in *Smith v. Allwright*, which ruled that "states must make voting in their primary elections equally accessible to voters of all races, even if they do not manage the election process themselves," thereby outlawing all-white primaries.[18]

A week later, "an unmasked band of twenty white men" led by "a tall dignified white man" killed four African Americans, two men, one of them a recently discharged World War II veteran, and their wives—George Dorsey and his wife Mae Murray Dorsey and Roger Malcom and his wife Dorothy Dorsey Malcom—near Moore's Ford Bridge on the Apalachee River in Walton County, just over 100 miles from where Maceo Snipes was killed.[19] The conservative senator William Knowland of California later said, to the displeasure of Southern senators, that the lynching in Georgia was "a blot on the whole United States," and intimated that feelings such as those leading to the killings were widespread across the country.[20] Leo Hurwitz's 1948 *Strange Victory* was a response to these incidents, capturing the post–World War II America and calling with a voice of a moral outrage and clarity for reckoning so the victory over fascism in May 1945 could become more than just a military victory.[21]

But the fate of the film epitomizes the fate of the efforts at that reckoning. The film opened for limited screenings in New York and Chicago and was panned by American critics, with the exception of left-leaning papers, which published positive reviews. The *Daily News* called it "the voice of Stalin."[22] The director, Leo Hurwitz, was blacklisted, and Virgil Richardson, the Tuskegee pilot, left the US. The country was not ready to look in the mirror. Anticommunism and cold war politics further helped kill, or at least thwart, whatever efforts toward reckoning and racial equality might have been taken, branding them communist.[23] Abroad, the film won the first prize in the Karlovy Vary film festival.

*Strange Victory* in its righteous outrage spoke the anti-fascist language and expressed sentiments voiced by Black activists already in the 1930s.[24] Black activists and press challenged the hypocrisy of Americans who touted the Four Freedoms and condemned the Nazis abroad while tolerating discrimination and violence against Black citizens at home.[25] For example, after Kristallnacht in December 1938, Walter White of the NAACP issued a statement, condemning "the unspeakable terror now being inflicted on the Jewish people in Germany by the sadistic Nazi regime" and warning that "unless all our citizens, white and black, Jew and Gentile, Protestant and Catholic, work together to strengthen democracy here the horrors that is Nazi Germany will obtain a foothold in the United States."[26] The December 1938 issue of *The Crisis*, a monthly published by the NAACP, published an editorial, "Negroes, Nazis and Jews," also in response to the anti-Jewish violence in Germany, expressing solidarity with Jews and outrage over Nazi attacks on them, but also adding moral indignation at the silence at the treatment of Black Americans at home.[27]

Many African Americans connected Nazi policies concerning Jews with the treatment of Black Americans in the United States already in the 1930s. The St. Louis *Argus* observed that there was "no consolation" from press reports about "police officials in Germany . . . asking for jim crow sections for Jews who travel by rail." Indeed, "the fact that these officials claim that they are merely taking pattern after the 'freest country in the world' the United States, calls for some serious thinking, not only on the part of Negroes and Jews but also on the part of the government itself."[28] And in October 1939, *The Crisis* reprinted an editorial titled "White Racialism in America," originally published in *The Reconstructionist*, an organ of the recently established Society for the Advancement of Judaism, arguing that "an Aryan racialism directed against Jews or a white racialism directed against Negroes" was wrong, and "now that America has assumed the role of champion of democracy and the equal rights of all citizens, it is high time that we put our own house in order and wipe out every last vestige of anti-Negro discrimination, which is a heritage from slavery days."[29] The NAACP hosted numerous events about the topic of "Jews in Germany and Negroes in America," featuring Black and Jewish speakers. And readers of *The Crisis* made further connections, already in the 1930s.[30]

As the war progressed, the historian Charles H. Wesley declared: "The Negro wants not only to win the war but also to win the peace."[31] A peace that would allow Black Americans "to be free of race and color restrictions, of imperialism and exploitation, and inclusive of the participation of minorities all over the world in their own governments." Wesley wondered "whether or not the struggle of World War II is one of freedom everywhere in the world or of freedom limited only to white people in the world and measured in broken doses to colored peoples." And what the outcome was would not only have an impact on people of color, but Wesley ominously concluded, "It may sound the tocsin of another of civilization's advances or the death knell of democratic western civilization."

These questions and expectations continued after the war. In December 1945, an editorial in *The Crisis* articulated the concern that no true peace had been achieved, despite the victory and the cost in lives:

We suffered a million casualties to defeat the master race theory in the East and the West, but we continue to follow the race superiority line at home and abroad, as our Congress strangles a bill which says simply that no man may be denied employment because of his race or religion, and fights inch by inch another bill which says the payment of a poll tax may not be a pre-requisite for voting. . . . But for the record the world has peace this Christmas. It does not have good will, but it does not have hand grenades, rockets, droning bombers and deadly fighters. And who said good will was the basis of peace?[32]

As war efforts were forcing the US government to mobilize Black citizens, Black activists hoped that contributions to the war at home and on the front would "lead to wider citizenship rights" and challenge "Southern, national, and global systems of race."[33]

But instead of "wider citizenship," there was a backlash violently limiting these citizenship rights; crucially, a backlash against voting rights, despite legal victories the NAACP brought in *Smith v. Allwright*. And there was the resurgence of the KKK, which Harold Preece, a white American writer, dubbed "the leading organization of the still-flourishing fascist internationale."[34] Moreover, the KKK recruited candidates from among war veterans, some of whom would further radicalize, as did George Lincoln Rockwell, who became the leader of a white power movement in the US. They now targeted both African Americans and Jews. According to Preece's reporting in *The Crisis*, some warned that "the South's Jewish minority, which has largely escaped oppression in the past because the Negro has been a handier victim, can look forward to the same treatment that his black neighbor is scheduled to receive during the post-war period. For the Klan credo, expressed by Georgia born Kleagle Stoner, is that 'Anti-semitism and white supremacy go hand in hand.'"[35] According to Stoner, "A politician who doesn't believe in white supremacy can't get very far. Antisemitism is stronger than before." Preece reported that Stoner was even circulating a petition "to disenfranchise and deport all Americans of Jewish faith."

Unabashed antisemitism was also expressed by another man Preece encountered, Ross Overton from Texas.[36] "We need a Hitler in this country," Overton reportedly said, "to clean out the kikes and niggers." Overton then rebuked Preece for having "picked up a lot of funny ideas that don't go in the South and won't go in the North before very long. . . . You are on the nigger side an' I know it. But you'd better cross over to yore own side which is the white side if you wanta keep on livin' to see yore boy grow up." (Spelling retained). Preece was taken aback. "I saw on his face," he wrote, "the same look which Jews, slated to be martyred by Hitler, must have seen in the faces of those merciless hooligans who started out by smashing Jewish stores and ended up by taking control of a nation which, in the duality of the Western soul, could produce both an Einstein and a Goebbels." But Ross Overton was not done. He shared with Preece his vision for America. It would be "a new kind of country," in which "hundred per cent Americans like me an' like yore kin-folks can have a dog's chance to get by without the niggers takin' all the jobs an' the Jews, lined up with the CIO [Congress of Industrial Organizations] an' the Com-mu-nists takin' all the money. We're gonna build a hundred per cent white white American party and a hundred per cent white American unions, an' maybe a hundred per cent white American church where the preachers preach the Bible an' not com-mu-nism."[37] This was, Preece noted, "the bitter fruit" spread by the white Southerners when they left the South to go north for jobs, a migration that helped fascism survive, for the white Southerners remained Southerners when they moved to "weld and rivet hate in Detroit as well as other cities in the North."

Preece lamented that few liberal organizations "understood the special background of Southern migrants" and few worked "to develop special program of orientation and democratic education for them." They failed, Preece remarked somewhat patronizingly, "to see the importance of getting down to the cultural level of people whose thinking had been influenced by the demagogue, speaking in chummy, homey folk talk on the courthouse lawn." But where the liberal organizations had failed, the Klan succeeded, organizing "industrial cells" in the UAW and other unions, staffed by men who "understood both the folk culture of the Southerner and his bewilderment in a huge industrial community where food and talk and habits were different" from what they knew from home. The Klan planned to establish similar units, Preece reported, "in white Protestant communities throughout the South" and circulate through them "tons of antisemitic, anti-Negro, and anti-[Russian] propaganda." Preece concluded that while there was no revolution in the US of "what is loosely called 'the Left'—meaning all of the liberal and humane forces of this country," there was "a revolution of the Right—the retrogressive, anti-human and profoundly anti-Christian forces financed and encouraged by Big Business—fermenting in the country." Fascism was threatening American Democracy. And the "rehearsal for this revolution was in the South, conditioned by human slavery to a perpetual semi-fascism with a grandiose *Herrenvolk* ideology of 'we're better than niggers.'"

But there was more, Preece argued, shining light onto white Christian churches in the South. People promoting fascism "feel that unsophisticated southern whites can be easily induced to swallow their poison if it is wrapped in distorted texts from . . . the Bible."[38] Southern pastors were preaching against Jews, Preece reported. One preacher—Reverend A. A. Smith of the Baptist Gospel Center in Tampa, Florida—is said to have preached to "poor whites" in 1946 that "ten million more Jews" were "doomed to die before the Second Coming of Christ." Smith offered to his faithful a modernized version of ancient Christian beliefs. Jews were doomed—"all but 'a remnant'" of them—because they "substituted atheism, evolution and materialism" for "the worship of God." The preacher added, "No Western nation wants the Jews and no Western nation can assimilate them." Smith and other Southerners were set to promote, and some even ran for office on, the platform of "white Christian Americanism," in such ideology neither Black nor Jewish Americans had a place.[39]

This "revolution of the Right" was troubling, Preece warned. These were men who were organized, who would "kneel before an open Bible and unfurled American flag, and promise to buy and store more arms for future use against Negroes" in "a coming race war."[40] They also organized youth groups, which, Preece warned, "with its fierce fundamentalism and its implied hypernationalism" had "all the possibilities of a *Hitler Jugend* movement." These groups along with the Klan were determined "to hold Dixie for fascism." White supremacist presses began to republish many turn-of-the-century racist and antisemitic books.[41] Klan members and other open white supremacists held public offices and were elected to the highest positions in society, feeling no shame to use derogatory racist and antisemitic language. They chaired Senate and House committees, doggedly working to stop the progress in civil rights by branding, as did the HUAC, any activism toward social justice as communist and un-American.[42] Some politicians even advocated abolishing the NAACP and publishing the names of its members "in the name of preventing secretive Communist activity."[43] Anticommunist ideology became a potent tool preventing racial justice and social reckoning—potent on both sides of the Atlantic.

The NAACP, with their star attorney Thurgood Marshall, had been working on chipping away racial injustice through the court system.[44] Despite the conservative nature of the courts, the NAACP's efforts led to the landmark decisions in *Smith v. Allwright* in 1944 and then ten years later in *Brown v. Board of Education*. But notwithstanding these legal victories, laws intended to provide more equal treatment were not enforced, and sometimes the implementation only affirmed the American segregated caste system. For example, in Atlanta, when Black officers were appointed to the police force after the war, they "were not allowed to arrest white people."[45] President Dwight Eisenhower never endorsed *Brown* and backtracked on government intervention on other racial justice issues. Roy Wilkins of NAACP once quipped about

Eisenhower that "if he had fought World War II the way he fought for civil rights, we would all be speaking German today."[46]

A deadly backlash followed these legal victories and any other steps Black Americans took in order to claim their citizenship. A year before *Brown*, the Howards, a Black family in Chicago, were repeatedly and violently attacked for moving into a white development. "Cops," Donald Howard recounted, "seemed more intent upon protecting white families from contact with us than in protecting my family from the white mobsters."[47] Black families were often, as *Strange Victory* showed a few years earlier, forced to live and work in substandard conditions, their children attending similarly inferior schools. As the court would assert in *Brown*, citing *Strauder v. West Virginia*, "Legal discriminations" signified "inferiority in civil society" and diminished "the security of [Black Americans'] enjoyment of the rights which others enjoy."[48] A year after *Brown*, Emmet Till was brutally murdered. As the self-confessed murderers later explained, "Niggers are gonna stay in their place. Niggers ain't going to vote where I live. . . . They ain't gonna go to school with my kids."[49] Emmet Till's murder and the subsequent acquittal of the perpetrators added fire to the ongoing struggle for equality and civil rights. And over the following years more violence against Black Americans followed: rapes, lynchings, fire bombings, and assassinations of civil rights leaders.

The deadly backlash that followed these legal gains along with the slowness of progress left many African Americans disillusioned. It was not only the violence of the backlash but also the silence of the majority of whites, sometimes asking Black Americans to be patient in their struggle for justice. As Martin Luther King Jr. said in his *Letter from Birmingham Jail*, Black Americans, "have waited for more than three hundred and forty years for our God-given and constitutional rights. The nations of Asia and Africa are moving with jetlike speed toward the goal of political independence, and we still creep at horse-and-buggy pace toward the gaining of a cup of coffee at a lunch counter." [50] But, in facing both the daily humiliations and violence, "there comes a time when the cup of endurance runs over and men are no longer willing to be plunged into an abyss of injustice where they experience the bleakness of corroding despair." King and other Black activists were frustrated not as much with the open white supremacists but, as King put it, with

> the white moderate who is more devoted to order than to justice; who prefers a negative peace which is the absence of tension to a positive peace which is the presence of justice; who constantly says, "I agree

with you in the goal you seek, but I can't agree with your methods of direct action"; who paternalistically feels that he can set the timetable for another man's freedom; who lives by the myth of time; and who constantly advises the Negro to wait until a "more convenient season." Shallow understanding from people of good will is more frustrating than absolute misunderstanding from people of ill will. Lukewarm acceptance is much more bewildering than outright rejection. [51]

But it was not just Black activism for civil rights and equality, also *Brown* and other legal and political gains that followed the Civil Rights Act passed in 1964 that tested white liberals' commitment to equal rights.[52] That commitment may have been there as long as equality and full civil rights remained in the realm of an idea—something to aspire to, to "wait" for. But when it became a legal reality, white Americans panicked much like the French did in the aftermath of the French Revolution when they realized that their banner of "liberty, fraternity, and equality" would have to apply to Black and Jewish citizens as well. White Americans, even committed liberals, began to feel uneasy about the effects of the application of these laws in their own lives. According to historian Stephen Tuck, "allies in the North supported rights rather than enforcement," while moderates "sought token changes to avoid confrontation rather than embrace integration."[53]

That is the sentiment James Baldwin expressed in *The Fire Next Time*. "White Americans," Baldwin wrote, "have contented themselves with gestures that are now described as 'tokenism.'"[54] Indeed, "white Americans congratulate themselves on the 1954 Supreme Court decision outlawing segregation in the schools; they suppose, in spite of the mountain of evidence that has since accumulated to the contrary, that this was proof of the change of heart," and of progress. But Baldwin objected that to solve the so-called "Negro problem" it was incumbent on Black Americans to "accept and adopt white standards."[55] White people could not be "models of how to live." Indeed, they themselves needed "new standards." He rebuked the perception of white superiority and "the notion" that white Americans were "in possession of some intrinsic value that Black people need, or want." For Baldwin and other Black intellectuals, "the only thing white people have that Black people need, or should want, is power."

Baldwin would continue to address the white audiences and plead with them to "liberate" themselves through "the liberation of the blacks— the total liberation, in the cities, in the towns, before the law, and in the mind."[56] But other Black activists turned inward, organizing around the principles of Black Power, a movement that further exposed the deep fissures in American society over issues of race and racial equality, together with the lackadaisical commitment to racial equality among white liberals. That disillusionment and political shift to Black Power did not go unnoticed in white circles. In 1960, Nathan Edelstein of the American Jewish Committee, which had been engaged in the civil rights movement, remarked that "the Negro community" was "completely dissatisfied with the present rate of progress toward equality" and was "reevaluating their alliances."[57] Edelstein added that there was "a mistrust of 'liberals' in the struggle for civil rights." The shift to Black Power increased white anxiety.[58] In 1968, the writer and civil rights activist Julius Lester remarked in 1968, "the white liberal has generally turned out to be more white than liberal whenever blacks assert themselves."[59]

Meanwhile, conservatives like William Buckley Jr. simply rejected the idea that Black Americans deserved equality and full citizenship and suggested defying the Reconstruction era amendments.[60] As Buckley wrote in 1957, the Fourteenth and Fifteenth Amendments, guaranteeing equal protection and the right to vote, were "regarded by much of the South as inorganic accretions to the original document, grafted upon it by a victor-at-war by force." In his white northeastern elitism, Buckley advocated disenfranchisement of Black voters, along with some whites whom he considered unprepared for full citizenship. This dual disenfranchisement would be a workaround of charges of racism, because it would "apply equally to blacks and whites." Buckley projected a white sense of privilege and ownership over American civilization. In his debate with James Baldwin in Cambridge in 1965, he was appalled that Baldwin had charged that "our civilization has failed him and his people, that our ideals are insufficient." Buckley claimed that in *The Fire Next Time* Baldwin "threatened America . . . with the necessity to jettison our entire civilization." In his polemical response to Baldwin, he sought to focus on Baldwin's individual experience—it was "the refusal of the American community to treat him other than as a Negro."[61] Baldwin was, Buckley implied, motivated by personal grievance. But in fact, Buckley noted further, revealing his ideas of social order, Baldwin was receiving the respect and honor "from coast to coast in the United States." This honor bestowed on Baldwin was, Buckley claimed, "a kind of unctuous servitude which, in point of fact, goes beyond anything that was ever expected from the most servile Negro creature by a southern family."

For Buckley, like for other conservatives, "American" meant white. Black Americans were not "the American people"—they were Negroes, or "Negro people whose fate was dependent on the will of whites. "I believe with absolute authority," Buckley said in his closing remarks, that "the fundamental friend of the Negro people in the United States is the good nature and is the generosity, and is the good wishes, is the decency, the fundamental decency that do lie at the reserves of the spirit of the American people."[62] The stark juxtaposition between "the Negro people" and "the American people" made it clear who belonged to the "We, the people." (Buckley would have likely objected to the term "Black Americans" used here.)

As conservatives like Buckley began to provide intellectual force behind the backlash through books and magazines like the *National Review,* which Buckley edited, they also began to organize to reverse, or at least thwart, the legal racial progress. They did so by designing lawsuits intended to reverse *Brown,* the Civil Rights Act, and the Voting Rights Act. They used racially neutral language and legal concepts to coopt white, often liberal, suburbanites. They spoke about school districts and "good schools," property taxes, individual rights and individual responsibility, "law and order," or welfare reform. And they chalked up some victories in *San Antonio Independent School District v. Rodriguez* (1973) and in *Milliken v. Bradley* (1974), both of which went directly after *Brown* and school desegregation.[63] The structures of racism, inequality, and built-in racial hierarchy have remained in place; the wealth gap between Black and white Americans has persisted, as has police brutality.[64]

The perception of Black inferiority, so deeply rooted in the history of racism and slavery, also continues to endure. White liberal parents in places like the Upper West Side in New York City fight "diversification" of schools, fearing, as they did as late as in 2018, that the schools' standards would decline if more students of color were admitted.[65] Commenting on the issue, a Columbia Teachers College professor said, "There's a lot of research that shows that the higher achieving kids, when they are in a more integrated space, are not negatively impacted." Though stated in effort to help the desegregation efforts and assuage the white parents' fears, this statement nevertheless voices several assumptions that reveal a racial hierarchy. Phrased as it was, "higher achieving kids" implied white children, who, if the school was "diversified," would be placed in "a more integrated space," that is, in the presence of students of color. Then the assertion that such placement has a potential to have a "negative" impact on those "high achieving kids" suggests that it was the students of color who might bring the standards down—a persistent and malignant manifestation of racial hierarchy. This is not dissimilar from the much more explicit assertions made by John Tyler Morgan in 1889 for whom a union between whites and Blacks would be tantamount to lowering "the whites to the level of the intellectual, moral, and social condition of the Negroes."[66] So, while Americans, to quote Baldwin, "congratulate themselves" on *Brown v. Board of Education*, remembering it as progress in racial relations, they forget *San Antonio Independent School District v. Rodriguez* (1973) and *Milliken v. Bradley* (1974), which have helped perpetuate school segregation and unequal distribution of resources, which ultimately lead to clashes such as the one on the Upper West Side.

In his book *Dreams of My Father*, Barack Obama remarked about "American mythology" and "America's hunger for any optimistic sign from the racial front—a morsel of proof that, after all, some progress has been made."[67] But perhaps it is not optimism, but rather an avoidance to look honestly at the past, choosing to look only at the moments of progress and obscuring the centuries-old dynamics that continue to grip the nation even today. Barack Obama's election in 2008 and the furious white supremacist backlash that followed can serve as testimony. So, too, can the election of Donald Trump in 2016 and the virulent white supremacist sentiments he allowed to come into the open, spurring violence. All this makes Baldwin's writings on race in America from the 1950s and 1960s resonate, with some even calling Baldwin "a prophet."[68] But that Baldwin's writing seems prophetic and that his clarion of moral outrage reverberates even in our era—still marked by police brutality against Black men and women, by backlash against an election of a Black man, against The 1619 Project that has sought to force Americans to look at American history through the lens of the experience of Black Americans, and by daily manifestations of white supremacy—is evidence that the reckoning in the US has not been successful.

So, too, in Europe, the reckoning after the war, despite the "rounding up" of Nazis and despite the prosecution of some of the most prominent ones at Nuremberg, was also rather stunted. The Nuremberg trial allowed the continent to move on but without deeper self-reflection because reckoning through law does not always lead to moral reckoning. As Martha Minow has pointed out, "Trials following mass violence can never establish full historical record," because trials focus on legal questions and their goal is not the establishment of full historical record.[69] This is what Leo Hurwitz captured in his film *Strange Victory*—there was no adequate punishment for the Nazis for what they did: "We only hanged them," the narrator said.

In August 1945, the so-called Nuremberg Charter that set guidelines for the prosecution of Nazi officials in Nuremberg defined three categories of crimes: crimes against peace, war crimes, and crimes against human-ity.[70] This framework of generally conceived "crimes against humanity" set an international precedent of obscuring the specificity of what happened to Jews during the war. The indictment, in Count Four—Crimes Against Humanity—did specify in paragraph B that "persecution on political, racial, and religious grounds" was "directed against Jews . . . also against persons whose political belief or spiritual aspirations were deemed to be in conflict with the aims of the Nazis"; and Jewish survivors helped gather evidence against Nazis, documenting the destruction of Jews in Europe, and testified during the trial.[71] Still, the universalization of Nazi crimes gave European countries cover to present the devastation of the war as Nazi, or "Hitlerite," crimes against humanity without having to acknowl-edge antisemitism and the Nazi obsession with Jews, and, thus, without reckoning with the key element of what made such crimes possible.

In places where local authorities tried to address antisemitism or to seek a deeper reckoning with these crimes, these efforts came to be seen as "victors' justice" imposed by occupying powers, the Americans in the west, and the Soviets in the east.[72] With little local impulse, the voices for justice and reckoning were gradually marginalized. Post-war pragmatism supplanted the moral duty. Some nations even began to refashion their own role. Austria, for example, soon began to present itself as Hitler's first victim, "its Nazi allegiance conveniently forgotten."[73] Even Germans were for decades after the war "obsessed with the suffering they'd endured, not the suffering they'd caused."[74] Post-war European history is, as Tony Judt put it, "a story shadowed by silences," as collective amnesia willfully pre-vailed in many European countries, now without or with greatly dimin-ished Jewish populations.[75]

These silences and amnesia have manifested themselves differently in different countries. In the Netherlands, historical museums pass over in silence, as Susan Neiman has shown, "the fact that, thanks to Dutch col-laboration with the Nazi occupation, a higher percentage of Jews were deported to concentration and death camps from Holland than from anywhere else in Europe."[76] (And only recently did the Dutch began to "face up their colonial past" and their role in the history of slavery.[77]) The French too avoided the question of responsibility for what happened to Jews, focusing their post-war trials on French collaboration with the Nazis against French resistance, which became the ethos of French memory of World War II, rather than on French assistance in the deportation of Jews to their deaths.[78] In West Germany, Austria, France, Belgium, and the Netherlands, people quickly moved on, reintegrating some of the war criminals into the society. Already two years after the war, a reporter noted that denazification was no longer "a moral problem"; it became "simply an administrative procedure, no longer a problem of right and wrong."[79] But in East Germany the denazification and the reckoning with antisemitism was fuller than elsewhere—it fit the Soviet ethos of victory over fascism.[80]

Less than a year after the Nuremberg trials ended, *The Commentary Magazine* published a report from Europe by David Bernstein.[81] In it, Bernstein remarked that there was "still plenty of fascism in Europe," and Hitler's ideas still festered. The "old world" may have been "gone, but nothing has yet taken its place. And the shredding of Europe's psychological fabric has left Western Europeans, at least, with little faith and less hope." Bernstein found "vestiges" of Nazism and antisemitism, and "a terrifying nostalgia for the good old days of Nazi splendor, a glib repudiation of all the evils of the recent past, an impelling desire for still another attempt to dominate the world." Germany was not alone, even in England, he reported, "a nation fighting for sheer survival" displayed "the first telltale symptoms of stagnation and disease, among them increasing anti-Semitism."

So, too, in Poland, a country that lost the highest proportion of its Jewish population, as Jewish survivors returning home reported and as Polish intellectuals confirmed, antisemitism after the war seems to have become worse than before the war.[82] Though Poland, on whose territories most of the killings took place, was the only occupied country without collaborative government—"Poland had no Quisling," one Polish intellectual wrote in September 1945—though it was a country whose occupation required a huge Nazi manpower, and one in which the punishment for helping Jews was a summary death penalty, the end of World War II was not met with cheers of victory and empathy for returning Jewish survivors.[83] Poland seemed to some, writer Kazimierz Wyka asserted, "the only country in Europe where antisemitism persists and leads to political and moral crimes." "Hitlerism," Wyka concluded, left in Poland "a cuckoo's egg," or, as a Polish sociologist Stanisław Ossowski put it, "Nessus's brown shirt."[84]

The situation became further complicated by the civil war between Soviet-backed forces and their opponents. The Soviet-backed authorities at first tried to fight antisemitism, which they saw as reactionary. But, when they sought punishment for Nazi collaborators and for antisemitic attacks, they were forced to retreat—antisemitism, as Adam Michnik has noted, was a "form of anticommunism and patriotism," and thus to condemn antisemitic attacks came to be seen as tantamount to support for the communist government.[85] This, together with international measures universalizing Nazi crimes, helped further repress reckoning with the role

Polish antisemitism played before, during, and even after the war in the fulfillment of Nazi genocidal policies on the Polish soil.[86]

In Poland, thus, the peace brought by German capitulation was no peace at all, and not only because the country came under Soviet control, leading to civil war that raged until at least 1947.[87] There could be no meaningful peace also because of the crimes committed by Poles against Jewish survivors returning home. In Poland, as Saul Levitt would have said, "the news was still bad" despite the war's end. Hostility toward returning survivors, individual killings, and outright massacres marked the first months following the German capitulation, with the largest massacre in Kielce on July 4, 1946, where over forty Jewish survivors, among them a mother with a newborn infant and a pregnant woman—a photo of her dead body became an iconic representation of this pogrom—were bludgeoned to death in a vicious frenzy that lasted over six hours.[88] The *New York Times* reported that the Polish government put a lid on the news "lest it by suggestion lead to repetition of such incidents in other cities," thus acknowledging "frankly and ashamedly that it was not safe for Jews to live in small Polish towns."[89] W. H. Lawrence, the *Times* reporter, compared the forces behind attacks on Jews in Poland to the KKK. "The best known band is the National Armed Forces, which keeps groups in the forests by day, while at night they emerge to raid and kill. It is probably not unlike the Ku Klux Klan at the height of its violent anti-Negro, anti-Catholic, and anti-Jewish campaign in the South of the United States."[90]

But unlike the authorities in the United States, which tended to ignore or excuse violent attacks against on Black Americans, the military authorities in Poland quickly arrested some of the perpetrators, and by July 11, nine of them were condemned to death and executed three days later. The swift punishment was greeted with a mixture of feelings in Poland and abroad. The American reporter for the *New York Times* observed that "the Government's decision to move against the mob members is as surprising in this country as would be the effective prosecution in the southern United States of members of a crowd who had lynched a Negro."[91] But the government's response was tainted because they used the Kielce pogrom as an opportunity to make a political statement against "reactionaries" and to place the blame for the massacres on their political opponents, not just the fascist militant groups. For some Poles the trial was just a show trial, another example of illegitimacy of the new government; others considered the event "an act of few individuals, who after all were condemned to death," denying any systemic problem.[92] But for some, it brought "relief" that punishment was meted out.[93]

Still, some intellectuals reflected on the superficiality of the punishment in face of the depth of the problem. Those sentenced were, historian Witold Kula observed at the time, only "the unlucky ones" who "in contrast to the rest of the crowd of several thousand" happened to be arrested by the authorities.[94] There were hundreds of thousands of potential "pogromists," Kula said, every day in trams, trains, factories, and universities.[95] Franciszek Gil, a Polish journalist reporting from Kielce, noted that the trial "took place in a vacuum outside of human and moral attitudes toward Jews."[96] Gil felt a palpable silence about the meaning of the events, and it seemed to him that at the end of the trial, after the sentences were announced, if people had been able to talk freely they would have expressed their unbelief "What is it all about? . . . what is it all for? After all, they only beat Jews."

Poles abroad were also following the news. The Jewish World News Service reported in late July that, apparently, "Polish officers and men of the Polish Army stationed in Scotland held a memorial service for the nine men" who were executed and proclaimed them "martyrs of the Judea [sic] communist regime in Poland," referencing the antisemitic canard that Jews were responsible for communism.[97] Also in Jerusalem, the papers reported, "Followers of Gen. Władysław Anders who are now in Palestine are arranging a memorial meeting for the nine Poles who were executed last Sunday for participation in the Kielce pogrom in Poland."[98]

This post-war Polish antisemitism baffled some intellectuals. The Polish sociologist Stanisław Ossowski noted that while one could have expected that "in view of the terrible suffering of the murdered masses and the horror of the extermination camps; hatred of a common enemy; blood jointly shed on numerous occasions; rejection of the ideology propagated by the defeated occupier; a sense of justice demanding some compensation for those who survived, for example, in the form of human kindness; and the radical numerical decline of the Jewish population," antisemitism would be gone in post-war Poland, but "compassion is not the only imaginable response to misfortune suffered by other people."[99] Ossowski also warned that "throwing high condemnations is not the most important thing."[100] Not even "the gallows issued by the judicial authorities for the captured perpetrators will remove the evil." What was necessary was "to undertake deeper educational work"; "a longer period of cleansing."[101] As another intellectual concluded in 1948, "Most people, not only in Poland but all over the world, have come to terms with this cruelest crime in history, with the same amoral shrug of the shoulders and washing of their hands as the German nation. Someone's tragedy does not move for a long time."[102] He called on rebuilding the nation not just physically but morally.

So did Stanisław Grabski, an influential politician, associated with *Endecja*, a right-wing nationalist faction, in the interwar period. After the Kielce massacre, Grabski focused on the issue of hatred and reminded his readers of a pastoral letter issued by the Polish Catholic bishops in February 1946, for Lent, which said that "Polish life must be cured of hatred, which is the seed of Satan, and stands in stark contrast to Christian teaching. In private and public life hatred is a disruptive and destructive force that cannot be utilized by Catholics."[103] Grabski acknowledged that the massacre in Kielce indicated that "the Polish life not been cured of the hatred born of the horrors of war, but that there is more of it than during the occupation, with every month more and more." And, he added, that was "our most horrifying tragedy," for hatred was "always a destructive force, seeded by Satan." According to Grabski, "healing Polish life from hatred" was the most effective protection not only of Jews—from antisemitic attacks—but also of "the good Polish name in the world."

A voice calling for the end of hatred and for commitment to "Christian morality" was also heard from Teodor Kubina, the bishop of Częstochowa, the town of the famous Black Madonna shrine. Bishop Kubina spoke with righteous clarity—since, after all, who could not agree that a brutal killing of dozens of innocent survivors, men, women, and infants was not a horrendous crime? Kubina's response, issued jointly with the local city officials on July 7, 1946, just days after the massacre in Kielce, was one of the earliest responses to the events.[104] "In Kielce," Bishop Kubina stated, "mass slaughter was committed on Polish citizens of Jewish nationality. More than forty Jews and two Poles, who survived the Hell of German occupation, looked at the deaths and torments of their loved ones, and themselves avoided death at the hands of the Nazis, not without the help of Polish Christian society, were murdered." The perpetrators, "moral and actual," the bishop continued, "trampled on human dignity and horribly violated the Christian commandment of love for one's neighbor and universal principle: 'Do not kill.' Nothing, absolutely nothing, justifies the Kielce crime, which is deserving of the wrath of God." The perpetrators had to "be absolutely and without objections condemned as criminals according to all divine and human laws." Bishop Kubina then appealed to "human consciousness and Christian and moral principles" and condemned both the violence and the ritual murder libel, rumor of which had triggered the pogrom and which the bishop called "lies." These were lone voices of moral outrage. Most people did not want to face the difficult-to-bear truth, preferring to push the moral questions aside, ejecting Jews, who were a daily reminder of those issues, out of the social realm. Anticommunism further complicated the matters.

Indeed, the Episcopate (the Polish Bishops' Conference), Cardinal August Hlond, the primate of Poland and archbishop of Warsaw, and Czesław Kaczmarek, the bishop of Kielce, were more circumspect in their responses to the Kielce massacre. On July 11, 1946, four days after Bishop Kubina's letter, Cardinal Hlond, held a press conference and issued a statement, condemning "all murders regardless if they targeted Poles, or Jews, in Kielce and in all parts of Poland."[105] He said that many Jews were saved by Poles, who themselves "were targeted" by Germans but who risked their lives hiding and rescuing Jews. Many Jews, he added, "owe their lives to Poles and Polish clergy." But then the archbishop switched his tone and blamed "Jews, who hold leading state positions and seek to establish a regime the vast majority of the nation does not want in Poland," for destroying "this great relationship." It was, he said, "a destructive game, because it leads to dangerous tensions. In fatal armed clashes on a political battlefield unfortunately some Jews perish, but so do immeasurably more Poles." The sentiment in Cardinal Hlond's statement illustrates that anticommunism was a key reason behind the Catholic Church's inability to speak with moral clarity against the massacre. Jews should have been grateful for being spared extermination, "owing their lives" to Poles—a phrase that implied indebtedness, but they returned "holding leading positions" in "a regime" that was undesired. This kind of anticommunism would become a major obstacle to Polish-Jewish relations and later efforts of reconciliation well into the twenty-first century.

The justification of anticommunist antisemitism through claims that Jews held leading positions in the new government reflected a more pernicious and deeply rooted unwillingness to accept Jews in positions of authority—a modern manifestation of the deeply ingrained theological trope of Jewish servitude and the subsequent prohibitions against Jews holding public office that had entered Christian jurisprudence many centuries earlier. A striking example comes from a reported meeting between Jewish leaders in Kielce and the bishop of Kielce, Czesław Kaczmarek, after someone threw hand grenades into a Jewish home in December 1945—seven months before the massacre.[106] The Jewish leaders were asking the bishop to intervene and tell the clergy, who, they hoped, would then convey the message to the faithful, that the "tiny handful of Jews who remained should not be persecuted." The bishop "smiled," saying, "We do not have any influence" to imply impotence in the face of communist authorities, adding: "You know, Jews are talented merchants, talented doctors, talented lawyers—Poland is destroyed, it needs strength—why don't Jews do what they are capable of, why do they engage in politics? Can you imagine what it looks like when a priest comes to the ministry and a Jewish woman is sitting there, God knows from where, and treats our clergy with superiority and insolence? What kind of impression does it make?"

Zacharia Schuster, the European director of the American Jewish Committee, confirmed this sentiment in his incisive report on the situation in Poland published in the August 1946 issue of *The Commentary*.[107] "In Poland," Schuster wrote, "with its traditional exclusion of Jews from public office, the mere fact that Jews occupy high government posts is startling. Accordingly, it becomes easy to call the pro-Soviet government Jewish, and all Jews Russian Communists." The perception that Jews held high positions of power in the communist government served to justify anti-Jewish massacres and made it more difficult for the tenuously established communist government to act more decisively. Some felt, Schuster observed, that the government "prefer[red] to 'go easy' in order not to bolster the charge that it is a Jewish government, and thus further prejudice and incite the populace against it."

In September 1946, two months after the massacre, Bishop Kaczmarek of Kielce doubled down on his justification for anti-Jewish violence in post-war Poland.[108] In a report he claimed that there had been there "no hostility towards Jews and no antisemitism" in Kielce before the war, and during the war "everyone empathized with Jews, even their biggest enemies. Many Poles saved Jews, since without Polish help they would have not survived." But things changed, the bishop asserted, in 1944 and 1945 when Soviet troops entered Poland and began to establish a Soviet-backed government. This was, according to Kaczmarek's report, the beginning of anti-Jewish sentiments. "Jews are not liked; indeed, they are hated all over Poland. This is a phenomenon that cannot be doubted at all." But this hatred, the bishop claimed, was not grounded in racist ideas but existed because "Jews are the main proponents of the communist regime, which the Polish nation rejects, but which is imposed on it with force and against its will." Bishop Kaczmarek's report then listed the evidence, a veritable list of antisemitic tropes: Jews occupied high-profile positions of power, they were successful in business and trade, they controlled the press and also were in charge of its censorship in Poland. "An average Pole," the report noted, "thinks (whether it is accurate or inaccurate) that among the only true and sincere supporters of communism in Poland are primarily Jews, because the vast majority of communist Poles are—according to this general opinion—only opportunists, without ideology, who are communists only because it is handsomely worthwhile for them [*że im się to sowicie opłaca*]." Moreover, he said without condemnation, rumors had been spreading earlier about Jews kidnapping children to take their blood, with the police doing nothing. These rumors affirmed for the "masses the belief that Jews in Poland are allowed to do anything, that they can get away with everything." And such rumors coupled with "the Jews communist activities" helped spread the hatred against Jews and were a backdrop to the "events in Kielce." Bishop Kaczmarek did not explain but rather excused anti-Jewish hatred in Poland and scorned the demands that the Polish Bishops' Council issue a statement condemning antisemitism. Such demands were "demeaning" to the Church. Jews spread communism, the bishop's report said, they were part of the secret police, which arrested people, beat them, even killed them like the Gestapo. The Poles were "fed up." Why then would the Church "solemnly announce that this hostility [toward Jews] within the society is unjustified, that the behavior of the Jews is completely innocent, that it was the Poles who were guilty of resenting them"? A demand for such a statement was tantamount, he asserted, to a demand that "the Church approve the system of terror that is currently used in Poland." Such virulent anticommunism and persistent association of communism in Poland with Jews prevented later reckoning with the past. Its legacy still festers in Poland.

But beyond the violence, there was also the antisemitism of everyday life—the rejection of Jews from the polity and social life in Poland.[109] This was manifested in the whispers, the language, gestures, humiliating jabs, and daily harassments. Jews were not called "Jews," *Żydzi* but rather *Żydki*, a diminutive "little Jews." They were, as the Polish writer Jerzy Andrzejewski observed, subject to "a huge scale of various reactions, starting from indulgent, almost friendly derision, joke and lighthearted humor, through mockery, satire and sarcasm, to clearly hostile reflexes of scorn, contempt and disgust."[110] These were manifestations of Polish superiority. While humor and laughter are healthy, Andrzejewski noted, "Whoever mocks another person can easily kick and beat him with a stick under favorable circumstances. The road from mockery to fist is not very far and not extremely difficult." People turn to mockery and laughter when they deal with those they consider "weaker and lesser people." After all, Andrzejewski concluded, "chuckling is retaliation for weakness, a weapon of the artificially exalted." As long as the Jew remained "poor, weak, and wretched," as long as he remained "funny and amusing," as long as "the little Jew" could be relied on to do the dirty work or could be ordered around, he could be tolerated. But once a Jew began to climb the social and political ladder he came to be seen as "a dangerous and harmful element" to be ejected from "the political organism."[111] What Andrzejewski described echoed anti-Black sentiments in the US and the link between Jim Crow era minstrel shows, "Sambo art," and violence against Black Americans exercising their citizenship rights.

But Jews who survived World War II and wanted to stay in Poland were not those "little Jews" mocked in jokes. They were highly Polonized, some holding positions of power as ministers or senior government advisors, further leading to rumors and whispers that "all high-ranking positions in Poland were occupied by Jews," that Jews "push themselves into these positions" in clear evidence of arrogance and insolence.[112] But then Andrzejewski stated the obvious: "What if they have the appropriate qualifications and if through their good work serve Poland well? Are they not citizens? Do Poles, who themselves went through so much, think that these few surviving Jews do not have the right to a full, normal life, and that when there is so much talk about democracy, they must live in a state a shameful vegetation in hiding?" It was clear, according to Andrzejewski, that the Polish nation needed to shake the old "habits of thinking and feeling" about Jews.[113] Empathy and feelings of solidarity were not possible if Poles considered themselves superior and looked down on Jews with contempt.

This was also the point raised by Franciszek Gil, reporting from Kielce. Gil explored the moral vacuum in which such attacks were possible after six years of German occupation and the destruction of Polish Jewish population. He listed, in random order, common associations and impressions of Jews from before the war that allowed Polish Christians to feel superior— Jews killed Jesus; circumcision; dark Jewish schools; ear locks; skullcaps; church teachings that Jews were a nation cursed by God; shops; inns; and others. "Eventually came the German ghettos, armbands, slave columns and death ditches for the entire nation. So, indeed, these Jews could not be good people, since God punished them in such a way, since such an end happened to them. . . . At the same time, the death of a Jew began to mean an apartment, a shop, some jewelry."[114] German murder of Jews, preceded by total deprecation of Jewish humanity only reinforced the Polish sense of superiority. To accept as equal "those returning ghosts," it would have taken a major emotional "revolt" or "a deep sense of equality with the slaves during their slavery." But the moment Jews were separated from Poles by their badges, such feeling of empathy became impossible.

Gil connected antisemitism of the prewar Poland with that which led to the Kielce pogrom. "The great Hitler was finishing in a gigantic style the work of the little Hitlers," Gil said, referring to pre-war Polish antisemitism, "of academic senates and faculty councils, which, by adopting resolutions on Jewish benches, taught the masses that Jews were different and inferior."[115] And so, when these "slaves, the unlawful, returned to the streets, took equal positions in the army and administration," and began to make a living, "the country became the scene of pogroms," the backlash was particularly violent. It was not about numbers and demographic proportions, which Gil dubbed "the delusional arithmetic attitude to the Jewish problem." But rather, it was all about "changing human-to-human attitude."

These massacres and violent attacks on Jewish survivors and the continuous existence of brazen antisemitism shocked many in Poland. Some of their voices were, like *Strange Victory* in the United States, *cris de cœur*, calling for deeper introspection, delving into the unpleasant truths. In May 1946, the Polish poet and writer Władysław Broniewski lamented that "the times of war did not teach Polish fascists anything, or rather—they did not unteach them anything."[116] The German crimes against many millions, "overwhelming in its horrors" the human imagination, should have "stopped anyone in whom the remnants of human feelings have not died out. On the contrary: the school of murder, the school of blind racist hatred, was victorious. The patterns are clear that they look like a continuation of a work unfinished by Hitler." The soul of the nation was poisoned, Broniewski concluded.

Poet Julian Przyboś was even more explicit:

> The slaughter of millions of Jews during the German occupation did not shock consciences, innocent blood did not purify the hearts. On the contrary: Nazism infected many with anti-human hatred, and hyenas prey on this hatred. Before the war, I looked at the man who tried to prove that a Jew was a pest because he was a Jew with pity, the way one looks at an insane man, with disgust, as if he were a barbarian. Today, after a terrible experience that revealed what this anti-human mindlessness and this unselfconscious lust for murder lead to—I consider an anti-Semite a potential murderer. I look into the faces of my friends and strangers, walk among people in Poland, listen to conversations—and how many times I am frightened that I live among the insane and among possible criminals.[117]

Jews should have been welcomed "with open arms and moved hearts." They were "fellow citizens" who "should have found in Poland the best fatherland." It was a country "in which for centuries their fate was bound with ours." Antisemitism was a "disgrace." It needed to be fought "with law and reason." Poland was not going to be truly free if that battle was not won. "Free, above all, from disgrace."

But antisemitic killings were not the only manifestation of how much the soul of the nation was "poisoned"; the treatment of Jewish children and individual Jews was another. "An average Polish intellectual does not realize," wrote Witold Kula, "that a Jew in Poland cannot drive a car; he is reluctant to travel by rail. That he is afraid to send his child to a sleep-away summer camp; that he will not dare to show in any small town; that he congregates only in the largest cities, because even in medium-sized cities he cannot walk quietly in the streets before dusk. It takes a hero to consent to live in such an atmosphere after six years of agony."[118] Stories of children ostracized and bullied in schools, coming home and asking if they were Jewish and what that meant, when other children pulled them into the bathrooms to check if they were circumcised or refused to sit with them because they were "little Jews"; some teachers only reinforcing this bench segregation.[119] It was precisely the "antisemitism of the gentle and good people" that was the most dangerous, Tadeusz Mazowiecki argued in 1960.[120] Antisemitism was about humiliation and the struggle against it was a struggle for dignity. Jews still felt insecure in Poland. In 1968, a new wave of politically motivated antisemitism erupted, leading to mass emi-gration of thousands of the remaining Jews from Poland, leaving an even smaller handful behind. Those who stayed were "Polish Polish Jews"; they became major actors in the 1980s and 1990s to work toward reconciliation and revival of the Jewish community in Poland.[121]

What was described about the hostility toward Jews in Poland in the years following World War II and the fear they felt on the streets, on the trains and buses, the humiliation they experienced in workplaces and schools is not dissimilar from some of the realities Black Americans expe-rienced in the first half of the twentieth century: white violence, school strikes protesting integration, as well as daily harassments.[122] But, in con-trast to the United States, as the *New York Times* reported, in Poland, for better or for worse, in the first years after the war the Polish authorities fought back. In the US, coming to terms with racism was slow, and legal discrimination did not end until the courts and the Congress stepped in in the second half of the century. But these legal measures, while rem-edying the *de jure* disabilities, failed to provide full reckoning with the country's history and racism. *De facto* discrimination remained and, one could argue, these legal victories provided an excuse to avoid deeper intro-spection on race and racism. Even today the specter of old racial dynamics persists as video after video repeatedly shows murders of unarmed Black men by white police officers.

In both Europe and the US, the period since the end of World War II was pivotal in forcing reckoning with issues of antisemitism and racism and with the questions about collective belonging: Who belonged to the social and political "we"? Both in the United States and in many European countries these issues remain unresolved because on both sides of the Atlantic, large portions of society are resistant to facing the unvarnished history, preferring a memory of an imagined past, or focusing on redemptive moments of progress, while explaining away the issues that do not fit with the neat memory. Thus persists the legacy of slavery and servitude, along with the heritage of European white Christian supremacy. A major difference is that in Europe significant Jewish communities only exist in a handful of countries, whereas in the United States, Black Americans remain a sizable and politically important minority.

# CHAPTER 11

# Reckoning with the Christian Legacy of Antisemitism and Racism

JUST AS SOME JEWISH and Catholic Poles were demanding that the Catholic Church in Poland acknowledge and address antisemitism among its clergy and faithful, in the United States racism among white American Christians was forcing into the public sphere questions about what it meant to be "Christian." Jim Crow was "renting the pews" and the "creeping dry-rot of racism" was "taint[ing] American Christianity and our churches," wrote James Farmer and James W. Ivy in *The Crisis* in 1946.[1] Segregation in churches was more "entrenched" than other types of segregation. After all, in many cities in the North, Farmer and Ivy observed, "Negroes and white[s] can and do attend the same public schools, eat in the same restaurants, go to the same theaters, play in the same parks and swim on the same beaches." On Sundays, however, "they go to separate churches and Sunday schools, listen to separate sets of sermons on brotherly love and Christian righteousness. It is in this way that segregation becomes invested with religious and moral values." And these could not be questioned. This kind of segregation was practiced "every Sunday" even by those "who are often the loudest to condemn discrimination against Negroes in hotels and restaurants." Only a small minority of white churches, Catholic among them, were willing to "welcome all races to worship," some on a conditional basis, still "entrapped in their own and their parishioners' prejudices." And though, the authors noted, "it might seem reasonable to suppose that the majority of northern ministers would at least see the elementary Christian implications of their religion—but they do not." Some simply lacked "the courage to fight for implementation of their beliefs in human brotherhood." Farmer and Ivy conceded that "one should not blame them too much, for after all they are men and they have churches to maintain, members to placate, apportionments to raise, and ambitions to fulfill." The clergy were open to "inviting Negro speakers and singers of spirituals, attending interracial conferences, and making donations to Negro congregations." But this was "a clumsy subterfuge" that might "ease the ministerial conscience" but did not "erase the shame of segregated congregations."

This dynamic was portrayed, in a powerful 1966 documentary by Barbara Connell and Bill Jersey called *A Time for Burning*. The film, shot in a year prior, tells the story of William Youngdahl, a minister of an all-white Augustana Lutheran Church in Omaha, Nebraska, seeking to facilitate integration of his church and foster dialogue between his congregation and a Black Lutheran congregation. The film follows discussions by church leadership, focus groups, and interracial committees, and painful attempts at integrated worship—everything that James Farmer and James W. Ivy discussed in 1946. The film documents the failure of an eager, idealistic young pastor overcome by his congregation, and ultimately leaving the Lutheran Church altogether. The film questions what it means to be a Christian.

The same question animated James Baldwin, who throughout his many essays, repeatedly and passionately confronted on moral grounds the label "Christian" when talking about white Christians in the United States and white Christian Europeans. "We have lost," Baldwin wrote in "We Can Change the Country" in 1963, "the right—by the murder of our brothers and sisters—to be called a Christian nation."[2] And Christian churches had to face their responsibility for perpetuating the oppression of Black Americans. In *The Fire Next Time*, Baldwin declared that "the Christian world has revealed itself as morally bankrupt and politically unstable."[3] He probed the association of "the terms 'civilized' and 'Christian,'" which had "a very strange ring, particularly in the ears of those who have been judged to be neither civilized nor Christian." According to Baldwin, World War II presented clear evidence of such moral bankruptcy of the Christian world, "when a Christian nation surrender[ed] to a foul and violent orgy, as Germany did during the Third Reich," sending millions "in the heart of Europe—God's citadel . . . to a death so calculated, so hideous, and so prolonged that no age before this enlightened one had been able to imagine it, much less achieve and record it." The Third Reich, thus, made "obsolete forever any question of Christian superiority, except in technological terms." And if "white people were, and are, astounded by the holocaust in Germany," for "they did not know they could act that way," he doubted whether Black people were equally shocked. "The fate of the Jews and the world's indifference" frightened Baldwin because he imagined that similar indifference would have been the reaction if "the United States decided to murder its Negroes systematically instead of little by little and catch-as-catch-can." Genocide was replicable, Baldwin argued, despite reassurances that "what had happened to the Jews in Germany could not happen to the Negroes in America." Baldwin's challenge has not been taken up. Churches remain largely segregated in the United States and Christian intellectuals and theologians still grapple with the history of Christian supremacy and racism. Theologian Jeannine Hill Fletcher has recently urged that "as a way forward, we must see how Whiteness and Christianness have been twin pillars of the dominant religio-racial project" and suggested that "if Christians desire a world of racial justice and religious integrity, understanding the sin of supremacy and theology's role within it is our only way forward."[4]

The Catholic Church, though doctrinally integrated—as Farmer and Ivy put it in 1946, "a Negro Catholic is acceptable in the eyes of God, but a white non-Catholic is a heretic"—has not been immune to segregation and racism.[5] Indeed, Farmer and Ivy noted that after the War, "racism was on the increase in Catholicism" and "within recent years many Negro Catholic churches have been developed throughout the nation and Negroes are being urged to leave the white churches to attend 'their own.'" Some priests were penalized for encouraging integration. The US Catholic Church struggled during the civil rights era. While the bishops recognized, in 1958, "the race question" as "moral and religious," they had to balance morality and pragmatism.[6] In 1968, Black Catholic clergy formed the National Black Catholic Clergy Caucus and demanded to be taken seriously and be placed in "rightful positions of leadership and ministry."[7] For too long, they declared, they "had been told . . . in so many ways by so many persons that we were second rate, that we were less than equal and would never amount to anything in society and the church."

In 1979, the US Catholic Bishops issued a strong statement against racism in a pastoral letter called *Brothers and Sisters to Us*.[8] The bishops called "attention to the persistent presence of racism and in particular to the relationship between racial and economic justice." They saw "racism and economic oppression" as "distinct but interrelated forces which dehumanize our society." To move "toward authentic justice demands a simultaneous attack on both evils." The bishops stressed that "an unresolved racism" still "permeates our society's structures and resides in the hearts of many among the majority." But since it was "less blatant, this subtle form of racism" was "in some respects even more dangerous—harder to combat and easier to ignore." The bishops called on each Catholic to "acknowledge a share in the mistakes and sins of the past. Many of us have been prisoners of fear and prejudice. We have preached the Gospel while closing our eyes to the racism it condemns. We have allowed conformity to social pressures to replace compliance with social justice."

While the letter condemned racism as a sin, its first words—"Racism is an evil which endures in our society and in our Church"—and the very title—*Brothers and Sisters to Us*—still reflect white domination. After all, as theologian Bryan Massingale asked, "Who is the 'us'?"[9] The implementation of *Brothers and Sisters to Us* lagged; the issues did not disappear, neither did the *in*ability to face them.[10] In 1999, during his visit to the United States, Pope John Paul II challenged American Catholics "to put an end to every form of racism . . . one of the most persistent and destructive evils of the nation."[11] But this remark by the pope was considered "curious," one commentator observed. The pope was "ill-served by his advisors, since racism is no longer a pressing social issue in the United States." In this light, Massingale urged that "slavery's legacy as African stigmata of inferiority needs to be forthrightly addressed in any adequate account or process of racial reconciliation in America."[12]

Still, the 1979 pastoral letter by the US Catholic Bishops was quite explicit in its treatment of racism and in its contemporary assessment of existing racism (though its assessment of legal and theological traditions underpinning American and Christian ideals was rather optimistic). The same forthrightness also took decades to achieve in the Catholic Church's approach to Jews in the aftermath of World War II. The murder of European Jews during the war demonstrated human capability of utmost brutality and ruthlessness leading many Christian thinkers to probe the extent to which Christian theological teaching may have contributed to the ruthless antisemitism that brought about the methodical murder of the Jews. Before the war, the British Anglican theologian and historian James Parkes, though not free from antisemitic assumptions himself, published several works probing the role Christianity had played in the history of antisemitism, laying foundations for a sustained Jewish-Christian dialogue that would only come after the war.[13]

And after the war, some Christian churches issued statements reflecting on the mass murder of Jews in Europe. In October 1945, the Council of the Protestant Church in Germany issued what came to be called "Stuttgart

Declaration of Guilt" about "not witnessing more courageously," "not praying more faithfully," "not believing more joyously," and "not loving more ardently."[14] The declaration admitted "endless suffering . . . brought to many peoples and countries," but it did not mention antisemitism and Jews specifically.

A year later, a committee of Protestant churches issued in Geneva a "Resolution on Antisemitism and the Jewish Situation."[15] This resolution was much more explicit in addressing a "deep sense of horror at the unprecedented tragedy which has befallen the Jewish people in consequence of the Nazi attempt to exterminate European Jewry." It also expressed "heartfelt sympathy with the survivors of this tragedy and their fellow-Jews throughout the world."

And in 1947, a group of Christian and Jewish thinkers met in Seelisberg in Switzerland to create a concrete action plan to pave way for a transformation of Christian attitudes toward Jews. They issued a ten-point task list for Christian churches and a report on "The Principal Objectives of Jewish-Christian Cooperation in Combating Antisemitism" that admitted at the very opening that "antisemitism is a world-wide problem" that could only be solved "by the cooperation of all men without distinction of race and creed."[16]

These early conversations were not easy, but they produced a foundation on which later reconciliation between Jews and Christians, and in particular between Jews and the Catholic Church would take place.[17] A year after Seelisberg, Gertrud Luckner, a German social worker and activist in Nazi resistance, founded a journal in Freiburg dedicated to Jewish-Christian reconciliation.[18] Around the same time, the French ambassador to the Vatican, Jacques Maritain entreated Pope Pius XII "to take lead in condemning the Holocaust atrocities and European antisemitism." And, in 1949, Jules Isaac, a French Jewish survivor and historian, met with Pope Pius XII and "pleaded with him to change certain injurious phrases concerning the Jews in Catholic prayers."[19] All to no avail. Indeed, the Church investigated Gertrud Luckner's group for potential heresy of "indifferentism."[20]

With lack of approval from the Vatican, Catholic journals, too, remained silent on the efforts at Jewish-Christian dialogue.[21] From 1958, after Pius XII died, and the new pope John XXIII was elected, a different approach marked the Catholic Church's attitudes toward Jewish-Catholic dialogue. In October 1960, as *L'Osservatore Romano* reported, Pope John XXIII met with a Jewish delegation. During that friendly meeting, the pope turned to a passage from the book of Genesis—of Joseph meeting his brothers, "who had come to seek him out. In the beginning, he used an innocent ruse almost to conceal himself from their sight: but then he could no longer contain what had been the yearning of his heart and, immediately after having hidden himself to conceal his sobbing, he cried out: 'It is I—Joseph, your brother!'"[22] Though an act of friendly gesture—calling Jews "brothers" was a departure from earlier attitudes—the story of Joseph was loaded with theological symbolism, as well, for in Catholic exegesis Joseph was seen through the lens of Christological typology.[23] Joseph had been sold by his elder brothers into slavery but instead the younger brother rose to power in Egypt. In this position, he was responsible for managing provisions and years later, during famine, which he predicted through his dreams, Joseph's brothers came to Egypt, before him, looking for food. Not recognizing him, they "bowed low to him, with their faces to the ground" (Gen 42:6, also 43:26). Drama ensued but at the end the brothers reconciled, with Joseph forgiving them for what they had done, interpreting their act as intended by God. What this well-intentioned gesture by Pope John XXIII made clear was that the metaphor of Jews and Christians as brothers needed a reinterpretation.

That same year, Pope John XXIII asked Cardinal Augustin Bea, a German Jesuit, already sympathetic to Jewish-Catholic reconciliation, to draft a document on the relations between Jews and the Church. A year later Bea proposed a *Decretum de Judaeis,* a self-standing decree concerning Jews, which focused on the roots of Christianity reaching the biblical patriarchs and prophets and expressed hope for "the union" of Jews and Christians in "one body." This was still a conversionist document, echoing ancient ecclesiastical histories, but it ended with a condemnation of anti-Jewish persecution: "As the Church, like a mother, condemns most severely injustices committed against innocent people everywhere, so she raises her voice in loud protest against all wrongs done to Jews, whether in the past or in our time. Whoever despises or persecutes this people does injury to the Catholic Church."[24]

Bea's text went over numerous revisions, and five years later—twenty years from the end of World War II—a final version was included in what became the declaration *Nostra aetate* "on the relation of the Church to non-Christian religions." The history of this text, its revisions, and the final version included in *Nostra aetate* attested to the Church's unease about its relationship to Jews. The proposed "decree concerning the Jews" was demoted to a "declaration," a document lower in rank of the three types of pronouncements issued by the Church during the council, with "constitutions" ranking the highest.[25] Not only had the document lost its rank, it was now also diluted, for political reasons, to address other non-Christian religions: Hinduism, Buddhism, Islam, and Judaism.[26]

The first three paragraphs of *Nostra aetate,* addressing non-Christian religions in general and Hinduism, Buddhism, and Islam in particular, expressed appreciation of what each of those religions can offer humanity. In Hinduism, the declaration said, "Men contemplate the divine mystery and express it through an inexhaustible abundance of myths and through searching philosophical inquiry" and "seek freedom from the anguish of our human condition either through ascetical practices or profound meditation or a flight to God with love and trust."[27] Buddhism "realizes the radical insufficiency of this changeable world" and "teaches a way by which men, in a devout and confident spirit, may be able either to acquire the state of perfect liberation, or attain, by their own efforts or through higher help, supreme illumination." Muslims, too, the Church held in "esteem," said paragraph 3:

> They adore the one God, living and subsisting in Himself; merciful and all-powerful, the Creator of heaven and earth, who has spoken to men; they take pains to submit wholeheartedly to even His inscrutable decrees, just as Abraham, with whom the faith of Islam takes pleasure in linking itself, submitted to God. Though they do not acknowledge Jesus as God, they revere Him as a prophet. They also honor Mary, His virgin Mother; at times they even call on her with devotion. In addition, they await the day of judgment when God will render their deserts to all those who have been raised up from the dead. Finally, they value the moral life and worship God especially through prayer, almsgiving and fasting.[28]

Despite past conflicts between Christianity and Islam, the Church urged "all to forget the past and to work sincerely for mutual understanding and to preserve as well as to promote together for the benefit of all mankind social justice and moral welfare, as well as peace and freedom."

But the tone was much different in paragraph 4, the "Jewish" paragraph. [29] No similar positive appreciation for living Judaism or Jews was expressed. Instead, the text focused on ancient Israel, emphasizing instead the "bond" between "the people of the New Covenant" and "Abraham's stock," and presenting Jews as merely instrumental to Christianity. The Church "received the revelation of the Old Testament through the people with whom God in His inexpressible mercy concluded the Ancient Covenant" and "draws sustenance from the root of that well-cultivated olive tree onto which have been grafted the wild shoots, the Gentiles." But Jews as Jews, detached from their connection to Christianity had nothing to offer, as did for example Islam, "for the benefit of all mankind."

The text continued to express supersessionism and Christological interpretation of stories from the Hebrew scriptures. It declared that "according to God's saving design, the beginnings of her faith and her election are found already among the Patriarchs, Moses and the prophets" and "that all who believe in Christ, Abraham's sons according to faith, are included in the same Patriarch's call, and likewise that the salvation of the Church is mysteriously foreshadowed by the chosen people's exodus from the land of bondage."[30] The declaration reminded the faithful of "the words of the Apostle about his kinsmen: 'theirs is the sonship and the glory and the covenants and the law and the worship and the promises; theirs are the fathers and from them is the Christ according to the flesh' [Rom. 9:4–5], the Son of the Virgin Mary." And so, though the effort was to demonstrate a bond between the Church and Jews, the trope of faith and flesh returned, as did a reminder about Jewish bondage and of the Jews' rejection of Christ.

But the revolutionary aspect of the declaration came in the paragraph addressing the centuries-old Church teaching about Jews' responsibility for Jesus's death—the root of so much anti-Jewish hatred. After expressing a desire "to foster" "mutual understanding and respect" through "biblical and theological studies" and "fraternal dialogues," the declaration switched gears, equivocally backing away from this doctrine. "True," the declaration admitted, "the Jewish authorities and those who followed their lead pressed for the death of Christ; still, what happened in His passion cannot be charged against all the Jews, without distinction, then alive, nor against the Jews of today." This wording echoed a comment by Archbishop John Heenan, who said that just as "it would doubtless be unjust were one to blame all the Christians of Europe for the murder of six million Jews in Germany and Poland in our own day," so "it is unjust to condemn the whole Jewish people for the death of Christ."[31] *Nostra aetate* did address hatred, persecution, and antisemitism, but without mentioning the war. And here, too, the language was diluted to make it more universal: "Furthermore, in her rejection of every persecution against any man, the Church, mindful of the patrimony she shares with the Jews and moved not by political reasons but by the Gospel's spiritual love, decries hatred, persecutions, displays of anti-Semitism, directed against Jews at any time and by anyone."

The "Jewish" paragraph of the declaration reveals a tension between the conciliatory voice of the Second Vatican Council and the voice of centuries of traditional Church teachings about Jews, which included a hope for the Jews' conversion, the motif of Jews as the killers of Christ and enemies of Christianity, and that of Jews as the elder brother. For centuries, these motifs had weighed heavily on the Jewish-Christian relation and on the

legal status of Jews in Christian Europe, leaving thus open wounds in Jewish collective memory. Ultimately, the declaration still reaffirmed that "the
Church is the new people of God," even though it urged the faithful not to
present Jews "as rejected or accursed by God." The *Ecclesia* still remained
the queen but now *Synagoga* was not to be publicly humiliated. In the
new post–World War II context, the declaration did "forge new theological
territory" in recasting the old language in a new way.[32] Religion does not
like ruptures—it relies on tradition and continuity. Indeed, the most effective change is one that is rooted in tradition. That was one of the reasons
why *Nostra aetate*, though a milestone, represents, in a complex way, *both*
continuity and change.

*Nostra aetate*, though the lowest in the rank after four constitutions
and nine decrees, became a springboard for new gestures and measures
that would turn Jews, to use John Connelly's words, from "enemies to
brothers," and hostile polemic to, what *Nostra aetate* calls, "fraternal dialogue."[33] For example, the equivocal tone about the Jews' role in the death
of Jesus was modified in the subsequent documents. The 1974 "Guidelines and Suggestions for Implementing the Conciliar Declaration Nostra
aetate, No. 4," issued by the Vatican Commission for Religious Relations
with Jews, dropped the sentence about the role of Jewish authorities, saying now: "With regard to the trial and death of Jesus, the Council recalled
that 'what happened in his passion cannot be blamed upon all the Jews
then living, without distinction, nor upon the Jews of today.'"[34] The
guidelines also further encouraged, "research into the problems bearing
on Judaism and Jewish-Christian relations . . . among specialists, particularly in the fields of exegesis, theology, history and sociology." It promoted
the creation of "chairs of Jewish studies" and "collaboration with Jewish
scholars" at higher institutions of Catholic research.

The depth of the impact of *Nostra aetate* became more obvious as time
went on and the relationship between Jews and the Catholic Church has
been transformed, as the 1974 guidelines put it, from a relationship historically "marked by mutual ignorance and frequent confrontation" to a
"sound" relationship "between Catholics and their Jewish brothers."[35] But
now the common relationship between Jews and Christians as brothers
required forgetting the traditional understanding of this brotherhood,
developed by Christian theologians through biblical sibling pairs: from
Cain and Abel, Ishmael and Isaac, Jacob and Esau, even to Joseph and
his elder brothers, who come and have to bow to him. In that traditional
interpretation, the younger brother became a symbol of Christianity, the
elder a symbol of the Jews, and the fateful phrase "the elder shall serve the

younger" in Christian exegesis has had profound ramifications for the history of anti-Jewish hatred. And yet, "in circumstances deeply affected by the memory of the persecution and massacre of Jews which took place in Europe just before and during the Second World War," as the 1974 guidelines stated, the trope of Jacob and Esau, despite its troubled history, became particularly useful. After all, in the end, these biblical brothers reconciled. As did Joseph and his brothers.

And, so, the Catholic Church and the Jewish community have continued to work toward a better relationship. In 1982, Pope John Paul II stated that "the faith and religious life of the Jewish people as they are professed and practiced still today, can greatly help us to understand better certain aspects of the life of the Church." And, three years later, in 1985, the Vatican Commission for Religious Relations with the Jews did address post-biblical Jewish history, stating that "the history of Israel did not end in 70 A. D. It continued, especially in a numerous Diaspora which allowed Israel to carry to the whole world a witness—often heroic—of its fidelity to the one God and to 'exalt Him in the presence of all the living' (Tobit 13:4), while preserving the memory of the land of their forefathers at the heart of their hope."[36] The commission also acknowledged that "the balance of relations between Jews and Christians over two thousand years has been negative" and instructed that "catechesis should on the other hand help in understanding the meaning for the Jews of the extermination during the years 1939–1945, and its consequences." Indeed, the role of Christianity in the history of antisemitism was explicitly addressed in 1998 in "We Remember: A Reflection on the Shoah."[37]

By 2015, the fiftieth anniversary of *Nostra aetate*, the tone of the Vatican-issued documents indicated a sense of greater ease with dealing with Jewish issues. "Over the past decades," the Vatican Commission for Religious Relations with the Jews stated, "Both the 'dialogue ad extra' and the 'dialogue ad intra' have led with increasing clarity to the awareness that Christians and Jews are irrevocably inter-dependent, and that the dialogue between the two is not a matter of choice but of duty as far as theology is concerned. Jews and Christians can enrich one another in mutual friendship."[38] The 2015 document—titled "'The Gifts and the Calling of God Are Irrevocable' (Rom 11:29): A Reflection on Theological Questions Pertaining to Catholic-Jewish Relations on the Occasion of the 50th Anniversary of "Nostra ætate" (No. 4)—conveys Jewish views, while simultaneously affirming the Church's teachings. It explicitly addressed supersessionism by disavowing it gently and replacing it with a new relationship of "constructive dialogue".

The *Reflection* stressed the unique relationship the Church and Christianity have had with Jews: "The dialogue with Judaism is for Christians something quite special, since Christianity possesses Jewish roots which determine relations between the two in a unique way (cf. "Evangelii gaudium," 247). In spite of the historical breach and the painful conflicts arising from it, the Church remains conscious of its enduring continuity with Israel. Judaism is not to be considered simply as another religion; the Jews are instead our 'elder brothers.'"[40] The statement acknowledged post-biblical history as well, stating that "Given Jesus' Jewish origins, coming to terms with Judaism in one way or another is indispensable for Christians. Yet, the history of the relationship between Judaism and Christianity has also been mutually influenced over time. . . . The soil that nurtured both Jews and Christians is the Judaism of Jesus' time, which not only brought forth Christianity but also, after the destruction of the temple in the year 70, post-biblical rabbinical Judaism which then had to do without the sacrificial cult and, in its further development, had to depend exclusively on prayer and the interpretation of both written and oral divine revelation. Thus Jews and Christians have the same mother and can be seen, as it were, as two siblings who—as is the normal course of events for siblings—have developed in different directions."

Moreover, crucially, the document shifted away from supercessionism. In paragraph 17, the *Reflection* declared: "On the part of many of the Church Fathers the so-called replacement theory or supersessionism steadily gained favour until in the Middle Ages it represented the standard theological foundation of the relationship with Judaism: the promises and commitments of God would no longer apply to Israel because it had not recognised Jesus as the Messiah and the Son of God, but had been transferred to the Church of Jesus Christ which was now the true 'new Israel', the new chosen people of God." This resulted in "a theological antagonism which was only to be defused at the Second Vatican Council," which offered "a new theological framework, the Jewish roots of Christianity. While affirming salvation through an explicit or even implicit faith in Christ, the Church does not question the continued love of God for the chosen people of Israel. A replacement or supersession theology which sets against one another two separate entities, a Church of the Gentiles and the rejected Synagogue whose place it takes, is deprived of its foundations." Although the framework of "the Jewish roots of Christianity" was not new—Augustine used it as a justification for the preservation of Jews, nonetheless, the move away from supersessionism and the reframing of the special role Jews had for the history of Christianity are manifestations of the success of decades of real, honest commitment to dialogue and understanding, and willingness to take painstaking steps to achieve that.

The shift away from supersessionism also represents a shift away from a hierarchical order that Christianity has constructed since its earliest centuries. Jews and Judaism, real and imagined, have played a key role in Christianity's self-identity. It was not only as "the foundation of [Christian] faith," but also in Christianity's self-perception of its own theological and political position.[41] And while for so many centuries, the relationship was framed around the idea of Christian dominance and Jewish submission, as per the interpretation of the *Synagoga* as inferior, humiliated, and rejected by God, the decades of dialogue between Jews and the Catholic Church turned that relationship into equal partnership, now embodied in a sculpture by Joshua Koffman unveiled in 2015 at St. John's University in Philadelphia, depicting *Synagoga* and *Ecclesia*, seated together, both donning crowns, and looking at each other's texts—the Torah scroll held by *Synagoga*, and the codex, symbolizing the New Testament, held by *Ecclesia* (fig. 30).

But what has been accomplished at the Vatican level has not always trickled down to other countries. The implementation, as the sculpture at St. John's illustrates, has been effective in the United States. This is not an accident. There are Jewish and Catholic organizations in the United States committed to sustaining this dialogue. In countries with smaller Jewish communities, and deeper antisemitism and distrust, the implementation has been less consistent.

In France, the first letter issued by French bishops came in 1973, eight years after *Nostra aetate*.[42] It was a bold theological affirmation of *Nostra aetate*, acknowledging Christianity's debt "to the Jewish people for the Five Books of the Law, the Prophets, and the other Scriptures, which complete the message" and affirming that "these precepts were received by Christians without, however, dispossessing the Jews." The French letters called for "respect" for Jews and their Jewishness and reminded the faithful that while both Jews and Christians "accomplish their vocation along dissimilar lines," "their paths cross incessantly" and their constant "vis-à-vis" is part of the divine plan. It was, therefore, "desirable" to "enter the road of mutual acceptance and appreciation and, repudiating their former enmity, turn toward the Father, with one and the same movement of hope, which will be a promise for the entire world." The letter condemned antisemitism and antisemitic stereotypes but spoke relatively little about the recent past, or about France, in particular.

It was only in September 1997, in the midst of the Maurice Papon trial, when the Catholic Bishops of France addressed World War II in a powerful

FIGURE 30. "*Synagoga* and *Ecclesia* in Our Time," by Joshua Koffman, was commissioned by Saint Joseph's University in Philadelphia to mark the golden jubilee of the Second Vatican Council, Declaration *Nostra Aetate* in 2015. Photo with permission from Joshua Koffman.

"Declaration of Repentance" in which they stated that "the time has come for the church to submit her own history, especially that of this period, to critical examination and to recognize without hesitation the sins committed by members of the church, and to beg forgiveness of God and humankind."[43] "The Declaration of Repentance" was a sincere document of moral reckoning with the past, addressing "questions of conscience, which no human can ignore." The bishops noted that "the Catholic Church, far from wanting to be forgotten, knows full well that conscience is formed in remembering and that just as no individual person can live with himself, neither can society live in peace with a repressed or untruthful memory." The Church had to reckon with choosing pragmatism over decisive moral stances when that choice mattered the most. When French Jews were in internment camps, the bishops noted, and "the country, which had been beaten, lay prostrate and was partially occupied, the hierarchy saw the protection of its own faithful as its first priority, assuring as much as possible its own institutions." This priority was "legitimate," the bishops acknowledged, but it was also a retreat to "a narrow vision of the church's mission" at a time when "many members of the church and many non-Catholics yearned for the church to speak out at a time of such spiritual confusion and to recall the message of Jesus Christ." Thus, "those in authority of the church, caught up in a loyalism and docility which went far beyond the obedience traditionally accorded to civil authorities, remained stuck in conformity, prudence and abstention." All this "out of fear of reprisals." The church leaders "failed to realize that the church, called at that moment to play the role of defender within a social body that was falling apart, did in fact have considerable power and influence, and that in the face of the silence of other institutions, its voice could have echoes loudly by taking a definitive stand against the irreparable." The bishops conceded that they could "pass no judgment on the consciences of the people of that era; we are not ourselves guilty of what took place in the past, but we must be fully aware of the cost of such behavior and actions. It is our church, and we are obliged to acknowledge objectively today that ecclesiastical interests understood in an overly restrictive sense, took priority over the demands of conscience, and we must ask ourselves why."

In examining the "why," the French bishops acknowledged the role Christian theology had played in spreading anti-Jewish prejudice. There were of course, "social, political, economic, and cultural factors," but "one of the essential factors was of religious nature." [44] According to "the judgment of historians, it is a well-proven fact that for centuries, up until Vatican Council II, an anti-Jewish tradition stamped its mark in differing ways on Christian doctrine and teaching, in theology, apologetics, preaching and in the liturgy. It was on such ground that the venomous plant of hatred for the Jews was able to flourish." All this was "heavy inheritance" to bear, "its consequences . . . so difficult to wipe out." The Church in France failed "in her mission as teacher of consciences and that therefore she carries along with the Christian people the responsibility for failing to lend their aid, from the very first moments, when protest and protection were still possible, as well as necessary, even if, subsequently, a great many acts of courage were performed. . . . For, this failing of the church of France and of her responsibility toward the Jewish people are part of our history. We confess this sin. We beg God's pardon, and we call upon the Jewish people to hear our words of repentance." The French bishops' letter, in its earnestness, provides a model for sincere reckoning with the past and probing moral questions with courage and maturity.

But in other countries, that road to reconciliation was even more bumpy than in France. In Poland, the impact of *Nostra aetate* and later efforts of reconciliation between Polish Jews and Catholics, and between Poles and Jews, have been hampered by communist and anticommunist politics. Given the speed with which of the message of *Nostra aetate* per-colated into individual countries, its implementation in Poland was made even more difficult, where in 1968, antisemitic purges lead to a wave of Jewish emigration and were followed by silence about anything Jewish. But the existence of the declaration *Nostra aetate* was known, and under-ground, among the opposition to the communist regime, a dialogue began. This dialogue was later amplified after Cardinal Karol Wojtyła became Pope John Paul II.

And while *Nostra aetate* and, later, Pope John Paul II provided tools and authority to those who wanted to pursue the path toward change, *Nostra aetate*, paradoxically, also provided a shield for those who did not: it focused only on theological matters, not subjects that touched the core of the more immediate past. And thus, in the texts produced in Poland in the late twentieth century through the efforts at dialogue between the Catho-lic Church and Jews, the two voices already heard in the aftermath of the Kielce pogrom continue to sound among Polish leaders of the Catholic Church. On the one hand, there is the voice of those genuinely interested in honest reckoning with the past, and, on the other, there is the voice of those who continue to hide behind the protective shields of Nazism, com-munism, and anticommunism. These voices, almost a duo-phonic back-and-forth chorus, are heard distinctly in most of the documents issued by the Catholic Church in Poland since 1986, when the first subcommittee for the dialogue with Judaism was established by the Polish Bishops' Confer-ence (the subcommittee was raised to the status of a full committee a year later).[45]

In 1991 the Polish bishops issued one of the earliest pastoral letters addressing Jews and Judaism. In that letter, published on the twenty-fifth anniversary of *Nostra aetate*, one could hear a voice, resembling that of Bishop Kubina of Częstochowa after the Kielce massacre. It regretted that some Catholics "remained indifferent" to the "incomprehensive tragedy" of the mass murder of Jews on Polish soil, or worse, that some Catholics "were the cause of the death of Jews."[46] Such Catholics, the bishops' let-ter stated, "will forever gnaw at our conscience. . . . If only one Christian could have helped and did not stretch out a helping hand to a Jew during the time of danger or caused his death, we must ask for forgiveness of our Jewish brothers and sisters." This sincere voice of reckoning was then immediately countered by a voice that echoed the sentiments expressed by Cardinal Hlond and Bishop Kaczmarek. "We are aware," this second voice interjected, "that many of our compatriots still remember the injustices and injuries committed by the postwar communist authorities, in which people of Jewish origin also took part. We must acknowledge, however, that the source of the inspiration of their activity was clearly neither their origin nor religion, but the communist ideology, from which the Jews themselves, in fact, suffered many injustices." The first voice then took its turn, expressing "regrets for all the incidents of antisemitism . . . committed at any time or by anyone on Polish soil." But then the second voice returned pushing back against the "untrue and deeply harmful" concept of "Polish antisemitism" and reminded the audience that "the Poles as a nation were one of the first victims of the same criminal racist ideology of Hitler's Nazism." This back-and-forth between the two voices weakened the impact of those most powerful passages that could have provided a clear direction to help Poland and Polish Catholics to move forward toward a better understanding of the past and toward a meaningful conversation on Polish-Jewish relations.

These opposing voices were still heard in the statement for the Jubilee of 2000 issued by the Polish Bishops' Conference, which forcefully called for "the purification of memory and [for] reconciliation" and noted, "in the spirit of the Jubilee's act of penance" that "along noble efforts by Poles to rescue many Jewish lives, there are also our sins from that period: indifference or enmity toward Jews."[47] The letter urged Polish Catholics to "overcome all expressions of anti-Jewishness, anti-Judaism (that is animosity stemming from erroneous interpretations of Church teachings), and antisemitism (that is hatred based on nationalistic or racial motives) that existed or exists among Christians." These powerful words, reflecting some of the sentiments expressed by Pope John Paul II and echoing those of the French bishops, were then somewhat muffled by a statement demanding that "anti-Polonism" should be fought with "equal determination."[48] Moreover, in a sentence condemning antisemitism, an awkward insertion was made to include "also anti-Christianism." This duo-phony of conflicted voices has once again blunted the moral message that is otherwise conveyed in these texts, stunting reconciliation, which is impossible without a sincere reckoning with history.

This inability to confront antisemitism and the past in a focused and straightforward way has resulted in occasional flare-ups, like during Easter in 2019, when Bishop Rafał Markowski, Chair of the Committee for Dialogue with Judaism within the Polish Bishops' Conference, was forced to react to an incident that took place on April 19, Good Friday in Pruchnik, a small town in southeastern Poland.[49] Catholics in Pruchnik marked the holiday with a beating and burning of an effigy of Judas in a ritual called the "judgment of Judas," an older tradition revived since the 1980s after a decades-long hiatus.[50] The effigy was made of potato sacks filled with straw, its head modeled according to stereotypical antisemitic tropes: a big nose, beard, peyes (earlocks), and a black hat. The effigy was clearly meant to be not only "Judas" but also a stand-in for Jews. The thirty lashes it got from children for the thirty silver coins Judas is said to have received were complemented by an additional five lashes, advocated by adults "because they [Jews] want reparations from Poland." This was a reaction to US Senate bill, S 447, "Justice for Uncompensated Survivors Today (JUST) Act," which passed in May 2018, but gained the coordinated attention of Polish nationalists in 2019.[51]

After a local newspaper reported the story of "Judas's judgment," the story gained traction in Poland and abroad, and elicited condemnation from the World Jewish Congress. On Easter Monday, Bishop Markowski issued a statement, "In the context of the events that took place in Pruchnik on April 19, the Church clearly expresses her disapproval of practices that violate human dignity. The Catholic Church will never tolerate manifestations of contempt [pogarda] towards members of any nation, including the Jewish people. At this Easter season, we recall the truth of faith that Christ gave his life for the salvation of all, from which results the Christian attitude of respect towards every human being."[52] Bishop Markowski was right— the ritual was meant to be humiliating, expressing contempt. In the prewar period, the effigy was hung near Jewish homes, while Jews hid behind closed shutters. When the press reported the response of the Polish Bishops' Conference, the backlash was strong; comments left on the newspaper articles showed virulent antisemitic sentiments, condemning the bishops' acquiescence to Jewish pressures (though sentiments expressing outrage about this local "tradition" were present as well). The Pruchnik incident illustrates the dilemma the Catholic Church has faced when confronting antisemitism (and before the modern era also earlier anti-Jewish animus).[53] The Church has been trapped between a need for a moral response condemning despicable acts and public sentiments that condoned such acts; the Church was sometimes encumbered by local politics.

Reckoning and change are hard and the process to accomplish them is slow and tedious. Bishop Ambrogio Spreafico, the President on Ecumenism and Interreligious Dialogue of the Italian Catholic Bishops' Conference, observed in 2020, in response to an antisemitic painting depicting Jews killing a Christian child: "Despite the numerous declarations published by the Church in recent years, despite the gestures and words spoken by all the pontiffs of the last fifty years, we must unfortunately conclude that part of the teaching of the Church on the unique and singular relationship of Christians with Judaism has not yet entered into the hearts and minds of some, who, although they are actually minorities, regrettably still manage to attract attention."[54] Bishop Spreafico urged the faithful in Italy to "recognize the precious presence of the Jewish community and Judaism in our cities and in the world" and he promised to "promote the knowledge of Judaism by every means in the catechesis and teaching of the Catholic religion. Only in this way, through the defeat of ignorance and prejudice can we prevent the manifestations of antisemitism that open doors to exclusion and racism."

But change is only possible with a truthful accounting of history and traditions, and an examination of the underlying mental habits history has created. As James Baldwin observed, "The great force of history comes from the fact that we carry it within us, are unconsciously controlled by it in many ways, and history is literally present in all that we do."[55] For Christians, of all denominations—in Europe and the United States, the history of Jews and Judaism is part of the history of Christianity and of the fabric making Christian identity and sense of dominance, roots of which stem from the trope of Jewish servitude that had emerged from Christian supersessionism. And that Christian sense of superiority and dominance had ramifications beyond Jewish-Christian relations.

For Americans, the legacy of slavery and racism is part of both history and American identity—not only that of Black Americans. "We cannot escape history," said President Abraham Lincoln, a month before signing the Emancipation Proclamation, even if we try. In January 2021, President Trump's White House released a report on the history of the United States prepared by the so-called 1776 Commission. The report was a response to the *New York Times*'s 1619 Project led by Nikole Hannah-Jones, which examined American history through the Black experience—both slavery and accomplishments—and its centrality in US history and culture.[56] The 1776 report, in contrast, was defensive. It asserted that "the most common charge levelled [*sic*] against the founders, and hence against our country itself, is that they were hypocrites who didn't believe in their stated principles, and therefore the country they built rests on a lie. This charge is untrue, and has done enormous damage, especially in recent years, with a devastating effect on our civic unity and social fabric."[57] As Alfred, Ruth, and Steven Blumrosen have demonstrated, "the issue of race and slavery played an integral part in the foundation of the republic in 1774 and we have borne the brunt of the compromises made to achieve a union ever since."[58] And, as the Blumrosens rightly noted, "our struggles demonstrate the difficulties involved." But the difficulties lie in part in the fact that the roots of these issues have been obscured, suppressed even by recounting a triumphant narrative of throwing tyranny and building a land of liberty, and, on race issues, by looking for redemption in specific historical events that meshed with the triumphant metanarrative: the abolition of slavery, *Brown v. Board of Education*, the Civil Rights Act of 1964, the election of President Obama, and perhaps also the election of Kamala Harris as the vice president of the United States. What has been silenced is the history that had led to, or had been behind these "redemptive" moments, making them feel so transformative.

Modern Christians have, in turn, also become used to a narrative of Christian faith and love, even when the historical reality clashes with these popular perceptions. And while some denominations have confronted these issues, even if, like the Catholic Church, imperfectly and gingerly, especially in places where the political consequences of facing antisemitism or racism are still grave, others continue to function within the same racist and antisemitic frameworks, in which both Jews and Black people remain disruptive outsiders, undeserving of their places in society but needed to bolster white and Christian identity. This was certainly the message conveyed in 2018, during the congressional elections, by the Republican National Congressional Committee, in an ad it ran in the first congressional district in Minnesota (MN-01). The ad featured images of chaos and anarchy, with George Soros, dubbed "a connoisseur of chaos" and sitting in front of pile of money, and Colin Kaepernick slightly behind, with burning cities in the background. This imagery was a racist and antisemitic dog whistle—or rather a bullhorn, affirming white Christian supremacy by focusing on a Jew and a Black man as outsiders creating disorder.

Antisemitism and anti-Black racism do not say anything meaningful about Jews and Black people, whose mental effigies were created to play a role in the drama created by the dominant white Christian society. As James Baldwin daringly stated: "It is the American Republic . . . which created something which they call a 'nigger.' They created it out of necessities of their own. The nature of the crisis is that I am not a 'nigger'—I never was. I am a man. The question with which the country is confronted is this: Why do you need a 'nigger' in the first place?"[59] The same question can extend to Christians—why do they need "the little Jew"? The Judas? The George Soros? Invented as they are for the needs of Christians, they are the fruits of the seeds planted almost two millennia ago: of Christian supersessionism, Christian superiority, and Christian supremacy.

This white Christian supremacy was unambiguously on display on Capitol Hill in Washington, DC, on January 6, 2021, when a mob of pro-Trump insurrectionists invaded the Capitol building, demanding that the Congress overturn the election Donald Trump had lost to Joe Biden. They carried Confederate flags, and some participants were spotted wearing antisemitic shirts, including one with "Camp Auschwitz." On the outside, the rioters installed a large cross and gallows with a hanging noose—powerful symbols of white Christian supremacy. Though the rioters' convictions were fed and inflamed by modern media and writings, they embodied ideas developed and gradually transformed over centuries from ancient innocuous theological statements into a deadly social force. What unfolded in Washington, DC, was indeed the embodiment of the expectations and hopes for white Christian America the writer Harold Preece recorded in 1946.[60]

Words and symbols matter. Though their meaning changes over time, they create concepts and deep and unconscious habits of thinking that are difficult to uproot. Uprooted, or at least weakened, they must be.

## Preface

1. James Baldwin and Raoul Peck, *I Am Not Your Negro: A Companion Edition to the Documentary Film Directed by Raoul Peck* (New York: Vintage Books, 2017), 108–9. For the video segment with James Baldwin in "The Negro and the American Promise," see https://www.pbs.org/video/american-experience-james-baldwin-from-the-negro-and-the-american-promise/.

2. Sara Lipton, *Dark Mirror: The Medieval Origins of Anti-Jewish Iconography* (New York: Metropolitan Books, 2014). Magda Teter, *Blood Libel: On the Trail of an Antisemitic Myth* (Cambridge, MA: Harvard University Press, 2020).

3. Debra Kaplan and Magda Teter, "Out of the (Historiographic) Ghetto: Jews and the Reformation," *Sixteenth Century Journal* 40, no. 2 (2009).

## Introduction: Enduring Marks of Inferiority

1. Joe Heim, "Recounting a Day of Rage, Hate, Violence and Death," *Washington Post*, August 14, 2017.

2. Ellie Silverman et al., "Spencer, Kessler, Cantwell and Other White Supremacists Found Liable in Deadly Unite the Right Rally," *Washington Post*, November 23, 2021.

3. James Loeffler, "Charlottesville Was Only a Preview," *Atlantic*, December 23, 2021.

4. George M. Fredrickson, *Racism: A Short History* (Princeton: Princeton University Press, 2002), 99, also 146. For the example of the return to Europe, see James Q. Whitman, *Hitler's American Model: The United States and the Making of Nazi Race Law* (Princeton: Princeton University Press, 2018).

5. Geraldine Heng, *The Invention of Race in the European Middle Ages* (Cambridge: Cambridge University Press, 2019), 5, 57; Geraldine Heng, *England and the Jews: How Religion and Violence Created the First Racial State in the West* (Cambridge: Cambridge University Press, 2019), 5–6. Heng's study of medieval English history deploys modern terms and frameworks to medieval events and developments that often obscure and distort historical conditions and contexts. For a lengthy critique of the book and its treatment of Jews and race, see Sarah J. Pearce, "The Inquisitor and the Moseret: The Invention of Race in the European Middle Ages and the New English Colonialism in Jewish Historiography," *Medieval Encounters* 26, no. 2 (2020): 145–90.

6. George Yancy, *Black Bodies, White Gazes: The Continuing Significance of Race in America* (Lanham, MD: Rowman & Littlefield, 2017), e.g., xxx and xxxii. Jesus's quote, Matthew 5:38.

7. Frank Rudy Cooper spoke about Black men as "contrast figures" in white society: Frank Rudy Cooper, "Masculinities, Post-Racialism and the Gates Controversy: The False Equivalence between Officer and Civilian," *Nevada Law Journal* 11, no. 1 (2010): 18.

8. The exceptions are legal scholars in the US who have worked on critical race theory. Still, historians have tended to discuss culture, even "political culture," when law played a key role.

9. Ian Haney López, *White by Law: The Legal Construction of Race* (New York: New York University Press, 2006), 13, 91–92.

10. Haney López, *White by Law*, 86–87.

11. Haney López, *White by Law*, 13, 91–92.

12. Haney López, *White by Law*, 85.

13. *Oxford English Dictionary*, "supremacy": "The condition of being supreme in authority, rank, or power; the position of supreme or highest authority or power. **a.** With reference to the authority of the sovereign, *spec.* the position of the sovereign as supreme head of the Church of England or as supreme governor of England in spiritual as well as temporal matters. **b.** With reference to the authority of the Pope or the Holy See in spiritual or temporal matters. **c.** *figurative*. Applied to any quality, phenomenon, practice, etc., enjoying a dominant or superior status. **2.** The fact of being superior in rank or authority or of having power over another person, state, etc.; dominance, overlordship; an instance of this. Also *figurative*."

14. Recently, M. Lindsey Kaplan has explored this theme in the medieval context, in her excellent study, M. Lindsay Kaplan, *Figuring Racism in Medieval Christianity* (New York, Oxford: Oxford University Press, 2019).

15. For a concise overview of the early Christian imagery of Blackness, see Paul H. Kaplan, "Introduction to the New Edition," in *The Image of the Black in Western Art, Volume 2: From the Early Christian Era to the "Age of Discovery," Part 2: Africans in the Christian Ordinance of the World*, ed. David Bindman and Henry Louis Gates. 5 vols. (Cambridge, MA: Belknap Press of Harvard University Press, 2010), 1–30, especially 12, 15.

16. Barbara J. Fields, "Slavery, Race, and Ideology in the United States of America," *New Left Review* 181, no. May–June (1990): 114; Tyler Edward Stovall, *White Freedom: The Racial History of an Idea* (Princeton: Princeton University Press, 2021).

17. On the ideology of racism and its relation to enslavement, see the classic essay, Fields, "Slavery, Race, and Ideology," quote on 114.

18. During the Crusades, Christians attacked Jews in the name of Christianity and Christ, while some Christian leaders, such as Bernard of Clairvaux, defended Jews against such violence. But Bernard of Clairvaux also used the term "judaize" to describe Christians lending money on interest. On Bernard of Clairvaux and the reception of his teachings, see below. For English translations of Bernard's responses to anti-Jewish violence and his use of "judaize" to mean "lend on interest," see Robert Chazan, *Church, State, and Jew in the Middle Ages*, Library of Jewish Studies (New York: Behrman House, 1980).

19. On evangelicals and Jews, see, for example, Stephen Spector, *Evangelicals and Israel: The Story of Christian Zionism* (New York: Oxford University Press, 2009). Yaakov Ariel, *An Unusual Relationship: Evangelical Christians and Jews* (New York: NYU Press, 2013). On evangelicals, racism, "feeling thermometer," Robert P. Jones, *White Too Long: The Legacy of White Supremacy in American Christianity* (New York: Simon & Schuster, 2021), 158–159, 170–171. See also Anthea D. Butler, *White Evangelical Racism: The Politics of Morality in America* (Chapel Hill: University of North Carolina Press, 2021). The complexity of the story of evangelical relations with

Jews is illustrated by Ariel who starts his *An Unusual Relationship* with a vignette of the meeting between Richard Nixon and Billy Graham, in which both expressed anti-semitic views at the time when Graham nonetheless "spoke and wrote favorably about Israel," for which he was awarded "The Torch of Liberty" by the Anti-Defamation League (ADL) and "The Inter-Religious Award" by the American Jewish Committee (AJC), Ariel, *An Unusual Relationship*, 1–2.

20. For example, J. Kameron Carter, *Race: A Theological Account* (Oxford; New York: Oxford University Press, 2008); Bryan N. Massingale, *Racial Justice and the Catholic Church* (Maryknoll: Orbis Books, 2010); and Jeannine Hill Fletcher, *The Sin of White Supremacy: Christianity, Racism, and Religious Diversity in America* (Maryknoll: Orbis Books, 2017). On contemporary Christian racism, see most recently a brief account by Butler, *White Evangelical Racism*.

21. For a reflection on "The Use and Abuse of Historical Comparison," see Susan Neiman, *Learning from the Germans: Race and the Memory of Evil* (New York: Ferrar, Straus and Giroux, 2020), ch. 1.

22. Yancy, *Black Bodies, White Gaze*, xix and 22. See also, for example, Barack Obama, "Remarks by the President on Trayvon Martin," in *Office of the Press Secretary*, The White House (July 19, 2013). Taylor Lewis, "6 Times President Obama Honestly Shared His Own Experiences with Racism," *Essence*, October 27, 2020. Abby Goodnough, "Harvard Professor Jailed; Officer Is Accused of Bias," *New York Times*, July 21, 2009. Also, Jones, *White Too Long*.

23. The social climb of Jews in post–World War II Western societies and, in the US, the evangelical support for Israel have often erased Jews from studies of white Christian supremacy in the United States. See, for example, recently, Butler, *White Evangelical Racism*. The book discusses the centrality of Christianity and race in the white evangelical identity, their anti-Black racism, and even their Islamophobia, without as much as a word about their antisemitism.

24. Angela Onwuachi-Willig, "From Emmett Till to Trayvon Martin: The Persistence of White Womanhood and the Preservation of White Manhood," *Du Bois Review: Social Science Research on Race* 15, no. 2 (2018): 260.

25. On Jews in classical antiquity, see Peter Schäfer, *Judeophobia: Attitudes toward the Jews in the Ancient World* (Cambridge, MA: Harvard University Press, 1997); Benjamin H. Isaac, *The Invention of Racism in Classical Antiquity* (Princeton, NJ: Princeton University Press, 2006), ch. 13.

26. See for example, Galatians 4 and Romans 12.

27. Genesis 25:23, Romans 9:12.

28. Orlando Patterson, *Slavery and Social Death: A Comparative Study, with a New Preface* (Cambridge, MA: Harvard University Press, 2018), 19–20. On "racial habits," mental and physical, of white privilege, see Shannon Sullivan, *Revealing Whiteness: The Unconscious Habits of Racial Privilege* (Bloomington: Indiana University Press, 2006).

29. To be sure, in the Middle Ages, Europe retained trading contacts with Asia and north Africa, and the Middle East, but the early modern period brought a dominant and exploitative relation with non-Europeans.

30. David M. Goldenberg, *The Curse of Ham: Race and Slavery in Early Judaism, Christianity, and Islam* (Princeton: Princeton University Press, 2004).

31. On color prejudice and Christian polemic, see Gay L. Byron, *Symbolic Blackness and Ethnic Difference in Early Christian Literature* (London; New York: Routledge, 2008), especially ch. 2. On the meaning attached to skin colors, see Goldenberg, *Curse of Ham*, especially, chs. 4, 7, and 10.

32. Kaplan, *Figuring Racism*, 135–36.

33. Kaplan, *Figuring Racism*, 136. Fields, "Slavery, Race, and Ideology," 102, 104.

34. Fields, "Slavery, Race, and Ideology," 104.

35. For English, see the Oxford English Dictionary, meaning 2, first used in 1526. Also, Matthew Sutcliffe, *A Treatise of Ecclesiastical Discipline: Wherein That Confused Forme of Government, Which Certeine . . . Do Strive to Bring into the Church of England, Is Examined, Etc* (London: G. Bishop, 1590), 19: "Let not the do & or be offended with me, though I denigrate his dignity"; 26 "Let not the doctor be offended with me, though I denigrate his dignitie." Fascinatingly, the word in English falls out of use only to return in the nineteenth century, after the American Civil War. In Italian, the word in the second figurative sense appears in the 1500s, and by 1617 makes it to a dictionary, Giacomo Pergamini, *Il memoriale della lingua italiana* (In Venetia: Gio. Battista Ciotti, 1617), 56. In Spanish, the word enters a dictionary with that specific meaning in 1732: "DENIGRAR. v. a. Deslustrar, infamar, manchar el crédito, opinión, honra y fama de alguna persona, con palabras o escritos. Viene del Latino Denigrare. Latín. Alterius nomini infamiam aspergere, ignominiae notam inurere. CHRON. DEL R. D. JUAN EL II. cap. 99. Porque la fama suya, y de Don Rui Lopez de Avalos . . . no quedasse denigrada, ni mancillada, siendo innocents" in *Diccionario de la lengua castellana, en que se explica el verdadero sentido de las voces, su naturaleza y calidad, con las phrases o modos de hablar, los proverbios o refranes, y otras cosas convenientes al uso de la lengua* (Madrid: En la Imprenta de la Real Academia Española: Por la viudad de Francisco del Hierro, 1732). For the medieval use, Jean Devisse, "Christians and Black," in *The Image of the Black in Western Art, Volume 2: From the Christian Era to the "Age of Discovery," Part 1: From the Demonic Threat to the Incarnation of Sainthood,* ed. David Bindman and Henry Louis Gates. 5 vols. (Cambridge, MA: Belknap Press of Harvard University Press, 2010), especially 53–55 and Latin sources in footnotes. For the use of the word "white" in the English colonial context, see Winthrop D. Jordan, *White over Black: American Attitudes toward the Negro, 1550–1812*, 2nd ed. (Chapel Hill, NC: University of North Carolina Press, 2012), 95.

36. George M. Fredrickson, *The Arrogance of Race: Historical Perspectives on Slavery, Racism, and Social Inequality* (Middletown, CT: Wesleyan University Press, 1988), 3.

37. W. E. B. Du Bois, "Dusk of Dawn," in *Writings* (New York: Literary Classics of the United States, 2007), 704. Quoted and discussed in Fredrickson, *The Arrogance of Race*, 4.

38. Christhard Hoffmann, Werner Bergmann, and Helmut Smith, *Exclusionary Violence: Antisemitic Riots in Modern German History* (Ann Arbor: University of Michigan Press, 2002).

39. Paul R. Mendes-Flohr and Jehuda Reinharz, *The Jew in the Modern World*, 3rd ed. (Oxford, NY: Oxford University Press, 2011), 131.

40. Hartwig von Hundt-Radowsky, *Judenspiegel. Schand- und Sittengemälde alter und neuer Zeit* (Reutlingen: Enßlin, 1821), 57. An English translation of a few

paragraphs from this book was published in Mendes-Flohr and Reinharz, *The Jew in the Modern World*, 288–89.

41. Mendes-Flohr and Reinharz, *The Jew in the Modern World*, 297–99.

42. For a recent discussion of the racialized character of the idea of "freedom" and "liberty," see Stovall, *White Freedom*. See also Maurice Samuels, *The Right to Difference: French Universalism and the Jews* (Chicago: University of Chicago Press, 2019). Samuels focuses on the role Jews played in French discourse about universalism and citizenship; he pays little attention to French colonies before the nineteenth and twentieth centuries.

43. A short selection of quotes is available in English in Lynn Hunt, *The French Revolution and Human Rights: A Brief History with Documents* (Boston, New York: Bedford/St. Martin's, 2016), 97–98; Valerie Quinney, "Decisions on Slavery, the Slave Trade and Civil Rights for Negroes in the Early French Revolution," *Journal of Negro History* 55, no. 2 (1970); Valerie Quinney, "The Problem of Civil Rights for Free Men of Color in the Early French Revolution," *French Historical Studies* 7, no. 4 (1972); and David Geggus, "Racial Equality, Slavery, and Colonial Secession during the Constituent Assembly," *American Historical Review* 94, no. 5 (1989): 1291. A similar contrast between the continental and colonial attitudes appeared in Britain when they were considering the question of slavery; the abolitionist voices were far louder in the metropole, Christer Petley, "Slavery, Emancipation and the Creole World View of Jamaican Colonists, 1800–1834," *Slavery and Abolition* 26, no. 1 (2005).

44. Henri Grégoire, *Mémoire en faveur des gens de couleur ou sang-mêlés de St. Domingue, & des autres isles françoises de l'Amérique, adressé à l'assemblée nationale* (Paris: Belin, 1789), 4. Selections in Hunt, *The French Revolution and Human Rights*, 99–100.

45. "Admission of Missouri," *Annals of the Congress of the United States* Proceedings and Debates of the House of Representatives of the United States, at the Second Session of the Sixteenth Congress, begun at the City of Washington, Monday, November 13, 1820, no. 37 (1820–1821): 550. For an extensive discussion about admission of Missouri and the question of Black citizenship, see Martha S. Jones, *Birthright Citizens: A History of Race and Rights in Antebellum America* (Cambridge: Cambridge University Press, 2018), ch. 1.

46. Judith N. Shklar, *American Citizenship: The Quest for Inclusion* (Cambridge, MA: Harvard University Press, 2001), 13.

47. Rogers M. Smith has explored these clashing ideas in the US in his monumental study, Rogers M. Smith, *Civic Ideals* (New Haven: Yale University Press, 1997).

48. Patterson, *Slavery and Social Death*, 44.

49. Plessy v. Ferguson, 163 U.S. 537 (1896), 560.

50. Frederick Douglass, "The Claims of the Negro Ethnologically Considered (1854)," in *The Portable Frederick Douglass* (New York: Penguin Classics, 2016), 230.

51. Neiman, *Learning from the Germans*, 34.

52. This notion reverberates in recent attacks on Critical Race Theory, which emerged in legal studies to explore the relationship between race, racism, power, and law, but which now is attacked as "un-American" for raising the issue of race in American history, society, and culture.

53. "'I Am American': Black Americans Use Social Media to Respond to McConnell's Comments on Voting," *Washington Post*, January 21, 2022, https://www.washingtonpost.com/politics/2022/01/21/i-am-american-black-americans-use-social-media-respond-mcconnells-comments-voting/.

54. Haney López, *White by Law*.

55. Shklar, *American Citizenship*, 13.

56. Jones, *White Too Long*.

57. Shannon Sullivan called it "unconscious racial habits" in the context of white racism in the United States, Shannon Sullivan, *Good White People: The Problem with Middle-Class White Anti-Racism* (Albany: State University of New York Press, 2014), 19. Also, Sullivan, *Revealing Whiteness*.

58. James Baldwin, "White Man's Guilt," *Ebony*, August 1965, 47.

59. Alfred W. Blumrosen, Ruth G. Blumrosen, and Steven Blumrosen, *Slave Nation: How Slavery United the Colonies and Sparked the American Revolution* (Naperville, IL: Sourcebooks, 2007), xi. Susanna Schrobsdorff, "It's Not Just . . . Kamala Harris' White Suit, It's Also the Power of Human-to-Human Giving," *Time*, November 8, 2020, https://time.com/5909122/its-not-just-kamala-harris-white-suit-its-also-the-power-of-human-to-human-giving/.

60. Frederic Raphael's quote—"the Jews are the margin that runs down the middle of the page of European history"—referred to Jews only, but the idea behind it applies also to the centrality of Black people in the white imagination. Cited in Anthony Paul Bale, *The Jew in the Medieval Book: English Antisemitisms, 1350–1500* (Cambridge, UK; New York, US: Cambridge University Press, 2006), 5.

61. Glynis Cousin and Robert Fine, "A Common Cause: Reconnecting the Study of Racism and Antisemitism," in *Antisemitism, Racism and Islamophobia: Distorted Faces of Modernity*, ed. Christine Achinger and Robert Fine (London: Routledge, 2017), 14–33, especially, 15, 17–20, and 28–30.

62. Jonathan Judaken, "Anti-Semitism (Historiography)," ed. Sol Goldberg, Scott Ury, and Keith Ian Weiser (Basingstoke: Palgrave Macmillan, 2020), 25–38; David Nirenberg, *Anti-Judaism: The Western Tradition* (New York: W. W. Norton & Co., 2013); and Samuels, *The Right to Difference*. The origins of the history of antisemitism as rooted in Christianity can be traced to James Parkes's landmark study *The Conflict of the Church and the Synagogue: A Study of the Origins of Antisemitism*, first published in 1934 (London: Soncino Press). But many of the early scholars who sensed Christian roots of antisemitism often focused on the idea of deicide as the key motif behind Christian anti-Jewish animus.

63. More recent studies on Christianity and race focus on theology, such as Carter, *Race: A Theological Account*; and Hill Fletcher, *The Sin of White Supremacy*. See also Richard T. Hughes, Robert N. Bellah, and Molefi Kete Asante, *Myths America Lives By: White Supremacy and the Stories That Give Us Meaning* (Champaign: University of Illinois Press, 2018); Butler, *White Evangelical Racism*, and, Jones, *White Too Long*.

64. There are some exceptions, most notably, Kaplan, *Figuring Racism*. Other studies tend not to explicitly tackle the comparison of racism and antisemitism, focusing on questions of identity and race, such as Karen Brodkin, *How Jews Became White Folks and What That Says about Race in America* (New Brunswick, NJ: Rutgers

University Press, 1998); Robert Philipson, *The Identity Question: Blacks and Jews in Europe and America* (Jackson: University Press of Mississippi, 2000); and Eric L. Goldstein, *The Price of Whiteness: Jews, Race, and American Identity* (Princeton: Princeton University Press, 2008). Geraldine Heng applies race theory to medieval Jews, for example, Heng, *England and the Jews*; and Heng, *The Invention of Race*. For examples of where connections between the two could have been made productively, see Goldenberg, *The Curse of Ham*, ch. 13; Byron, *Symbolic Blackness*, especially the discussion of odor. Given the topic of "emancipation," addressing the issue of Black slavery and emancipation would have been appropriate, David Sorkin, *Jewish Emancipation: A History across Five Centuries* (Princeton: Princeton University Press, 2019). Samuels, *The Right to Difference*.

65. Cousin and Fine, "A Common Cause," 20–24.

66. Kaplan, *Figuring Racism*.

67. There is much scholarship on the lack of visible difference between Jews and Christians in premodern Europe, despite laws to mark Jews. Indeed, the IV Lateran Council issued a canon mandating the marking of Jews (and "Saracens" Muslims) precisely because there was no marked difference, leading to close social and sexual relations between Jews and Christians. See, for example, Lipton, *Dark Mirror*, 20–21, and ch. 24; Sara Lipton, "Isaac and Antichrist in the Archives," *Past and Present* 232, no. 1 (2016): 12–14; Debra Kaplan, *Beyond Expulsion: Jews, Christians, and Reformation Strasbourg* (Stanford: Stanford University Press, 2011), ch. 3; Magda Teter, "The Legend of Ger Zedek of Wilno as Polemic and Reassurance," *AJS Review* 29, no. 2 (2005); Magda Teter, *Jews and Heretics in Catholic Poland: A Beleaguered Church in the Post-Reformation Era* (Cambridge; New York: Cambridge University Press, 2006), ch. 4; Magda Teter, "'There Should Be No Love between Us and Them': Social Life and the Bounds of Jewish and Canon Law in Early Modern Poland," in *Social and Cultural Boundaries in Pre-Modern Poland*, ed. Adam Teller, Magda Teter, and Antony Polonsky (Oxford; Portland, OR: Littmann Library of Jewish Civilization, 2010). Jews, as Heng notes, were "figures" of difference, though their difference was not unambiguous (Heng, *England and the Jews*, 5. Also, Heng, *The Invention of Race*, 57). Heng rightly calls attention to legal structures applied to Jews' social existence, though it would be a mistake to see the existence of restrictive laws as evidence of such restrictions applied in life. Markings and efforts at segregation across Christian Europe were frequently but marks on parchment or paper—a dead letter. Still, even the restrictive structures in place, or on the books, did not confine Jews to, to use Lloyd Thompson's phrase, "inferior and unalterable roles and rights." Their roles and rights were alterable, and not just because of "state power," to use Heng's term. Jews, of flesh and blood not the "figures," had agency and often negotiated those across Europe, even if they continued to be deployed as symbols for social ills in Christian rhetoric and art. Jews, in all periods, in fact, were able to achieve high social positions, something that was jarring to those familiar with the theological concept of Jewish servitude and humiliation, resulting from supposed, as Christians believed, rejection of Jews by God. And of course, Jews could always convert to Christianity, though for the medieval period it is not clear it would always be a sign of social climb. Moreover, premodern legal and social framework did not leave much space for social climb even among Christians. See also the Lloyd Thompson discussion of race, racial prejudice,

and color prejudice, Lloyd A. Thompson, *Romans and Blacks* (London: Routledge, 2015), 17–18. For Winthrop Jordan's comment, Jordan, *White over Black: American Attitudes toward the Negro, 1550–1812*, xxix.

## Chapter One: The Sketches of Social Hierarchy in Early Christian Thought

1. Romans 11:13 (self-description as apostle to Gentiles), Romans 3:29–30, declaration about God's relationship to Jews and non-Jews. There is plenty of literature on Paul, see, for example, Daniel Boyarin, *A Radical Jew: Paul and the Politics of Identity* (Berkeley: University of California Press, 1994); Alan Segal, *Paul the Convert: The Apostolate and Apostasy of Saul the Pharisee* (New Haven: Yale University Press, 1992). And, more recently, Paula Fredriksen, *Paul the Pagan's Apostle* (New Haven; London: Yale University Press, 2017); Matthew V. Novenson and Barry Matlock, *The Oxford Handbook of Pauline Studies* (Oxford, UK; New York: Oxford University Press, 2022).

2. Romans 8:8.

3. Romans 9:6–8.

4. Romans 9:10–13.

5. On Paul's view of slavery, see Peter Garnsey, *Ideas of Slavery from Aristotle to Augustine* (Cambridge: Cambridge University Press, 1996), 173–88.

6. Galatians 4:22–26. On how those who wanted to become Christians first "had to" become Jews in ancient Roman Empire, see most recently, Christopher Stroup, *The Christians Who Became Jews: Acts of the Apostles and Ethnicity in the Roman City* (New Haven; London: Yale University Press, 2020).

7. Galatians 4:28–5:1.

8. On Graeco-Roman thought, see, Isaac, *The Invention of Racism in Classical Antiquity*, 184.

9. Jeremy Cohen, *Living Letters of the Law: Ideas of the Jew in Medieval Christianity* (Berkeley: University of California Press, 1999), 6. Nirenberg, *Anti-Judaism*, ch. 3.

10. Isaac, *The Invention of Racism in Classical Antiquity*, ch. 13. On the differences between the legal status of Jews and Christians, see especially, 484–91.

11. Jews were described as "anterior" and "maior" and Christian gentiles as "posterior" and "minor," Tertullian and Hermann Tränkle, *Q. S. F. Tertulliani Adversus Iudaeos* (Wiesbaden: F. Steiner, 1964), section I.

12. Nirenberg, *Anti-Judaism*, 130.

13. There are striking similarities between Augustine's exegesis and Tertullian's *Adversus Iudaeos*, Tertullian and Tränkle, *Q. S. F. Tertulliani Adversus Iudaeos*.

14. Cohen, *Living Letters*, 1, 33, and ch. 31. Paula Fredriksen, *Augustine and the Jews: A Christian Defense of Jews and Judaism* (New Haven; London: Yale University Press, 2010). A notable exception is Kaplan, *Figuring Racism*, especially, ch. 1.

15. Kaplan, *Figuring Racism*, 33.

16. Augustine, *Answer to Faustus, a Manichean* (Hyde Park, NY: New City Press, 2007), 12:9.

17. Scholars of American history are aware of the metaphor of Cain as deployed against Black people, but they do not know that it developed first in the context of Christian exegesis concerning Jews. See, for example, Jones, *White Too Long*.

18. Augustine, *Answer to Faustus*, 12:11–12.

19. The reference here is to Gen. 4:13–15.

20. Augustine, *Answer to Faustus*, 12:13.

21. Augustine, *Answer to Faustus*, 12:13. Conversion will remain a key strain in premodern Christianity, a marker of Jews' "mutability"; whatever characteristics Jews as people of individuals were ascribed would cease upon conversion.

22. The "curse of Cain" in some Christian texts became "a curse of blackness," Isaac, *The Invention of Racism in Classical Antiquity*, ch. 13. See also Kaplan, *Figuring Racism*, ch. 2.

23. Augustine, *The City of God*, trans. Henry Bettenson (London, New York: Penguin Books, 1984), Book XV, 1–2, 7.

24. Augustine, *City of God*, Book XVI, 34.

25. Genesis 25:23. Paul in Romans 9:10–13, Augustine, *City of God*, Book XVI, 35.

26. Augustine, *City of God*, Book XVI, 35. For Tertullian's interpretation, see Tertullian and Tränkle, *Q. S. F. Tertulliani Adversus Iudaeos*, Book I.

27. Augustine, *City of God*, Book XVII:7. Cicero referred to Jews as "natio nata servituti" but he considered both Jews and Syrians "born to be slaves." This language was used in the context of a Roman military campaign, with war captives frequently taken as slaves, Isaac, *The Invention of Racism in Classical Antiquity*, 172, 463, also figs. 8 a–d. For Augustine the victory was not only military but also religious.

28. Augustine, *City of God*, Book XVIII: 46.

29. Reference to Isaiah 10:20, which reads: "Even if your people, O Israel, Should be as the sands of the sea, Only a remnant of it shall return. Destruction is decreed; Retribution comes like a flood!"

30. Psalm 59:10–11, Augustine, *City of God*, Book XVIII, 46.

31. Augustine, *City of God*, Book XVIII, 46.

32. For example, Nirenberg, *Anti-Judaism*; Fredriksen, *Augustine and the Jews*; Cohen, *Living Letters*.

33. Kaplan, *Figuring Racism*, 33. Also his "distillation" of the figure of the Jew as a murderer, enemy of Christ, blind, in servitude to Christians, Nirenberg, *Anti-Judaism*, 119.

34. Isaac, *The Invention of Racism in Classical Antiquity*, figs. 8 a–d.

35. Garnsey, *Ideas of Slavery from Aristotle to Augustine*, 220–35.

36. Garnsey, *Ideas of Slavery from Aristotle to Augustine*, 206.

37. For an overview, see Anna Sapir Abulafia, *Christian-Jewish Relations, 1000–1300: Jews in the Service of Medieval Christendom*, ed. Julia Smith, The Medieval World (Harlow, UK: Pearson, 2011), ch. 1.

38. For a succinct discussion of the Jews' legal position within the Roman Empire, see Isaac, *The Invention of Racism in Classical Antiquity*, 447–50, also 461–62.

39. Isaac, *The Invention of Racism in Classical Antiquity*, 449.

40. Amnon Linder, *The Jews in Roman Imperial Legislation* (Detroit, MI; Jerusalem: Wayne State University Press; Israel Academy of Sciences and Humanities, 1987), 100.

41. I have slightly modified the translation found in Linder, *The Jews in Roman Imperial Legislation*, 104.

42. The legal measure is found in an anonymous work known as *Pauli Sententiae*, attributed to a well-known third-century jurist, Julius Paulus Prudentissimus, Isaac, *The Invention of Racism in Classical Antiquity*, 463, the text is cited in Latin in n.99.

43. Isaac, *The Invention of Racism in Classical Antiquity*, 488.

44. Linder, *The Jews in Roman Imperial Legislation*, 140.

45. Sapir Abulafia, *Christian-Jewish Relations, 1000–1300*, 12.

46. Linder, *The Jews in Roman Imperial Legislation*, 176.

47. Linder, *The Jews in Roman Imperial Legislation*, 141.

48. Linder, *The Jews in Roman Imperial Legislation*, 281–82.

49. Linder, *The Jews in Roman Imperial Legislation*, 327–31.

50. Linder, *The Jews in Roman Imperial Legislation*, 326–27, 329, 332–33.

51. Amnon Linder, *The Jews in the Legal Sources of the Early Middle Ages* (Detroit: Wayne State University Press, 1997), 474, 567–69, 597, 673.

52. Jones, *Birthright Citizens*, 4.

53. Linder, *The Jews in Roman Imperial Legislation*, 190.

54. Linder, *The Jews in Roman Imperial Legislation*, 285.

55. Honorius and Theodosius II, 414, in Linder, *The Jews in Roman Imperial Legislation*, 264–65.

56. On the argument about Augustine and contemporary Jews, see Cohen, *Living Letters*, 20; and more broadly, Fredriksen, *Augustine and the Jews*.

57. Linder, *Jews in Legal Sources*, 423.

58. Linder, *Jews in Legal Sources*, 434.

59. Linder, *Jews in Legal Sources*, 426–27.

60. Linder, *Jews in Legal Sources*, 440–41.

61. Linder, *Jews in Legal Sources*, 491.

62. Linder, *Jews in Legal Sources*, 662.

63. On canon law and Jews more broadly, see William Pakter, *Medieval Canon Law and the Jews* (Ebelsbach: R. Gremer, 1988).

64. Garnsey, *Ideas of Slavery from Aristotle to Augustine*, 7, 97–98, also, legal examples, 90–93; Patterson, *Slavery and Social Death*, 30–32; Isaac, *The Invention of Racism in Classical Antiquity*, 170–73.

65. Denise Eileen McCoskey, *Race: Antiquity and Its Legacy* (London, New York: Bloomsbury, 2019), 54–56.

66. Garnsey, *Ideas of Slavery from Aristotle to Augustine*, 5; Goldenberg, *The Curse of Ham*, 131; Isaac, *The Invention of Racism in Classical Antiquity*, 172.

67. See chapter 3 in this volume, also, Kaplan, *Figuring Racism*, on application of the anti-Jewish discourse to other groups, Muslims and Africans, see ch. 5. Goldenberg, *The Curse of Ham*, chs. 9 and 12.

68. Goldenberg, *The Curse of Ham*, 95.

69. Byron, *Symbolic Blackness*, 39. Goldenberg, *The Curse of Ham*, 95.

70. Goldenberg, *The Curse of Ham*, especially chs. 5 and 8. On skin color in Greek art, McCoskey, *Race: Antiquity and Its Legacy*, ch. 3.

71. Goldenberg, *The Curse of Ham*, ch. 10, esp. 152–52.

72. Byron, *Symbolic Blackness*, 35.

73. Goldenberg, *The Curse of Ham*, ch. 4, esp. 47–51.

74. Byron, *Symbolic Blackness*, 43–44; Goldenberg, *The Curse of Ham*, 48–51; Devisse, "Christians and Black," 53–55.

75. Goldenberg, *The Curse of Ham*, ch. 5.

76. Byron, *Symbolic Blackness*, 43.

77. Saint Jerome, *The Homilies of Saint Jerome, Volume 1 (1–59 on the Psalms)*, The Fathers of the Church (Washington, DC: Catholic University of America Press, 1964), 140.

78. Byron, *Symbolic Blackness*, 43; Jerome, *The Homilies of Saint Jerome*, 140.

79. Jerome, *The Homilies of Saint Jerome*, 139; Byron, *Symbolic Blackness*, 55–56.

80. Byron, *Symbolic Blackness*, 17; also, briefly, Goldenberg, *The Curse of Ham*, 134.

81. Byron, *Symbolic Blackness*, 97–98.

82. Susan Ashbrook Harvey, "On Holy Stench: When Odor of Sanctity Sickens," *Studia Patristica* 25 (2001): 91. Also, Byron, *Symbolic Blackness*, 97–102.

83. Pierluigi Lanfranchi, "*Foetor Judaicus*: Archéologie d'un préjugé," *Pallas* 104 (2017), http://journals.openedition.org/pallas/7397.

84. Kaplan, *Figuring Racism*, especially ch. 3.

85. *Bible moralisée/Bible de Saint Louis* (Facsimile edition, M. Moleiro, 2000–2004; original, 13th century, between 1226 and 1234, now at Santa Iglesia Catedral Primada, in Toledo), vol. 3, passion scenes in the Gospel section of the manuscript.

86. *Bible moralisée/Bible de Saint Louis* (Facsimile edition, M. Moleiro, 2000–2004; original, 13th century, between 1226 and 1234, now at Santa Iglesia Catedral Primada, in Toledo), vol. 1, Exodus. See also a discussion of English psalter illuminations, Kaplan, *Figuring Racism*, ch. 3.

87. Kaplan, "Introduction to the New Edition," 12.

88. Goldenberg, *The Curse of Ham*, 155.

## Chapter Two: Christian Supersessionism Becomes Christian Supremacy

1. Kaplan, *Figuring Racism*, especially ch. 3. See figs. 29 of Marbach-Schwarzenthann *Evangelistary* and fig. 35 in the *Sarum Missal* in Devisse, "Christians and Black," 65, [69]. While tormentors of Jesus were often depicted as dark-skinned, the skin pigment only meant to signify evilness and was not associated with any particular ethnic group—only with sinners, who rejected Christ. In fig. 29 of this late twelfth-century *Evangelistary*, the figure is dark-skinned and wearing a pointed hat. This is a dark-skinned Jew. As Sara Lipton has demonstrated, by 1140–1150 that iconographic marker came to be associated with Jews, Lipton, *Dark Mirror*, chapter 1. Devisse, however, mistakenly identified this figure as "simply a 'foreigner,'" thus erasing the significance of Christian anti-Jewish animus and connection between blackness and Jews. Devisse did acknowledge "religious hostility toward Jews" in the depiction of Judas's betrayal of Jesus from the *Sarum Missal*. Here, both Judas and Jesus are depicted as white, but the captors are shown of dark-skinned figures, some with deformed faces and large noses, typical of anti-Jewish iconography. The missal's depiction of the flagellation of Jesus also shows dark-skinned characters; their darkness here is more in line with the association with infidelity and evil than with Jews. This can be contrasted with the depiction of Jesus's followers. For the images, see *Missal (Sarum)* (Latin MS 24), John Rynolds Library, Manchester, fol. 150v, 151r,

151v, 152r, https://www.digitalcollections.manchester.ac.uk/view/MS-LATIN-00024 /308, and through https://www.digitalcollections.manchester.ac.uk/view/MS-LATIN -00024/311. The Salisbury *Sarum Missal* was created in the middle of the thirteenth century, exactly the point when anti-Jewish iconography focused on the Jewish face solidified, Lipton, *Dark Mirror*, 109–10, 172–73.

2. Goldenberg, *The Curse of Ham*, 175.

3. Jean Devisse, "The Black and His Color: From Symbols to Realities," in *The Image of the Black in Western Art, Volume 2: From the Early Christian Era to the "Age of Discovery,"* Part 1: From the Demonic Threat to the Incarnation of Sainthood, ed. David Bindman and Henry Louis Gates. 5 vols. (Cambridge, MA: Belknap Press of Harvard University Press, 2010), 73–74, 78.

4. Arguably, this can be said of Pope Alexander II's letter to bishops of Spain sent during his pontificate, 1061–1073, which also entered Ivo of Chartres's *Decretum*, Linder, *Jews in Legal Sources*, 452, 671. Also, Kaplan, *Figuring Racism*, 34–35.

5. Cohen, *Living Letters*, ch. 6, the letter translated on 234–36.

6. Cohen, *Living Letters*, 35.

7. Solomon Grayzel's classic article on *Sicut Iudaeis* is still very useful. The bull was reissued in 1120 by Pope Calixtus II, but it is the version by Pope Alexander III (1159–1181) that has survived and is published in the English translation in Solomon Grayzel, "The Papal Bull *Sicut Judaeis*," in *Studies and Essays in Honor of Abraham A. Neuman*, ed. Meir Ben-Horin, Bernard D. Weinryb, and Solomon Zeitlin (Leiden: Brill, 1962), 252. For the text by Gregory I and its mentions in canonical collections, see Linder, *Jews in Legal Sources*, 434–35, 622–25, 646, 647, 681.

8. Solomon Grayzel, *The Church and the Jews in the XIIIth Century: A Study of Their Relations during the Years 1198–1254* (Philadelphia: The Dropsie College, 1933), 92–95.

9. "Perpetue servitutis" is a recurring phrase; for a most recent discussion of this bull and more broadly of this issue, see Kaplan, *Figuring Racism*.

10. Grayzel, *The Church and the Jews*, no. 14, 104–9.

11. Grayzel, *The Church and the Jews*, no. 18, 114–17. I follow here, by and large, the modified and more accurate translation by M. Lindsay Kaplan, Kaplan, *Figuring Racism*, 43–44.

12. Haney López, *White by Law*, 13–14.

13. Kaplan, *Figuring Racism*, 45.

14. Grayzel, *The Church and the Jews*, no. 49, 166–67.

15. Grayzel, *The Church and the Jews*, no. 61, 184–87.

16. Grayzel, *The Church and the Jews*, no. 69, 198–201.

17. The Latin text and translation are in Kenneth R. Stow, *Catholic Thought and Papal Jewry Policy, 1555–1593* (New York: Jewish Theological Seminary of America, 1977), 294–98.

18. Especially section 3.3 "Since it is absurd," 72ff. See also Gerald Pattender, *Pius IV and the Fall of the Carafa: Nepotism and Papal Authority in Counter-Reformation Rome* (Oxford: Oxford University Press, 2013), 23–24. Most recently on Pope Paul IV and Jews, see Martina Mampieri, *Living under the Evil Pope: The Hebrew Chronicle of Pope Paul IV by Benjamin Nehemiah Ben Elnathan from Civitanova Marche (16th Cent.)* (Leiden: Brill, 2020).

19. Teter, *Jews and Heretics*, especially chs. 1–2. On Jews and nobles in Poland, see also Murray Jay Rosman, *The Lords' Jews: Magnate-Jewish Relations in the*

*Polish-Lithuanian Commonwealth during the Eighteenth Century* (Cambridge, MA: Harvard University Press, 1990); Adam Teller, *Money, Power, and Influence in Eighteenth-Century Lithuania: The Jews on the Radziwill Estates* (Stanford, CA: Stanford University Press, 2016), first published in Hebrew in 2006.

20. On Benedict XIV and the Jews, Mario Rosa, "La Santa Sede e gli ebrei nel settecento," in *Storia d'Italia: Annali* 11/2, "Gli ebrei in Italia" (1997), ch. 8; Marina Caffiero, *Battesimi forzati: storie di ebrei, cristiani e convertiti nella Roma dei papi* (Roma: Viella, 2004); Rebecca Marie Messbarger, Christopher M. S. Johns, and Philip Gavitt, eds., *Benedict XIV and the Enlightenment: Art, Science, and Spirituality* (Toronto: University of Toronto Press, 2016); Teter, *Blood Libel*, ch. 8.

21. Pope Benedict XIV, *Benedicti XIV Pont. Opt. Max. Olim Prosperi Cardinalis de Lambertinis Bullarium*, 17 vols., vol. 3/1 (Prati: Typographia Aldina, 1847), § 4–5 on 298–99.

22. For an extensive study of this iconographic typology, see Nina Rowe, *The Jew, the Cathedral, and the Medieval City: Synagoga and Ecclesia in the Thirteenth Century* (New York: Cambridge University Press, 2014). For examples of fifteenth-century representations in paintings, see Konrad Witz's diptych, *Ecclesia* and *Synagoga*, Kunstmuseum, Basel, ca. 1435, or Fernando Gallego's *Cristo bendiciendo*, ca. 1494–1496, Museo del Prado, Madrid. For an example of *Ecclesia* holding a church, illumination of "Ecclesia and Synagoga" in British Library, Royal 3 D VI, f.93| Petrus Comestor (index Peter Comestor, Pierra le Mangeur) also the south-east transept at Rochester Cathedral, England. For a *Synagoga* with an exposed breast, see a painting of the living cross in the Benedictine Abbey of St. Lambrecht in Austria, Alfred Raddatz, "Zur Geschichte eines Christlichen Bildmotivs: Ecclesia und Synagoge," in *Die Macht der Bilder antisemitische Vorurteile und Mythen*, ed. Elisabeth Klamper (Vienna: Picus-Verl, 1995), 58.

23. For examples of the synagogue holding a head of a goat instead of tablets with commandments, see *Historienbibel—Staat und Stadtsbibliothek*, Augsburg, 2 Cod 50 (Cim 74), Straßburg, 1422, https://daten.digitale-sammlungen.de/bsb00087190 /image_510 and *"De laudibus sanctae crucis,"* Württembergische Landesbibliothek, Cod.theol.et phil.fol.122, http://digital.wlb-stuttgart.de/purl/bsz330594400. For a continuation of this imagery into the eighteenth century, see *Synagoga and Ecclesia*, engraving print on paper, François Boucher and Gabriel Huquier, *Livre de Cartouches*, 18th-century, Victoria and Albert Museum, London, E.507–1991.

24. On Jewish badge and its color and meaning, see Flora Cassen, *Marking the Jews in Renaissance Italy: Politics, Religion, and the Power of Symbols* (Cambridge, New York: Cambridge University Press, 2017).

25. Hans-Martin Kirn, "The 'Freedom of a Christian'—'Servitude of the Jews'?: Martin Luther's Theology of Christian Freedom and His Early Attitude Towards Jews and Judaism against the Background of Medieval Ambiguities," *NTT* 72, no. 2 (2018): 137–51.

26. The Latin translation calls them Cain-like murderers, "prophetarum Caynici mactatores," Martin Luther, *Von den Juden und iren Lugen. D.M. Luth. zum andernmal gedruckt, und mehr dazu gethan. M.D. XLIII* (Wittemberg: durch Hans Lufft, 1543), [112]; Martin Luther, *De iudaeis et eorum mendaciis*, trans. Justus Jonas (Francofurti: Expressit Petrus Brubachius, 1544), 29.

27. Luther, *Von den Juden und iren Lugen*, [121]; Luther, *De iudaeis et eorum mendaciis*, 31.

28. On the complex topic of Luther and Jews, see Thomas Kaufmann, "Luther and the Jews," in *Jews, Judaism, and the Reformation in Sixteenth-Century Germany*, ed. Dean Phillip Bell and Stephen G. Burnett (Leiden; Boston: Brill Academic Publishers, 2006). *On the Jews and Their Lies* was published first in German in 1543 and then in a Latin adaptation in 1544, there was no other independent edition until the 1930s, though in the nineteenth century this work was included in an edition of all his works, giving it new exposure, Martin Luther, *Dr. Martin Luther's Sämmtliche Werke*, ed. Johann Conrad Irmischer and Johann Georg Plochmann (Erlangen: C. Heyder, 1826–1857). "Jesus Christ Was Born a Jew" was published in volume 29 in 1841 and "On the Jews and Their Lies" in 1842, in volume 32. Three years prior, in 1838, a preacher from Leipzig, Ludwig Fischer, published an abridged edition of Luther's 1543 pamphlet, Martin Luther and Ludwig Fischer, *Dr. Martin Luther von den Jüden und ihren Lügen: Ein crystallisirter Auszug aus dessen Schriften über der Juden Verblendung, Jammer, Bekehrung und Zukunft: Ein Beitrag zur Charakteristik dieses Volks* (Leipzig: B. Tauchnitz, 1838).

29. On the depictions of Jews in European chronicles and cosmographies, see Teter, *Blood Libel*, ch. 4.

30. Bale, *The Jew in the Medieval Book*, 6.

31. Quoted in Sapir Abulafia, *Christian-Jewish Relations, 1000–1300*, 56.

32. This point was made decades ago in a groundbreaking essay by Salo Baron, Salo Wittmayer Baron, "Ghetto and Emancipation," *Menorah Journal* 14 (1928): 515–26. For a most recent succinct discussion, Miri Rubin, *Cities of Strangers: Making Lives in Medieval Europe* (Cambridge: Cambridge University Press, 2020), ch 3. On the debates over whether Jews were slaves, see Kaplan, *Figuring Racism*, especially, 49–53.

33. Joel Sirkes, *Beit ḥadash (he-yeshanot)*, responsum no. 61, Bar-Ilan Responsa Project.

34. Kaplan, *Beyond Expulsion*.

35. See most recently, Federica Francesconi, *Invisible Enlighteners: The Jewish Merchants of Modena, from the Renaissance to the Emancipation* (Philadelphia: University of Pennsylvania Press, 2021).

36. Nirenberg, *Anti-Judaism*, 85. See also Bale, *The Jew in the Medieval Book*, 6.

37. Most recently on the badge and the ghetto, see Cassen, *Marking the Jews in Renaissance Italy*.and Daniel B. Schwartz, *Ghetto: The History of a Word* (Cambridge, MA: Harvard University Press, 2019).

## Chapter Three: A White European
### Christian Identity Emerges

1. William D. Phillips, *Slavery in Medieval and Early Modern Iberia* (Philadelphia: University of Pennsylvania Press, 2014), 11. See also Katharine Gerbner, *Christian Slavery: Conversion and Race in the Protestant Atlantic World* (Philadelphia: University of Pennsylvania Press, 2018), 14, 16.

2. Phillips, *Slavery in Medieval and Early Modern Iberia*, 6, 10.

3. Leslie Peirce, *A Spectrum of Unfreedom: Captives and Slaves in the Ottoman Empire* (Budapest, New York: Central European University Press, 2021), 1.

4. Phillips, *Slavery in Medieval and Early Modern Iberia*, 6, 10.

5. Phillips, *Slavery in Medieval and Early Modern Iberia*, ch. 2.

6. John Wright, *The Trans-Saharan Slave Trade* (London, New York: Routledge, 2010), ch. 3.

7. On the geographic origins of enslaved laborers in the Ottoman Empire, Peirce, *A Spectrum of Unfreedom*, 4–6.

8. Phillips, *Slavery in Medieval and Early Modern Iberia*, 14, 56.

9. Phillips, *Slavery in Medieval and Early Modern Iberia*, 13, 48.

10. Robert L. Paquette and Mark M. Smith, "Slavery in the Americas," in *The Oxford Handbook of Slavery in the Americas*, ed. Robert L. Paquette and Mark M. Smith (Oxford: Oxford University Press, 2016), 4. Phillips, *Slavery in Medieval and Early Modern Iberia*, ch. 1.

11. Phillips, *Slavery in Medieval and Early Modern Iberia*, 5, 10, 14, 18–22.

12. Phillips, *Slavery in Medieval and Early Modern Iberia*, 14.

13. Phillips, *Slavery in Medieval and Early Modern Iberia*, 55–58.

14. Phillips, *Slavery in Medieval and Early Modern Iberia*, 21–22, 60–61.

15. Gerbner, *Christian Slavery*, 16.

16. Norman P. Tanner, *Decrees of the Ecumenical Councils* (London, Washington, DC: Sheed & Ward, Georgetown University Press, 1990), Canon 26 in vol. 1: 223–24. See also Kaplan, *Figuring Racism*, 138.

17. Phillips, *Slavery in Medieval and Early Modern Iberia*, 58–62.

18. Gerbner, *Christian Slavery*, 14.

19. Pius Onyemechi Adiele, *The Popes, the Catholic Church and the Transatlantic Enslavement of Black Africans 1418–1839* (Hildesheim, Zürich, New York: Georg Olms Verlag, 2017), 367–70.

20. Adiele, *The Popes*, 284–87, text in English on 287 and in Latin 501–2. Also, Gomes Eannes de Azurara, Charles Raymond Beazley, and Edgar Prestage, *The Chronicle of the Discovery and Conquest of Guinea, Volume 1* (London: Hakluyt Society, 1896), 53. Available at https://www.gutenberg.org.

21. Azurara, Beazley, and Prestage, *The Chronicle of the Discovery and Conquest of Guinea, Volume 1*, 52–54.

22. Adiele, *The Popes*, 306–7.

23. Adiele, *The Popes*, sections translated into English on 311–13, Latin 502–3. See also Jean Devisse and Michel Mollat, "The Frontiers in 1460," in *The Image of the Black in Western Art, Volume 2: From the Early Christian Era to the "Age of Discovery," Part 2: Africans in the Christian Ordinance of the World*, ed. David Bindman and Henry Louis Gates. 5 vols. (Cambridge, MA: Belknap Press of Harvard University Press, 2010), 153–84, especially 153.

24. The Latin text and the English translation are available in Michael Cotta-Schønberg, "Oration 'Cum Bellum Hodie' of Pope Pius II (26 September 1459, Mantua). Edited and Translated by Michael von Cotta-Schönberg. 6th Version. (Orations of Enea Silvio Piccolomini / Pope Pius II; 45)," (2019), 39–167. The analysis follows that text, available at https://hal.archives-ouvertes.fr/hal-01184169/document.

25. Cotta-Schønberg, "Oration "Cum Bellum Hodie" of Pope Pius II," 39–167.

26. On the idea of just war and servitude in Christian law, see Kaplan, *Figuring Racism*, 146–52.

27. E.g., Pope Innocent III, Grayzel, *The Church and the Jews*, nos. 14 and 18, on 104–109 and 114–117.

28. See chapters 1 and 2 above.

29. Kaplan, *Figuring Racism*, ch. 5, especially 140–46.

30. See above and Grayzel, *The Church and the Jews*, no. 18, 114–17, M. Lindsay Kaplan, Kaplan, *Figuring Racism*, 43–44, 141.

31. Kaplan, *Figuring Racism*, 143–46, quote on 144.

32. Kaplan, *Figuring Racism*, 151.

33. Kaplan, *Figuring Racism*, 154.

34. Kaplan, *Figuring Racism*, 159, 165.

35. See also Kaplan, *Figuring Racism*, 162–65.

36. Quotation from Adiele, *The Popes*, 319, Latin 505–12.

37. Adiele, *The Popes*, 319, Latin 505–12.

38. Phillips, *Slavery in Medieval and Early Modern Iberia*, 62–65.

39. Phillips, *Slavery in Medieval and Early Modern Iberia*, 65.

40. Phillips, *Slavery in Medieval and Early Modern Iberia*, 65, 149.

41. Jean Devisse and Michel Mollat, "The African Transposed," in *The Image of the Black in Western Art, Volume 2: From the Christian Era to the "Age of Discovery," Part 2: Africans in the Christian Ordinance of the World*, ed. David Bindman and Henry Louis Gates. 5 vols. (Cambridge, MA: Belknap Press of Harvard University Press, 2010), 185.

42. Phillips, *Slavery in Medieval and Early Modern Iberia*, 94.

43. Peter Blanchard, "Spanish South American Mainland," in *The Oxford Handbook of Slavery in the Americas*, ed. Robert L. Paquette and Mark M. Smith (Oxford: Oxford University Press, 2016), 73–75.

44. Alan Gallay, "Indian Slavery," in *The Oxford Handbook of Slavery in the Americas*, ed. Robert L. Paquette and Mark M. Smith (Oxford: Oxford University Press, 2016), 314–16.

45. Adiele, *The Popes*, 371.

46. Gallay, "Indian Slavery," 316, 318. Blanchard, "Spanish South American Mainland," 70.

47. Blanchard, "Spanish South American Mainland," 70. Jeffrey Robert Young, "Proslavery Ideology," in *The Oxford Handbook of Slavery in the Americas*, ed. Robert L. Paquette and Mark M. Smith (Oxford: Oxford University Press, 2016), 402. Juan Friede and Benjamin Keen, *Bartolomé de Las Casas in History: Toward an Understanding of the Man and His Work* (DeKalb, IL: Northern Illinois University Press, 2008), 291, 416–17. On the opposition to African slavery in Iberia, Phillips, *Slavery in Medieval and Early Modern Iberia*, 157.

48. Timothy Lockley, "Race and Slavery," in *The Oxford Handbook of Slavery in the Americas*, ed. Robert L. Paquette and Mark M. Smith (Oxford: Oxford University Press, 2016), 340.

49. Phillips, *Slavery in Medieval and Early Modern Iberia*, 152–53.

50. Lockley, "Race and Slavery," 338. Also, Gerbner, *Christian Slavery*, 14 and Trevor Burnard, "British West Indies and Bermuda," in *The Oxford Handbook of Slavery in the Americas*, ed. Robert L. Paquette and Mark M. Smith (Oxford: Oxford University Press, 2016), 136.

51. Goldenberg, *The Curse of Ham*, 197. Also, Henk Den Heijer, "Dutch Caribbean," in *The Oxford Handbook of Slavery in the Americas*, ed. Robert L. Paquette and Mark M. Smith (Oxford: Oxford University Press, 2016), 162.

52. Goldenberg, *The Curse of Ham*, 175.

53. Friede and Keen, *Bartolomé de Las Casas in History*, 417.

54. Lockley, "Race and Slavery," 341. Also, Daniel C. Littlefield, "Colonial and Revolutionary United States," in *The Oxford Handbook of Slavery in the Americas*, ed. Robert L. Paquette and Mark M. Smith (Oxford: Oxford University Press, 2016), 203.

55. Den Heijer, "Dutch Caribbean," 154–72.

56. Den Heijer, "Dutch Caribbean," 155–56. Rebecca Anne Goetz, *Baptism of Early Virginia: How Christianity Created Race* (Baltimore: Johns Hopkins University Press, 2016).

57. Kaplan, *Figuring Racism*, 22.

58. For example, Phillips, *Slavery in Medieval and Early Modern Iberia*, 72–75; Byron, *Symbolic Blackness*; Goldenberg, *The Curse of Ham*. Isaac, *The Invention of Racism in Classical Antiquity*.

59. David Nirenberg, "Mass Conversion and Genealogical Mentalities: Jews and Christians in Fifteenth-Century Spain," *Past and Present*, no. 174 (2002): 6–7.

60. Nirenberg, "Mass Conversion and Genealogical Mentalities," 3, 13.

61. Nirenberg, "Mass Conversion and Genealogical Mentalities," 25.

62. Nirenberg, "Mass Conversion and Genealogical Mentalities," 31–32.

63. Robert Bernasconi, "Racism," in *Key Concepts in the Study of Antisemitism*, ed. Sol Goldberg, Scott Ury, and Keith Ian Weiser (Basingstoke: Palgrave Macmillan, 2020), 252–53.

64. Jean-Paul Zuñiga, "La voix du sang: du métis à l'idée de métissage en Amérique espagnole," *Annales. Histoire, Sciences Sociales* 54, no. 2 (1999): 427. See also Alexandre Coello de la Rosa, "El estatuto de limpieza de sangre de la Compañía de Jesús (1593) y su influencia en el Perú colonial," *Archivum Historicum Societatis Iesu* 80, no. 159 (2011); Elena Martínez, "The Black Blood of New Spain: Limpieza de Sangre, Racial Violence, and Gendered Power in Early Colonial Mexico," *The William and Mary Quarterly* 61, no. 3 (2004). Sometimes those ideas were appropriated and exploited by indigenous leaders to claim their social status, for example, Peter B. Villella, "'Pure and Noble Indians, Untainted by Inferior Idolatrous Races': Native Elites and the Discourse of Blood Purity in Late Colonial Mexico," *Hispanic American Historical Review* 91, no. 4 (2011): 633–63.

65. John Garrigus, "French Caribbean," in *The Oxford Handbook of Slavery in the Americas*, ed. Robert L. Paquette and Mark M. Smith (Oxford: Oxford University Press, 2016), 187.

66. Lockley, "Race and Slavery," 348.

67. Garrigus, "French Caribbean," 187.

68. Garrigus, "French Caribbean," 187.

69. Gerbner, *Christian Slavery*. Also, Goetz, *Baptism of Early Virginia*. Katherine Gerbner terms it Protestant Supremacy, but it was indeed white Protestant Supremacy.

70. The Dutch began to make overtures to wrestle the slave trade from the Portuguese and the English to challenge the Spanish colonial possessions already in the 1590s, but they had become dominant in the seventeenth century.

71. Den Heijer, "Dutch Caribbean," 156–157.

72. Burnard, "British West Indies and Bermuda," 136.

73. Gerbner, *Christian Slavery*, 11.

74. Goetz, *Baptism of Early Virginia*, ch. 2.

75. Goetz, *Baptism of Early Virginia*, 59–60.

76. Goetz, *Baptism of Early Virginia*, 69–70.

77. Gerbner, *Christian Slavery*, 14, 27, 30.

78. Gerbner, *Christian Slavery*, 30.

79. Gerbner, *Christian Slavery*, 44–45.

80. Goetz, *Baptism of Early Virginia*, 1.

81. Gerbner, *Christian Slavery*, 42ff.

82. Gerbner, *Christian Slavery*; Goetz, *Baptism of Early Virginia*.

83. William Rawlin, *The Laws of Barbados, Collected in One Volume, by William Rawlin, of the Middle-Temple, London, Esquire. And Now Clerk of the Assembly of the Said Island* (London: printed for William Rawlin, Esq., 1699), 203–7. Also, Gerbner, *Christian Slavery*, 74. The text of the act is available online, http://name.umdl.umich.edu/A30866.0001.001.

84. Gerbner, *Christian Slavery*, 74.

85. *Acts of Assembly: Passed in the Island of Barbadoes, from 1648, to 1718* (London: printed by John Baskett, Printer to the King's most Excellent Majesty, and by the assigns of Thomas Newcomb, and Henry Hills, deceas'd, 1721), 266–74. Also, Gerbner, *Christian Slavery*, 193.

86. Karl Watson, "Shifting Identities: Religion, Race, and Creolization among the Sephardi Jews of Barbados, 1654–1900," in *The Jews in the Caribbean*, ed. Jane S. Gerber (London: The Littman Library of Jewish Civilization, 2018).

87. Watson, "Shiftting Identities," 198–99.

88. Yancy, *Black Bodies, White Gaze*, 19–20.

89. Warren Eugene Milteer, *Beyond Slavery's Shadow: Free People of Color in the South* (Chapel Hill: University of North Carolina Press, 2021), 18–24, especially 18 and 23.

90. "An Act concerning Servants and Slaves," 1705, https://encyclopediavirginia.org/entries/an-act-concerning-servants-and-slaves-1705/.

91. Milteer, *Beyond Slavery's Shadow*, 19–20.

92. Paul Finkelman, "United States Slave Law," in *The Oxford Handbook of Slavery in the Americas*, ed. Robert L. Paquette and Mark M. Smith (Oxford: Oxford University Press, 2016), 429.

93. Goetz, *Baptism of Early Virginia*, 63.

94. Milteer, *Beyond Slavery's Shadow*, 15.

95. Article I, and IV, "An Act concerning Servants and Slaves" (1705).

96. Article II, "An Act concerning Servants and Slaves" (1705). Also, Goetz, *Baptism of Early Virginia*, 137.

97. Goetz, *Baptism of Early Virginia*, 137.

98. Jean Michel Massing, *The Image of the Black in Western Art, Volume 3: From the "Age of Discovery" to the Age of Abolition, Part 2: Europe and the World Beyond*, ed. David Bindman and Henry Louis Gates. 5 vols. (Cambridge, MA; London: Belknap, 2011). For the presence of Black individuals in Europe, see most recently, Olivette

Otele, *African Europeans: An Untold History* (New York: Basic Books, 2021). Also, Bernardus Paludanus, "Album Amicorum," KB Nationale Bibliothek, Netherlands, KW 133 M 63, fol. 167r. I thank Mark Ponte for introducing me to this image when he posted it on Twitter, https://twitter.com/voetnoot/status/1316704228954570765.

99. For example, the German editions, first and last, Sebastian Münster, *Cosmographia: Beschreibung aller Lender durch Sebastianum Münsterum: in welcher begriffen aller Voelker, Herrschaften, Stetten, und namhafftiger Flecken, herkommen: Sitten, Gebreüch, Ordnung, Glauben, Secten und Hantierung durch die gantze Welt und fürnemlich Teütscher Nation* (Basel: Getruckt durch Henrichum Petri, 1544), for example, dcxxii, dcxxviii; dcxxix, dcxxxix; Sebastian Münster, *Cosmographey oder Beschreibung aller Lander, Herrschafften, fürnem[b]sten Stetten, Geschichten, Gebreüche[n], Handtierungen* (Basel: Henri Petri, 1567), mccclxxviii, mccclxxxi, mccclxxviii; mcccxcix; mcccci; mccccxiii, mccccxx. There were also editions in Latin and Italian, also including these images and stories. On Sebastian Münster's *Cosmographia*, see Mathew Adam McLean, *The Cosmographia of Sebastian Münster: Describing the World in the Reformation*, St. Andrews Studies in Reformation History (Aldershot, UK: Ashgate, 2007). On Jews in Münster's work, Teter, *Blood Libel*, 158–59, 167–69.

100. On the depiction of Jews in printed books, see Teter, *Blood Libel*, ch. 4.

101. Cesare Ripa, *Iconologia ouero descrittione di diuerse imagini cauate dall' antichità, & di propria inuentione, trouate, & dichiarate da Cesare Ripa ... di nuouo reuista, & dal medesimo ampliata di 400 & più imagini* (Roma: Appresso Lepido Facij, 1603), 332–34. Cesare Ripa, *Della novissima iconologia* (Padova: P. P. Tozzi, 1625), 418–19. On the depiction of the four continents, with a focus on Africa, see David Bindman, Bruce Boucher, and Helen Weston, "The Theater of Court and Church: Blacks as Figures of Fantasy," in *The Image of the Black in Western Art, Volume 3: From the "Age of Discovery" to the Age of Abolition, Part 3: The Eighteenth Century*, ed. David Bindman and Henry Louis Gates. 5 vols. (Cambridge, MA: Belknap Press of Harvard University Press, 2011), 17–32.

102. Ripa, *Iconologia (1603)*, 334; Ripa, *Della novissima iconologia*, 420.

103. Ripa, *Iconologia (1603)*, 335; Ripa, *Della novissima iconologia*, 420.

104. Ripa, *Iconologia (1603)*, 338–39; Ripa, *Della novissima iconologia*, 421–22.

105. The Dutch edition of 1699 included only a few rhymed stanzas about each continent, Cesare Ripa, *Iconologia, of Uitbeeldinge des Verstands* (t'Amsterdam: By Timotheus ten Hoorn, boekverkoper in de Nes, in 't Sinnebeelt, 1699), 195–98. See also Cesare Ripa and Cornelis Danckertsz, *Iconologia, of uytbeeldinge des verstands: waar in verscheiden afbeeldingen van deugden, ondeugden ... werden verhandelt* (t' Amsteldam: uytgegeven door Cornelis Danckerts voor aan op de Nieuwendyck in den Atlas#, 1700), 274–276. Cesare Ripa, *Iconologia: Or, Moral Emblems: By Caesar Ripa Wherein Are Express'd, Various Images of Virtues, Vices, Passions, Arts, Humours, Elements and Celestial Bodies; as Design'd by the Ancient Egyptians, Greeks, Romans, and Modern Italians: Useful for Orators, Poets, Painters, Sculptors, and All Lovers of Ingenuity: Illustrated with Three Hundred Twenty-Six Humane Figures, with Their Explanations ; Newly Design'd, and Engraven on Copper, by I. Fuller, Painter, and Other Masters. By the Care and A* (London: Printed by Benj. Motte, 1709), 47, 53. But, Cesare Ripa, Giovanni Zaratino Castellini, and Dirck Pietersz Pers, *Iconologia*

*of uytbeeldingen des verstands: waer in verscheiden afbeeldingen van deughden,*
*ondeughden ... werden verhandelt ... : een werck dat dienstigh is ... ook om te spreecken,*
*van allerley toerustingen, 't zy op bruyloften ... en zeegefeesten* (Amstelredam: D. P.
Pers, 1644), 602–3.

106. François Bernier, "Nouvelle division de la terre par les différentes espèces ou
races qui l'habitent," *Journal des sçavans* 12, no. April 24 (1684); quote in Siep Stuurman, "François Bernier and the Invention of Racial Classification," *History Workshop
Journal*, no. 50 (2000): 4. Also, Stovall, *White Freedom*, 108.

107. Stuurman, "François Bernier and the Invention of Racial Classification," 3.

108. *Le Code Noir ou Edit du Roy: servant de reglement pour le gouvernement &*
*l'administration de la justice, police, discipline & le commerce des esclaves negres,*
*dans la province & colonie de la Louisianne. Donné à Versailles au mois de Mars 1724*
(Paris: De l'Imprimerie royale, 1727).

109. *Le Code Noir* 14, nos. 52, 54.

110. See, for example, Africans from Mozambique in Johannn Theodor de Bry and
Johann Israel de Bry, *Pars Indiæ Orientalis, in qva Iohan. Hvgonis Lintscotani Naui-*
*gatio in Orientem* (Frankfurt: Ex Officina Richteri, 1599), plate III; Africans on the
coast of Guinea in Pieter de Marees, *Beschryvinge ende historische verhael van't goudt*
*koninckrijck van Guinea* (Amsterdam: C. Claesz, 1602), between 14 and 15; a captain and two soldiers in Guinea, in Pieter de Marees, *Beschryvinge van de goudt-kust*
*Guinea, als mede een voyagie naer de selve* (Amsterdam: Joost Hartgers, 1650), 55; Con-
golese warriors in Duarte Lopez and Filippo Pigafetta, *Beschryvinge van't Koningkrijck*
*Congo, met't aenpalende Landt Angola* (Amsterdam: Joost Hartgers, 1650). 55. On the
"take-off of plantation economies," see Robin Blackburn, *The Making of New World*
*Slavery: From the Baroque to the Modern, 1492–1800* (London: Verso, 1997), quotes on
8 and 10. For a study of the pictorial representation of non-Europeans, see the richly
illustrated Massing, *The Image of the Black in Western Art*, 3/2, chapter 5, and Benjamin Schmidt, *Inventing Exoticism: Geography, Globalism, and Europe's Early Modern*
*World* (Philadelphia: University of Pennsylvania Press, 2019).

111. Olfert Dapper, *Naukeurige beschrijvinge der Afrikaensche Eylanden: als*
*Madagaskar, of Sant Laurens, Sant Thomee, d'eilanden van Kanarien, Kaep de Verd,*
*Malta, en andere: vertoont in de Benamingen, gelegentheit, Steden, Revieren, Gewas-*
*sen, Dieren, Zeeden, Drachten, Talen, Rijkdommen, Godsdiensten en Heerschappyen*
(T'Amsterdam: Jacob van Meurs, 1668); Olfert Dapper and John Ogilby, *Africa: Being*
*an Accurate Description of the Regions of Aegypt, Barbary, Lybia, and Billedulgerid,*
*the Land of Negroes, Guinee, Aethiopia, and the Abyssines, with All the Adjacent*
*Islands, Either in the Mediterranean, Atlantick, Southern, or Oriental Sea, Belonging*
*Thereunto ; with the Several Denominations of Their Coasts, Harbors, Creeks, Rivers,*
*Lakes, Cities, Towns, Castles, and Villages; Their Customs, Modes, and Manners, Lan-*
*guages, Religions, and Inexhaustible Treasure; with Their Governments and Policy,*
*Variety of Trade and Barter ; and Also of Their Wonderful Plants, Beasts, Birds, and*
*Serpents; Collected and Translated from Most Authentick Authors, and Augmented*
*with Later Observations; Illustrated with Notes, and Adorn'd with Peculiar Maps,*
*and Proper Sculptures* (London: Johnson, 1670); Olfert Dapper, *Umbständliche*
*und Eigentliche Beschreibung von Africa, Und denen darzu gehörigen Königreichen*
*und Landschaften:als Egypten, Barbarien, Libyen, Biledulgerid, dem Lande der*

*Negros, Guinea, Ethiopien, Abyßina und den Africanischen Insulen: zusamt deren Verschiedenen Nahmen, Grentzen, Städten . . . Wobey Die Land-Carten, und Abrisse der Städte, Trachten, [et]c. in Kupfer* (Amsterdam: Jacob von Meurs, 1671); Olfert Dapper, *Description de L'Afrique, contenant les noms, la situation & les confins de toutes ses parties, leurs rivières, leurs villes & leurs habitations, leurs plantes & leurs animaux, les moeurs, les co°tumes, la langue, les richesses, la religion & le gouvernement de ses peuples* (Amsterdam: Wolfgang, Waesberge, Boom & van Someren, 1686).

112. Dapper, *Naukeurige Beschrijvinge der Afrikaensche Eylanden*, 322ff. Some images of the French edition were published in Andrew S. Curran, *The Anatomy of Blackness: Science and Slavery in an Age of Enlightenment* (Baltimore: Johns Hopkins University Press, 2011), 151, 153. On representations of non-Europeans as dangerous, see Schmidt, Inventing Exoticism, especially ch. 3.

113. David Bindman, Bruce Boucher, and Helen Weston, "Africa and the Slave Trade," in *The Image of the Black in Western Art, Volume 3: From the "Age of Discovery" to the Age of Abolition, Part 3: The Eighteenth Century*, ed. David Bindman and Henry Louis Gates. 5 vols. (Cambridge, MA: Belknap Press of Harvard University Press, 2011), 206–40.

114. David Bindman, "Introduction," in *The Image of the Black in Western Art, Volume 3: From the "Age of Discovery" to the Age of Abolition, Part 3: The Eighteenth Century*, ed. David Bindman and Henry Louis Gates. 5 vols. (Cambridge, MA: Belknap Press of Harvard University Press, 2011), 6; see also Bindman, Boucher, and Weston, "The Theater of Court and Church."

115. Emmanuel Chukwudi Eze, *Race and the Enlightenment: A Reader* (Cambridge, MA: Blackwell, 1997), 33. Also quoted in Ibram X. Kendi, *Stamped from the Beginning: The Definitive History of Racist Ideas in America* (New York: Nation Books, 2017), 95–96.

116. Kendi, *Stamped from the Beginning*, 95–96.

117. Eze, *Race and the Enlightenment*, 38–64, quote on 63. See also, Dossa Shiraz, "Liberals and Muslims: Philosophy and Conquest," *Arab Studies Quarterly* 37, no. 1 (2015): 64, and Kendi, *Stamped from the Beginning*, 102.

118. Eze, *Race and the Enlightenment*, 46, 48, 64.

119. Giovanni Battista Tiepolo, *Allegory of the Planets and Continents*, a model for the decoration of the ceiling above the grand staircase in the bishop's residence in in Würzburg, oil on canvas, 1752, The Met Museum, Gift of Mr. and Mrs. Charles Wrightsman, 1977, Accession number, 1977.1.3. Mark Ashton, "Allegory, Fact, and Meaning in Giambattista Tiepolo's Four Continents in Würzburg," *Art Bulletin* 60, no. 1 (1978): 109. Also, Bindman, Boucher, and Weston, "The Theater of Court and Church," 26–31.

120. After the French Revolution, Europe would resemble the personification of Liberty, while America may be represented as white and triumphant, see for example, Jean Jacques François Le Barbier's *The Four Continents*, designed ca. 1786, woven 1790–91, The Met Museum, 1978.404.1–4.

121. Stovall, *White Freedom*, especially ch. 2.

122. On liberty and Christianity, see above and passim, Kaplan, *Figuring Racism*.

123. Curran, *The Anatomy of Blackness*.

124. Bernard Picart and Jean-Frédéric Bernard, *Cérémonies et coutumes religieuses de tous les peuples du monde: Représentées par des figures* (Amsterdam:

Chez J. F. Bernard, 1723); on the importance of this work, see Lynn Hunt, Margaret Jacob, and Wijnand Mijnhardt, *Bernard Picart and the First Global Vision of Religion* (Los Angeles: The Getty Research Institute, 2010); Lynn Hunt, Margaret C. Jacob, and Wijnand Mijnhardt, *The Book That Changed Europe: Picart and Bernard's Religious Ceremonies of the World* (Cambridge, MA: Belknap Press, 2010).

125. Curran, *The Anatomy of Blackness*, esp. ch. 3.

126. Curran, *The Anatomy of Blackness*, 120.

127. Bernier, "Nouvelle Division de la Terre Par les Différentes Espèces ou Races Qui L'habitent," 135. Curran, *The Anatomy of Blackness*, 141, 146, 154, 157. Bernier ended saying, "I will not tell you anything about the beauties of Europe, you probably know as much as I do" (140).

128. Patricia Bradley, *Slavery, Propaganda, and the American Revolution* (Jackson: University Press of Mississippi, 1999), xiii. See also Eric Foner, *The Second Founding: How the Civil War and Reconstruction Remade the Constitution* (New York: W. W. Norton & Company, 2019), 33.

129. Curran, *The Anatomy of Blackness*, 122ff.

130. Curran, *The Anatomy of Blackness*, 130–33, Eze, *Race and the Enlightenment*, 70–78.

131. Peter the Venerable wrote: "But because my discussion is with a Jew—I do not know whether he is a human—still other things must be added. Surely I do not know whether a Jew, who does not submit to human reason nor acquiesce to proof-texts that are both divine and his own, is a human. I do not know, I say, whether one is human from whose flesh a heart of stone has not yet been removed, to whom a heart of flesh has not yet been granted, within whom the divine spirit has not yet been placed, without which a Jew can never be converted to Christ." Peter the Venerable, *Against the Inveterate Obduracy of Jews*, trans. Irven M. Resnick (Washington, DC: Catholic University of America Press, 2013), quote on 123, see also 120.

132. For a detailed discussion of regional epistemological communities in Europe, see Teter, *Blood Libel*, ch. 4.

133. Claude Fleury, *Les Moeurs des Israélites* (Paris: Veuve G. Clouzier, 1681), 1–2.

134. Fleury, *Les Moeurs des Israélites*, 3.

135. L. P. Hartley, *The Go-Between* (London: Hamish Hamilton, 1953), 9. This is also a title of David Lowenthal's book about social attitudes toward the past, David Lowenthal, *The Past Is a Foreign Country* (New York: Cambridge University Press, 1985). A recent and expanded edition came out in 2015 as *The Past Is a Foreign Country—Revisited.*

136. Fleury, *Les Moeurs des Israélites*, 9. Later editions add "Turks," as well.

137. Fleury, *Les Moeurs des Israélites*, 341.

138. Fleury, *Les Moeurs des Israélites*, 343.

139. De La Créquinière, *The Agreement of the Customs of the East-Indians, with Those of the Jews, and Other Ancient People: Being the First Essay of This Kind, Towards the Explaining of Several Difficult Passages in Scripture, and Some of the Most Ancient Writers* (London: Printed for W. Davis, 1705). The text was then included also in the 1733 English edition of Bernard Picart's highly influential *Cérémonies et coutumes religieuses de tous les peuples du monde.*

140. Richard S. Levy, *Antisemitism in the Modern World: An Anthology of Texts* (Lexington, MA; Toronto: D. C. Heath and Company, 1991), 40.

141. Mendes-Flohr and Reinharz, *The Jew in the Modern World*, 27–34.

142. Mendes-Flohr and Reinharz, *The Jew in the Modern World*, 132.

143. Mendes-Flohr and Reinharz, *The Jew in the Modern World*, 137.

144. Mendes-Flohr and Reinharz, *The Jew in the Modern World*, 142.

145. Jonathan M. Hess, *Germans, Jews, and the Claims of Modernity* (New Haven: Yale University Press, 2002), chapter 2; Oded Y. Steinberg, *Race, Nation, History: Anglo-German Thought in the Victorian Era* (Philadelphia: University of Pennsylvania Press, 2019). Ernest Renan, for example, argued that "the languages of the Aryans and the Semites differed essentially," with the Aryan languages "immensely superior," Steinberg, *Race, Nation, History*, 66. In 2021, The Human Rights Watch issued a report called *A Threshold Crossed: Israeli Authorities and the Crimes of Apartheid and Persecution* in which they visually *Europeanize* Jews as blond Nordic types. I thank my student Maya Bentovim for pointing out this visual racialization of Jews as Europeans or Euro-Americans, with blond straight hair, to score political points in visually contrasting Jews as white against Palestinians as people of color.

## Chapter Four: European Christian Supremacy and Modern Citizenship

1. These words come from the American Declaration of Independence of 1776 and the French Declaration of the Rights of Man and Of the Citizen of 1789.

2. Christian Wilhelm von Dohm, "Concerning the Amelioration of the Civil Status of the Jews (1781)" in Mendes-Flohr and Reinharz, *The Jew in the Modern World*, 27–34.

3. Ibram X. Kendi discussed the topic of "uplift suasion" in the context of Black people and debates over their status, Kendi, *Stamped from the Beginning*, ch. 10.

4. Johann David Michaelis, "Arguments against Dohm (1782)," in Mendes-Flohr and Reinharz, *The Jew in the Modern World*, 34–36.

5. Hunt, *The French Revolution and Human Rights*, 18.

6. Emmanuel-Joseph Sieyès, *Préliminaire de la constitution françoise. reconnoissance et exposition raisonnée des droits de l'homme et du citoyen. par m. l'abbé Sieyès* (Paris: Baudouin, 1789), 7.

7. Sieyès, *Préliminaire de la constitution françoise.*

8. Sieyès, *Préliminaire de la constitution françoise*, 36–37. Also in Hunt, *The French Revolution and Human Rights*, 78.

9. Hunt, *The French Revolution and Human Rights*, 81–82.

10. Hunt, *The French Revolution and Human Rights*, 85–86. See also Sorkin, *Jewish Emancipation*, 95.

11. Anne-Louis-Henri de La Fare, *Opinion de M. l'évêque de Nancy, Député de Lorraine, sur l'admissibilité des Juifs à la plénitude de l'état-civil, et des droits de citoyens actifs* (Paris: Librarie au Palace Marchand, 1790).

12. La Fare, *Opinion de M. l'éveque de Nancy*, 3–4.

13. La Fare, *Opinion de M. l'éveque de Nancy*, 6. This passage is translated in Hunt, *The French Revolution and Human Rights*, 92.

14. La Fare, *Opinion de M. l'éveque de Nancy*, 7–8.

15. La Fare, *Opinion de M. l'éveque de Nancy*, 10.

16. On Henri Grégoire and Jews, see, for example, Ruth F. Necheles, "The Abbé Grégoire and the Jews," *Jewish Social Studies* 33, nos. 2/3 (1971); Lawrence Scott Lerner, "Beyond Grégoire: A Third Discourse on Jews and the French," *Modern Judaism: A Journal of Jewish Ideas and Experience* 21, no. 3 (2001); Michael Alpert, "The French Enlightenment and the Jews: An Essay by the Abbe Grégoire," *Patterns of Prejudice* 31, no. 1 (1997).

17. Henri Baptiste Grégoire, *Essai sur la régénération physique, morale et politique des Juifs* (Metz: Claude Lamort, 1789), 44.

18. Grégoire, *Essai sur la régénération physique*, 131–34.

19. Grégoire, *Essai sur la régénération physique*, 164.

20. Grégoire, *Essai sur la régénération physique*, 191–94.

21. Grégoire, *Essai sur la régénération physique*, 125–26.

22. Mendes-Flohr and Reinharz, *The Jew in the Modern World*, 55, 124.

23. Mendes-Flohr and Reinharz, *The Jew in the Modern World*, 126–27.

24. Mendes-Flohr and Reinharz, *The Jew in the Modern World*, 283–84.

25. "Debate on Jewish Emancipation (August 22–31, 1796)" in Mendes-Flohr and Reinharz, *The Jew in the Modern World*, 131–44.

26. "Debate on Jewish Emancipation (August 22–31, 1796)" in Mendes-Flohr and Reinharz, *The Jew in the Modern World*, 131–44.

27. "Report by the Prussian District Government in Koblenz on the Civic Condition of the Jewish population (1820)" in *German History in Documents and Images*, vol. 3. From Vormärz to Prussian Dominance, 1815–1866, available at http://ghdi.ghi-dc.org/sub_document.cfm?document_id=434.

28. "Report by the Prussian District Government in Koblenz," http://ghdi.ghi-dc.org/sub_document.cfm?document_id=434.

29. Apsley Pellatt and Joseph Hume, *Brief Memoir of the Jews in Relation to Their Civil and Municipal Disabilities: With an Appendix Containing the Jews' Petition to Oliver Cromwell, the Russian Ukase and Ordinance of the King of Wurtemberg Affecting the Civil and Religious Liberty of the Hebrew Nation* (London: Printed for Hatchard and Son . . . by Richard Taylor, 1829), iv, 5.

30. *Statement of the Civil Disabilities and Privations Affecting Jews in England* (London: G. Taylor, printer, 1829); it was soon reprinted in "Statement of the Civil Disabilities and Privations Affecting Jews in England," *Edinburgh Review* 52 (1830): 363–74; and again "Civil Disabilities of the Jews," in *Selections from the Edinburgh Review Comprising the Best Articles in That Journal from Its Commencement to the Present Time* (London: Longman, Rees, Orma, Brown, Green, & Longman, 1833), 667–75. The attribution is found in a footnote in "Civil Disabilities of the Jews," 675.

31. "Statement of the Civil Disabilities (1830)," 363–64; "Civil Disabilities of the Jews," 667.

32. "Statement of the Civil Disabilities (1830)," 364; "Civil Disabilities of the Jews," 668.

33. "Statement of the Civil Disabilities (1830)," 364; "Civil Disabilities of the Jews," 668.

34. "Statement of the Civil Disabilities (1830)," 365; "Civil Disabilities of the Jews," 668.

35. "Statement of the Civil Disabilities (1830)," 365; "Civil Disabilities of the Jews," 668.

36. "Statement of the Civil Disabilities (1830)," 366; "Civil Disabilities of the Jews," 669.

37. "Statement of the Civil Disabilities (1830)," 366; "Civil Disabilities of the Jews," 669.

38. "Statement of the Civil Disabilities (1830)," 367–69; "Civil Disabilities of the Jews," 670–71.

39. "Statement of the Civil Disabilities (1830)," 372; "Civil Disabilities of the Jews," 674.

40. "Statement of the Civil Disabilities (1830)," 374; "Civil Disabilities of the Jews," 675.

41. Pellatt and Hume, *Brief Memoir of the Jews*, 6.

42. Sorkin, *Jewish Emancipation*, 211–12.

43. Sections of the debate have been published in English in *German History in Documents and Images*, vol. 3. From Vormärz to Prussian Dominance, 1815–1866, http://ghdi.ghi-dc.org/sub_document.cfm?document_id=436 and http://ghdi.ghi-dc.org/sub_document.cfm?document_id=341, as well as in brief excerpts in Mendes-Flohr and Reinharz, *The Jew in the Modern World*, 166–67.

44. Heinrich Paulus, *Die jüdische Nationalabsonderung nach Ursprung, Folge und Besserungsmitteln* (1831), translated by Jeremiah Riemer in *German History in Documents and Images*, http://ghdi.ghi-dc.org/sub_document.cfm?document_id=436.

45. Gabriel Riesser, *Vertheidigung der bürgerlichen Gleichstellung der Juden gegen die Entwürfe des Herrn Dr. H. E. G. Paulus* (1831), translated by Jeremiah Riemer in *German History in Documents and Images*, http://ghdi.ghi-dc.org/sub_document.cfm?document_id=341.

46. Mendes-Flohr and Reinharz, *The Jew in the Modern World*, 166–67. Reisser's statement anticipates the pained *cri de cœur* written in 1944 by Julian Tuwim, "We, The Polish Jews," Julian Tuwim and Madeline G. Levine, "'We, the Polish Jews . . .'" *The Polish Review* 17, no. 4 (1972): 82–89.

## Chapter Five: Slavery, Citizenship, and the Legal Status of Free Blacks

1. Kendi, *Stamped from the Beginning*, 98.

2. Patterson, *Slavery and Social Death*, ix, 38. For a critique of Patterson and his idea of "social death," see for example, Franklin W. Knight, "The Haitian Revolution," *American Historical Review* 105, no. 1 (2000): 105; Paquette and Smith, "Slavery in the Americas," 4.

3. Frederick Douglass, *My Bondage and My Freedom* (New York; Auburn: Miller, Orton & Mulligan, 1855), 173.

4. Douglass, *My Bondage and My Freedom*, 174–75.

5. "From Thomas Jefferson to John Wayles Eppes, 30 June 1820," *Founders Online*, National Archives, https://founders.archives.gov/documents/Jefferson/98-01-02-1352. See also Kendi, *Stamped from the Beginning*, 136.

6. See for example, a recent work, Sophie White, *Voices of the Enslaved: Love, Labor, and Longing in French Louisiana* (Williamsburg, Chapel Hill: University of North Carolina Press, 2019).

7. Douglass, *My Bondage and My Freedom*, 175.

8. Frederick Douglass, *The Portable Frederick Douglass* (New York: Penguin Classics, 2016), 16.

9. Patterson, *Slavery and Social Death*, x.

10. See for example, Heidemarie Petersen, "Die Rechtsstellung der Judengemeinden von Krakau und Prag um 1500: Beispiele jüdischer Existenz in Ostmitteleuropa," *Zeitschrift für Ostmitteleuropa-Forschung* 46, no. 1 (1997). Adam Teller, "Some Comparative Perspectives on the Jews' Legal Status in the Polish-Lithuanian Commonwealth and the Holy Roman Empire," in *Polin: Social and Cultural Boundaries in Pre-Modern Poland*, ed. Adam Teller, Magda Teter, and Antony Polonsky (Oxford; Portland, OR: Littmann Library of Jewish Civilization, 2010); Jacob Goldberg, *Jewish Privileges in the Polish Commonwealth: Charters of Rights Granted to Jewish Communities in Poland-Lithuania in the Sixteenth to Eighteenth Centuries*, 3 vols. (Jerusalem: The Israel Academy of Sciences and Humanities, 1985–2001).

11. For an overview of the process of acquisition of citizenship rights, see Sorkin, *Jewish Emancipation*. This slippage happens even in the context of scholarship of Jews within slave societies, for example, Stanley Mirvis, *The Jews of Eighteenth-Century Jamaica a Testamentary History of a Diaspora in Transition* (New Haven: Yale University Press, 2020), 10, 197.

12. Patterson, *Slavery and Social Death*, 44.

13. On free people of color in the US and their exclusion by white European Americans, Milteer, *Beyond Slavery's Shadow*.

14. Haney López, *White by Law*.

15. Stovall, *White Freedom*.

16. Geggus, "Racial Equality," 1291.

17. *L'esclavage des nègres aboli ou moyens d'améliorer leur sort* (Paris: Froullé, 1789). A short selection of quotes is available in English in Hunt, *The French Revolution and Human Rights*, 97–98; Geggus, "Racial Equality," 1291. A similar contrast between the continental and colonial attitudes appeared in Britain when they were considering the question of slavery; the abolitionist voices were far louder in the metropole, Petley, "Slavery, Emancipation and the Creole World View of Jamaican Colonists, 1800–1834."

18. *L'esclavage des nègres aboli*, 3–4.

19. *L'esclavage des nègres aboli*, 5.

20. *L'esclavage des nègres aboli*, 6–7.

21. *L'esclavage des nègres aboli*, 8–9.

22. The estimate was not exaggerated. According to Herbert S. Klein, in the 1780s, in Saint-Domingue alone there were an estimated 460,000 slaves, nearly 50 percent of the total slave population in the Caribbean colonies, Herbert S. Klein, *The Atlantic Slave Trade* (Cambridge: Cambridge University Press, 1999), 33.

23. On the efforts to circumscribe the number of free or freed people of color, including schemes to keep some perpetually indentured, see Milteer, *Beyond Slavery's Shadow*. On the workings of the American Colonization Society, see Eric

Burin, *Slavery and the Peculiar Solution: A History of the American Colonization Society* (Gainesville: University Press of Florida, 2005). See also Allan E. Yarema, *The American Colonization Society: An Avenue to Freedom?* (Lanham, Md.: University Press of America, 2006), for example, 3–5, 8: "repatriation," "resettlement" and "deportation." James Madison claimed that the US could raise enough funds from the sale of public lands to deport "all blacks to Africa over a fifty-year period, John Stauffer, "Abolition and Antislavery," in *The Oxford Handbook of Slavery in the Americas*, ed. Robert L. Paquette and Mark M. Smith (Oxford: Oxford University Press, 2016), 562.

24. Grégoire, *Mémoire en faveur des gens de couleur ou sang-mêlés*, 4. Selections in Hunt, *The French Revolution and Human Rights*, 99–100.

25. For a broader discussion of this debate and the impact of colonial interests, see Quinney, "Decisions on Slavery," 117–30.

26. *Dénonciation de la secte des Amis des Noirs, par les habitants des colonies françaises*, 1789.

27. *Observations pour servir de réponse aux différens faits avancés par les préten-dus amis des noirs, et notamment une lettre du 4 janvier 1790, qui se trouve dans le Supplément du Journal de Paris, du 13 dudit mois. Par les capitaines du Havre-de-Grâce, navigans à la Côte d'Afrique* (Paris: Impr. de P.-F. Didot jeune, 1790).

28. *Observations*, 6. This point was then repeated by a delegation of the local National Guard at the National Assembly in March, 1790, Quinney, "Decisions on Slavery," 124.

29. *Observations*, 5.

30. *Observations*, 5–6.

31. *Observations*, 4. This argument would become popular beyond France. See, for example, a point made in an essay in the *Edinburgh Review*, "To take only one other example, the line of argument now under consideration furnished a favourite topic to the slave-traders, for many a long year of successful sophistry and misrepresentation. The negroes were so miserable in their own barbarous country; so comfortable and happy in our polished dominions!" *Selections from the Edinburgh Review Comprising the Best Articles in That Journal from Its Commencement to the Present Time*, vol. 3 (London: Longman, Rees, Orma, Brown, Green, & Longman, 1833), 257.

32. Others included Marquis la Fayette, Frédéric de Liancourt de la Rouchefou-cault, Henri Grégoire, Marquis de Condorcet, Jacques Pierre Brissot, Jean Philippe Garran de Coulon, and Emmanuel-Joseph Sieyès.

33. Grégoire, *Mémoire en faveur des gens de couleur ou sang-mêlés*, 17.

34. Grégoire, *Mémoire en faveur des gens de couleur ou sang-mêlés*, 7.

35. Grégoire, *Mémoire en faveur des gens de couleur ou sang-mêlés*, 8–10. Garrigus, "French Caribbean," 187.

36. Grégoire, *Mémoire en faveur des gens de couleur ou sang-mêlés*, 8–10.

37. A royal decree forbidding the immigration of Black or mixed-race people, free or enslaved, was issued in 1777, David Brion Davis, *The Problem of Slavery in the Age of Revolution, 1770–1823* (New York: Oxford University Press, 1999), 24.

38. Grégoire, *Mémoire en faveur des gens de couleur ou sang-mêlés*, 9–10.

39. Grégoire, *Mémoire en faveur des gens de couleur ou sang-mêlés*, 12.

40. Grégoire, *Mémoire en faveur des gens de couleur ou sang-mêlés*, 17–18.

41. Grégoire, *Mémoire en faveur des gens de couleur ou sang-mêlés*, 27.

42. Grégoire, *Mémoire en faveur des gens de couleur ou sang-mêlés*, 29.

43. Grégoire, *Mémoire en faveur des gens de couleur ou sang-mêlés*, 38.

44. Grégoire, *Mémoire en faveur des gens de couleur ou sang-mêlés*, 45–46.

45. Grégoire, *Mémoire en faveur des gens de couleur ou sang-mêlés*, 47.

46. Quinney, "Decisions on Slavery," 121.

47. He later vehemently opposed slave trade and slavery, and supported the independence of Haiti; he also published several works extolling intellectual accomplishments of people of color. Henri Grègoire, *De la littérature des nègres, ou recherches sur leurs facultés intellectuelles, leurs qualités morales et leur littérature: suivies de notices sur la vie et les ouvrages des nègres qui se sont distingués dans les sciences, les lettres et les arts* (Paris: Maradan, 1808). On French abolitionism after Napoleon's reestablishment of slave trade and colonial slavery, see Lawrence Jennings, *French Anti-Slavery: The Movement for the Abolition of Slavery in France, 1802–1848* (Cambridge: Cambridge University Press, 2000).

48. Hunt, *The French Revolution and Human Rights*, 100–102.

49. Quinney, "Decisions on Slavery," 121.

50. Quinney, "Decisions on Slavery," 122.

51. Quinney, "The Problem of Civil Rights for Free Men of Color in the Early French Revolution," 556.

52. Knight, "The Haitian Revolution," 112.

53. Knight, "The Haitian Revolution," 113.

54. Knight, "The Haitian Revolution," 113–14. On the backlash in the US, see Milteer, *Beyond Slavery's Shadow*, ch. 3.

55. Knight, "The Haitian Revolution," 114; Petley, "Slavery, Emancipation and the Creole World View of Jamaican Colonists, 1800–1834," 100.

56. Milteer, *Beyond Slavery's Shadow*, ch. 1.

57. On the statement "slavery is distinctive as a relation of domination" and the "idiom" of power and slavery, Patterson, *Slavery and Social Death*, 2, and ch. 1.

58. Thomas Carlyle, *Occasional Discourse on the Nigger Question* (London: Thomas Bosworth, 1853), 21.

59. Blumrosen, Blumrosen, and Blumrosen, *Slave Nation*, 34. See also, Milteer, *Beyond Slavery's Shadow*.

60. "An Act directing the trial of Slaves, committing capital crimes; and for the more effectual punishing conspiracies and insurrections of them; and for the better government of Negros, Mulattos, and Indians, bond or free," William Waller Hening, ed. *The Statutes at Large: Being a Collection of All the Laws of Virginia, from the First Session of the Legislature, in the Year 1619*, vol. 4 (Richmond: Franklin Press,1820), 126–34, par. XVII on 132. The manumission law was only repealed in 1782 but in 1806 Virginia passed a law forcing manumitted slaves to leave, and in 1852, it passed a constitutional amendment, permanently banning manumissions, Finkelman, "United States Slave Law," 430, 433, 437; Goetz, *Baptism of Early Virginia*, 150–151. Also, Milteer, *Beyond Slavery's Shadow*, Chapter 3.

61. "An Act directing the trial of Slaves" (1723), par. XXIII on 133–34.

62. On the *Somerset* case and its implications, see Blumrosen, Blumrosen, and Blumrosen, *Slave Nation*, ch. 1; on the coverage of the Somerset case in American

press, Bradley, *Slavery, Propaganda, and the American Revolution*, ch. 4. See also Davis, *The Problem of Slavery*, 471–83.

63. Some colonies threatened the metropole to secede should slavery be abolished, see, for example, Petley, "Slavery, Emancipation and the Creole World View of Jamaican Colonists, 1800–1834," 93–114. Stovall, *White Freedom*, for example, 72.

64. For an overview, see Blumrosen, Blumrosen, and Blumrosen, *Slave Nation*.

65. Blumrosen, Blumrosen, and Blumrosen, *Slave Nation*, ch. 7, Mason's quote, 125–26.

66. Blumrosen, Blumrosen, and Blumrosen, *Slave Nation*, 137.

67. Milteer, *Beyond Slavery's Shadow*, 37.

68. Blumrosen, Blumrosen, and Blumrosen, *Slave Nation*, 220. Kendi, *Stamped from the Beginning*, 207. For this issue as expressed in *Dred Scott*, see Dred Scott v. Sandford, 60 U.S. 393 (1856), 414, 545.

69. Blumrosen, Blumrosen, and Blumrosen, *Slave Nation*, 84–86. On the language and rhetoric of slavery in the Revolutionary era, see Bradley, *Slavery, Propaganda, and the American Revolution*.

70. Blumrosen, Blumrosen, and Blumrosen, *Slave Nation*, 91.

71. "Admission of Missouri," 546. Barbour referred to the law passed in 1806, Finkelman, "United States Slave Law," 433.

72. Milteer, *Beyond Slavery's Shadow*, 67.

73. H. R. 40, Naturalization Bill, March 4, 1790, Records of the U.S. Senate, National Archives and Records Administration.

74. On whiteness and naturalization, Haney López, *White by Law*. For a discussion of inclusion of Christianity in state constitutions, see David J. Brewer, *The United States: A Christian Nation* (Philadelphia: Winston, 1905). On Justice David J. Brewer, Linda Przybyszewski, "Judicial Conservatism and Protestant Faith: The Case of Justice David J. Brewer," *Journal of American History* 91, no. 2 (2004). Also, Edward J. Blum, *Reforging the White Republic: Race, Religion, and American Nationalism 1865–1898* (Baton Rouge: Louisiana State University Press, 2015), 10.

75. Jones, *Birthright Citizens*, 1.

76. Milteer, *Beyond Slavery's Shadow*, 61–62. For a longer discussion of slave badges in Charleston, see Harlan Greene, Harry S. Hutchins and Brian E Hutchins, *Slave Badges and the Slave-Hire System in Charleston, South Carolina, 1783–1865* (Jefferson, NC: McFarland, 2008), this regulation is quoted extensively on 22–23.

77. David Brion Davis, *The Problem of Slavery in the Age of Emancipation* (New York: Vintage Books, 2015), 64.

## Chapter Six: The Fault Lines on Race, Religion, and American Citizenship

1. "Admission of Missouri," 555. On the Missouri debate, see also Jones, *Birthright Citizens*, ch.1, especially, 27–28.

2. "Admission of Missouri," 529–30.

3. Blumrosen, Blumrosen, and Blumrosen, *Slave Nation*, 89–90.

4. "Admission of Missouri," 534–36.

5. "Admission of Missouri," 524.

6. "Admission of Missouri," 530.

7. "Admission of Missouri," 536–37.

8. "Admission of Missouri," 541.

9. "Admission of Missouri," 545.

10. "Admission of Missouri," 545–48. Quote on 545.

11. Blum, *Reforging the White Republic*, 7.

12. "Admission of Missouri," 547–49.

13. "Admission of Missouri," 549–50.

14. "Admission of Missouri," 549.

15. Finkelman, "United States Slave Law," 433. Also, Milteer, *Beyond Slavery's Shadow*, 73–74.

16. "Admission of Missouri," 550.

17. Milteer, *Beyond Slavery's Shadow*, 78–79.

18. "Admission of Missouri," 550.

19. Stovall, *White Freedom*. Because the Naturalization Act limited citizenship to white Europeans, in the first half of the nineteenth century, the Democrats embraced immigrant voters because it guaranteed white voters. On Democrats courting immigrant voters, though without mentioning the race aspect of this issue, see Alexander Keyssar, *The Right to Vote: The Contested History of Democracy in the United States* (New York: Basic Books, 2009), 33–34, 52–53. Keyssar discusses the issue of voting and "whiteness and citizenship," elsewhere, for example, 47.

20. "Debate on Jewish Emancipation (August 22–31, 1796)" in Mendes-Flohr and Reinharz, *The Jew in the Modern World*, 131–44.

21. Mendes-Flohr and Reinharz, *The Jew in the Modern World*, 297–99.

22. "Admission of Missouri," 555–56.

23. Luke E. Harlow, *Religion, Race, and the Making of Confederate Kentucky, 1830–1880*, Cambridge Studies on the American South (Cambridge University Press, 2014), 4, 13, 17, 52–53. Also, Jones, *White Too Long*, ch. 3.

24. "Admission of Missouri," 557.

25. Timothy Garton Ash, *Free World: America, Europe, and the Surprising Future of the West* (New York: Vintage Books, 2005), 3.

26. Cited in Charles H. Wesley, "Creating and Maintaining an Historical Tradition," *Journal of Negro History* 49, no. 1 (1964): 15–16.

27. Edward J. Blum and Paul Harvey, *The Color of Christ: The Son of God and the Saga of Race in America* (Chapel Hill: University of North Carolina Press, 2012), 83. Also, Harlow, *Religion, Race*.

28. "Admission of Missouri," 565–74.

29. "Admission of Missouri," 570.

30. "Admission of Missouri," 570–71.

31. "Admission of Missouri," 596–97.

32. "Admission of Missouri," 598–99. On the complexity of the issue of birthright citizenship and the status of free Black people in antebellum America, see Jones, *Birthright Citizens*. For the 1619 Project see, "The 1619 Project," *New York Times Magazine*, August 18, 2019. Nikole Hannah-Jones, ed., *The 1619 Project: A New Origin Story* (New York: One Word, 2021).

33. "Admission of Missouri," 600.

34. "Admission of Missouri," 613–14.

35. "Admission of Missouri," 614.

36. "Admission of Missouri," 615–16.

37. "Admission of Missouri," 616.

38. See above chapter 5 for the discussion of the 1723 "Act directing the trial of Slaves, committing capital crimes; and for the more effectual punishing conspiracies and insurrections of them; and for the better government of Negros, Mulattos, and Indians, bond or free," Hening, ed. *The Statutes at Large: Being a Collection of All the Laws of Virginia, from the First Session of the Legislature, in the Year 1619*, 126–34, par. XVII on 132. While the manumission law was repealed in 1782, in 1806 Virginia passed a law forcing manumitted slaves to leave the state. This is what was discussed here. In 1852, Virginia would permanently ban manumissions through a constitutional amendment, Finkelman, "United States Slave Law," 430, 433, 437; Goetz, *Baptism of Early Virginia*, 150–51. Virginia, however, had been until 1800, the only state "to prohibit free people of color from entering its borders," Milteer, *Beyond Slavery's Shadow*, 77.

39. "Admission of Missouri," 616–617.

40. On exclusion from political rights in the colonial and early republican period, see Keyssar, *The Right to Vote*, 5, 11, 16.

41. "Admission of Missouri," 618.

42. "Admission of Missouri," 619–20, also 625.

43. On the invention of the term "racism," see Pierre-André Taguieff, *The Force of Prejudice: On Racism and Its Doubles* (Minneapolis: University of Minnesota Press, 2001), ch. 3. Bernasconi, "Racism."

44. Intermarriage was an issue in Jewish-Christian relations in premodern times, manifesting fears of Jewish proselytism, and was thus prohibited by law. During the debates over citizenship, the emphasis shifted to the Jewish reluctance for intermarriage in an effort to prove that Jews were ineligible for citizenship due to their refusal to join the civil community.

45. "Admission of Missouri," 619.

46. "Admission of Missouri," 616, 622.

47. "Admission of Missouri," 626.

48. "Admission of Missouri," 632. For the text of Vermont's state constitution, see https://sos.vermont.gov/vsara/learn/constitution/1793-constitution/.

49. "Admission of Missouri," 635. On Vermont, see also Keyssar, *The Right to Vote*, 15.

50. "Admission of Missouri," 635–39.

51. Rufus Pettibone and Henry Sheffie Geyer, *Laws of the State of Missouri: Revised and Digested by Authority of the General Assembly*, 2 vols., vol. 2 (St. Louis: E. Charles, 1825), 600–602.

52. This classification is similar to that applied by the Nazis to Jews in the Nuremberg Laws of 1935. This is not surprising, Nazi lawyers studied US race laws before enacting the Nuremberg laws concerning Jews, see Whitman, *Hitler's American Model*.

53. Pettibone and Geyer, *Laws of the State of Missouri*, 600–601.

54. See for example, Jane S. Gerber, ed. *The Jews in the Caribbean* (London: The Littman Library of Jewish Civilization, 2018), part 4: "Jews and Slave Society."

Especially, Aviva Ben-Ur, "The Cultural Heritage of Eurafrican Sephardi Jews in Suriname," in *The Jews in the Caribbean*, ed. Jane S. Gerber (London: The Littman Library of Jewish Civilization, 2018); Watson, "Shifting Identities." Most recently on Jamaica, Mirvis, *The Jews of Eighteenth-Century Jamaica*. Hasia R. Diner, *The Jews of the United States, 1654 to 2000* (Berkeley: University of California Press, 2004), 25–26, 48–53, 164–65. On Maryland, see Edward Eitches, "Maryland's 'Jew Bill,'" *American Jewish Historical Quarterly* 60, no. 3 (1971). For a list of legal disabilities Jews had, see Leonard Dinnerstein, *Antisemitism in America* (New York, Oxford: Oxford University Press, 1995), 14–15.

55. Laura Arnold Leibman, *Once We Were Slaves: The Extraordinary Journey of a Multiracial Jewish Family* (New York: Oxford University Press, 2021).

56. Blum and Harvey, *The Color of Christ*, chs. 3 and 4; in ch. 2, especially on 73–75.

57. Harlow, *Religion, Race*, 26–28, 48. Also, Jones, *White Too Long*, 1–2, 5–6, 81–92.

58. "Admission of Missouri," 555–56.

59. Harlow, *Religion, Race*, 17.

60. Harlow, *Religion, Race*, 108.

61. John H. Van Evrie, *Negroes and Negro "Slavery": The First an Inferior Race, the Latter Its Normal Condition* (Baltimore: J. D. Toy, Printer, 1853), 27.

62. John H. Van Evrie, *Negroes and Negro Slavery: The First, an Inferior Race: The Latter, Its Normal Condition* (New York: Van Evrie, Horton, 1861), 141–42.

63. Updegraph v. Commonwealth (Pa.) (1824), 11 Serg. & Rawle 394 Pa. 1824, accessible online at https://press-pubs.uchicago.edu/founders/documents/amendI_speechs30.html.

64. William Penn, "An Act for Freedom of Conscience," (1682).

65. William Penn, "Charter of Privileges Granted by William Penn, Esquire, to the Inhabitants of Pennsylvania and Territories October 28, 1701" (1701).

66. Updegraph v. Commonwealth (Pa.) (1824).

67. Ezra Stiles Ely, *The Duty of Christian Freemen to Elect Christian Rulers. A Discourse [on Ps. I1. 10–12] Delivered on the Fourth of July, 1827* (Philadelphia, 1828).

68. Ely, *The Duty of Christian Freemen*, 6–7.

69. Ely, *The Duty of Christian Freemen*, 11.

70. Ely, *The Duty of Christian Freemen*, 14.

71. Ely, *The Duty of Christian Freemen*, 16.

72. Kendi, *Stamped from the Beginning*, 195.

73. Blum and Harvey, *The Color of Christ*, 118. Decades later, Frederick Douglass commented on the visual trope showing Black men in a crouching, subservient position. In his letter to the editor, published in the *National Republican*, Frederick Douglass wrote, reacting to the Emancipation monument in Washington, DC, which shows a Black man on his knees before Abraham Lincoln: "Admirable as is the monument by Mr. Ball in Lincoln Park, it does not, as it seems to me, tell the whole truth, and perhaps no one monument could be made to tell the whole truth of any subject which it might be designed to illustrate. The mere act of breaking the negro's chains was the act of Abraham Lincoln, and is beautifully expressed in this monument. But the act by which the negro was made a citizen of the United States and invested with

the elective franchise was pre-eminently the act of President U. S. Grant, and this is nowhere seen in the Lincoln monument. The negro here, though rising, is still on his knees and nude. What I want to see before I die is a monument representing the negro, not couchant on his knees like a four-footed animal, but erect on his feet like a man. There is room in Lincoln park for another monument, and I throw out this suggestion to the end that it may be taken up and acted upon." Frederick Douglass, "A Suggestion." *National Republican*, April 19, 1876, 4, https://chroniclingamerica.loc .gov/lccn/sn86053573/1876-04-19/ed-1/seq-4/.

74. Naomi W. Cohen, *Jews in Christian America: The Pursuit of Religious Equality* (New York: Oxford University Press, 1992), 56–63.

75. Dinnerstein, *Antisemitism in America*, 16–17.

76. James William Hagy, *This Happy Land: The Jews of Colonial and Antebellum Charleston* (Tuscaloosa: University of Alabama Press, 1992), 40.

77. For the text, see Gary Phillip Zola and Marc Dollinger, *American Jewish History: A Primary Source Reader* (Waltham: Brandeis University Press, 2014), 73–74.

78. For the text, see Zola and Dollinger, *American Jewish History*, 73–74.

79. Hagy, *This Happy Land*, 40–41. Cohen, *Jews in Christian America*, 49–50. The discussion here is based on the documents published in "The Israelites of South Carolina," *Occident and American Jewish Advocate* 2, no. 10 (1845): 496–510.

80. On James Henry Hammond, see Drew Gilpin Faust, *James Henry Hammond and the Old South: A Design for Mastery* (Baton Rouge: Louisiana State University Press, 2010), on the incident 249ff.

81. "The Israelites of South Carolina," 501–4.

82. "The Israelites of South Carolina," 503.

83. "The Israelites of South Carolina," 504–6.

84. "The Israelites of South Carolina," 505–6.

85. Haney López, *White by Law*, 111.

86. Cohen, *Jews in Christian America*, 104.

87. "The Israelites of South Carolina," 506–10.

88. "The Israelites of South Carolina," 508–9.

89. "The Israelites of South Carolina," 508–9.

90. "The Israelites of South Carolina," 496–510, the phrase is on 496.

91. "The Israelites of South Carolina," 497–98.

92. Harlow, *Religion, Race*, 109.

93. Shklar, *American Citizenship*, 3.

## Chapter Seven: Contesting Black Citizenship and Equality

1. Dred Scott v. Sandford, 60 U.S. 393 (1856), 407, available on Justia Online Database, https://supreme.justia.com/cases/federal/us/60/393/. A short section of this quote in Blumrosen, Blumrosen, and Blumrosen, *Slave Nation*, 250. Kendi, *Stamped from the Beginning*, 204. One of the most comprehensive studies of the case is Don E. Fehrenbacher, *The Dred Scott Case: Its Significance in American Law and Politics* (Oxford; New York: Oxford University Press, 2001). Regarding Taney's exclusion of Black Britons from protection of Anglo-American treaties prior to *Dred Scott*, see Michael A. Schoeppner, "Status across Borders: Roger Taney, Black British Subjects,

and a Diplomatic Antecedent to the Dred Scott Decision," *Journal of American History* 100 (2013): 46–67.

2. Dred Scott v. Sandford, 60 U.S. 393 (1856). The Missouri debate of 1820 is discussed in chapter 6 above.

3. As quoted in dissent by Justice John McLean in *Dred Scott v. Sandford*, 60 U.S. 393 (1856), 550.

4. Dred Scott v. Sandford, 60 U.S. 393 (1856), 407.

5. Dred Scott v. Sandford, 60 U.S. 393 (1856), 403.

6. Dred Scott v. Sandford, 60 U.S. 393 (1856), 404–5.

7. Dred Scott v. Sandford, 60 U.S. 393 (1856), 407–8.

8. Dred Scott v. Sandford, 60 U.S. 393 (1856), 409.

9. Dred Scott v. Sandford, 60 U.S. 393 (1856), 409.

10. Dred Scott v. Sandford, 60 U.S. 393 (1856), 410.

11. Dred Scott v. Sandford, 60 U.S. 393 (1856), 410–11.

12. Dred Scott v. Sandford, 60 U.S. 393 (1856), 412.

13. Dred Scott v. Sandford, 60 U.S. 393 (1856), 414–16.

14. Dred Scott v. Sandford, 60 U.S. 393 (1856), 416–17

15. Dred Scott v. Sandford, 60 U.S. 393 (1856), 425–26.

16. Dred Scott v. Sandford, 60 U.S. 393 (1856), 419–20.

17. Dred Scott v. Sandford, 60 U.S. 393 (1856), 502.

18. Dred Scott v. Sandford, 60 U.S. 393 (1856), 533–34.

19. Dred Scott v. Sandford, 60 U.S. 393 (1856), 548–557.

20. Dred Scott v. Sandford, 60 U.S. 393 (1856), 569.

21. Dred Scott v. Sandford, 60 U.S. 393 (1856), 571–72.

22. Dred Scott v. Sandford, 60 U.S. 393 (1856), 571–72. See also Bradley, *Slavery, Propaganda, and the American Revolution*, ch. 1, esp. 6.

23. Dred Scott v. Sandford, 60 U.S. 393 (1856), 573.

24. Dred Scott v. Sandford, 60 U.S. 393 (1856), 574.

25. Dred Scott v. Sandford, 60 U.S. 393 (1856), 574–76. On added voting restrictions, see Keyssar, *The Right to Vote*, 27.

26. Dred Scott v. Sandford, 60 U.S. 393 (1856), 581.

27. Dred Scott v. Sandford, 60 U.S. 393 (1856), 582–83.

28. Jones, *Birthright Citizens*, 128.

29. Blum, *Reforging the White Republic*, 7. See also Jones, *White Too Long*.

30. Harlow, *Religion, Race*, 15.

31. Harlow, *Religion, Race*, 13.

32. Harlow, *Religion, Race*, 165.

33. Harlow, *Religion, Race*, 15. While Harlow focused on Kentucky, the same issues apply more broadly, Jones, *White Too Long*; Blum, *Reforging the White Republic*.

34. Blum, *Reforging the White Republic*, 88.

35. Blum, *Reforging the White Republic*, 89.

36. Blum, *Reforging the White Republic*, 1.

37. Horatio Bateman, *Explanation of Bateman's National Picture of Reconstruction Together with the Declaration of Independence and the Constitution of the United States* (New York: Published by H. Bateman, 171 Broadway; Blackwell, printer, 45 Cortlandt Street [1867]), 2.

38. Blum, *Reforging the White Republic*, 100.

39. Harlow, *Religion, Race*, 191–92.

40. Harlow, *Religion, Race*, 196.

41. Harlow, *Religion, Race*, 201.

42. Harlow, *Religion, Race*, 206–8.

43. Harlow, *Religion, Race*, 210–11.

44. Stovall, *White Freedom*, ch. 3. Milteer, *Beyond Slavery's Shadow*.

45. As quoted in Brook Thomas, *Plessy v. Ferguson: A Brief History with Documents* (Boston, New York: Bedford Books, 1997), 13.

46. Haney López, *White by Law*, 111. There is much scholarship on culture and whiteness, but Edward J. Blum's and Paul Harvey's *The Color of Christ* provides a useful analysis of what can be seen as the epitome of religion and culture—the image of Christ, which became "refashioned" as a white Christ to become "a symbol of white national unity and power," Blum and Harvey, *The Color of Christ*, 10.

47. Michael Perman and Amy Murrell Taylor, *Major Problems in the Civil War and Reconstruction: Documents and Essays* (Boston: Houghton Mifflin Co., 2011), 395. See also Henry Louis Gates, *Stony the Road: Reconstruction, White Supremacy, and the Rise of Jim Crow* (New York: Penguin, 2019), 21–22.

48. On the history of these three amendments, see Foner, *The Second Founding*.

49. Perman and Taylor, *Major Problems in the Civil War and Reconstruction*, 395.

50. Gates, *Stony the Road*, 8.

51. W. E. B. Du Bois, *Black Reconstruction in America: Toward a History of the Part Which Black Folk Played in the Attempt to Reconstruct Democracy in America, 1860–1880* (New York: Taylor & Francis, 2017), 381. The speech served as inspiration to an essay published by Ta-Nehisi Coates in *The Atlantic*, and became part of his book, Ta-Nehisi Coates, *We Were Eight Years in Power: A Journey through the Obama Era* (New York: Random House Inc, 2017).

52. Foner, *The Second Founding*, xxii.

53. *Harper's Weekly*, March 14, 1874, https://lccn.loc.gov/91705051. The image is discussed in Gates, *Stony the Road*, 153–54.

54. Du Bois, *Black Reconstruction in America*, 381.

55. Harlow, *Religion, Race*, 190.

56. On the Colfax massacre, LeeAnna Keith, *The Colfax Massacre: The Untold Story of Black Power, White Terror, and the Death of Reconstruction* (New York: Oxford University Press, 2008). Also, Eric Foner, *A Short History of Reconstruction* (New York: HarperPerennial, 1990), 184–91.

57. Blum and Harvey, *The Color of Christ*, 10.

58. Charles Reagan Wilson, *Baptized in Blood: The Religion of the Lost Cause, 1865–1920* (Athens: University of Georgia Press, 2009), 100, 110–11.

59. Neil R. McMillen, *Dark Journey: Black Mississippians in the Age of Jim Crow* (Urbana, IL; Chicago: University of Illinois Press, 1990), 41.

60. McMillen, *Dark Journey*, 43.

61. McMillen, *Dark Journey*, 43.

62. See the numerous laws restricting voting passed in many states following 2008 through 2020 elections. Most recently *Brnovich v. DNC* (2021), which also addresses the issue of the use of neutral language with racial intent remains current. In her

dissent in *Brnovich v. DNC*, Justice Elena Kagan noted that the Voting Rights Act of 1965, which the majority opinion in *Brnovich v. DNC* now undermined, was passed to remedy laws that "states and localities contrived . . . mostly neutral on their face but discriminatory in operation, to keep minority voters from the polls." Brnovich v. DNC, 594 U.S. ___ (2021), J. Kagan dissenting, 2, https://www.supremecourt.gov/opinions /20pdf/19-1257_g204.pdf.

63. *Harper's Weekly*, October 21, 1876, https://www.facinghistory.org/resource -library/image/course-he-votes-democratic-ticket-1876.

64. *Harper's Weekly*, October 28, 1876, https://www.loc.gov/item/2010644412 / and https://www.facinghistory.org/resource-library/image/he-wants-change-too -1876. See also September 2, 1876, https://www.loc.gov/resource/cph.3c16355/.

65. "Limited Sovereignty in the United States," *The Atlantic*, February 1879, https://www.theatlantic.com/magazine/archive/1879/02/limited-sovereignty-in-the -united-states/632104/. See also, Keyssar, *The Right to Vote*, 62–63. *The Atlantic's* editors asserted that "No other people ever displayed political talents of so high an order as that derived from the Anglo-Saxon stock. They have surpassed even the Romans in the practical art of government, and in adapting political systems to new conditions and changing times."

66. Quoted in Keyssar, *The Right to Vote*, 63.

67. Blum, *Reforging the White Republic*, ch. 3, quote on 100.

68. On Jews see below, and Cohen, *Jews in Christian America*, 104.

69. *Civil Rights Cases*, 109 U.S. 3 (1883), 4, the decisions are available online at https://supreme.justia.com/cases/federal/us/109/3/. On these cases and their significance, see Foner, *The Second Founding*, 151–67.

70. "An Act to Protect All Citizens in Their Civil and Legal Rights," Forty-Third Congress, Session II, ch. 114, March 1, 1875.

71. HR 796 (1875): Section 1 stated: "That all persons within the jurisdiction of the United States shall be entitled to the full and equal enjoyment of the accommodations, advantages, facilities, and privileges of inns, public conveyances on land or water, theaters, and other places of public amusement; subject only to the conditions and limitations established by law, and applicable alike to citizens of every race and color, regardless of any previous condition of servitude. Section 2 enumerated sanctions for violation of Section 1." The original document can be seen at https://www.senate.gov/artandhistory/history/resources/pdf/Civil_Rights _Act_1875.pdf.

72. *Civil Rights Cases*, 109 U.S. 3 (1883), 9–10.

73. "No State shall make or enforce any law which shall abridge the privileges or immunities of citizens of the United States; nor shall any State deprive any person of life, liberty, or property without due process of law; nor deny to any person within its jurisdiction the equal protection of the laws."

74. *Civil Rights Cases*, 109 U.S. 3 (1883), 11.

75. *Civil Rights Cases*, 109 U.S. 3 (1883), 16.

76. *Civil Rights Cases*, 109 U.S. 3 (1883), 17.

77. *Civil Rights Cases*, 109 U.S. 3 (1883), 17.

78. *Civil Rights Cases*, 109 U.S. 3 (1883), 20–21. The Thirteenth Amendment allows for "slavery and servitude" as "a punishment for crime whereof the party shall

have been duly convicted." This became a loophole that has been exploited to criminalize Black Americans, Muhammad Khalil Gibran, *The Condemnation of Blackness: Race, Crime, and the Making of Modern Urban America, with a New Preface* (Cambridge, MA: Harvard University Press, 2019).

79. *Civil Rights Cases*, 109 U.S. 3 (1883), 22–24.

80. *Civil Rights Cases*, 109 U.S. 3 (1883), 25.

81. Bradwell v. State 83 U.S. 130 (1873), https://supreme.justia.com/cases/federal /us/83/130/.

82. *Civil Rights Cases*, 109 U.S. 3 (1883), 26. The recent voting rights cases issued by the Roberts court similarly interpret the Constitution very narrowly and limit the power of Congress to pass voting rights laws. The Roberts court, like the Waite court in the *Civil Rights Cases*, issued reactionary rulings halting progress made through congressional legislation.

83. *Civil Rights Cases*, 109 U.S. 3 (1883), 28–29.

84. *Civil Rights Cases*, 109 U.S. 3 (1883), 34–35.

85. *Civil Rights Cases*, 109 U.S. 3 (1883), 34.

86. *Civil Rights Cases*, 109 U.S. 3 (1883), 35.

87. *Civil Rights Cases*, 109 U.S. 3 (1883), 36.

88. *Civil Rights Cases*, 109 U.S. 3 (1883), 40–41.

89. *Civil Rights Cases*, 109 U.S. 3 (1883), 42.

90. *Civil Rights Cases*, 109 U.S. 3 (1883), 48–49.

91. *Civil Rights Cases*, 109 U.S. 3 (1883), 56.

92. *Civil Rights Cases*, 109 U.S. 3 (1883), 58.

93. *Civil Rights Cases*, 109 U.S. 3 (1883), 59.

94. *Civil Rights Cases*, 109 U.S. 3 (1883), 61–62.

95. Gates, *Stony the Road*, 32–33.

96. Shelley v. Kraemer, 334 U.S. 1 (1948), 13.

97. The Chinese Exclusion Act (1882), https://www.ourdocuments.gov/doc.php ?doc=47&page=transcript.

98. Gabriel Jackson Chin, "Segregation's Last Stronghold: Race Discrimination and the Constitutional Law of Immigration," *UCLA Law Review* 46, no. 1 (1998): 10.

99. Thomas Nast, "Which color is to be tabooed next?" *Harper's Weekly*, March 25, 1882, 192, https://lccn.loc.gov/91793231. On the legal exclusion of different religious and national groups, see Chin, "Segregation's Last Stronghold," 6–7.

100. *Church of the Holy Trinity v. United States*, 143 U.S. 457 (1892), https:// supreme.justia.com/cases/federal/us/143/457/. Also, Cohen, *Jews in Christian America*, 100–101; Blum, *Reforging the White Republic*, 10.

101. This was, of course, not an entirely new notion, Foner, *The Second Founding*, 3.

102. On the legal cases around naturalization and whiteness, see Haney López, *White by Law*, the Ozawa case on 56–61.

103. On the legal cases around naturalization and whiteness, see Haney López, *White by Law*, 57.

104. Takao Ozawa v. United States, 260 U.S. 178 (189), available on https:// supreme.justia.com/cases/federal/us/260/178/.

105. Takao Ozawa v. United States, 260 U.S. 178 (195).

106. Takao Ozawa v. United States, 260 U.S. 178 (197).

107. On the legal cases around naturalization and whiteness, see Haney López, *White by Law*, 59–60.

108. Richard Delgado, Jean Stefancic, and Angela P. Harris, *Critical Race Theory: An Introduction* (New York: NYU Press, 2017), 80.

109. John Tyler Morgan, "Shall Negro Majorities Rule?," *The Forum* February (1889): 586–99.

110. Morgan, "Shall Negro Majorities Rule?," 593.

111. Morgan, "Shall Negro Majorities Rule?," 587, 591.

112. Morgan, "Shall Negro Majorities Rule?," 588.

113. Morgan, "Shall Negro Majorities Rule?," 587–89. On Jews, see above chapter 4 and below chapter 8.

114. Morgan, "Shall Negro Majorities Rule?," 593–95.

115. Morgan, "Shall Negro Majorities Rule?," 593.

116. Morgan, "Shall Negro Majorities Rule?," 595–96.

117. This idea was promoted by the Nazis in Europe and after World War II by American white supremacists such as George Lincoln Rockwell, *White Power* (Dallas: Ragnarok Press, 1967). See also an ad run by the RNC in 2018 in MN-01, featuring George Soros and Colin Kaepernick as "agents of chaos."

118. Morgan, "Shall Negro Majorities Rule?," 591.

119. Morgan, "Shall Negro Majorities Rule?," 591–92.

120. Thomas, *Plessy v. Ferguson*, 62–76.

121. Morgan was comparing Black people unfavorably to Native Americans.

122. Thomas, *Plessy v. Ferguson*, 62–76.

123. "Address of Mr. Clayton of Alabama" and "Address of Mr. Heflin of Alabama," in *John Tyler Morgan and Edmund Winston Pettus (Late Senators from Alabama): Memorial Addresses, Sixtieth Congress, First Session, Senate of the United States, April 18, 1908, House of Representatives, April 25, 1908* (Washington, DC: United States Government Printing Office, 1909), 137, 189.

124. *Civil Rights Cases*, 109 U.S. 3 (1883), and Plessy v. Ferguson, 163 U.S. 537 (1896), https://supreme.justia.com/cases/federal/us/163/537/, for Plessy v. Ferguson, see also other documents in Thomas, *Plessy v. Ferguson*.

125. Plessy v. Ferguson, 163 U.S. 537 (1896), 541.

126. Plessy v. Ferguson, 163 U.S. 537 (1896), 543.

127. Plessy v. Ferguson, 163 U.S. 537 (1896), 544.

128. "Admission of Missouri," 619.

129. Plessy v. Ferguson, 163 U.S. 537 (1896), 544.

130. Plessy v. Ferguson, 163 U.S. 537 (1896), 548.

131. Plessy v. Ferguson, 163 U.S. 537 (1896), 544. This is still the case, as evidence suggests about income and wealth gaps, suggests Stephen Miller, in "Black Workers Still Earn Less than Their White Counterparts," *Society for Human Resource Management*, June 11, 2020, https://www.shrm.org/resourcesandtools/hr-topics /compensation/pages/racial-wage-gaps-persistence-poses-challenge.aspx; and Kriston McIntosh et al., "Examining the Black-White Wealth Gap" (Brookings Institute, 2020), https://www.brookings.edu/blog/up-front/2020/02/27/examining-the-black -white-wealth-gap/.

132. Plessy v. Ferguson, 163 U.S. 537 (1896), 551–52.

133. Plessy v. Ferguson, 163 U.S. 537 (1896), 554–55.

134. Plessy v. Ferguson, 163 U.S. 537 (1896), 555–56.

135. Plessy v. Ferguson, 163 U.S. 537 (1896), 557.

136. Plessy v. Ferguson, 163 U.S. 537 (1896), 559.

137. Plessy v. Ferguson, 163 U.S. 537 (1896), 559–60.

138. Plessy v. Ferguson, 163 U.S. 537 (1896), 560.

139. Plessy v. Ferguson, 163 U.S. 537 (1896), 560.

140. Plessy v. Ferguson, 163 U.S. 537 (1896), 562.

141. Plessy v. Ferguson, 163 U.S. 537 (1896), 562–64.

142. Plessy v. Ferguson, 163 U.S. 537 (1896), 563.

143. Neiman, *Learning from the Germans*, 19.

144. Chin, "Segregation's Last Stronghold," 3.

## Chapter Eight: Backlash against Jewish Equality

1. A good concise overview can be found in Richard Levy, "Political Antisemitism in Germany and Austria, 1848–1914," in *Antisemitism*, ed. Alfred Lindemann and Richard Levy (Oxford, New York: Oxford University Press, 2010). For a more detailed study, see Shulamit Volkov, *Germans, Jews, and Antisemites: Trials in Emancipation* (Cambridge; New York: Cambridge University Press, 2006).

2. Mendes-Flohr and Reinharz, *The Jew in the Modern World*, 308.

3. Mendes-Flohr and Reinharz, *The Jew in the Modern World*, 308.

4. Shulamit Volkov, "Antisemitism as a Cultural Code: Reflections on the History and Historiography of Antisemitism in Imperial Germany," *Leo Baeck Institute Year Book* (1978), 25–46.

5. Levy, "Political Antisemitism," 123.

6. Levy, *Antisemitism in the Modern World*, 79.

7. Levy, *Antisemitism in the Modern World*, 58–59.

8. Wilhelm Marr, *Der Sieg des Judenthums über das Germanenthum: vom nicht confessionellen Standpunkt aus Betrachtet* (Bern: Rudolph Costenoble, 1879), 10. Sections of this pamphlet were published in English in Levy, *Antisemitism in the Modern World*, 76–93.

9. Marr, *Der Sieg des Judenthums*, 11, 21; Levy, *Antisemitism in the Modern World*, 81, 84.

10. Marr, *Der Sieg des Judenthums*, 17–20; Levy, *Antisemitism in the Modern World*, 83.

11. Marr, *Der Sieg des Judenthums*, 21; Levy, *Antisemitism in the Modern World*, 84.

12. Marr, *Der Sieg des Judenthums*, 21; Levy, *Antisemitism in the Modern World*, 84.

13. Marr, *Der Sieg des Judenthums*, 28–30; Levy, *Antisemitism in the Modern World*, 87–88.

14. Marr, *Der Sieg des Judenthums*, 43; Levy, *Antisemitism in the Modern World*, 91.

15. Marr, *Der Sieg des Judenthums*, 47–48; Levy, *Antisemitism in the Modern World*, 93.

16. Reported in "Cronaca Mensile Italiana," *L'Educatore Israelita* (1873): 149–50.

17. Patterson, *Slavery and Social Death*, ch. 1, esp. pages, 18–21, 28. Patterson used the term "mental structures."

18. Patterson, *Slavery and Social Death*, 79.

19. Petley, "Slavery, Emancipation and the Creole World View of Jamaican Colonists, 1800–1834," 98.

20. The English translation of the petition was published in Levy, *Antisemitism in the Modern World*, 125–27. And online with some additions, *German History in Documents and Images (GHDI): Forging an Empire: Bismarckian Germany (1866–1890), Religion, Education, Social Welfare*, document 13, http://ghdi.ghi-dc.org/.

21. Adolf Stöcker "Our Demands on Modern Jewry" (1879) in Levy, *Antisemitism in the Modern World*, 61.

22. Levy, *Antisemitism in the Modern World*, 65.

23. Levy, *Antisemitism in the Modern World*, 66.

24. Heinrich von Treitschke, "A Word about Our Jews (1879–1880)" in Levy, *Antisemitism in the Modern World*, 71. The essays were originally published as a monthly column in 1879, and were then republished in a separate pamphlet in 1880, Heinrich von Treitschke, *Ein Wort über unser Judentum* (Berlin: Reimer, 1880).

25. Treitschke, *Ein Wort über unser Judentum*, 4, 8.

26. "unbeschreiblich freche und hämische Ton," Treitschke, *Ein Wort über unser Judentum*, 14.

27. Treitschke, *Ein Wort über unser Judentum*, 15. Other examples of his concern with Jews' "haughtiness" (*Übermuth*), 18, and in the essay he published in December 1880, which was included in the later editions of the work.

28. Treitschke, *Ein Wort über unser Judentum*, 19.

29. Treitschke, *Ein Wort über unser Judentum*, 27.

30. Theodor Mommsen, *Auch Ein Wort über unser Judenthum* (Berlin: Weidmann, 1880), on that particular point, 6–7. Selections were printed in the English translation, in Mendes-Flohr and Reinharz, *The Jew in the Modern World*, 322–24.

31. "Unterdrückung der deutschen Semiten durch die deutschen Christen," Mommsen, *Auch Ein Wort*, 8.

32. Mommsen, *Auch Ein Wort*, 10.

33. Mommsen, *Auch Ein Wort*, 11–13.

34. Mommsen, *Auch Ein Wort*, 15–16.

35. Robert F. Byrnes, "Edouard Drumont and *La France Juive*," *Jewish Social Studies* 10, no. 2 (1948): 167.

36. Samuels, *The Right to Difference*, 5.

37. Samuels, *The Right to Difference*, 12, 52–53.

38. James McAuley, *The House of Fragile Things: A History of Jewish Art Collectors in France, 1870–1945* (New Haven: Yale University Press, 2021), 52. On the number of deputies, see Samuels, *The Right to Difference*, 52.

39. McAuley, *The House of Fragile Things*, 6–8.

40. Quoted in Samuels, *The Right to Difference*, 61.

41. Robert S. Wistrich, *Antisemitism: The Longest Hatred* (New York: Schoken Books, 1994), 129. Pierre-André Taguieff, "L'invention du «Complot Judéo-Maçonnique»: avatars d'un mythe apocalyptique moderne," *Revue d'histoire de la Shoah* 198, no. 1 (2013): 26. In 1869, for example, Henri Roger Gougenot des Mousseaux published a book in which he called attention to "Judaization of the Christian people," Taguieff, "L'invention du «Complot Judéo-Maçonnique»," 33–34.

42. McAuley, *The House of Fragile Things*, 51.

43. Jacob Katz, *From Prejudice to Destruction: Anti-Semitism, 1700–1933* (Cambridge; London: Harvard University Press, 1997), 293–94. McAuley, *The House of Fragile Things*, 54–55.

44. Samuels, *The Right to Difference*, ch. 4.

45. François Soyer, *Antisemitic Conspiracy Theories in the Early Modern Iberian World: Narratives of Fear and Hatred* (Leiden: Brill, 2019), ch. 2, especially 84–85.

46. Taguieff, "L'invention du «Complot Judéo-Maçonnique»," 34–35. Also, Byrnes, "Edouard Drumont and *La France Juive*," 171.

47. Emmanuel Chabauty, *Les Juifs, Nos Maîtres!: documents et développements nouveaux sur la question juive* (Paris: Société Générale de Librairie Catholique, 1882), 1.

48. Chabauty, *Les Juifs, Nos Maîtres!*, 2.

49. Chabauty, *Les Juifs, Nos Maîtres!* 132, 134–37.

50. Byrnes, "Edouard Drumont and *La France Juive*," 178.

51. Francis Magnard, "Echoes de Paris: La Politique," *Le Figaro*, April 19 1886, 1.

52. Byrnes, "Edouard Drumont and *La France Juive*," 179. Soyer, *Antisemitic Conspiracy Theories*, 85.

53. Byrnes, "Edouard Drumont and *La France Juive*," 184.

54. Édouard Drumont, *La France Juive: Devant L'opinion* (Paris: C. Marpon & E. Flammarion, 1886).

55. McAuley, *The House of Fragile Things*, 12, 59–61, quote on 59.

56. McAuley, *The House of Fragile Things*, 12, 59–61.

57. Katz, *From Prejudice to Destruction*, 296–97.

58. Drumont, *La France Juive: Devant L'opinion*, 11.

59. Samuels, *The Right to Difference*, 99.

60. Drumont, *La France Juive: Devant L'opinion*, 87. On Zola's views, Samuels, *The Right to Difference*, 100–101.

61. Katz, *From Prejudice to Destruction*, 298.

62. McAuley, *The House of Fragile Things*, 12.

63. McAuley, *The House of Fragile Things*, 16, 22, 48.

64. McAuley, *The House of Fragile Things*, 47–48. See also the reactions to the casting of a Jewish actor in a role of a marquis in 1939, Samuels, *The Right to Difference*, 127.

65. McAuley, *The House of Fragile Things*, 3.

66. McAuley, *The House of Fragile Things*.

67. Alexander Orbach and John Klier, *Perspectives on the 1881–1882 Pogroms in Russia* (Pittsburgh, PA: Russian and East European Studies Program, University of Pittsburgh, 1984); Irwin Michael Aronson, *Troubled Waters: The Origins of the 1881 Anti-Jewish Pogroms in Russia* (Pittsburgh, PA: University of Pittsburgh Press, 1990).

68. Monty Noam Penkower, "The Kishinev Pogrom of 1903: A Turning Point in Jewish History," *Modern Judaism* 24, no. 3 (2004): 216. For a similar argument recently, see Steven J. Zipperstein, *Pogrom: Kishinev and the Tilt of History* (New York: Liveright Publishing Corporation, 2018). For a detailed study of the pogrom, see Edward H. Judge, *Easter in Kishinev: Anatomy of a Pogrom* (New York: NYU Press, 1992).

69. Zipperstein, *Pogrom*.

70. Levy, *Antisemitism in the Modern World*, 154–55, 160, 161.

71. Whitman, *Hitler's American Model*.

72. On pauperization of Jews in eastern Europe and its impact on Jewish culture, see Natan M. Meir, *Stepchildren of the Shtetl: The Destitute, Disabled, and Mad of Jewish Eastern Europe, 1800–1939* (Stanford: Stanford University Press, 2020).

73. Jerzy Andrzejewski, "Zagadnienia polskiego antysemityzmu," in Adam Michnik, *Przeciw antysemityzmowi 1936–2009*, 3 vols. (Cracow: Universitas, 2010), vol. 2: 63.

74. Blum, *Reforging the White Republic*, 7.

75. Ian Haney López has discussed extensively the idea of being "white by law" based on the naturalization act in his book *White by Law*, but he does not address Jews, except in passing, for example, Haney López, *White by Law*, 74.

76. Leo Hurwitz's powerful film *Strange Victory* (1948) illustrates this anxiety and hostility as persisting in the aftermath of World War II. See below, chapter 10.

77. Linda, "Judicial Conservatism and Protestant Faith," 471–73.

78. Brewer, *The United States: A Christian Nation*, especially 32 and 50.

79. Cohen, *Jews in Christian America*, especially 100–104.

80. Thomas Nast, "Religious liberty is guaranteed: but can we allow foreign reptiles to crawl all over us?" unpublished cartoon, Library of Congress, https://lccn.loc.gov/2010717281.

81. See for example, Johan Phillips's request in 1787 to modify the wording in the constitution of Pennsylvania that acknowledged "the Scriptures of the Old and New Testaments to be given by divine inspiration," or the debate over the so called "Jew Bill" in 1819 in Maryland, Zola and Dollinger, *American Jewish History*, 40–41, 49–50.

82. On the history of Jews in Charleston, SC, see Hagy, *This Happy Land*.

83. Hagy, *This Happy Land*, 42.

84. *An Act to Protect All Citizens in Their Civil and Legal Rights*, Forty Third Congress, Session II (March 1, 1875), Chapter 114, on 336.

85. John H. Davis, *The Guggenheims: An America Epic* (New York: S. P. I. Books, 1994), 79–80. Dinnerstein, *Antisemitism in America*, 39–40. The affair is also briefly described in Sharon B. Oster, *No Place in Time: The Hebraic Myth in Late-Nineteenth-Century American Literature* (Detroit: Wayne State University Press, 2018), Introduction. Oster examines the "Hebraic myth" that allowed Henry Hilton to distinguish between "Hebrews" and "Jews."

86. "A Sensation at Saratoga: New Rules for the Grand Union," *New York Times*, June 19, 1877: 1.

87. "A Sensation at Saratoga," 1.

88. "Judge Hilton's Statement," *New York Times*, June 19, 1877: 1.

89. "Hotel Discrimination: The Right to Refuse Applicants," *New York Times*, June 20, 1877: 1.

90. "Judge Hilton's Position: The Step He Has Taken Was Forced Upon Him," *New York Times*, June 20, 1877, 1.

91. "Judge Hilton's Position," 1.

92. Oster, *No Place in Time*, introduction.

93. "Judge Hilton's Position," 1.

94. On sound pollution and Jews, see Ruth HaCohen, *The Music Libel against the Jews* (New Haven: Yale University Press, 2011).

95. "A Reply to Judge Hilton." *New York Times*, June 20, 1877, 1.

96. "Judge Hilton's Course Sustained," *New York Times*, June 21, 1877: 8

97. "A Reply to Judge Hilton."

98. "A Pending Combination: Hotel-Keepers' Union," *New York Times*, June 23, 1878, 12.

99. "A Reply to Judge Hilton."

100. "Judge Hilton's Course Sustained," 8.

101. "Judge Hilton's Course Sustained," 8.

102. Quoted in Judaken, "Anti-Semitism (Historiography)," 3.

103. Yancy, *Black Bodies, White Gaze*, xx.

104. Yancy, *Black Bodies, White Gaze*, 20.

105. Yancy, *Black Bodies, White Gaze*, 43.

106. "The Hebrew Controversy," *New York Times*, July 19, 1877, 5; "An Interview with Mr. Hilton," *New York Times*, July 19, 1877, 5; "The Hebrew Controversy," *New York Times*, July 22 1877, 2; "A Pending Combination," 12. For the obituary, see "Henry Hilton Is Dead: Suffered a Relapse and Expired at Saratoga," *New York Times*, August 25 1899: 3.

107. For a contemporary account, see *Coney Island and the Jews: A History of This Development and Success of This Famous Seaside Resort, Together with a Full Account of the Recent Jewish Controversy* (New York: G. W. Carleston & Co., 1879). For a song about it, Mailliw J. Rolyat, "Extra! Jews at Manhattan Beach," New York: s.n., 1879, Division of Rare and Manuscripts Collection, Cornell University, Rare Books, F129.C75 E96 +.

108. *Coney Island and the Jews*, 20.

109. Lake Placid Club, *Lake Placid Club, Organized 1895 Morningside, Moose Island, Adirondack Lodge, 'Heart of the Adirondacks': Handbook* (Morningside, NY, 1901), 23; Lake Placid Club, *Handbook, 1914* (Lake Placid, NY: Lake Placid Club, 1914), 468. The club also advertised having a "piggery."

110. Lake Placid, *Handbook, 1914*, 468.

111. "Ask Regents to Depose State Librarian Dewey," *New York Times* (1857–1922), January 21, 1905. Also quoted in Wayne A. Wiegand, "'Jew Attack': The Story Behind Melvil Dewey's Resignation as New York State Librarian in 1905," *American Jewish History* 83, no. 3 (1995): 359.

112. Wiegand, "'Jew Attack.'"

113. "Ask Regents to Depose State Librarian Dewey."

114. "Ask Regents to Depose State Librarian Dewey." On some Jews' support for Dewey and opposition to Marshall and the petitioners, see Wiegand, "'Jew Attack.'"

115. "Did Not Use Position to Boom Club, Dewey: State Librarian's Defense against Charges of Jews," *New York Times*, January 24, 1905.

116. For an account of the hearing, see Wiegand, "'Jew Attack.'"

117. Wiegand, "'Jew Attack,'" 372–73.

118. Wiegand, "'Jew Attack,'" 374–75.

119. Wiegand, "'Jew Attack,'" 374–75.

120. "Jews Protest Aid by State for Club," *New York Times*, November 7, 1930; "Mosessohn Disputes Dewey's Club Reply," *New York Times*, November 8, 1930; "Lake Placid Club Ends Olympic Row: Citizens of Village Make Peace with Jewish Tribune— Slide Deeded to Township," *New York Times*, December 4, 1930.

121. "Dr. Wise Attacks Fifth Avenue Clubs," *New York Times*, May 22, 1911, 5; Gretchen Sorin, *Driving While Black: African American Travel and the Road to Civil Rights* (New York: Liveright Publishing Corporation, 2020), 184–85. On Mohonk, Cindy Sondik Aron, *Working at Play: A History of Vacations in the United States* (New York: Oxford University Press, 2001), 54–55.

122. "Dr. Wise Attacks Fifth Avenue Clubs."

123. "Dr. Wise Attacks Fifth Avenue Clubs."

124. A similar sentiment was voiced in the aftermath of the Dewey affair. For example, as Wayne Wiegand has shown, Rabbi Joseph Friedlander of Temple Emmanuel in Beaumont, Texas, declared that Jews who acquiesced and bore the indignities "had 'to be fought even more than the Melvil Deweys.' Until 'you implant or restore self-respect to the character of the Jew,' he concluded, 'he will always remain the object of scorn and the target of assault for the baser elements of our mixed humanity.'" Wiegand, "'Jew Attack,'" 373.

125. "Dr. Wise Attacks Fifth Avenue Clubs."

126. This is signaled in Rabbi Wise's sermon and discussed in Wiegand, "'Jew Attack,'" 365, 367–68, 370, 373. On the backlash after Jews responded to Brewer's publication, Cohen, *Jews in Christian America*, 102. One Baptist minister said, "If you don't like conditions in . . . our Christian country, then go back, you don't have to stay. But if you do stay, you stay as those who stay in Christian America."

127. "Look to America to Lead for Peace: Our Cosmopolitan Population Makes It Incumbent on Us, Many Pastors Assert. Here for Mohonk Meeting Dean of Worcester Says the Churches Can Do Much to Aid in the Movement to End War," *New York Times* May 23, 1911, 10.

128. Aron, *Working at Play*, 217.

129. Aron, *Working at Play*, 218.

130. Aron, *Working at Play*, 238–39.

131. Some of the lyrics to the song were as follows: "Borkum der Nordsee schönste Zier/bleib du von Juden rein/laß Rosenthal und Levysohn/in Norderney allein." See Jerome Forman, *Graphic History of Antisemitism* (Atglen, PA: Schiffer Publishing, 2014), 106.

132. Frank Bajohr, *"Unser Hotel ist judenfrei": Bäder-Antisemitismus im 19. und 20. Jahrhundert* (Frankfurt am Main: Fischer Taschenbuch Verlag, 2003).

133. Forman, *Graphic History of Antisemitism*, 107.

134. Bajohr, *"Unser Hotel ist judenfrei".*

135. On this, Sorin, *Driving While Black*. For examples of anti-Jewish ads and postcards, see Forman, *Graphic History of Antisemitism*, 95–101. Private restrictive covenants in real estate were challenged in *Shelley v. Kraemer* in 1948, a landmark case originating in Missouri. Previous cases addressing such covenants and cited in *Shelley v. Kraemer* dealt with state or local laws, which were ruled by the Supreme Court as violating the Fourteenth Amendment rights. Shelley v. Kraemer, 334 U.S. 1 (1948).

136. Reports on the case and Crum's confirmation controversy, "The Crum Case," *New York Times*, April 28, 1904; John L. McLaurin, "McLaurin on Race Problem: South Carolina Ex-Senator Says Crisis Is Near, Crum Case," *New York Times*, September 12, 1904; "W. D. Crum Confirmed: Senate Acts after Debate on Question of Constructive Recesses," *New York Times*, January 7, 1905; "Crum Refused a Chair: After a White Lad to Push It Was Refused to the Negro Collector," *New York Times*, August 15, 1905. The case is mentioned but wrongly dated to August 1904 in Aron, *Working at Play*, 213.

137. "Crum Refused a Chair."

138. "Negro Colonel 'Stirs San Antonio Camp," *New York Times*, April 5, 1911.

139. "Negro Troops Will Go to Brownsville," *New York Times*, April 6, 1911.

140. "Topics of the Times: 'A Theory Confronts a Condition,'" *New York Times*, April 5, 1911, 8.

141. Ruth Hampton, "A Negro Soldier," *New York Times*, April 7, 1911, 12.

142. "Danger to Nation in Race Prejudice," *New York Times*, March 5, 1911, 5.

143. Quoted in Cousin and Fine, "A Common Cause," 19.

144. Dinnerstein, *Antisemitism in America*, 15.

145. "Would Abolish Negro Votes: Georgia Representative Wants Fourteenth Amendment Repealed," *New York Times*, April 15, 1911, 5.

146. Michnik, *Przeciw antysemityzmowi*, vol. 1: 19–20.

147. Jan Nepomucen Miller, "Dyplomatyczna drzemka," in Michnik, *Przeciw antysemityzmowi*, vol. 1: 71.

148. "A Reply to Judge Hilton."

149. Seeking to explain what made Nazi murder of Jews possible, Shulamit Volkov argued that political antisemitism transformed in a short time into "a cultural code"; it became wrapped in "a radical anti-modern mentality, rejecting liberalism, capitalism, and socialism; in a nostalgic passion for a long-lost world." Antisemitism became, as Friedrich Lange stated in 1893 "an element and by no means the most important of a much broader and higher reaching national worldview and politics," or as Volkov put it, "a short-hand for an entire set of ideas and attitudes having little if anything to do with direct affection or dislike of Jews." Volkov, "Antisemitism as a Cultural Code," esp. 31–32, 35.

150. Wilson, *Baptized in Blood*, 117.

151. Deborah E. Lipstadt, *Antisemitism: Here and Now* (New York: Schocken, 2019).

152. For a detailed study, see Whitman, *Hitler's American Model*.

153. Whitman, *Hitler's American Model*, 70.

154. Whitman, *Hitler's American Model*, 71, 144.

155. Whitman, *Hitler's American Model*, 117.

156. Whitman, *Hitler's American Model*, 70.

157. Whitman, *Hitler's American Model*, 43–44.

158. Quoted in Whitman, *Hitler's American Model*, 45.

159. See, for example, a photograph by Otto Schönstein from Behringersdorf, 1933, Deutsches Historisches Museum, Berlin, Inv.-Nr.: Schönstein 2506, https://www.dhm.de/lemo/bestand/objekt/juden-nicht-erwuenscht-1933.html. See also "The Motorcycle Album" at the Wiener Holocaust Library, objects: WL14522, WL5973, WL6139, WL10375, https://www.wienerlibrary.co.uk/The-Motorcycle-Album.

160. Joel Cang, "The Opposition Parties in Poland and Their Attitude Towards the Jews and the Jewish Problem," *Jewish Social Studies* 1, no. 2 (1939): 243–44.

161. Quoted in Cang, "The Opposition Parties," 245.

162. A succinct explanation of the unprecedented but *not* unique nature of the Nazi murder of Jews, see Yehuda Bauer, *Rethinking the Holocaust* (New Haven: Yale University Press, 2001).

## Chapter Nine: Visualizing Social Hierarchy

1. For a mirror view of the question, see Aston Gonzalez, *Visualizing Equality: African American Rights and Visual Culture in the Nineteenth Century* (Chapel Hill: University of North Carolina Press, 2020).

2. For an unsympathetic comparison between Jews and Chinese, see William Trant, "Jew and Chinaman," *North American Review* 195, no. 675 (1912).

3. Bernier, "Nouvelle division de la terre par les différentes espèces ou races qui l'habitent," 136; Stuurman, "François Bernier and the Invention of Racial Classification," 4.

4. Helen H. Jun, "Black Orientalism: Nineteenth-Century Narratives of Race and U.S. Citizenship," *American Quarterly* 58, no. 4 (2006): 1047.

5. Chin, "Segregation's Last Stronghold," 5.

6. Plessy v. Ferguson, 163 U.S. 537 (1896), 561.

7. Thomas Nast., "Chinese Question," *Harper's Weekly*, February 18, 1871, 149.

8. *Life*, July 14, 1887, 22–23.

9. *Life*, July 9, 1885, 36–37. Digitized on Google Books.

10. *Life*, August 20, 1885, 106–107.

11. Gates, *Stony the Road*, 126.

12. The Blavatnik Archive online has a large collection of nearly six hundred antisemitic postcards, https://www.blavatnikarchive.org/.

13. Lipton, *Dark Mirror*. Gates, *Stony the Road*, 126.

14. Elisabeth Klamper, *Die Macht der Bilder antisemitische Vorurteile und Mythen* (Vienna: Picus-Verl, 1995).

15. Gérard Silvain, Joël Kotek, and Marie-Anne Matard-Bonucci, *La carte postale antisémite: de l'affaire Dreyfus à la Shoah* (Paris: Berg International Editeurs, 2005), 124. On other examples of antisemitic postcards, see Salo Aizenberg, *Hatemail: Anti-Semitism on Picture Postcards* (Philadelphia: Jewish Publication Society, 2013). See also The Blavatnik Archive, https://www.blavatnikarchive.org/.

16. Silvain, Kotek, and Matard-Bonucci, *La carte postale antisémite*, 126.

17. Quoted in Fredrickson, *Racism*, 120.

18. "DEY IS SHUST A LITTLE SHORT, BUT DEN YOU IS A GROWIN' POY / BUT WOANT DEY BE SHOTAH WHEN I GROWS, BOSS? / MEIN KRACIOUS ! DO YOU TINK YOUR FEET VILL GROW DOWN THE FLOOR INTO? YOU VAS A CRAZY, EH? OF COURSE YOU GROW UP INTO 'EM." *Life*, July 9, 1885, 24.

19. *Life*, September 17, 1885, 159.

20. Frederick Douglass, "Lessons of the Hour (1894)," in *The Portable Frederick Douglass* (New York: Penguin Classics, 2016), 393.

21. Charles Carroll, *"The Negro a Beast," or, "in the Image of God"... The Negro Not the Son of Ham* (St. Louis: American Book and Bible House, 1900). Images also published in Gates, *Stony the Road*, 114–17.

22. Carroll, *"The Negro a Beast,"* 8.

23. Carroll, *"The Negro a Beast,"* 44.

24. Douglass, "Lessons of the Hour (1894)," 378–90.

25. Gates, *Stony the Road*, 148–50.

26. As quoted in Gates, *Stony the Road*, 152.

27. As quoted in Gates, *Stony the Road*, 154.

28. Douglass, "Lessons of the Hour (1894)," 378–90.

29. Christina von Braun, "Antisemitische Stereotype und Sexualphantasien," in *Die Macht der Bilder antisemitische Vorurteile und Mythen*, ed. Elisabeth Klamper (Vienna: Picus-Verl, 1995), 180–91.

30. See, for example, issues of *Der Stürmer* published in the 1920s.

31. Elvira Bauer, *Trau keinem Fuchs auf grüner Heid und keinem Jud auf seinem Eid: Ein Bilderbuch für Gross und Klein* (Nuremberg: Stürmer Verlag, 1936). Translation of the text by Randall L. Bytwerk, https://research.calvin.edu/german-propaganda-archive/fuchs.htm.

32. Gates, *Stony the Road*, 132. See also Yancy, *Black Bodies, White Gaze.*

33. Gates, *Stony the Road*, 128.

34. On naturalizing the image of the black person as subhuman, Gates, *Stony the Road*, 130. I extended it to Jews as well.

35. Quoted in Gates, *Stony the Road*, 131.

36. Gates, *Stony the Road*, 134.

37. Aizenberg, *Hatemail*, 44.

38. Nahum Wolf, "Are the Jews an Inferior Race?," *North American Review* 195, no. 677 (1912): 492–95.

39. Douglass, "The Claims of the Negro Ethnologically Considered (1854)," 235.

40. Douglass, "Lessons of the Hour (1894)," 393.

41. Michael Stanislawski, *Zionism and the Fin-de-Siècle: Cosmopolitanism and Nationalism from Nordau to Jabotinsky* (Berkeley: University of California Press, 2001), ch. 4, especially, 91–93. Presner Todd Samuel, "'Clear Heads, Solid Stomachs, and Hard Muscles': Max Nordau and the Aesthetics of Jewish Regeneration," *Modernism/Modernity* 10, no. 2 (2003). And Presner's more recent monograph, Todd Samuel Presner, *Muscular Judaism: The Jewish Body and the Politics of Regeneration* (London: Routledge, 2010).

42. Stanislawski, *Zionism and the Fin-de-Siècle*, ch. 5.

43. Alma Rachel Heckman and Frances Malino, "Packed in Twelve Cases: The Alliance Israélite Universelle and the 1893 Chicago World's Fair," *Jewish Social Studies* 19, no. 1 (2012): 57–58.

44. "Report of the U.S. Secretary of the Interior," ed. United States Department of the Interior (Washington: Government Printing Office, 1895), vol. 5: 501, 651–52, 1152–53.

45. "Report of the U.S. Secretary of the Interior," vol. 5: 651–52.

46. Gates, *Stony the Road*, ch. 4.

47. "Report of the U.S. Secretary of the Interior," vol. 5: 495.

48. Douglass, "Lessons of the Hour (1894)," 393.

49. Deborah Willis and David Levering Lewis, *A Small Nation of People: W. E. B. Du Bois and African American Portraits of Progress* (New York: Amistad, 2003). See also Gates, *Stony the Road*, 196–98.

50. Willis and Lewis, *A Small Nation*, 13. Also, W. E. B. Du Bois, Whitney Battle-Baptiste, and Britt Rusert, *W. E. B. Du Bois's Data Portraits Visualizing Black America: The Color Line at the Turn of the Twentieth Century* (Hudson, NY: Princeton Architectural Press, 2018).

51. Willis and Lewis, *A Small Nation*, 33.

52. Willis and Lewis, *A Small Nation*, 30.

53. Shawn Michelle Smith, *Photography on the Color Line: W. E. B. Du Bois, Race, and Visual Culture* (Durham: Duke University Press, 2004), 2.

54. James Van der Zee and Deborah Willis-Braithwaite, *Van Der Zee: Photographer, 1886–1983* (New York: Harry N. Abrams, 1993). On respectability, also see Gates, *Stony the Road*, 193–96, 199–200.

55. Gates, *Stony the Road*, 131–32.

56. Gates, *Stony the Road*, 203.

57. Du Bois quoted in Gates, *Stony the Road*, 125. On lynchings statistics, David Rigby and Charles Seguin, "National Crimes: A New National Data Set of Lynchings in the United States, 1883 to 1941," *Socius: Sociological Research for a Dynamic World* 5 (2019).

## Chapter Ten: The (Stunted) Reckoning

1. This is the title of chapter 3 in his Fredrickson, *Racism*.

2. *Strange Victory* (1948), directed by Leo Hurwitz, narrated by Saul Levitt, 49:21–49:39, https://leohurwitz.com/movie/strange-victory/.

3. John H. Johnson, "Publisher's Statement," *Ebony*, August 1965, 27.

4. *Strange Victory* (1948), 14:10–16:45.

5. *Strange Victory* (1948), 9:52–9:58.

6. Charles Abrams, "Homes for Aryans Only: The Restrictive Covenant Spreads Legal Racism in America," *The Commentary*, May 1947.

7. *Strange Victory* (1948), 27:03–30:00.

8. *Strange Victory* (1948), 30:01–32:55.

9. *Strange Victory* (1948), 32:56–36:50, 38:12–40:19. A similar point would be made decades later, Julia Fletcher Carney, "Racism and Sexism and Children's Books," *The Crisis* 82, no. 1 (1975): 21–23.

10. *Strange Victory* (1948), 36:51-37-57. For a similar sentiment, expressed in 1963, see James Baldwin, "A Talk to Teachers," in *Collected Essays* (New York: The Library of America, 1998), 678–86, esp. 680.

11. *Strange Victory* (1948), 52:11–53:25. See also a story about Black pilots after the war, Will Thomas, "Hill to Climb," *The Crisis* 53, no. 6 (1946).

12. Stephen Tuck, *We Ain't What We Ought to Be: The Black Freedom Struggle from Emancipation to Obama* (Cambridge: Belknap Harvard, 2011), 236–37.

13. Neiman, *Learning from the Germans*, 153.

14. "The People vs. Discrimination," *Commentary Magazine*, March 1946.

15. Thomas, "Hill to Climb," 173–74.

16. Patricia Sullivan, "Movement Building during the World War II Era: The NAACP's Legal Insurgency in the South," in *Fog of War: The Second World War and the Civil Rights Movement*, ed. Kevin M. Kruse and Stephen Tuck (New York: Oxford University Press, 2012), 76.

17. Patrick Novotny, *This Georgia Rising: Education, Civil Rights, and the Politics of Change in Georgia in the 1940s* (Macon, GA: Mercer University Press, 2007), 198–200. George Hatcher, "Rural Vote Gave Talmadge Victory in Georgia Test: Few Negroes Outside Chief Urban Centers Appear to Have Cast Ballots in Primary First Negro Vote," *New York Times*, July 21, 1946, E1.

18. Smith v. Allwright, 321 U.S. 649 (1944). https://supreme.justia.com/cases /federal/us/321/649/ For a discussion of the case and the election season, Sullivan, "Movement Building," 74–78.

19. "Georgia Mob of 20 Men Massacres 2 Negroes, Wives," *New York Times*, July 27, 1946, 1; Novotny, *This Georgia Rising*, 203–15.

20. "Lynchings Declared 'Blot on Whole U.S.,'" *New York Times*, July 28, 1946.

21. The image of a funeral for the four victims of the Moore's Ford lynching is in *Strange Victory* (1948), 40:54–41:05, and the reference to the killing of Maceo Snipes at 38:36–38:42. There were other incidents as well, see a report about a meeting of protest in Harlem, "3 Meetings Protest Cruelty to Negroes," *New York Times*, July 30, 1946, 13.

22. Tanya Goldman, "The Strange Lives of Leo Hurwitz's *Strange Victory*," *Cinéaste* 44, no. 1 (2018): 39.

23. Julian E. Zelizer, "Confronting the Roadblock: Congress, Civil Rights, and World War II," in *Fog of War: The Second World War and the Civil Rights Movement*, ed. Kevin M. Kruse and Stephen Tuck (New York: Oxford University Press, 2012), 44–45; James T. Sparrow, "Freedom to Want: Federal Government and Politicized Consumption in World War II," in *Fog of War: The Second World War and the Civil Rights Movement*, ed. Kevin M. Kruse and Stephen Tuck (New York: Oxford University Press, 2012), 15; Sullivan, "Movement Building," 81; Stephen Tuck, "'You Can Sing and Punch . . . but You Can't Be a Soldier or a Man': African American Struggles for a New Place in Popular Culture," in *Fog of War: The Second World War and the Civil Rights Movement*, ed. Kevin M. Kruse and Stephen Tuck (New York: Oxford University Press, 2012), 119.

24. Thomas Sugrue, "Hillburn, Hattiesburg, and Hitler: Wartime Activists Think Globally Act Locally," in *Fog of War: The Second World War and the Civil Rights Movement*, ed. Kevin M. Kruse and Stephen Tuck (New York: Oxford University Press, 2012), 89–91.

25. See, for example: "We are ready to bring Germany to task for her misdeeds but we have 'Hands Off' on our own doorsteps" in Layle Lane, "The Land of the Noble Free," *The Crisis* 46, no. 7 (1939): 208. Charles H. Wesley, "The Negro Has Always Wanted the Four Freedoms," in *What the Negro Wants*, ed. Rayford W. Logan (Chapel Hill: University of North Carolina Press, 1944), 90–112. Also, Sullivan, "Movement Building," 71. Tuck, "'You Can Sing and Punch,'" 108.

26. "Walter White Scores Persecution of Jews," *The Crisis* 45, no. 12 (December 1938), 399–400.

27. "Negroes, Nazis and Jews," *The Crisis* 45, no. 12 (December 1938), 393.

28. Reprinted in *The Crisis* 46, no. 2 (February 1939), 51.

29. "White Racialism in America," *The Crisis* 46, no.10, 308.

30. One David Pierce of Cleveland Heights, Ohio, noted that "the fascists" ignored "the Negro for the time being. . . . Meanwhile, our Coughlins and their sponsors, the labor hating Ford and the less obstrusive men of wealth, will endeavor to inculcate a feeling of superiority in downtrodden, dispossessed, pitiful white Gentile shop-keepers, clerks and poverty stricken professional men who are, like the majority of Negroes and Jews, victims of the world economic crisis," "Letters," *The Crisis* 46, no. 3 (March 1939), 90–91.

31. Wesley, "The Negro Has Always Wanted the Four Freedoms," 111–12.

32. "Confusion for Christmas," *The Crisis* 52, no. 12 (1945): 345.

33. Kevin M. Kruse and Stephen Tuck, *Fog of War: The Second World War and the Civil Rights Movement* (New York: Oxford University Press, 2012), 11. Also, Sparrow, "Freedom to Want."

34. Harold Preece, "The Klan's 'Revolution of the Right,'" *The Crisis* 53, no. 7 (1946): 202.

35. Preece, "The Klan's 'Revolution of the Right,'" 202.

36. Preece, "The Klan's 'Revolution of the Right,'" 202–3.

37. Preece, "The Klan's 'Revolution of the Right,'" 203.

38. Preece, "The Klan's 'Revolution of the Right,'" 203.

39. Preece, "The Klan's 'Revolution of the Right,'" 220.

40. Preece, "The Klan's 'Revolution of the Right,'" 220.

41. Charles Carroll, *"The Negro a Beast" or, "in the Image of God"; the Reasoner of the Age, the Revelator of the Century! The Bible as It Is! The Negro and His Relation to the Human Family! . . . The Negro Not the Son of Ham* (Savannah, GA: Thunder-bolt, Inc., 1968). T. T. Timayenis and Edward R. Fields, *The Jew Comes to America: An Exposé of His Career, Profusely Illustrated* (Savannah, GA: Thunderbolt, 1960s).

42. Zelizer, "Confronting the Roadblock," 43. *Strange Victory (1948)*, 19:11–22:14. On anti-communism as an obstacle to racial justice, see also Tuck, *We Ain't What We Ought to Be*, 233, 243, 259–62, 286.

43. Tuck, *We Ain't What We Ought to Be*, 262.

44. Sullivan, "Movement Building"; Jason Morgan Ward, "'A War for States' Rights': The White Supremacist Vision of Double Victory," in *Fog of War: The Second World War and the Civil Rights Movement*, ed. Kevin M. Kruse and Stephen Tuck (New York: Oxford University Press, 2012). These efforts were covered in *The Crisis*. See also Roy Wilkins, "The Negro Wants Full Equality," in *What the Negro Wants*, ed. Rayford W. Logan (Chapel Hill: University of North Carolina Press, 1944).

45. Tuck, *We Ain't What We Ought to Be*, 258.

46. Quoted in Tuck, *We Ain't What We Ought to Be*, 242, 263.

47. Tuck, *We Ain't What We Ought to Be*, 247–50.

48. Brown v. Board of Education of Topeka, 347 U.S. 483 (1954), Footnote 5 quoting Strauder v. West Virginia, 100 U. S. 303, 307–308 (1880).

49. Quoted in Nicholas Buccola, *The Fire Is Upon Us: James Baldwin, William F. Buckley Jr., and the Debate over Race in America* (Princeton: Princeton University Press, 2019), 74.

50. Martin Luther King Jr. "The Negro Is Your Brother: A Letter from a Birmingham Jail," *The Atlantic Monthly*, 1963, henceforth, "A Letter from a Birmingham Jail."

51. King, "A Letter from a Birmingham Jail."

52. The journalist Louis Lomax discussed this issue in an essay published in *Ebony* in August 1965, and then republished in a self-contained volume a year later, Louis Lomax, "The White Liberal," in *The White Problem in America*, ed. editors of *Ebony* (Chicago: Johnson, 1966), 39–46.

53. Tuck, *We Ain't What We Ought to Be*, 274, 335–36. On the complexity of Jewish-Black relations in the US, see Cheryl Lynn Greenberg, *Troubling the Waters: Black-Jewish Relations in the American Century* (Princeton: Princeton University Press, 2006), chapter 6 deals with the fallout of the civil rights era and beyond. On the retreat of Jewish liberals, see Marc Dollinger, *Black Power, Jewish Politics: Reinventing the Alliance in the 1960s* (Waltham: Brandeis University Press, 2018); Nancy Sinkoff, *From Left to Right: Lucy S. Dawidowicz, the New York Intellectuals, and the Politics of Jewish History* (Detroit: Wayne State University Press, 2020). See also, a recent podcast "School Colors" hosted by Max Freedman and Mark Winston Griffith and produced by the Code Switch team of the WNYC.

54. James Baldwin, "The Fire Next Time," in *Collected Essays* (New York: The Library of America, 1998), 336.

55. Baldwin, "The Fire Next Time," 340–41.

56. Baldwin, "The Fire Next Time," 342. Baldwin even pushed for white self-love to solve the racial problem, Sullivan, *Good White People*, 9–10. See also ch. 4 on "white self-love."

57. Greenberg, *Troubling the Waters*, 205.

58. Sinkoff, *From Left to Right*, 121–36.

59. Quoted in Tuck, *We Ain't What We Ought to Be*, 335.

60. Buccola, *The Fire Is Upon Us*, 97–100.

61. Buccola, *The Fire Is Upon Us*, 387–89.

62. Buccola, *The Fire Is Upon Us*, 398.

63. San Antonio Independent School District v. Rodriguez, 411 U.S. 1 (1973) went after the question of distribution of property taxes, https://supreme.justia.com/cases/federal/us/411/1/; and Milliken v. Bradley, 418 U.S. 717 (1974) addressed the question of redrawing school district lines to combat segregation https://supreme.justia.com/cases/federal/us/418/717/. On the organized conservative backlash to civil rights, see Tuck, *We Ain't What We Ought to Be*, 356–59.

64. McIntosh et al., "Examining the Black-White Wealth Gap."

65. Christopher Robbins, "Upper West Side Uproar as City Tries to Diversify Schools," *The Gothamist*, May 1, 2018.

66. Morgan, "Shall Negro Majorities Rule?," 588.

67. Barack Obama, *Dreams of My Father* (New York: Three Rivers Press, 2005), xiii. The passage is discussed in Tuck, *We Ain't What We Ought to Be*, 418.

68. See for example, James Baldwin and Gwendolyn Brooks, *James Baldwin Reading from His Works* (Library of Congress: 1986), https://www.loc.gov/item/88752473/; and Coates, *We Were Eight Years in Power*, 219.

69. Martha Minow, *Between Vengeance and Forgiveness: Facing History after Genocide and Mass Violence* (Boston: Beacon Press, 1998), 9, 47. See also Lawrence

Douglas, *The Memory of Judgment: Making Law and History in the Trials of the Holocaust* (New Haven: Yale University Press, 2001), especially ch. 2.

70. Richard J. Golsan, *Memory, the Holocaust, and French Justice: The Bousquet and Touvier Affairs* (Hanover, NH: University Press of New England, 1996), 110–112. On the limitations of trials in pursuit of reckoning and justice, see Minow, *Between Vengeance and Forgiveness*, ch. 3. For the US, see Renee Romano, *Racial Reckoning: Prosecuting America's Civil Rights Murders* (Cambridge, MA: Harvard University Press, 2014).

71. Michael Robert Marrus, *The Nuremberg War Crimes Trial, 1945–46: A Brief History with Documents* (Boston, New York: Bedford/St. Martin's, 2018), indictment on 121.

72. Neiman, *Learning from the Germans*, 47–48.

73. Tony Judt, *Postwar: A History of Europe since 1945* (New York: Penguin Books, 2006), 2.

74. Neiman, *Learning from the Germans*, 42–44. See also Frank Biess, "Between Amnesty and Anti-Communism: The West German Kameradenschinder Trials, 1948–1960," in *Crimes of War: Guilt and Denial in the Twentieth Century*, ed. Omer Bartov, Atina Grossman, and Mary Nolan (New York: Norton, 2003).

75. Judt, *Postwar*, 8.

76. Neiman, *Learning from the Germans*, 372.

77. The Rijksmuseum in Amsterdam recently opened an exhibition on slavery and Dutch colonial history, https://www.rijksmuseum.nl/en/whats-on/exhibitions/slavery.

78. Golsan, *Memory, the Holocaust, and French Justice*, 1–49.

79. Franz Neumann, "Re-Educating the Germans:The Dilemma of Reconstruction," *The Commentary*, June, 1947.

80. Neiman, *Learning from the Germans*.

81. David Bernstein, "Europe's Jews, Summer, 1947: A Firsthand Report by an American Observer," *The Commentary*, August, 1947.

82. For example, W. H. Lawrence, "Poles Kill 26 Jews in Kielce Pogrom," *New York Times*, July 5, 1946, 1. Witold Kula, "Nasza w tym rola (głos pesymisty)," in Michnik, *Przeciw antysemityzmowi*, vol. 2: 145.

83. Kazimierz Wyka, "Potęga ciemnoty potwierdzona," in Michnik, *Przeciw antysemityzmowi*, vol. 2: 33.

84. Wyka, "Potęga ciemnoty potwierdzona," 33. Stanisław Ossowski, "Na tle wydarzeń kieleckich," in Michnik, *Przeciw antysemityzmowi*, vol. 2: 123.

85. Adam Michnik, "Pogrom kielecki: dwa rachunki sumienia," in Michnik, *Przeciw antysemityzmowi*, vol. 2: 184. The *New York Times*, reporting on the Kielce massacre in July 1946, noted: "What the Kielce events illustrate is that there is a large minority segment in the Polish population committed to the use of illegal means to exterminate Jews and to oppose the Soviet Union—which means they are, of course, against the present Government," W. H. Lawrence, "Poles Declare Two Hoaxes Caused High Toll in Pogrom," *New York Times*, July 6, 1946, 1. On post-war trials in Poland, see Gabriel N. Finder and Alexander Victor Prusin, *Justice Behind the Iron Curtain: Nazis on Trial in Communist Poland* (Toronto: University of Toronto Press, 2018).

86. A large body of scholarship has been inspired by Jan Tomasz Gross's seminal book *Neighbors: The Destruction of the Jewish Community in Jedwabne, Poland* (Penguin Books, 2002).

87. On this period, see Marcin Zaremba, *Wielka Trwoga: Polska 1944-1947, Ludowa Reakcja Na Kryzys* (Cracow: Wydawnictwo Znak, 2012).

88. See for example, Jan Tomasz Gross, *Fear: Anti-Semitism in Poland after Auschwitz: An Essay in Historical Interpretation* (New York: Random House, 2006). Joanna Tokarska-Bakir, *Pod Klątwą: Społeczny Portret Pogromu Kieleckiego*, 2 vols. (Warsaw: Wydawnictwo Czarna Owca, 2018). Volume 2 in Tokarska-Bakir's study consists of primary sources related to the Kielce massacre of 1946. Some responses from 1945-1947 to the anti-Jewish violence are available in Michnik, *Przeciw antysemityzmowi*, vol. 2: 2-266.

89. Lawrence, "Poles Kill 26 Jews in Kielce Pogrom," 1.

90. Lawrence, "Poles Declare Two Hoaxes Caused High Toll in Pogrom."

91. "9 Sentenced to Die in Kielce Pogrom: 3 Others, Including Woman, Get Prison Terms in a Rare Prosecution in Poland," *New York Times*, July 12, 1946, 8.

92. Stanisław Grabski, "Groźna przestroga," in Michnik, *Przeciw antysemityzmowi*, 102.

93. Kula, "Nasza w tym rola," 141.

94. Kula, "Nasza w tym rola," 141.

95. Kula, "Nasza w tym rola," 143.

96. Franciszek Gil, "Powrót z Kielc," in Michnik, *Przeciw antysemityzmowi*, vol. 2: 109-10.

97. "Polish Army in Scotland Calls 9 Executed Pogromists 'Martyrs,'" *Jewish Post*, July 26, 1946.

98. "Poles in Palestine to Hold Memorial for Executed," *Jewish Post*, July 26, 1946.

99. Ossowski, "Na tle wydarzeń kieleckich," 118-19; the English translation of this passage is in Gross, *Fear*, 130-31.

100. Ossowski, "Na tle wydarzeń kieleckich," 122.

101. Ossowski, "Na tle wydarzeń kieleckich," 122, 128.

102. Edmund Jan Osmańczyk, "Antypolonizm," in Michnik, *Przeciw antysemityzmowi*, vol. 2: 136.

103. Stanisław Grabski, "Groźna przestroga," in Michnik, *Przeciw antysemityzmowi*, vol. 2: 102-3.

104. Michnik, *Przeciw antysemityzmowi*, vol. 2: 169-70.

105. Michnik, *Przeciw antysemityzmowi*, vol. 2: 166-67; also, Gross, *Fear*, 137-38. This is not unlike today's innocuous sounding cry "All lives matter" in response to "Black Lives Matter."

106. Michnik, *Przeciw antysemityzmowi*, vol. 2: 165.

107. Zachariah Schuster, "Between the Millstones in Poland: The Jews of Poland Are on the March," *Commentary Magazine*, August, 1946, Online archive: https://www.commentary.org/issues/1946-august/.

108. Michnik, *Przeciw antysemityzmowi*, vol. 2: 159-61.

109. Gross, *Fear*, ch. 2.

110. Jerzy Andrzejewski, "Zagadnienie polskiego antysemityzmu," in Michnik, *Przeciw antysemityzmowi*, vol. 2: 58-60.

111. Andrzejewski, "Zagadnienie polskiego antysemityzmu," 62-63.

112. "Arogancja, tupet," Andrzejewski, "Zagadnienie polskiego antysemityzmu," 64, also 66.

113. Andrzejewski, "Zagadnienie polskiego antysemityzmu," 49, 68.

114. Gil, "Powrót z Kielc," 110–12.

115. Gil's language echoes Adam Clayton Powell Jr.'s quip: "We recognized [Hitler] immediately, because he is like minor Hitlers here," quoted in Tuck, "'You Can Sing and Punch,'" 108.

116. Władysław Broniewski, "Wstęp do książki Juliana Bendy," in Michnik, *Przeciw antysemityzmowi*, 46.

117. Julian Przyboś, "Hańba antysemityzmu," in Michnik, *Przeciw antysemityz- mowi*, vol. 2: 225–27.

118. Kula, "Nasza w tym rola," 145–46.

119. "Wyznanie Żyda," in Michnik, *Przeciw antysemityzmowi*, vol. 2: 298. A. Minkowski, "Sprawa Hanki," in Michnik, *Przeciw antysemityzmowi*, vol. 2: 301–6. Henryk Kollat, "Nie kryjmy się po bramach . . . ," in Michnik, *Przeciw antysemityzmowi*, vol. 2: 407–8. Compare that to what took place in the United States as efforts at inte- grating schools intensified after the war into the 1950s, Clarence A. Laws, "Nine Cour- agous Students," *The Crisis* 65, no. 5 (1958): 267–72, 318.

120. Tadeusz Mazowiecki, "Antysemityzm ludzi łagodnych i dobrych," in Mich- nik, ed *Przeciw antysemityzmowi*, vol. 2: 471–90; Mazowiecki, "Antisemitism of the Good and Gentle People" in Adam Michnik, *Against Anti-Semitism: An Anthology of Twentieth-Century Polish Writings*, trans. Agnieszka Marczyk (Oxford, New York: Oxford University Press, 2018), 170–87.

121. Stanisław Krajewski, *Poland and the Jews: Reflections of a Polish Polish Jew* (Kraków: Wydawnictwo Austeria, 2005).

122. For example, Thelma Thurston Gorham, "Negroes and Japanese Evacuees," *The Crisis* 52, no. 11 (1945): 353–54. James Farmer and James W. Ivy, "Jim Crow Rents a Pew," *The Crisis* 53, no. 6 (1946). On dangers of travel, Sorin, *Driving While Black*.

## Chapter Eleven: Reckoning with the Christian Legacy of Antisemitism and Racism

1. Farmer and Ivy, "Jim Crow Rents a Pew," 170–72.

2. James Baldwin, *The Cross of Redemption: Uncollected Writings* (New York: Vintage Books, 2011), 59.

3. Baldwin, "The Fire Next Time," 316–17. In his "Letter from a Birmingham Jail," Martin Luther King Jr. noted that many "have lost faith in America, who have absolutely repudiated Christianity, and who have concluded that the white man is an incurable devil."

4. Hill Fletcher, *The Sin of White Supremacy*, 5.

5. Farmer and Ivy, "Jim Crow Rents a Pew," 172. Farmer and Ivy were correct; in 1946 the Catholic Church was still quite strict about its faithful relations with Prot- estant denominations, John W. O'Malley and David G. Schultenover, *Vatican II: Did Anything Happen?* (New York: Continuum, 2007), 9.

6. The Catholic Church struggled during the civil rights era, and continues to face these issues, Massingale, *Racial Justice and the Catholic Church*, esp. ch. 2.

7. Massingale, *Racial Justice and the Catholic Church*, 57.

8. "Brothers and Sisters to Us" is accessible on the website of the US Conference of Catholic Bishops, https://www.usccb.org/committees/african-american-affairs/brothers-and-sisters-us.

9. Massingale, *Racial Justice and the Catholic Church*, 75.

10. Massingale, *Racial Justice and the Catholic Church*, 68. Also, Jones, *White Too Long*, 69.

11. Massingale, *Racial Justice and the Catholic Church*, 46.

12. Massingale, *Racial Justice and the Catholic Church*, 100.

13. See a review of his books pointing to some deeply embedded antisemitic assumptions despite good intentions, Marie Jahoda, "An Enemy of the People: Anti-Semitism; and the Jewish Problem in the Modern World, by James Parkes," *The Commentary*, January 1947.

14. Franklin Sherman, *Bridges: Documents of the Christian-Jewish Dialogue*, 2 vols., vol. 1 (New York: Paulist Press, 2011), 41–42.

15. Sherman, *Bridges*, 43–44.

16. Sherman, *Bridges*, 338–43.

17. John Connelly, *From Enemy to Brother: The Revolution in Catholic Teaching on the Jews, 1933–1965* (Cambridge, MA: Harvard University Press, 2012), ch. 5.

18. O'Malley and Schultenover, *Vatican II: Did Anything Happen?*, 110–12.

19. "Vatican II and the Jews," *The Commentary*, January, 1965.

20. O'Malley and Schultenover, *Vatican II: Did Anything Happen?*, 111.

21. Connelly, *From Enemy to Brother*, 179–82.

22. "Giovanni XXIII: 'Io sono Giuseppe, il vostro fratello,'" *L'Osservatore Romano*, October 19, 1960. English translation available at Council of Centers on Jewish-Christian Relations, https://www.ccjr.us/dialogika-resources/documents-and-statements/roman-catholic/second-vatican-council/naprecursors/j231960oct19. See also John M. Oesterreicher, *The New Encounter: Between Christians and Jews* (New York: Philosophical Library, 1986), 112–13.

23. Kathryn A. Smith, "History, Typology and Homily: The Joseph Cycle in the Queen Mary Psalter," *Gesta* 32, no. 2 (1993): 152.

24. Oesterreicher, *The New Encounter*, 158–59.

25. O'Malley and Schultenover, *Vatican II: Did Anything Happen?*, 7.

26. John W. O'Malley, *What Happened at Vatican II* (Cambridge; London: The Belknap Press of Harvard University Press, 2008), 220–22.

27. "The Declaration *Nostra aetate* on the Church's Relation with non-Christian Religions," http://www.vatican.va/archive/hist_councils/ii_vatican_council/documents/vat-ii_decl_19651028_nostra-aetate_en.html.

28. "The Declaration *Nostra aetate* on the Church's Relation with non-Christian Religions."

29. "The Declaration *Nostra aetate* on the Church's Relation with non-Christian Religions."

30. "The Declaration *Nostra aetate* on the Church's Relation with non-Christian Religions."

31. Oesterreicher, *The New Encounter*, 211.

32. This phrase was used to describe recent steps taken by Pope Francis, Jordan Denari, "'In our time': Francis moves beyond Nostra aetate" in *Commonweal*

*Magazine,* December 8, 2013, https://www.commonwealmagazine.org/blog/our-time
-francis-moves-beyond-nostra-aetate. Accessed January 31, 2015.

33. O'Malley and Schultenover, *Vatican II: Did Anything Happen?*, 7. On the
history of this process, Connelly, *From Enemy to Brother.* "Nostra aetate" 1965. Also,
Pope John Paul II, "Address to Representatives of Jewish Organizations," March 12,
1979: "a sign of understanding and fraternal love already achieved," available at
http://www.ccjr.us/dialogika-resources/documents-and-statements/roman-catholic
/pope-john-paul-ii/.

34. The Vatican Commission for Religious Relations with the Jews, "Guidelines
and Suggestions for Implementing the Conciliar Declaration Nostra aetate, No. 4,"
December 1, 1974 (henceforth, "Guidelines 1974").

35. "Guidelines 1974."

36. The Vatican Commission for Religious Relations with the Jews, "Notes on
the Correct Way to Present the Jews and Judaism in Preaching and Catechesis in the
Roman Catholic Church," June 24, 1985.

37. The Vatican Commission for Religious Relations with the Jews, "We Remember: A Reflection on the Shoah," March 16, 1998.

38. The Vatican Commission for Religious Relations with the Jews, "'The
Gifts and the Calling of God Are Irrevocable' (Rom 11:29): A Reflection on Theological Questions Pertaining to Catholic-Jewish Relations on the Occasion of the
50th Anniversary of Nostra aetate (No. 4)." December 10, 2020, available online:
http://www.christianunity.va/content/unitacristiani/en/commissione-per-i-rapporti
-religiosi-con-l-ebraismo/commissione-per-i-rapporti-religiosi-con-l-ebraismo-crre
/documenti-della-commissione/en.html.

39. "The Gifts and the Calling of God Are Irrevocable" (2015), paragraph 17.

40. "The Gifts and the Calling of God Are Irrevocable" (2015), paragraph 20.

41. "The Gifts and the Calling of God Are Irrevocable" (2015), paragraph 20.

42. The text was published in Marie Therese Hoch and Bernard Dominique Dupuy, *Les
eglises devant le judaisme: documents officiels, 1948–1978* (Paris: Editions du Cerf, 1980).
It is available online at https://www.paris.catholique.fr/391-L-attitude-des-chretiens-a-l
.html#nb2-1, and in the English translation on the website of Council of Centers of Jewish-
Christian Relations, https://www.ccjr.us/dialogika-resources/documents-and-statements
/roman-catholic/other-conferences-of-catholic-bishops/cefr1973.

43. "Declaration de Repentance," available in French: https://www.paris
.catholique.fr/Declaration-de-repentance-de-l.html and in the English Translation on
the website of Council of Centers of Jewish-Christian Relations https://www.ccjr.us
/dialogika-resources/documents-and-statements/roman-catholic/other-conferences
-of-catholic-bishops/cefr1997.

44. "Declaration de Repentance."

45. For an account of these early years, see Abp Henryk Józef Muszyński, *Początek
wspólnej drogi: dialog katolicko-żydowski w Polsce w latach 1986–1994* (Gniezno: Pelplin, 2015).

46. The English translation of the pastoral letter was published in "A Polish Pastoral Letter on the Jews," *New York Times,* January 20, 1991.

47. "List Rady Episkopatu Polski do Spraw Dialogu Religijnego z okazji
Wielkiego Jubileuszu Roku 2000 zaakceptowany przez 307. Zebranie Plenarne

Konferencji Episkopatu Polski," August 25, 2000, available at https://www.prchiz
.pl/prchizwypKoscListWlkJubpopup.

48. The issue of anti-Polonism returns in many statements by Polish bishops,
even those that sincerely seek Polish-Jewish reconciliation and dialogue. It is true
that "anti-Polonism" exists among Jews. But one also has to be mindful that "anti-
Polonism" is also an antisemitic trope developed at the end of World War I. It
reframed the old trope of Jews as enemies of Christianity in a new national mold
presenting "Jews enemies of Poland." As my student Agata Sobczak has shown in
her research, the idea that Jews sought to "slander" Poland and to turn "the opinion of the whole world against Poland" was already deployed as an antisemitic
argument against Jews in in Polish nationalist press in 1919–1921.

49. "Statement of Bishop Rafał Markowski on the events that took place on
April 19 in Pruchnik," English https://episkopat.pl/en/statement-of-bishop-rafal
-markowski-on-the-events-that-took-place-on-april-19-in-pruchnik/. Polish: https:
//episkopat.pl/bp-markowski-kosciol-jednoznacznie-wyraza-dezaprobate-wobec
-praktyk-ktore-godza-w-godnosc-czlowieka-komunikat/.

50. On this tradition and its revival, see Joanna Tokarska-Bakir, "'Wieszanie
Judasza,' czyli tematy żydowskie dzisiaj," in *Przeciw antysemityzmowi 1936–2009*, ed.
Adam Michnik (Cracow: Universitas, 2010), vol. 3: 313–321.

51. Available at https://www.congress.gov/bill/115th-congress/senate-bill/447.

52. "Statement of Bishop Rafał Markowski."

53. On the Church's lackluster response to blood libel accusations, see Teter, *Blood
Libel*.

54. Ambrogio Spreafico, "A proposito di un dipinto su Simonino di Trento," April 2,
2020, *SIR*, https://www.agensir.it/chiesa/2020/04/02/a-proposito-di-un-dipinto-su
-simonino-di-trento/. The English translation is available on the website of the Council of Centers for Jewish-Christian Relations, https://www.ccjr.us/dialogika-resources
/documents-and-statements/roman-catholic/other-conferences-of-catholic-bishops
/spreafico-2020apr2.

55. Baldwin, "White Man's Guilt," 47.

56. "The goal of *The 1619 Project*, a major initiative from The New York Times that
this issue of the magazine inaugurates, is to reframe American history by considering
what it would mean to regard 1619 as our nation's birth year. Doing so requires us to
place the consequences of slavery and the contributions of black Americans at the
very center of the story we tell ourselves about who we are as a country." Editor's Note
to "The 1619 Project," *New York Times Magazine*, August 18, 2019, 4–5.

57. The President's Advisory 1776 Commission, *The 1776 Report*. The project was
available at https://www.whitehouse.gov/briefings-statements/1776-commission
-takes-historic-scholarly-step-restore-understanding-greatness-american-founding/
but has since been removed, and placed on an archived site: https://trumpwhitehouse
.archives.gov/wp-content/uploads/2021/01/The-Presidents-Advisory-1776
-Commission-Final-Report.pdf

58. Blumrosen, Blumrosen, and Blumrosen, *Slave Nation*, 252, 254.

59. Baldwin, *The Cross of Redemption*, 60.

60. Preece, "The Klan's 'Revolution of the Right.'"

# BIBLIOGRAPHY

## Primary Sources

### FILM:

*The Birth of a Nation*. A film directed by D. W. Griffith (1915).

*Strange Victory*. A film directed by Leo Hurwitz (1948), https://leohurwitz.com/movie/strange-victory/.

*A Time for Burning*. A film directed by Barbara Connell and Bill Jersey (1966), https://archive.org/details/atimeforburning.

### PRINTED:

"3 Meetings Protest Cruelty to Negroes." *New York Times*, July 30, 1946, 13.

"9 Sentenced to Die in Kielce Pogrom: 3 Others, Including Woman, Get Prison Terms in a Rare Prosecution in Poland." *New York Times*, July 12, 1946, 8.

Abrams, Charles. "Homes for Aryans Only: The Restrictive Covenant Spreads Legal Racism in America." *The Commentary*, May 1947, Online Archive.

*An Act to Protect All Citizens in Their Civil and Legal Rights*. Forty-Third Congress, Session 2, March 1, 1875.

*Acts of Assembly: Passed in the Island of Barbadoes, from 1648, to 1718*. London: printed by John Baskett, Printer to the King's most Excellent Majesty, and by the assigns of Thomas Newcomb, and Henry Hills, deceas'd, 1721.

"Admission of Missouri." *Annals of the Congress of the United States* Proceedings and Debates of the House of Representatives of the United States, at the Second Session of the Sixteenth Congress, begun at the City of Washington, Monday, November 13, 1820, no. 37 (1820–1821): 509–640.

Aizenberg, Salo. *Hatemail: Anti-Semitism on Picture Postcards*. Philadelphia: Jewish Publication Society, 2013.

Andrzejewski, Jerzy. "Zagadnienie polskiego antysemitizmu." In *Przeciw antysemi-tyzmowi 1936–2009*, edited by Adam Michnik, 49–70. Cracow: Universitas, 2010.

"Ask Regents to Depose State Librarian Dewey." *New York Times (1857–1922)*, January 21, 1905, 5.

Augustine. *Answer to Faustus, a Manichean*. Hyde Park, NY: New City Press, 2007.

———. *The City of God*. Translated by Henry Bettenson. London, New York: Penguin Books, 1984.

Azurara, Gomes Eannes de, Charles Raymond Beazley, and Edgar Prestage. *The Chronicle of the Discovery and Conquest of Guinea. Vol. 1*. London: Hakluyt Society, 1896.

Baldwin, James. *The Cross of Redemption: Uncollected Writings*. New York: Vintage Books, 2011.

———. "The Fire Next Time." In *Collected Essays*, 283–347. New York: The Library of America, 1998.

——. "A Talk to Teachers." In *Collected Essays*, 678–86. New York: The Library of America, 1998.

——. "White Man's Guilt." *Ebony*, August 1965, 47–50.

Baldwin, James, and Gwendolyn Brooks. *James Baldwin Reading from His Works*. Library of Congress, 1986.

Baldwin, James, and Raoul Peck. *I Am Not Your Negro: A Companion Edition to the Documentary Film Directed by Raoul Peck*. New York: Vintage Books, 2017.

Bateman, Horatio. *Explanation of Bateman's National Picture of Reconstruction Together with the Declaration of Independence and the Constitution of the United States*. New York: Published by H. Bateman, 171 Broadway; Blackwell, printer, 45 Cortlandt Street [1867].

Bauer, Elvira. *Trau keinem Fuchs auf Grüner Heid und keinem Jud bei seinem Eid: Ein Bilderbuch für Gross und Klein*. Nuremberg: Strürmer-Verlag, 1936.

Benedict XIV, Pope. *Benedicti XIV Pont. Opt. Max. Olim Prosperi Cardinalis de Lambertinis Bullarium*. 17 vols. Vol. 3/1. Prati: Typographia Aldina, 1847.

Bernier, François. "Nouvelle division de la terre par les différentes espèces ou races qui l'habitent." *Journal des sçavans* 12, no. April 24 (1684): 133–40.

Bernstein, David. "Europe's Jews, Summer, 1947: A Firsthand Report by an American Observer." *The Commentary*, August 1947, Online Archive.

*Bible moralisée/Bible de Saint Louis* (Facsimile edition, M. Moleiro, 2000–2004), 3 vols.

Bindman, David, Henry Louis Gates, Karen C. C. Dalton, and Jean Michel Massing, eds. *From the "Age of Discovery" to the Age of Abolition*. Vol. 3, part 2, of *The Image of the Black in Western Art*. Cambridge, MA: Belknap Press of Harvard University Press, 2011.

Brewer, David J. *The United States: A Christian Nation*. Philadelphia: Winston, 1905.

Broniewski, Władysław. "Wstęp do książki Juliana Bendy 'Antysemita z przekonania.'" In *Przeciw antysemityzmowi 1936–2009*, edited by Adam Michnik, 44–48. Cracow: Universitas, 2010.

*Brown v. Board of Education of Topeka*. 347 U.S. 483, 1954.

Bry, Johann Theodor de, Johann Israel de Bry, and Jan Huygen van Linschoten. *II. Pars Indiæ Orientalis, in Qva Iohan. Hvgonis Lintscotani Nauigatio in Orientem, Item Regna . . . Moresque Indorum & Lusitanorum Pariter in Oriente Degentium . . . Proponuntur. Ea Lintscotvs . . . Primùm . . . Belgice in Publicum Dedit . . . Nunc . . . Latine . . . Reddita Enunciauit Tevcrides Annævs Lonicervs. Uniform Title: India Orientalis. Pars 2*. Frankfurt: Ex officina W Richteri, 1599.

Cang, Joel. "The Opposition Parties in Poland and Their Attitude Towards the Jews and the Jewish Problem." *Jewish Social Studies* 1, no. 2 (1939): 241–56.

Carlyle, Thomas. *Occasional Discourse on the Nigger Question*. London: Thomas Bosworth, 1853.

Carroll, Charles. *"The Negro a Beast," or, "in the Image of God" . . . The Negro Not the Son of Ham*. St. Louis: American Book and Bible House, 1900.

——. *"The Negro a Beast" or, "in the Image of God"; the Reasoner of the Age, the Revelator of the Century! The Bible as It Is! The Negro and His Relation to the Human Family! . . . The Negro Not the Son of Ham*. Savannah, GA: Thunderbolt, Inc., 1968.

Chabauty, Emmanuel. *Les Juifs, Nos Maîtres!: documents et développements nouveaux sur la question juive.* Paris: Société Générale de Librairie Catholique, 1882.

Chazan, Robert. *Church, State, and Jew in the Middle Ages,* Library of Jewish Studies. New York: Behrman House, 1980.

"Civil Disabilities of the Jews." In *Selections from the Edinburgh Review Comprising the Best Articles in That Journal from Its Commencement to the Present Time,* 667–75. London: Longman, Rees, Orma, Brown, Green, & Longman, 1833.

Coates, Ta-Nehisi. *We Were Eight Years in Power: A Journey through the Obama Era.* New York: Random House Inc, 2017.

*The Commentary Magazine.* 1946–present.

*Coney Island and the Jews: A History of This Development and Success of This Famous Seaside Resort, Together with a Full Account of the Recent Jewish Controversy.* New York: G. W. Carleston & Co., 1879.

"Confusion for Christmas." *The Crisis* 52, no. 12 (1945): 345.

Cotta-Schönberg, Michael von. "Oration 'Cum Bellum Hodie' of Pope Pius II (26 September 1459, Mantua). Edited and Translated by Michael von Cotta-Schönberg. 6th Version. (Orations of Enea Silvio Piccolomini / Pope Pius II; 45)." 2019.

*The Crisis. A Magazine of the NAACP.* 1910–present.

"Cronaca Mensile Italiana." *L'Educatore Israelita* (1873): 149–50.

"The Crum Case." *New York Times,* April 28, 1904, 8.

"Crum Refused a Chair: After a White Lad to Push It Was Refused to the Negro Collector." *New York Times,* August 15, 1905, 1.

"Danger to Nation in Race Prejudice." *New York Times,* March 5, 1911, 5.

Dapper, Olfert. *Description de L'Afrique, contenant les noms, la situation & les confins de toutes ses parties, leurs rivières, leurs villes & leurs habitations, leurs plantes & leurs animaux; les mœurs, les coûtumes, la langue, les richesses, la religion & le gouvernement de ses peuples. avec des cartes des états, des provinces & des villes, & des figures en taille-douce, qui representent les habits & les principales ceremonies des habitans, les plantes & les animaux les moins connus.* Amsterdam: Wolfgang, Waesberge, Boom & van Someren, 1686.

——. *Naukeurige beschrijvinge der Afrikaensche Eylanden: als Madagaskar, of Sant Laurens, Sant Thomee, d'eilanden van Kanarien, Kaep de Verd, Malta, en andere: vertoont in de Benamingen, gelegentheit, Steden, Revieren, Gewassen, Dieren, Zeeden, Drachten, Talen, Rijkdommen, Godsdiensten en Heerschappyen.* T'Amsterdam: Jacob van Meurs, 1668.

——. *Umbständliche und Eigentliche Beschreibung von Africa, Und denen darzu gehörigen Königreichen und Landschaften: als Egypten, Barbarien, Libyen, Biledulgerid, dem Lande der Negros, Guinea, Ethiopien, Abyßina und den Africanischen Insulen: zusamt deren Verschiedenen Nahmen, Grentzen, Städten ... Wobey Die Land-Carten, und Abrisse der Städte, Trachten, [et]c.* Amsterdam: Jacob von Meurs, 1671.

Dapper, Olfert, and John Ogilby. *Africa: Being an Accurate Description of the Regions of Aegypt, Barbary, Lybia, and Billedulgerid, the Land of Negroes, Guinee, Aethiopia, and the Abyssines, with All the Adjacent Islands, Either in the Mediterranean, Atlantick, Southern, or Oriental Sea, Belonging Thereunto ; with the Several Denominations of Their Coasts, Harbors, Creeks, Rivers, Lakes, Cities, Towns,*

*Castles, and Villages; Their Customs, Modes, and Manners, Languages, Religions, and Inexhaustible Treasure; with Their Governments and Policy, Variety of Trade and Barter; and Also of Their Wonderful Plants, Beasts, Birds, and Serpents ; Collected and Translated from Most Authentick Authors, and Augmented with Later Observations; Illustrated with Notes, and Adorn'd with Peculiar Maps, and Proper Sculptures*. London: Johnson, 1670.

*Dénonciation de la secte des Amis des Noirs, par les habitants des colonies françaises.* 1789.

*Diccionario de la lengua castellana, en que se explica el verdadero sentido de las voces, su naturaleza y calidad, con las phrases o modos de hablar, los proverbios o refranes, y otras cosas convenientes al uso de la lengua.* Madrid: En la Imprenta de la Real Academia Española: Por la viudad de Francisco del Hierro, 1732.

"Did Not Use Position to Boom Club, Dewey: State Librarian's Defense against Charges of Jews." *New York Times*, January 24, 1905, 5.

Douglass, Frederick. "The Claims of the Negro Ethnologically Considered (1854)." In *The Portable Frederick Douglass*. New York: Penguin Classics, 2016.

———. "Lessons of the Hour (1894)." In *The Portable Frederick Douglass*. New York: Penguin Classics, 2016.

———. *My Bondage and My Freedom*. New York; Auburn: Miller, Orton & Mulligan, 1855.

———. *The Portable Frederick Douglass*. New York: Penguin Classics, 2016.

———. "A Suggestion." *National Republican*, April 19, 1876, 4. https://chroniclingamerica .loc.gov/lccn/sn86053573/1876-04-19/ed-1/seq-4/

"Dr. Wise Attacks Fifth Avenue Clubs." *New York Times*, May 22, 1911, 5.

Drumont, Édouard. *La France juive: devant l'opinion*. Paris: C. Marpon & E. Flammarion, 1886.

Du Bois, W. E. B. *Black Reconstruction in America: Toward a History of the Part Which Black Folk Played in the Attempt to Reconstruct Democracy in America, 1860–1880*. New York: Taylor & Francis, 2017.

———. "Dusk of Dawn." In *Writings*. New York: Literary Classics of the United States, 2007.

Ely, Ezra Stiles. *The Duty of Christian Freemen to Elect Christian Rulers. A Discourse [on Ps. II. 10–12] Delivered on the Fourth of July, 1827*. Philadelphia, 1828.

Eze, Emmanuel Chukwudi. *Race and the Enlightenment: A Reader*. Cambridge, MA: Blackwell, 1997.

Farmer, James, and James W. Ivy. "Jim Crow Rents a Pew." *The Crisis* 53, no. 6 (1946): 170–72.

Fleury, Claude. *Les moeurs des Israélites*. Paris: Veuve G. Clouzier, 1681.

Forman, Jerome. *Graphic History of Antisemitism*. Atglen, PA: Schiffer Publishing, 2014.

"Georgia Mob of 20 Men Massacres 2 Negroes, Wives." *New York Times*, July 27, 1946, 1.

Gil, Franciszek. "Powrót z Kielc." In *Przeciw antysemityzmowi 1936–2009*, edited by Adam Michnik, 104–15. Cracow: Universitas, 2010.

"Giovanni XXIII: 'Io Sono Giuseppe, Il Vostro Fratello.'" *L'Osservatore Romano*, October 19, 1960.

Goldberg, Jacob. *Jewish Privileges in the Polish Commonwealth: Charters of Rights Granted to Jewish Communities in Poland-Lithuania in the Sixteenth to Eighteenth*

*Centuries*. 3 vols. Jerusalem: The Israel Academy of Sciences and Humanities, 1985–2001.

Goodnough, Abby. "Harvard Professor Jailed; Officer Is Accused of Bias." *New York Times*, July 21, 2009.

Gorham, Thelma Thurston. "Negroes and Japanese Evacuees." *The Crisis* 52, no. 11 (1945): 314–16.

Grabski, Stanisław. "Groźna przestroga." In *Przeciw Antysemityzmowi 1936–2009*, edited by Adam Michnik, 101–3. Cracow: Universitas, 2010.

Grayzel, Solomon. *The Church and the Jews in the XIIIth Century: A Study of Their Relations During the Years 1198–1254*. Philadelphia: The Dropsie College, 1933.

Grégoire, Henri. *De la littérature des nègres, ou recherches sur leurs facultés intellectuelles, leurs qualités morales et leur littérature: suivies de notices sur la vie et les ouvrages des nègres qui se sont distingués dans les sciences, les lettres et les arts*. Paris: Maradan, 1808.

——. *Mémoire en faveur des gens de couleur ou sang-mêlés de St. Domingue, & des autres isles françoises de l'Amérique, adressé à l'Assemblée Nationale*. Paris: Belin, 1789.

——. *Essai sur la régénération physique, morale et politique des Juifs*. Metz: Claude Lamort, 1789.

Hampton, Ruth. "The Negro Soldier." *New York Times*, April 7, 1911, 12.

*Harper's Weekly, A Journal of Civilization*. 1857–1916.

Hartley, L. P. *The Go-Between*. London: Hamish Hamilton, 1953.

Hatcher, George. "Rural Vote Gave Talmadge Victory in Georgia Test: Few Negroes Outside Chief Urban Centers Appear to Have Cast Ballots in Primary First Negro Vote." *New York Times*, July 21, 1946, 1.

"The Hebrew Controversy." *New York Times*, July 19, 1877, 5.

"The Hebrew Controversy." *New York Times*, July 22, 1877, 2.

Heim, Joe. "Recounting a Day of Rage, Hate, Violence and Death." *Washington Post*, August 14, 2017, Online Archive.

Hening, William Waller, ed. *The Statutes at Large: Being a Collection of All the Laws of Virginia, from the First Session of the Legislature, in the Year 1619*. Vol. 4. Richmond: Franklin Press, 1820.

"Henry Hilton Is Dead: Suffered a Relapse and Expired at Saratoga." *New York Times*, August 25, 1899, 1.

Hoch, Marie Therese, and Bernard Dominique Dupuy. *Les Eglises devant le Judaisme: documents officiels, 1948–1978*. Paris: Editions du Cerf, 1980.

"Hotel Discrimination: The Right to Refure Applicants." *New York Times*, June 20 1877, 1.

The Human Rights Watch. *A Threshold Crossed: Israeli Authorities and the Crimes of Apartheid and Persecution*. Online report, 2021.

Hunt, Lynn. *The French Revolution and Human Rights: A Brief History with Documents*. Boston, New York: Bedford/St. Martin's, 2016.

"'I Am American': Black Americans Use Social Media to Respond to McConnell's Comments on Voting," *Washington Post*, January 21, 2022.

"An Interview with Mr. Hilton." *New York Times*, July 19, 1877, 5.

"The Israelites of South Carolina." *Occident and American Jewish Advocate* 2, no. 10 (1845): 496–511.

Jahoda, Marie. "An Enemy of the People: Anti-Semitism; and the Jewish Problem in the Modern World, by James Parkes." *The Commentary*, January 1947, Online Archive.

Jerome, Saint. *The Homilies of Saint Jerome, Volume 1 (1–59 on the Psalms)*, The Fathers of the Church. Washington, DC: Catholic University of America Press, 1964.

"Jews Protest Aid by State for Club." *New York Times*, November 7, 1930, 25.

*John Tyler Morgan and Edmund Winston Pettus (Late Senators from Alabama): Memorial Addresses, Sixtieth Congress, First Session, Senate of the United States, April 18, 1908, House of Representatives, April 25, 1908.* Washington, DC: United States Government Printing Office, 1909.

Johnson, John H. "Publisher's Statement." *Ebony*, August 1965, 27–28.

"Judge Hilton's Course Sustained." *New York Times*, June 21, 1877, 8.

"Judge Hilton's Position: The Step He Has Taken Was Forced Upon Him." *New York Times*, June 20, 1877, 1.

"Judge Hilton's Statement," *New York Times*, June 19, 1877, 1.

King, Martin Luther, Jr. "The Negro Is Your Brother: A Letter from a Birmingham Jail." *The Atlantic Monthly*, 1963.

Kula, Witold. "Nasza w tym rola (głos pesymisty)." In *Przeciw antysemityzmowi 1936–2009*, edited by Adam Michnik, 141–51. Cracow: Universitas, 2010.

La Créquinière, De. *The Agreement of the Customs of the East-Indians, with Those of the Jews, and Other Ancient People: Being the First Essay of This Kind, Towards the Explaining of Several Difficult Passages in Scripture, and Some of the Most Ancient Writers*. London: Printed for W. Davis, 1705.

*L'esclavage des Nègres aboli ou moyens d'améliorer leur sort*. Paris: Froullé, 1789.

La Fare, Anne-Louis-Henri de. *Opinion de M. l'évêque de Nancy, député de Lorraine, sur l'admissibilité des Juifs à la plénitude de l'état-civil, et des droits de citoyens actifs*. Paris: Librarie au Palace Marchand, 1790.

Lake Placid Club. *Handbook, 1914*. Lake Placid, NY: Lake Placid Club, 1914.

——. *Lake Placid Club, Organized 1895 Morningside, Moose Island, Adirondack Lodge, 'Heart of the Adirondacks': Handbook*. Morningside, NY, 1901.

"Lake Placid Club Ends Olympic Row: Citizens of Village Make Peace with Jewish Tribune—Slide Deeded to Township." *New York Times*, December 4, 1930, 50.

Lane, Layle. "The Land of the Noble Free." *The Crisis* 46, no. 7 (1939): 207–9, 210.

Lawrence, W. H. "Poles Declare Two Hoaxes Caused High Toll in Pogrom." *New York Times*, July 6, 1946, 1.

——. "Poles Kill 26 Jews in Kielce Pogrom." *New York Times*, July 5, 1946, 1.

Laws, Clarence A. "Nine Couragous Students." *The Crisis* 65, no. 5 (1958): 267–72, 318.

*Le Code Noir ou Edit du Roy: servant de reglement pour le gouvernement & l'administration de la justice, police, discipline & le commerce des esclaves negres, dans la province & colonie de la Louisianne. donné à Versailles au mois de Mars 1724*. Paris: De l'Imprimerie royale, 1727.

Levy, Richard S. *Antisemitism in the Modern World: An Anthology of Texts*. Lexington, MA; Toronto: D. C. Heath and Company, 1991.

Lewis, Taylor. "6 Times President Obama Honestly Shared His Own Experiences with Racism." *Essence*, October 27, 2020.

"Librarians Annual Meeting in the Adirondacks of the New York State Assotiation: "Library Week" Established." *New York Times*, September 29, 1900, BR16.

"Limited Sovereignty in the United States." *The Atlantic*, February 1879.

Linder, Amnon. *The Jews in the Legal Sources of the Early Middle Ages*. Detroit: Wayne State University Press, 1997.

——. *The Jews in Roman Imperial Legislation*. Detroit, MI; Jerusalem: Wayne State University Press; Israel Academy of Sciences and Humanities, 1987.

*Life Magazine*. 1883–1972.

Loeffler, James. "Charlottesville Was Only a Preview." *Atlantic*, December 23, 2021.

Lomax, Louis. "The White Liberal." In *The White Problem in America*, edited by editors of *Ebony*, 39–46. Chicago: Johnson, 1966.

"Look to America to Lead for Peace: Our Cosmopolitan Population Makes It Incumbent on Us, Many Pastors Assert. Here for Mohonk Meeting Dean of Worcester Says the Churches Can Do Much to Aid in the Movement to End War." *New York Times* May 23, 1911, 10.

Lopez, Duarte, Filippo Pigafetta, and Marten Everart. *Beschryvinge van 't Koningkrijck Congo, met 't aenpalende landt Angola. Zijnde het tweede deel van de Goudt-Kust*. Amstelredam: voor Joost Hartgers, 1650.

Luther, Martin. *De Iudaeis et eorum mendaciis*. Translated by Justus Jonas. Francofurti: Expressit Petrus Brubachius, 1544.

——. *Dr. Martin Luther's Sämmtliche Werke*. Edited by Johann Conrad Irmischer and Johann Georg Plochmann. Erlangen: C. Heyder, 1826–1857.

——. *Von den Juden und iren Lugen. D.M. Luth. zum Andernmal gedruckt, und mehr dazu gethan. M.D. XLIII*. Wittemberg: durch Hans Lufft, 1543.

Luther, Martin, and Ludwig Fischer. *Dr. Martin Luther von den Jüden und ihren Lügen: Ein crystallisirter Auszug aus dessen Schriften über der Juden Verblendung, Jammer, Bekehrung und Zukunft: Ein Beitrag zur Charakteristik dieses Volks*. Leipzig: B. Tauchnitz, 1838.

"Lynchings Declared 'Blot on Whole U.S.'" *New York Times*, July 28, 1946, 12.

Magnard, Francis. "Echoes de Paris: La Politique." *Le Figaro*, April 19 1886.

Marees, Pieter de. *Beschryvinge Ende Historische Verhael, Vant Gout Koninckrijck Van Gunea*. Amsterdam: ghedruct by C Claesz, 1602.

——. *Beschryvinge Van de Goudt-Kust Guinea*. Amsterdam: Joost Hartgers, 1650.

Marr, Wilhelm. *Der Sieg des Judenthums über das Germanenthum: vom nicht confessionellen Standpunkt aus Betrachtet*. Bern: Rudolph Costenoble, 1879.

Marrus, Michael Robert. *The Nuremberg War Crimes Trial, 1945–46: A Brief History with Documents*. Boston, New York: Bedford/St. Martin's, 2018.

Mazowiecki, Tadeusz. "Antisemitism of Good and Gentle People." In *Against Anti-Semitism: An Anthology of Twentieth-Century Polish Writings*, edited by Adam Michnik, 170–87. Oxford: Oxford University Press, 2018.

——. "Antysemityzm ludzi łagodnych i dobrych." In *Przeciw antysemityzmowi 1936–2009*, edited by Adam Michnik, 471–90. Cracow: Universitas, 2010.

McLaurin, John L. "McLaurin on Race Problem: South Carolina Ex-Senator Says Crisis Is Near, Crum Case." *New York Times*, September 12, 1904, 8.

Mendes-Flohr, Paul R., and Jehuda Reinharz. *The Jew in the Modern World*. 3rd ed. Oxford, NY: Oxford University Press, 2011.

Michnik, Adam, ed. *Against Anti-Semitism: An Anthology of Twentieth-Century Polish Writings*. Translated by Agnieszka Marczyk. Oxford: Oxford University Press, 2018.

———. "Pogrom kielecki: dwa rachunki sumienia." In *Przeciw antysemityzmowi 1936–2009*, edited by Adam Michnik, 152–84. Cracow: Universitas, 2010.

———. *Przeciw antysemityzmowi, 1936–2009*. 3 vols. Kraków: Universitas, 2010.

Miller, Jan Napomucen. "Dyplomatyczna Drzemka." In *Przeciw antysemityzmowi 1936–2009*, edited by Adam Michnik, 70–71. Cracow: Universitas, 2010.

Mommsen, Theodor. *Auch ein Wort über unser Judenthum*. Berlin: Weidmann, 1880.

Morgan, John Tyler. "Shall Negro Majorities Rule?" *The Forum* February, (1889): 586–99.

"Mosessohn Disputes Dewey's Club Reply." *New York Times*, November 8, 1930, 3.

Münster, Sebastian. *Cosmographey oder Beschreibung aller Lander, Herrschafften, fürnem[b]sten Stetten, Geschichten, Gebreüche[n], Handtierungen*. Basel: Henri Petri, 1567.

———. *Cosmographia: Beschreibung aller Lender durch Sebastianum Münsterum: in welcher begriffen aller Voelker, Herrschaften, Stetten, und namhafftiger Flecken, herkommen: Sitten, Gebreüch, Ordnung, Glauben, Secten und Hantierung durch die gantze Welt und fürnemlich Teütscher Nation*. Basel: Getruckt durch Henrichum Petri, 1544.

Muszyński, Abp Henryk Józef. *Początek wspólnej drogi: Dialog katolicko-żydowski w Polsce w latach 1986–1994*. Gniezno: Pelplin, 2015.

Nast, Thomas. "Chinese Question," *Harper's Weekly*, February 18, 1871, 149.

———. "'Religious Liberty Is Guaranteed: But Can We Allow Foreign Reptiles to Crawl All over Us?'": Library of Congress, 1870s–1890s.

"Negro Colonel 'Stirs San Antonio Camp." *New York Times*, April 5, 1911, 3.

"Negro Troops Will Go to Brownsville." *New York Times*, April 6, 1911, 2.

"Negroes, Nazis and Jews," *The Crisis* 45, no. 12 (December 1938): 393.

Neumann, Franz. "Re-Educating the Germans: The Dilemma of Reconstruction." *The Commentary*, June 1947, Online Archive.

Obama, Barack. *Dreams of My Father*. New York: Three Rivers Press, 2005.

———. "Remarks by the President on Trayvon Martin." In *Office of the Press Secretary*, edited by The White House, July 19, 2013.

*Observations pour servir de réponse aux différens faits avancés par les prétendus Amis des Noirs, et notamment une lettre du 4 Janvier 1790, qui se trouve dans le supplément du Journal de Paris, du 13 dudit mois. Par les Capitaines du Havre-de-Grâce, navigans à la Côte D'Afrique*. Paris: Impr. de P.-F. Didot jeune, 1790.

Oesterreicher, John M. *The New Encounter: Between Christians and Jews*. New York: Philosophical Library, 1986.

Osmańczyk, Edmund Jan. "Antypolonizm." In *Przeciw Antysemityzmowi 1936–2009*, edited by Adam Michnik, 129–40. Cracow: Universitas, 2010.

Ossowski, Stanisław. "Na tle wydarzeń kieleckich." In *Przeciw Antysemityzmowi 1936–2009*, edited by Adam Michnik, 116–28. Cracow: Universitas, 2010.

Paulus, Heinrich Eberhard. *Die Jüdische Nationalabsonderung nach Ursprung, Folgen und Besserungsmitteln: oder über Pflichten, Rechte und Verordnungen zur Verbesserung der jüdischen Schutzbürgerschaft in Teutschland*. Heidelberg,1831.

Pellatt, Apsley, and Joseph Hume. *Brief Memoir of the Jews in Relation to Their Civil and Municipal Disabilities: With an Appendix Containing the Jews' Petition to Oliver Cromwell, the Russian Ukase and Ordinance of the King of Wurtemberg*

*Affecting the Civil and Religious Liberty of the Hebrew Nation*. London: Printed for Hatchard and Son . . . by Richard Taylor, 1829.

"A Pending Combination: Hotel-Keepers' Union." *New York Times*, June 23, 1878, 12.

Penn, William. "An Act for Freedom of Conscience." 1682.

——. "Charter of Privileges Granted by William Penn, Esquire, to the Inhabitants of Pennsylvania and Territories October 28, 1701."

"The People vs. Discrimination." *Commentary Magazine*, March, 1946, Online Archive.

Pergamini, Giacomo. *Il memoriale della lingua italiana*. In Venetia: Gio. Battista Ciotti, 1617.

Perman, Michael, and Amy Murrell Taylor. *Major Problems in the Civil War and Reconstruction: Documents and Essays*. Boston: Houghton Mifflin Co., 2011.

Peter the Venerable. *Against the Inveterate Obduracy of Jews*. Translated by Irven M. Resnick. Washington, DC: Catholic University of America Press, 2013.

Pettibone, Rufus, and Henry Sheffie Geyer. *Laws of the State of Missouri: Revised and Digested by Authority of the General Assembly*. 2 vols. Vol. 2. St. Louis: E. Charles, 1825.

Picart, Bernard, and Jean-Frédéric Bernard. *Cérémonies et coutumes religieuses de tous les peuples du monde: Représentées par des figures*. Amsterdam: Chez J. F. Bernard, 1723.

Pierce, David. "Letters," *The Crisis* 46, no. 3 (March 1939), 90–91.

"Poles in Palestine to Hold Memorial for Executed." *Jewish Post*, July 26, 1946, 5.

"Polish Army in Scotland Calls 9 Executed Pogromists 'Martyrs.'" *Jewish Post*, July 26th, 1946, 5.

"A Polish Pastoral Letter on the Jews." *New York Times*, January 20, 1991, Online Archive.

Preece, Harold. "The Klan's 'Revolution of the Right.'" *The Crisis* 53, no. 7 (1946): 202–3, 219.

Przyboś, Julian. "Hańba antysemitizmu." In *Przeciw antysemityzmowi 1936–2009*, edited by Adam Michnik, 225–27. Cracow: Universitas, 2010.

Rawlin, William. *The Laws of Barbados, Collected in One Volume, by William Rawlin, of the Middle-Temple, London, Esquire. And Now Clerk of the Assembly of the Said Island*. London: printed for William Rawlin, Esq., 1699.

Riemer, Jeremiah, *German History in Documents and Images*. Online resource: http:// ghdi.ghi-dc.org/sub_document.cfm?document_id=341.

Riesser, Gabriel. *Vertheidigung der bürgerlichen Gleichstellung der Juden: gegen die Einwürfe des Herrn. Dr. H.E.G. Paulus : den gesetzgebenden Versammlungen Deutschlands gewidmet*. Altona: In Commission bei J. F. Hammerich, 1831.

"A Reply to Judge Hilton." *New York Times*, June 20, 1877, 1.

"Report of the U.S. Secretary of the Interior." edited by United States Department of the Interior. Washington: Government Printing Office, 1895.

Ripa, Cesare. *Della novissima iconologia*. Padova: P. P. Tozzi, 1625.

——. *Iconologia, of uitbeeldinge des verstands*. t'Amsterdam: By Timotheus ten Hoorn, boekverkoper in de Nes, in 't Sinnebeelt, 1699.

——. *Iconologia: Or, Moral Emblems: By Caesar Ripa Wherein Are Express'd, Various Images of Virtues, Vices, Passions, Arts, Humours, Elements and Celestial Bodies ; as Design'd by the Ancient Egyptians, Greeks, Romans, and Modern Italians: Useful for Orators, Poets, Painters, Sculptors, and All Lovers of Ingenuity: Illustrated with Three Hundred Twenty-Six Humane Figures, with Their Explanations ; Newly Design'd, and Engraven on Copper, by I. Fuller, Painter, and Other Masters. By the Care and A.* London: Printed by Benj. Motte, 1709.

———. *Iconologia ouero descrittione di diuerse imagini cauate dall' antichità, & di propria inuentione, trouate, & dichiarate da Cesare Ripa . . . di nuouo reuista, & dal medesimo ampliata di 400 & più imagini.* Roma: Appresso Lepido Facij, 1603.

Ripa, Cesare, and Cornelis Danckertsz. *Iconologia, of uytbeeldinge des verstands: waar in verscheiden afbeeldingen van deugden, ondeugden . . . werden verhandelt.* t' Amsteldam: uytgegeven door Cornelis Danckerts#voor aan op de Nieuwendyck in den Atlas, 1700.

Ripa, Cesare, Giovanni Zaratino Castellini, and Dirck Pietersz Pers. *Iconologia of uytbeeldingen des verstands: waer in verscheiden afbeeldingen van deughden, ondeughden . . . werden verhandelt . . . : een werck dat dienstigh is . . . ook om te spreecken, van allerley toerustingen, 't zy op bruyloften . . . en zeegefeesten.* Amstelredam: D. P. Pers, 1644.

Robbins, Christopher. "Upper West Side Uproar as City Tries to Diversify Schools." *The Gothamist,* May 1, 2018, Online.

Rockwell, George Lincoln. *White Power.* Dallas: Ragnarok Press, 1967.

Rolyat, Mailliw J. "Extra! Jews at Manhattan Beach," New York: s.n., 1879, Division of Rare and Manuscripts Collection, Cornell University.

"Say Dewey Offered to Quit Club Office." *New York Times,* February 3, 1905, 3.

Schuster, Zachariah. "Between the Millstones in Poland: The Jews of Poland Are on the March." *Commentary Magazine,* August 1946, Online Archive.

*Selections from the Edinburgh Review Comprising the Best Articles in That Journal from Its Commencement to the Present Time.* London: Longman, Rees, Orma, Brown, Green, & Longman, 1833.

"A Sensation at Saratoga: New Rules for the Grand Union." *New York Times,* June 19 1877, 1.

Sherman, Franklin. *Bridges: Documents of the Christian-Jewish Dialogue.* 2 vols. Vol. 1. New York: Paulist Press, 2011.

Sieyès, Emmanuel-Joseph. *Préliminaire de la constitution françoise. reconnoissance et exposition raisonnée des droits de l'homme et du citoyen. par M. l'abbé Sieyès.* Paris: Baudouin, 1789.

Silvain, Gérard, Joël Kotek, and Marie-Anne Matard-Bonucci. *La carte postale antisémite: de l'affaire Dreyfus à la Shoah.* Paris: Berg International Editeurs, 2005.

Sirkes, Joel. *Beit ḥadash (he-yeshanot)* in Bar-Ilan Responsa Project.

*Smith v. Allwright.* In 321 U.S. 649, 1944.

"State Librarian Dewey Is Rebuked by Regents." *New York Times,* February 16, 1905, 1.

*Statement of the Civil Disabilities and Privations Affecting Jews in England.* London: G. Taylor, printer, 1829.

"Statement of the Civil Disabilities and Privations Affecting Jews in England." *Edinburgh Review* 52 (1830): 363–74.

Sutcliffe, Matthew. *A Treatise of Ecclesiastical Discipline: Wherein That Confused Forme of Government, Which Certeine . . . Do Strive to Bring into the Church of England, Is Examined, Etc.* London: G. Bishop, 1590.

Tanner, Norman P. *Decrees of the Ecumenical Councils*. London, Washington, DC: Sheed & Ward, Georgetown University Press, 1990.

Tertullian, and Hermann Tränkle. *Q. S. F. Tertulliani Adversus Iudaeos*. Wiesbaden: F. Steiner, 1964.

Thomas, Brook. *Plessy v. Ferguson: A Brief History with Documents*. Boston, New York: Bedford Books, 1997.

Thomas, Will. "Hill to Climb." *The Crisis* 53, no. 6 (1946): 173–74.

Timayenis, T. T., and Edward R. Fields. *The Jew Comes to America: An Exposé of His Career, Profusely Illustrated*. Savannah, GA: Thunderbolt, 1960s.

"Topics of the Times: 'A Theory Confronts a Condition.'" *New York Times*, April 5, 1911, 8.

Trant, William. "Jew and Chinaman." *North American Review* 195, no. 675 (1912): 249–60.

Treitschke, Heinrich von. *Ein Wort über unser Judentum*. Berlin: Reimer, 1880.

Tuwim, Julian, and Madeline G. Levine. "'We, the Polish Jews . . .'" *The Polish Review* 17, no. 4 (1972): 82–89.

Van der Zee, James, and Deborah Willis-Braithwaite. *Van Der Zee: Photographer, 1886–1983*. New York: Harry N. Abrams, 1993.

Van Evrie, John H. *Negroes and Negro "Slavery": The First an Inferior Race; the Latter Its Normal Condition*. Baltimore: J.D. Toy, Printer, 1853.

———. *Negroes and Negro Slavery: The First, an Inferior Race: The Latter, Its Normal Condition*. New York: Van Evrie, Horton, 1861.

"Vatican II and the Jews." *The Commentary*, January, 1965, Online Archive.

The Vatican Commission for Religious Relations with the Jews, "'The Gifts and the Calling of God Are Irrevocable' (Rom 11:29): A Reflection on Theological Questions Pertaining to Catholic-Jewish Relations on the Occasion of the 50th Anniversary of Nostra aetate (No. 4)." December 10, 2020.

———. "Guidelines and Suggestions for Implementing the Conciliar Declaration Nostra aetate, No. 4," December 1, 1974.

———. "Notes on the Correct Way to Present the Jews and Judaism in Preaching and Catechesis in the Roman Catholic Church," June 24, 1985.

———. "We Remember: A Reflection on the Shoah," March 16, 1998.

von Hundt-Radowsky, Hartwig. *Judenspiegel. Schand- und Sittengemälde alter und neuer Zeit*. Reutlingen: Enßlin, 1821.

"W. D. Crum Confirmed: Senate Acts after Debate on Question of Constructive Recesses." *New York Times*, January 7, 1905, 5.

"Walter White Scores Persecution of Jews," *The Crisis* 45, no. 12 (December 1938): 399–400.

Wesley, Charles H. "Creating and Maintaining an Historical Tradition." *Journal of Negro History* 49, no. 1 (1964): 13–33.

———. "The Negro Has Always Wanted the Four Freedoms." In *What the Negro Wants*, edited by Rayford W. Logan, 90–112. Chapel Hill: University of North Carolina Press, 1944.

"White Racialism in America," *The Crisis* 46, no.10 (October, 1938): 308.

Wilkins, Roy. "The Negro Wants Full Equality." In *What the Negro Wants*, edited by Rayford W. Logan, 113–32. Chapel Hill: University of North Carolina Press, 1944.

Willis, Deborah, and David Levering Lewis. *A Small Nation of People: W. E. B. Du Bois and African American Portraits of Progress*. New York: Amistad, 2003.

Wolf, Nahum. "Are the Jews an Inferior Race?" *The North American Review* 195, no. 677 (1912): 492–95.

"Would Abolish Negro Votes: Georgia Representative Wants Fourteenth Amendment Repealed." *New York Times*, April 15, 1911, 5.

Wyka, Kazimierz. "Potęga ciemnoty potwierdzona." In *Przeciw antysemityzmowi 1936-2009*, edited by Adam Michnik, 29–34. Cracow: Universitas, 2010.

"Wyznanie Żyda." In *Przeciw antysemityzmowi 1936-2009*, edited by Adam Michnik, 297–300. Cracow: Universitas, 2010.

Zola, Gary Phillip, and Marc Dollinger. *American Jewish History: A Primary Source Reader*. Waltham: Brandeis University Press, 2014.

## Secondary Sources

"The 1619 Project." *New York Times Magazine*, August 18, 2019.

Achinger, Christine, and Robert Fine. *Antisemitism, Racism and Islamophobia: Distorted Faces of Modernity*. London: Routledge, 2017.

Adiele, Pius Onyemechi. *The Popes, the Catholic Church and the Transatlantic Enslavement of Black Africans 1418–1839*. Hildesheim, Zürich, New York: Georg Olms Verlag, 2017.

Alpert, Michael. "The French Enlightenment and the Jews: An Essay by the Abbe Grégoire." *Patterns of Prejudice* 31, no. 1 (1997): 31–41.

Ariel, Yaakov. *An Unusual Relationship: Evangelical Christians and Jews*. New York: NYU Press, 2013.

Aron, Cindy Sondik. *Working at Play: A History of Vacations in the United States*. New York: Oxford University Press, 2001.

Aronson, Irwin Michael. *Troubled Waters: The Origins of the 1881 Anti-Jewish Pogroms in Russia*. Pittsburgh, PA: University of Pittsburgh Press, 1990.

Ashbrook Harvey, Susan. "On Holy Stench: When the Odor of Sanctity Sickens." *Studia Patristica* 25, (2001): 90–101.

Ashton, Mark. "Allegory, Fact, and Meaning in Giambattista Tiepolo's Four Continents in Würzburg." *Art Bulletin* 60, no. 1 (1978): 109–25.

Bajohr, Frank. *"Unser Hotel ist judenfrei": Bäder-Antisemitismus im 19. und 20. Jahrhundert*. Frankfurt am Main: Fischer Taschenbuch Verlag, 2003.

Bale, Anthony Paul. *The Jew in the Medieval Book: English Antisemitisms, 1350–1500*. Cambridge, UK; New York, US: Cambridge University Press, 2006.

Baron, Salo Wittmayer. "Ghetto and Emancipation." *Menorah Journal* 14 (1928): 515–26.

Bauer, Yehuda. *Rethinking the Holocaust*. New Haven: Yale University Press, 2001.

Ben-Ur, Aviva. "The Cultural Heritage of Eurafrican Sephardi Jews in Suriname." In *The Jews in the Caribbean*, edited by Jane S. Gerber, 169–94. London: The Littman Library of Jewish Civilization, 2018.

Bernasconi, Robert. "Racism." In *Key Concepts in the Study of Antisemitism*, edited by Sol Goldberg, Scott Ury and Keith Ian Weiser, 245–56. Basingstoke: Palgrave Macmillan, 2020.

Biess, Frank. "Between Amnesty and Anti-Communism: The West German Kameradenschinder Trials, 1948–1960." In *Crimes of War: Guilt and Denial in the*

*Twentieth Century*, edited by Omer Bartov, Atina Grossman and Mary Nolan. New York: Norton, 2003.

Bindman, David. "Introduction." In *The Image of the Black in Western Art, Volume 3: From the "Age of Discovery" to the Age of Abolition, Part 3: The Eighteenth Century*, edited by David Bindman and Henry Louis Gates, 1–16. 5 vols. Cambridge, MA: Belknap Press of Harvard University Press, 2011.

Bindman, David, Bruce Boucher, and Helen Weston. "Africa and the Slave Trade." In *The Image of the Black in Western Art, Volume 3: From the "Age of Discovery" to the Age of Abolition, Part 3: The Eighteenth Century*, edited by David Bindman and Henry Louis Gates, 206–40. 5 vols. Cambridge, MA: Belknap Press of Harvard University Press, 2011.

———. "The Theater of Court and Church: Blacks as Figures of Fantasy." In *The Image of the Black in Western Art, Volume 3: From the "Age of Discovery" to the Age of Abolition, Part 3: The Eighteenth Century*, edited by David Bindman and Henry Louis Gates, 16–76. 5 vols. Cambridge, MA: Belknap Press of Harvard University Press, 2011.

Bindman, David, and Henry Louis Gates. *The Image of the Black in Western Art*. 10 vols. Cambridge, MA: Belknap Press of Harvard University Press, 2010–2014.

Bindman, David, and Henry Louis Gates, eds. *The Image of the Black in Western Art, Volume 2: From the Early Christian Era to the "Age of Discovery," Part 2: Africans in the Christian Ordinance of the World*. 5 vols. Cambridge, MA: Belknap Press of Harvard University Press, 2010.

———, eds. *The Image of the Black in Western Art, Volume 2: From the Early Christian Era to the "Age of Discovery," Part 1: From the Demonic Threat to the Incarnation of Sainthood*. 5 vols. Cambridge, MA: Belknap Press of Harvard University Press, 2010.

———, eds. *The Image of the Black in Western Art, Volume 3: From the "Age of Discovery" to the Age of Abolition," Part 3: The Eighteenth Century*. 5 vols. Cambridge, MA: Belknap Press of Harvard University Press, 2011.

———, eds. *The Image of the Black in Western Art, Volume 3: From the "Age of Discovery" to the Age of Abolition, Part 2: Europe and the World Beyond*. 5 vols. Cambridge, MA: London: Belknap, 2011.

Bindman, David, Henry Louis Gates, Karen C. C. Dalton, and Jean Michel Massing, eds. *From the "Age of Discovery" to the Age of Abolition*. Vol. 3, part 2, of *The Image of the Black in Western Art*. Cambridge, MA: Belknap Press of Harvard University Press, 2011.

Blackburn, Robin. *The Making of New World Slavery: From the Baroque to the Modern, 1492–1800*. London: Verso, 1997.

Blanchard, Peter. "Spanish South American Mainland." In *The Oxford Handbook of Slavery in the Americas*, edited by Robert L. Paquette and Mark M. Smith, 68–89. Oxford: Oxford University Press, 2016.

Blum, Edward J. *Reforging the White Republic: Race, Religion, and American Nationalism 1865–1898*. Baton Rouge: Louisiana State University Press, 2015.

Blum, Edward J., and Paul Harvey. *The Color of Christ: The Son of God and the Saga of Race in America*. Chapel Hill: University of North Carolina Press, 2012.

Blumrosen, Alfred W., Ruth G. Blumrosen, and Steven Blumrosen. *Slave Nation: How Slavery United the Colonies and Sparked the American Revolution*. Naperville, IL: Sourcebooks, 2007.

Boyarin, Daniel. *A Radical Jew: Paul and the Politics of Identity*, Contraversions. Berkeley: University of California Press, 1994.

Bradley, Patricia. *Slavery, Propaganda, and the American Revolution*. Jackson, MS: University Press of Mississippi, 1999.

Brodkin, Karen. *How Jews Became White Folks and What That Says about Race in America*. New Brunswick, NJ: Rutgers University Press, 1998.

Buccola, Nicholas. *The Fire Is Upon Us: James Baldwin, William F. Buckley Jr., and the Debate over Race in America*. Princeton: Princeton University Press, 2019.

Burin, Eric. *Slavery and the Peculiar Solution: A History of the American Colonization Society*. Gainesville: University Press of Florida, 2005.

Burnard, Trevor. "British West Indies and Bermuda." In *The Oxford Handbook of Slavery in the Americas*, edited by Robert L. Paquette and Mark M. Smith, 134–53. Oxford: Oxford University Press, 2016.

Butler, Anthea D. *White Evangelical Racism: The Politics of Morality in America*. Chapel Hill: University of North Carolina Press, 2021.

Byrnes, Robert F. "Edouard Drumont and *La France Juive*." *Jewish Social Studies* 10, no. 2 (1948): 165–84.

Byron, Gay L. *Symbolic Blackness and Ethnic Difference in Early Christian Literature*. London; New York: Routledge, 2008.

Caffiero, Marina. *Battesimi forzati: storie di ebrei, cristiani e convertiti nella Roma dei papi*. Roma: Viella, 2004.

Carney, Julia Fletcher. "Racism and Sexism and Children's Books." *The Crisis* 82, no. 1 (1975): 21–23.

Carter, J. Kameron. *Race: A Theological Account*. Oxford; New York: Oxford University Press, 2008.

Cassen, Flora. *Marking the Jews in Renaissance Italy: Politics, Religion, and the Power of Symbols*. Cambridge, New York: Cambridge University Press, 2017.

Chin, Gabriel Jackson. "Segregation's Last Stronghold: Race Discrimination and the Constitutional Law of Immigration." *UCLA Law Review* 46, no. 1 (1998): 1–74.

Cohen, Jeremy. *Living Letters of the Law: Ideas of the Jew in Medieval Christianity*. Berkeley: University of California Press, 1999.

Cohen, Naomi W. *Jews in Christian America: The Pursuit of Religious Equality*. New York: Oxford University Press, 1992.

Connelly, John. *From Enemy to Brother: The Revolution in Catholic Teaching on the Jews, 1933–1965*. Cambridge, MA: Harvard University Press, 2012.

Cooper, Frank Rudy. "Masculinities, Post-Racialism and the Gates Controversy: The False Equivalence between Officer and Civilian." *Nevada Law Journal* 11, no. 1 (2010): 1–43.

Cousin, Glynis, and Robert Fine. "A Common Cause: Reconnecting the Study of Racism and Antisemitism." In *Antisemitism, Racism and Islamophobia: Distorted Faces of Modernity*, edited by Christine Achinger and Robert Fine, 14–33. London: Routledge, 2017.

Curran, Andrew S. *The Anatomy of Blackness: Science and Slavery in an Age of Enlightenment*. Baltimore: Johns Hopkins University Press, 2011.

Dahl, Curtis. "The Clergyman, the Hussy, and Old Hickory: Ezra Stiles Ely and the Peggy Eaton Affair." *Journal of Presbyterian History (1962-1985)* 52, no. 2 (1974): 137-55.

Davis, David Brion. *The Problem of Slavery in the Age of Emancipation*. New York: Vintage Books, 2015.

———. *The Problem of Slavery in the Age of Revolution, 1770-1823*. New York: Oxford University Press, 1999.

Davis, John H. *The Guggenheims: An America Epic*. New York: S. P. I. Books, 1994.

De la Rosa, Alexandre Coello. "El Estatuto de Limpieza de Sangre de la Compañía de Jesús (1593) y su influencia en el Perú colonial." *Archivum Historicum Societatis Iesu* 80, no. 159 (2011): 45-93.

Delgado, Richard, Jean Stefancic, and Angela P. Harris. *Critical Race Theory: An Introduction*. New York: NYU Press, 2017.

Den Heijer, Henk. "Dutch Caribbean." In *The Oxford Handbook of Slavery in the Americas*, edited by Robert L. Paquette and Mark M. Smith, 154-72. Oxford: Oxford University Press, 2016.

Devisse, Jean. "The Black and His Color: From Symbols to Realities." In *The Image of the Black in Western Art, Volume 2: From the Early Christian Era to the "Age of Discovery," Part 1: From the Demonic Threat to the Incarnation of Sainthood*, edited by David Bindman and Henry Louis Gates, 73-137. 5 vols. Cambridge, MA: Belknap Press of Harvard University Press, 2010.

———. "Christians and Black." In *The Image of the Black in Western Art, Volume 2: From the Early Christian Era to the "Age of Discovery," Part 1: From the Demonic Threat to the Incarnation of Sainthood*, edited by David Bindman and Henry Louis Gates, 31-72. 5 vols. Cambridge, MA: Belknap Press of Harvard University Press, 2010.

Devisse, Jean, and Michel Mollat. "The African Transposed." In *The Image of the Black in Western Art, Volume 2: From the Early Christian Era to the "Age of Discovery," Part 2: Africans in the Christian Ordinance of the World*, edited by David Bindman and Henry Louis Gates, 185-279. 5 vols. Cambridge, MA: Belknap Press of Harvard University Press, 2010.

———. "The Frontiers in 1460." In *The Image of the Black in Western Art, Volume 2: From the Early Christian Era to the "Age of Discovery," Part 2: Africans in the Christian Ordinance of the World*, edited by David Bindman and Henry Louis Gates, 153-84. 5 vols. Cambridge, MA: Belknap Press of Harvard University Press, 2010.

Diner, Hasia R. *The Jews of the United States, 1654 to 2000*. Berkeley: University of California Press, 2004.

Dinnerstein, Leonard. *Antisemitism in America*. New York, Oxford: Oxford University Press, 1995.

Dollinger, Marc. *Black Power, Jewish Politics: Reinventing the Alliance in the 1960s*. Waltham: Brandeis University Press, 2018.

Douglas, Lawrence. *The Memory of Judgment: Making Law and History in the Trials of the Holocaust*. New Haven: Yale University Press, 2001.

Du Bois, W. E. B., Whitney Battle-Baptiste, and Britt Rusert. *W. E. B. Du Bois's Data Portraits Visualizing Black America: The Color Line at the Turn of the Twentieth Century*. Hudson, NY: Princeton Architectural Press, 2018.

Eitches, Edward. "Maryland's 'Jew Bill.'" *American Jewish Historical Quarterly* 60, no. 3 (1971): 258–79.

Espelt-Bombín, Silvia. "Notaries of Color in Colonial Panama: Limpieza de Sangre, "Legislation, and Imperial Practices in the Administration of the Spanish Empire"." *The Americas* 71, no. 1 (2014): 37–69.

Faust, Drew Gilpin. *James Henry Hammond and the Old South: A Design for Mastery.* Baton Rouge: Louisiana State University Press, 2010.

Fehrenbacher, Don E. *The Dred Scott Case: Its Significance in American Law and Politics.* Oxford; New York: Oxford University Press, 2001.

Fields, Barbara J. "Slavery, Race, and Ideology in the United States of America." *New Left Review* 181 (May–June 1990): 95–118.

Finder, Gabriel N., and Alexander Victor Prusin. *Justice Behind the Iron Curtain: Nazis on Trial in Communist Poland.* Toronto: University of Toronto Press, 2018.

Finkelman, Paul. "United States Slave Law." In *The Oxford Handbook of Slavery in the Americas*, edited by Robert L. Paquette and Mark M. Smith, 424–46. Oxford: Oxford University Press, 2016.

Foner, Eric. *A Short History of Reconstruction.* New York: HarperPerennial, 1990.

——. *We Were Eight Years in Power: A Journey through the Obama Era The Second Founding: How the Civil War and Reconstruction Remade the Constitution.* New York: W. W. Norton & Company, 2019.

Francesconi, Federica. *Invisible Enlighteners: The Jewish Merchants of Modena, from the Renaissance to the Emancipation.* Philadelphia: University of Pennsylvania Press, 2021.

Fredrickson, George M. *The Arrogance of Race: Historical Perspectives on Slavery, Racism, and Social Inequality.* Middletown, CT: Wesleyan University Press, 1988.

——. *Racism: A Short History.* Princeton: Princeton University Press, 2002.

Fredriksen, Paula. *Augustine and the Jews: A Christian Defense of Jews and Judaism.* New Haven; London: Yale University Press, 2010.

——. *Paul the Pagan's Apostle.* New Haven; London: Yale University Press, 2017.

Friede, Juan, and Benjamin Keen. *Bartolomé de Las Casas in History: Toward an Understanding of the Man and His Work.* DeKalb, IL: Northern Illinois University Press, 2008.

Gallay, Alan. "Indian Slavery." In *The Oxford Handbook of Slavery in the Americas*, edited by Robert L. Paquette and Mark M. Smith, 312–35. Oxford: Oxford University Press, 2016.

Garnsey, Peter. *Ideas of Slavery from Aristotle to Augustine.* Cambridge: Cambridge University Press, 1996.

Garrigus, John. "French Caribbean." In *The Oxford Handbook of Slavery in the Americas*, edited by Robert L. Paquette and Mark M. Smith, 173–95. Oxford: Oxford University Press, 2016.

Garton Ash, Timothy. *Free World: America, Europe, and the Surprising Future of the West.* New York: Vintage Books, 2005.

Gates, Henry Louis. *Stony the Road: Reconstruction, White Supremacy, and the Rise of Jim Crow.* New York: Penguin, 2019.

Geggus, David. "Racial Equality, Slavery, and Colonial Secession during the Constituent Assembly." *American Historical Review* 94, no. 5 (1989): 1290–1308.

Gerber, Jane S., ed. *The Jews in the Caribbean*. London: The Littman Library of Jewish Civilization, 2018.

Gerbner, Katharine. *Christian Slavery: Conversion and Race in the Protestant Atlantic World*. Philadelphia: University of Pennsylvania Press, 2018.

Goetz, Rebecca Anne. *Baptism of Early Virginia: How Christianity Created Race*. Baltimore: Johns Hopkins University Press, 2016.

Goldenberg, David M. *The Curse of Ham: Race and Slavery in Early Judaism, Christianity, and Islam*. Princeton: Princeton University Press, 2004.

Goldman, Tanya. "The Strange Lives of Leo Hurwitz's *Strange Victory*." *Cinéaste* 44, no. 1 (2018): 37–40.

Goldstein, Eric L. *The Price of Whiteness: Jews, Race, and American Identity*. Princeton: Princeton University Press, 2008.

Golsan, Richard J. *Memory, the Holocaust, and French Justice: The Bousquet and Touvier Affairs*. Hanover, NH: University Press of New England, 1996.

Gonzalez, Aston. *Visualizing Equality: African American Rights and Visual Culture in the Nineteenth Century*. Chapel Hill: University of North Carolina Press, 2020.

Grayzel, Solomon. "The Papal Bull *Sicut Judaeis*." In *Studies and Essays in Honor of Abraham A. Neuman*, edited by Meir Ben-Horin, Bernard D. Weinryb, and Solomon Zeitlin, 243–80. Leiden: Brill, 1962.

Greenberg, Cheryl Lynn. *Troubling the Waters: Black-Jewish Relations in the American Century*. Princeton: Princeton University Press, 2006.

Greene, Harlan, Harry S. Hutchins, and Brian E. Hutchins. *Slave Badges and the Slave-Hire System in Charleston, South Carolina, 1783–1865*. Jefferson NC: McFarland, 2008.

Greene, Larry A. "Race in the Reich: The African American Press on Nazi Germany." In *Germans and African Americans: Two Centuries of Exchange*, edited by Larry A. Greene and Anke Ortlepp. Jackson: University Press of Mississippi, 2010.

Gross, Jan Tomasz. *Fear: Anti-Semitism in Poland after Auschwitz: An Essay in Historical Interpretation*. New York: Random House, 2006.

——. *Neighbors: The Destruction of the Jewish Community in Jedwabne, Poland*: Penguin Books, 2002.

HaCohen, Ruth. *The Music Libel against the Jews*. New Haven: Yale University Press, 2011.

Hagy, James William. *This Happy Land: The Jews of Colonial and Antebellum Charleston*. Tuscaloosa: University of Alabama Press, 1992.

Haney López, Ian. *White by Law: The Legal Construction of Race*. New York: New York University Press, 2006.

Hannah-Jones, Nikole, ed. *The 1619 Project: A New Origin Story*. New York: One Word, 2021.

Harlow, Luke E. *Religion, Race, and the Making of Confederate Kentucky, 1830–1880*, Cambridge Studies on the American South: Cambridge University Press, 2014.

Heckman, Alma Rachel, and Frances Malino. "Packed in Twelve Cases: The Alliance Israélite Universelle and the 1893 Chicago World's Fair." *Jewish Social Studies* 19, no. 1 (2012): 53–69.

Heng, Geraldine. *England and the Jews: How Religion and Violence Created the First Racial State in the West*. Cambridge: Cambridge University Press, 2019.

——. *The Invention of Race in the European Middle Ages*. Cambridge: Cambridge University Press, 2019.

Hess, Jonathan M. *Germans, Jews, and the Claims of Modernity*. New Haven: Yale University Press, 2002.

Hill Fletcher, Jeannine. *The Sin of White Supremacy: Christianity, Racism, and Religious Diversity in America*. Maryknoll: Orbis Books, 2017.

Hoffmann, Christhard, Werner Bergmann, and Helmut Smith. *Exclusionary Violence: Antisemitic Riots in Modern German History*. Ann Arbor: University of Michigan Press, 2002.

Hughes, Richard T., Robert N. Bellah, and Molefi Kete Asante. *Myths America Lives By: White Supremacy and the Stories That Give Us Meaning*. Champaign: University of Illinois Press, 2018.

Hunt, Lynn, Margaret C. Jacob, and Wijnand Mijnhardt. *The Book That Changed Europe: Picart and Bernard's Religious Ceremonies of the World*. Cambridge, MA: Belknap Press, 2010.

Hunt, Lynn, Margaret Jacob, and Wijnand Mijnhardt. *Bernard Picart and the First Global Vision of Religion*. Los Angeles: The Getty research Institute, 2010.

Isaac, Benjamin H. *The Invention of Racism in Classical Antiquity*. Princeton, NJ: Princeton University Press, 2006.

Jennings, Lawrence. *French Anti-Slavery: The Movement for the Abolition of Slavery in France, 1802–1848*. Cambridge: Cambridge University Press, 2000.

Jones, Martha S. *Birthright Citizens: A History of Race and Rights in Antebellum America*. Cambridge: Cambridge University Press, 2018.

Jones, Robert P. *White Too Long: The Legacy of White Supremacy in American Christianity*. New York: Simon & Schuster, 2021.

Jordan, Winthrop D. *White over Black: American Attitudes toward the Negro, 1550–1812*. 2nd ed. Chapel Hill, NC: University of North Carolina Press, 2012.

Judaken, Jonathan. "Anti-Semitism (Historiography)." edited by Sol Goldberg, Scott Ury, and Keith Ian Weiser, 25–38. Basingstoke: Palgrave Macmillan, 2020.

Judge, Edward H. *Easter in Kishinev: Anatomy of a Pogrom*. New York: NYU Press, 1992.

Judt, Tony. *Postwar: A History of Europe since 1945*. New York: Penguin Books, 2006.

Jun, Helen H. "Black Orientalism: Nineteenth-Century Narratives of Race and U.S. Citizenship." *American Quarterly* 58, no. 4 (2006): 1047–66.

Kaplan, Debra. *Beyond Expulsion: Jews, Christians, and Reformation Strasbourg*. Stanford: Stanford University Press, 2011.

Kaplan, Debra, and Magda Teter. "Out of the (Historiographic) Ghetto: Jews and the Reformation." *Sixteenth Century Journal* 40, no. 2 (2009): 365–93.

Kaplan, M. Lindsay. *Figuring Racism in Medieval Christianity*. New York, Oxford: Oxford University Press, 2019.

Kaplan, Paul H. "Introduction to the New Edition." In *The Image of the Black in Western Art, Volume 2: From the Early Christian Era to the "Age of Discovery," Part 2: Africans in the Christian Ordinance of the World*, edited by David Bindman and Henry Louis Gates, 1–30. 5 vols. Cambridge, MA: Belknap Press of Harvard University Press, 2010.

Katz, Jacob. *From Prejudice to Destruction: Anti-Semitism, 1700–1933*. Cambridge; London: Harvard University Press, 1997.

Kaufmann, Thomas. "Luther and the Jews." In *Jews, Judaism, and the Reformation in Sixteenth-Century Germany*, edited by Dean Phillip Bell and Stephen G. Burnett, 61–104. Leiden; Boston: Brill Academic Publishers, 2006.

Keith, LeeAnna. *The Colfax Massacre: The Untold Story of Black Power, White Terror, and the Death of Reconstruction*. New York: Oxford University Press, 2008.

Kendi, Ibram X. *Stamped from the Beginning: The Definitive History of Racist Ideas in America*. New York: Nation Books, 2017.

Keyssar, Alexander. *The Right to Vote: The Contested History of Democracy in the United States*. New York: Basic Books, 2009.

Khalil Gibran, Muhammad. *The Condemnation of Blackness: Race, Crime, and the Making of Modern Urban America, with a New Preface*. Cambridge, MA: Harvard University Press, 2019.

Kirn, Hans-Martin. "The 'Freedom of a Christian'—'Servitude of the Jews'?: Martin Luther's Theology of Christian Freedom and His Early Attitude Towards Jews and Judaism against the Background of Medieval Ambiguities." *NTT* 72, no. 2 (2018): 137–51.

Klamper, Elisabeth. *Die Macht der Bilder antisemitische Vorurteile und Mythen*. Vienna: Picus-Verl, 1995.

Klein, Herbert S. *The Atlantic Slave Trade*. Cambridge: Cambridge University Press, 1999.

Knight, Franklin W. "The Haitian Revolution." *American Historical Review* 105, no. 1 (2000): 103.

Krajewski, Stanisław. *Poland and the Jews: Reflections of a Polish Polish Jew*. Kraków: Wydawnictwo Austeria, 2005.

Kruse, Kevin M., and Stephen Tuck. *Fog of War: The Second World War and the Civil Rights Movement*. New York: Oxford University Press, 2012.

Lanfranchi, Pierluigi. "*Foetor Judaicus*: archéologie d'un préjugé," *Pallas* (2017), http://journals.openedition.org/pallas/7397.

Leibman, Laura Arnold. *Once We Were Slaves: The Extraordinary Journey of a Multiracial Jewish Family*. New York: Oxford University Press, 2021.

Lerner, Lawrence Scott. "Beyond Grégoire: A Third Discourse on Jews and the French." *Modern Judaism: A Journal of Jewish Ideas & Experience* 21, no. 3 (2001): 199–215.

Levy, Richard. "Political Antisemitism in Germany and Austria, 1848–1914." In *Antisemitism*, edited by Alfred Lindemann and Richard Levy, 121–135. Oxford, New York: Oxford University Press, 2010.

Lipstadt, Deborah E. *Antisemitism: Here and Now*. New York: Schocken, 2019.

Lipton, Sara. *Dark Mirror: The Medieval Origins of Anti-Jewish Iconography*. New York: Metropolitan Books, 2014.

———. "Isaac and Antichrist in the Archives." *Past and Present* 232, no. 1 (2016): 3–44.

Littlefield, Daniel C. "Colonial and Revolutionary United States." In *The Oxford Handbook of Slavery in the Americas*, edited by Robert L. Paquette and Mark M. Smith, 201–26. Oxford: Oxford University Press, 2016.

Lockley, Timothy. "Race and Slavery." In *The Oxford Handbook of Slavery in the Americas*, edited by Robert L. Paquette and Mark M. Smith, 336–56. Oxford: Oxford University Press, 2016.

Lowenthal, David. *The Past Is a Foreign Country*. New York: Cambridge University Press, 1985.

Mampieri, Martina. *Living under the Evil Pope: The Hebrew Chronicle of Pope Paul IV by Benjamin Nehemiah Ben Elnathan from Civitanova Marche (16th Cent.)*. Leiden: Brill, 2020.

Martínez, Elena. "The Black Blood of New Spain: Limpieza de Sangre, Racial Violence, and Gendered Power in Early Colonial Mexico." *The William and Mary Quarterly* 61, no. 3 (2004): 479–520.

Massing, Jean Michel. *The Image of the Black in Western Art, Volume 3: From the "Age of Discovery" to the Age of Abolition," Part 2: Europe and the World Beyond*. Edited by David Bindman and Henry Louis Gates. 5 vols. Cambridge, MA: Belknap Press of Harvard University Press, 2011.

Massingale, Bryan N. *Racial Justice and the Catholic Church*. Maryknoll: Orbis Books, 2010.

McAuley, James. *The House of Fragile Things: A History of Jewish Art Collectors in France, 1870–1945*. New Haven: Yale University Press, 2021.

McCoskey, Denise Eileen. *Race: Antiquity and Its Legacy*. London, New York: Bloomsbury, 2019.

McIntosh, Kriston, Emily Moss, Ryan Nunn, and Jay Shambaugh. "Examining the Black-White Wealth Gap." Brookings Institute, 2020.

McLean, Mathew Adam. *The Cosmographia of Sebastian Münster: Describing the World in the Reformation*, St. Andrews Studies in Reformation History. Aldershot, UK: Ashgate, 2007.

McMillen, Neil R. *Dark Journey: Black Mississippians in the Age of Jim Crow*. Urbana, IL; Chicago: University of Illinois Press, 1990.

Meir, Natan M. *Stepchildren of the Shtetl: The Destitute, Disabled, and Mad of Jewish Eastern Europe, 1800–1939*. Stanford: Stanford University Press, 2020.

Messbarger, Rebecca Marie, Christopher M. S. Johns, and Philip Gavitt, eds. *Benedict XIV and the Enlightenment: Art, Science, and Spirituality*. Toronto: University of Toronto Press, 2016.

Miki, Yuko. *Frontiers of Citizenship: A Black and Indigenous History of Postcolonial Brazil*. Cambridge: Cambridge University Press, 2019.

Milteer, Warren Eugene. *Beyond Slavery's Shadow: Free People of Color in the South*. Chapel Hill: University of North Carolina Press, 2021.

Minow, Martha. *Between Vengeance and Forgiveness: Facing History after Genocide and Mass Violence*. Boston: Beacon Press, 1998.

Mirvis, Stanley. *The Jews of Eighteenth-Century Jamaica a Testamentary History of a Diaspora in Transition*. New Haven: Yale University Press, 2020.

Necheles, Ruth F. "The Abbé Grégoire and the Jews." *Jewish Social Studies* 33, no. 2/3 (1971): 120–40.

Neiman, Susan. *Learning from the Germans: Race and the Memory of Evil*. New York: Ferrar, Straus and Giroux, 2020.

Nirenberg, David. *Anti-Judaism: The Western Tradition*. New York: W. W. Norton & Co., 2013.

———. "Mass Conversion and Genealogical Mentalities: Jews and Christians in Fifteenth-Century Spain." *Past and Present* no. 174 (2002): 3–41.

Novenson, Matthew V., and Barry Matlock. *The Oxford Handbook of Pauline Studies*. Oxford, UK; New York: Oxford University Press, 2022.

Novotny, Patrick. *This Georgia Rising: Education, Civil Rights, and the Politics of Change in Georgia in the 1940s*. Macon, GA: Mercer University Press, 2007.

O'Malley, John W. *What Happened at Vatican II*. Cambridge; London: The Belknap Press of Harvard University Press, 2008.

——, and David G. Schultenover. *Vatican II: Did Anything Happen?* New York: Continuum, 2007.

Onwuachi-Willig, Angela. "From Emmett Till to Trayvon Martin: The Persistence of White Womanhood and the Preservation of White Manhood." *Du Bois Review: Social Science Research on Race* 15, no. 2 (2018): 257–94.

Orbach, Alexander, and John Klier. *Perspectives on the 1881–1882 Pogroms in Russia*. Pittsburgh, PA: Russian and East European Studies Program University of Pittsburgh, 1984.

Oster, Sharon B. *No Place in Time: The Hebraic Myth in Late-Nineteenth-Century American Literature*. Detroit: Wayne State University Press, 2018.

Otele, Olivette. *African Europeans: An Untold History*. New York: Basic Books, 2021.

Paquette, Robert L., and Mark M. Smith. *The Oxford Handbook of Slavery in the Americas*. Oxford: Oxford University Press, 2016.

——. "Slavery in the Americas." In *The Oxford Handbook of Slavery in the Americas*, edited by Robert L. Paquette and Mark M. Smith, 3–17. Oxford: Oxford University Press, 2016.

Pattender, Gerald. *Pius IV and the Fall of the Carafa: Nepotism and Papal Authority in Counter-Reformation Rome*. Oxford: Oxford University Press, 2013.

Patterson, Orlando. *Slavery and Social Death: A Comparative Study, with a New Preface*. Cambridge, MA: Harvard University Press, 2018.

Pearce, Sarah J. "The Inquisitor and the Moseret: The Invention of Race in the European Middle Ages and the New English Colonialism in Jewish Historiography." *Medieval Encounters* 26, no. 2 (2020): 145–90.

Peirce, Leslie. *A Spectrum of Unfreedom: Captives and Slaves in the Ottoman Empire*. Budapest; New York: Central European University Press, 2021.

Penkower, Monty Noam. "The Kishinev Pogrom of 1903: A Turning Point in Jewish History." *Modern Judaism* 24, no. 3 (2004): 187–225.

Petersen, Heidemarie. "Die Rechtsstellung der Judengemeinden von Krakau und Prag um 1500: Beispiele jüdischer Existenz in Ostmitteleuropa." *Zeitschrift für Ostmitteleuropa-Forschung* 46, no. 1 (1997): 63–77.

Petley, Christer. "Slavery, Emancipation and the Creole World View of Jamaican Colonists, 1800–1834." *Slavery and Abolition* 26, no. 1 (2005): 93–114.

Philipson, Robert. *The Identity Question: Blacks and Jews in Europe and America*. Jackson: University Press of Mississippi, 2000.

Phillips, William D. *Slavery in Medieval and Early Modern Iberia*. Philadelphia: University of Pennsylvania Press, 2014.

Poole, Stafford. "The Politics of Limpieza de Sangre: Juan de Ovando and His Circle in the Reign of Philip II." *The Americas* 55, no. 3 (1999): 359–89.

Presner, Todd Samuel. *Muscular Judaism: The Jewish Body and the Politics of Regeneration*. London: Routledge, 2010.

Przybyszewski, Linda. "Judicial Conservatism and Protestant Faith: The Case of Justice David J. Brewer." *Journal of American History* 91, no. 2 (2004): 471–96.

Quinney, Valerie. "Decisions on Slavery, the Slave Trade and Civil Rights for Negroes in the Early French Revolution." *Journal of Negro History* 55, no. 2 (1970): 117–30.

———. "The Problem of Civil Rights for Free Men of Color in the Early French Revolution." *French Historical Studies* 7, no. 4 (1972): 544.

Pakter, Walter. *Medieval Canon Law and the Jews*. Ebelsbach: R. Gremer, 1988.

Parkes, James. *The Conflict of the Church and the Synagogue: A Study in the Origins of Antisemitism*. London: Soncino Press, 1934.

Raddatz, Alfred. "Zur Geschichte eines christlichen Bildmotivs: Ecclesia und Synagoge." In *Die Macht der Bilder Antisemitische Vorurteile und Mythen*, edited by Elisabeth Klamper, 53–59. Vienna: Picus-Verl, 1995.

Rigby, David, and Charles Seguin. "National Crimes: A New National Data Set of Lynchings in the United States, 1883 to 1941." *Socius: Sociological Research for a Dynamic World* 5, (2019): 1–9.

Romano, Renee. *Racial Reckoning: Prosecuting America's Civil Rights Murders*. Cambridge, MA: Harvard University Press, 2014.

Rosa, Mario. "La Santa Sede e gli ebrei nel settecento." *Storia d'Italia: Annali* 11/2, "Gli ebrei in Italia" (1997): 1069–87.

Rosman, Murray Jay. *The Lords' Jews: Magnate-Jewish Relations in the Polish-Lithuanian Commonwealth During the Eighteenth Century*. Cambridge, MA: Harvard University Press, 1990.

Rowe, Nina. *The Jew, the Cathedral, and the Medieval City: Synagoga and Ecclesia in the Thirteenth Century*. New York: Cambridge University Press, 2014.

Rubin, Miri. *Cities of Strangers: Making Lives in Medieval Europe*. Cambridge: Cambridge University Press, 2020.

Samuels, Maurice. *The Right to Difference: French Universalism and the Jews*. Chicago: University of Chicago Press, 2019.

Sapir Abulafia, Anna. *Christian-Jewish Relations, 1000–1300: Jews in the Service of Medieval Christendom*. Harlow, UK: Pearson, 2011.

Schäfer, Peter. *Judeophobia: Attitudes toward the Jews in the Ancient World*. Cambridge, MA: Harvard University Press, 1997.

Schmidt, Benjamin. *Inventing Exoticism: Geography, Globalism, and Europe's Early Modern World*. Philadelphia: University of Pennsylvania Press, 2019.

Schoeppner, Michael A. "Status across Borders: Roger Taney, Black British Subjects, and a Diplomatic Antecedent to the Dred Scott Decision." *Journal of American History* 100, (2013): 46–67.

"School Colors" Podcast in *Code Switch*, hosted by Max Freedman and Mark Winston Griffith. New York: WNYC, 2022.

Schwartz, Daniel B. *Ghetto: The History of a Word*. Cambridge, MA: Harvard University Press, 2019.

Segal, Alan F. *Paul the Convert: The Apostolate and Apostasy of Saul the Pharisee*. New Haven: Yale University Press, 1992.

Shiraz, Dossa. "Liberals and Muslims: Philosophy and Conquest." *Arab Studies Quarterly* 37, no. 1 (2015): 54–72.

Shklar, Judith N. *American Citizenship: The Quest for Inclusion*. Cambridge, MA: Harvard University Press, 2001.

Silverman, Ellie, Ian Shapira, Tom Jackman, and John Woodrow Cox. "Spencer, Kessler, Cantwell and Other White Supremacists Found Liable in Deadly Unite the Right Rally." *Washington Post*, November 23, 2021.

Sinkoff, Nancy. *From Left to Right: Lucy S. Dawidowicz, the New York Intellectuals, and the Politics of Jewish History*. Detroit: Wayne State University Press, 2020.

Smith, Kathryn A. "History, Typology and Homily: The Joseph Cycle in the Queen Mary Psalter." *Gesta* 32, no. 2 (1993): 147–59.

Smith, Rogers M. *Civic Ideals*. New Haven: Yale University Press, 1997.

Smith, Shawn Michelle. *Photography on the Color Line: W. E. B. Du Bois, Race, and Visual Culture*. Durham: Duke University Press, 2004.

Sorin, Gretchen. *Driving While Black: African American Travel and the Road to Civil Rights*. New York: Liveright Publishing Corporation, 2020.

Sorkin, David. *Jewish Emancipation: A History across Five Centuries*. Princeton: Princeton University Press, 2019.

Soyer, François. *Antisemitic Conspiracy Theories in the Early Modern Iberian World: Narratives of Fear and Hatred*. Leiden: Brill, 2019.

Sparrow, James T. "Freedom to Want: Federal Government and Politicized Consumption in World War II." In *Fog of War: The Second World War and the Civil Rights Movement*, edited by Kevin M. Kruse and Stephen Tuck, 15–31. New York: Oxford University Press, 2012.

Spector, Stephen. *Evangelicals and Israel: The Story of Christian Zionism*. New York: Oxford University Press, 2009.

Stanislawski, Michael. *Zionism and the Fin-de-Siècle: Cosmopolitanism and Nationalism from Nordau to Jabotinsky*. Berkeley: University of California Press, 2001.

Stauffer, John. "Abolition and Antislavery." In *The Oxford Handbook of Slavery in the Americas*, edited by Robert L. Paquette and Mark M. Smith, 556–77. Oxford: Oxford University Press, 2016.

Steinberg, Oded Y. *Race, Nation, History: Anglo-German Thought in the Victorian Era*. Philadelphia: University of Pennsylvania Press, 2019.

Stovall, Tyler Edward. *White Freedom: The Racial History of an Idea*. Princeton: Princeton University Press, 2021.

Stow, Kenneth R. *Catholic Thought and Papal Jewry Policy, 1555–1593*. New York: Jewish Theological Seminary of America, 1977.

Stroup, Christopher. *The Christians Who Became Jews: Acts of the Apostles and Ethnicity in the Roman City*. New Haven; London: Yale University Press, 2020.

Stuurman, Siep. "François Bernier and the Invention of Racial Classification." *History Workshop Journal* no. 50 (2000): 1–21.

Sugrue, Thomas. "Hillburn, Hattiesburg, and Hitler: Wartime Activists Think Globally Act Locally." In *Fog of War: The Second World War and the Civil Rights Movement*, edited by Kevin M. Kruse and Stephen Tuck, 87–102. New York: Oxford University Press, 2012.

Sullivan, Patricia. "Movement Building During the World War II Era: The NAACP's Legal Insurgency in the South." In *Fog of War: The Second World War and the Civil Rights Movement*, edited by Kevin M. Kruse and Stephen Tuck, 70–86. New York: Oxford University Press, 2012.

Sullivan, Shannon. *Good White People: The Problem with Middle-Class White Anti-Racism*. Albany: State University of New York Press, 2014.

——. *Revealing Whiteness: The Unconscious Habits of Racial Privilege*. Bloomington: Indiana University Press, 2006.

Taguieff, Pierre-André. *The Force of Prejudice: On Racism and Its Doubles*. Minneapolis: University of Minnesota Press, 2001.

——. "L'invention du «Complot Judéo-Maçonnique»: Avatars d'un mythe apocalyptique moderne." *Revue d'Histoire de la Shoah* 198, no. 1 (2013): 23–97.

Teller, Adam. *Money, Power, and Influence in Eighteenth-Century Lithuania: The Jews on the Radziwill Estates*. Stanford, CA: Stanford University Press, 2016.

——. "Some Comparative Perspectives on the Jews' Legal Status in the Polish-Lithuanian Commonwealth and the Holy Roman Empire." In *Polin:Social and Cultural Boundaries in Pre-Modern Poland*, edited by Adam Teller, Magda Teter, and Antony Polonsky, 109–41. Oxford; Portland, OR: Littmann Library of Jewish Civilization, 2010.

Teter, Magda. *Blood Libel: On the Trail of an Antisemitic Myth*. Cambridge, MA: Harvard University Press, 2020.

——. *Jews and Heretics in Catholic Poland: A Beleaguered Church in the Post-Reformation Era*. Cambridge; New York: Cambridge University Press, 2006.

——. "The Legend of Ger Zedek of Wilno as Polemic and Reassurance." *AJS Review* 29, no. 2 (2005): 237–64.

——. "'There Should Be No Love between Us and Them': Social Life and the Bounds of Jewish and Canon Law in Early Modern Poland." In *Polin: Social and Cultural Boundaries in Pre-Modern Poland*, edited by Adam Teller, Magda Teter, and Antony Polonsky, 249–70. Oxford; Portland, OR: Littmann Library of Jewish Civilization, 2010.

Thompson, Lloyd A. *Romans and Blacks*. London: Routledge, 2015.

Todd Samuel, Presner. "'Clear Heads, Solid Stomachs, and Hard Muscles': Max Nordau and the Aesthetics of Jewish Regeneration." *Modernism/Modernity* 10, no. 2 (2003): 269–96.

Tokarska-Bakir, Joanna. *Pod Klątwą: Społeczny Portret Pogromu Kieleckiego*. 2 vols. Warsaw: Wydawnictwo Czarna Owca, 2018.

——. "'Wieszanie Judasza,' Czyli Tematy Żydowskie Dzisiaj." In *Przeciw Antysemityzmowi 1936-2009*, edited by Adam Michnik, 302–328. Cracow: Universitas, 2010.

Tuck, Stephen. *We Ain't What We Ought to Be: The Black Freedom Struggle from Emancipation to Obama*. Cambridge: Belknap Harvard, 2011.

——. "'You Can Sing and Punch . . . but You Can't Be a Soldier or a Man': African American Struggles for a New Place in Popular Culture." In *Fog of War: The Second World War and the Civil Rights Movement*, edited by Kevin M. Kruse and Stephen Tuck, 103–25. New York: Oxford University Press, 2012.

Villella, Peter B. "'Pure and Noble Indians, Untainted by Inferior Idolatrous Races': Native Elites and the Discourse of Blood Purity in Late Colonial Mexico." *Hispanic American Historical Review* 91, no. 4 (2011): 633–63.

Vinson, Ben. *Flight: The Story of Virgil Richardson, a Tuskegee Airman in Mexico*. New York: Palgrave Macmillan, 2004.

Volkov, Shulamit. "Antisemitism as a Cultural Code: Reflections on the History and Historiography of Antisemitism in Imperial Germany." *Leo Baeck Institute Year Book*, 25–46 (1978).

———. *Germans, Jews, and Antisemites: Trials in Emancipation*. Cambridge; New York: Cambridge University Press, 2006.

von Braun, Christina. "Antisemitische Stereotype und Sexualphantasien." In *Die Macht Der Bilder Antisemitische Vorurteile und Mythen*, edited by Elisabeth Klamper, 180–191. Vienna: Picus-Verl, 1995.

Ward, Jason Morgan. "'A War for States' Rights': The White Supremacist Vision of Double Victory." In *Fog of War: The Second World War and the Civil Rights Movement*, edited by Kevin M. Kruse and Stephen Tuck, 126–44. New York: Oxford University Press, 2012.

Watson, Karl. "Shifting Identities: Religion, Race, and Creolization among the Sephardi Jews of Barbados, 1654–1900." In *The Jews in the Caribbean*, edited by Jane S. Gerber, 195–222. London: The Littman Library of Jewish Civilization, 2018.

White, Sophie. *Voices of the Enslaved: Love, Labor, and Longing in French Louisiana*. Williamsburg, Chapel Hill: University of North Carolina Press, 2019.

Whitman, James Q. *Hitler's American Model: The United States and the Making of Nazi Race Law*. Princeton: Princeton University Press, 2018.

Wiegand, Wayne A. "'Jew Attack'": The Story Behind Melvil Dewey's Resignation as New York State Librarian in 1905." *American Jewish History* 83, no. 3 (1995): 359–79.

Wilson, Charles Reagan. *Baptized in Blood: The Religion of the Lost Cause, 1865–1920*. Athens: University of Georgia Press, 2009.

Wistrich, Robert S. *Antisemitism: The Longest Hatred*. New York: Schoken Books, 1994.

Wright, John. *The Trans-Saharan Slave Trade*. London, New York: Routledge, 2010.

Yancy, George. *Black Bodies, White Gazes: The Continuing Significance of Race in America*. Lanham, MD: Rowman & Littlefield, 2017.

Yarema, Allan E. *The American Colonization Society: An Avenue to Freedom?* Lanham, Md.: University Press of America, 2006.

Young, Jeffrey Robert. "Proslavery Ideology." In *The Oxford Handbook of Slavery in the Americas*, edited by Robert L. Paquette and Mark M. Smith, 399–423. Oxford: Oxford University Press, 2016.

Zaremba, Marcin. *Wielka trwoga: Polska 1944–1947, Ludowa reakcja na kryzys*. Cracow: Wydawnictwo Znak, 2012.

Zelizer, Julian E. "Confronting the Roadblock: Congress, Civil Rights, and World War II." In *Fog of War: The Second World War and the Civil Rights Movement*, edited by Kevin M. Kruse and Stephen Tuck, 32–50. New York: Oxford University Press, 2012.

Zipperstein, Steven J. *Pogrom: Kishinev and the Tilt of History*. New York: Liveright Publishing Corporation, 2018.

Zuñiga, Jean-Paul. "La voix du sang: du métis à l'idée de métissage en Amérique espagnole." *Annales. Histoire, Sciences Sociales* 54, no. 2 (1999): 425–52.

Page numbers in *italics* indicate illustrations.